LOOKING OUT WINDOWS

LOOKING OUT WINDOWS

The True Adventures of an Uncommon Life

SCOTTY R. HAZEL

authorHOUSE®

AuthorHouse™
1663 Liberty Drive
Bloomington, IN 47403
www.authorhouse.com
Phone: 1-800-839-8640

Published by AuthorHouse 10/23/2012

ISBN: 978-1-4772-5255-0 (sc)
ISBN: 978-1-4772-7525-2 (e)

Library of Congress Control Number: 2012917925

This book is printed on acid-free paper.

COVER DESIGN: Photograph by Darcy Olson. White Pine Trail; Rockford, Michigan

INTRODUCTION

Looking Out Windows is a true story; my story. As best as my memory allowed, I have written down the key events and people of my life. It goes without saying that over the years I have forgotten some details and maybe even forgotten a name or two. But the gist of every story is true and the characters, correct name or not, really exist. In some cases I have deliberately changed names as a courtesy to those who may not want their involvement with me known. Apologies to those who had an impact in my life, but whose names are not mentioned. For the sake of keeping *Looking Out Windows* at a comfortable length, I chose to omit some people and events that certainly could have been included.

As well as names, there may also be some slight inaccuracies with dates and timelines, but the events are factual; nothing in these pages are contrived or made up. In many cases, I remember verbatim things that were said and done, in others I have filled in the cracks with what I recall was said in the spirit of the dialogue or the basis of the event. Forgive the occasional profanity, but sugar-coating the language would not do justice to the tale. My hope is that you as a reader might find something in my story encouraging, entertaining, and inspirational. With my compliments, enjoy *Looking Out Windows.*

Scott Hazel

For those who made a difference.

TABLE OF CONTENTS

THE AWAKENING

CHAPTER 1

It was the autumn of 1974. I was a sophomore at Flint Southwestern High School. Sometime during the previous year Scott had changed to Scotty. I wasn't sure if I liked it or not, but it seemed endearing, and I did not discourage it. I was a drummer in the marching band, and the pettiness of junior high had somehow vanished. In the summer separating Zimmerman Junior High from Southwestern, I outgrew much of my pubescent awkwardness and was actually not a bad-looking guy. This was a giant transformation, considering how I battled to be accepted in spite of many physical flaws.

I had a double crown, which made my hair hard to manage since it swirled in two different directions. I was thin and a little bony, but fast and coordinated. I was born with a mouthful of unruly teeth, featuring two abnormally large "corn strippers" center stage. I had the wonderful bronze skin of my Indian ancestors, but I also had the prominent nose of Crazy Horse. Even though I was smart, funny, and athletic, all of my features translated into "dorky, goofy, and awkward." Because of all this, my self-image had suffered. But that was in 1973; now in 1974, longer hair calmed my double crown. Years of dental work and the miracle of porcelain caps had minimized my choppers and straightened my smile. I had filled out some, thanks to years of playing the drums and several sports . . . mostly soccer. Plus, I was a bicycle fanatic! I rode everywhere. I can't tell you how much riding a bike can help your thighs and tush! The love of riding a bike would play an important role in my life . . . but not quite yet. In the meantime, my Native skin tanned easily, and

I think my body finally caught up with my nose . . . somewhat. I was amazed at the attention I was receiving from girls in high school that I longed for when I was younger, but never got. I was not really sure how to handle it, but I sure liked it. I was popular.

The fact that something had changed for the better happened like a thunderclap at a party after a football game one Friday night. As a sophomore, I was at the bottom of the high school food chain because in the Flint school system, ninth graders were still attending their junior high buildings. Kids didn't actually attend the high school until they were tenth graders. I faced my first big decision when entering Southwestern. I was a pretty good athlete and had made a name for myself playing football, soccer, basketball, and track. When I was younger, I was the only student in my school to be awarded the Presidential Physical Fitness Award. Surprisingly, I chose to become a band kid. I think the deciding factor was the five siblings before me that had great experiences in the music department. This was my situation at that first Friday night party of the year.

I was young and naïve and still feeling like the awkward adolescent from junior high. The party was being held at Phil's house, a trumpet player whose parents were gone for the weekend. I'm sure there was booze there, but I was not drinking that night. Not that the presence of alcohol offended me; Lord knows at the age of sixteen I had already developed an appreciation for a cold beer. Being from a large Irish-Catholic family with a grandfather who owned a pub, drinking was part of who we were. No, the reason I was not drinking at Phil's that night was because of an uncomfortable sense of fear that gripped me. I had been to many events where the booze flowed freely and I was sneaking drinks, but I always knew that my family was close by. For the first time, I was not at home or at a family wedding, reunion, graduation, or camping . . . I was out on my own. It was all new territory for me, and I was actually trying to just take it all in. I had never been to a *real* party alone before, a party with tons of kids and no adult safety net watching from afar. Like a small bird on the edge of the nest, I was trying to decide whether or not to jump.

There was a cute girl named Barb who played flute in the band giving me a great deal of attention. I didn't realize until later that she was flirting with me . . . heavily. Barb had wavy shoulder-length light brown hair that she parted in the middle. Two large curls left her forehead exposed but then returned to the corners of her green eyes before falling to her shoulders. She was short, had smooth olive skin, and perfect teeth that immediately caught your eye when she smiled. She was tiny, and thin, but not skinny. I had noticed her before, but never thought she had noticed me in return; after all, she was a senior, two years older than I. With an entire school of choices out there and a band filled with marching hormones, why would she even give me a second thought? Away from marching band, I don't think I ever gave her much thought other than a voice in my head acknowledging, "Man, that chick is hot!"

At Phil's party, somehow I found myself sitting in a chair in the corner of a den with Barb sitting on the floor facing me. With her knees together and her bare feet underneath her butt, she had both her hands lying flat, palms down on her thighs. Occasionally when someone said something funny, she would reach up and touch my knee while she laughed. It was as if she was using the laughter as an excuse to touch me. A couple times after the laughter stopped, she left the hand for a few moments. "She is doing that on purpose," I thought, "or is she?" Whether she was or not, one thing was for sure: She was totally oblivious to anyone in the room but me, and I was diggin' the attention. I was trying to act older than I was and certainly more together. But I had little experience in trying to be charming, and I am sure I was obviously awkward. Barb knew this before she ever plopped down on the floor in front of me. Months later, it dawned on me that she had taken advantage. No matter, somewhere along the line cooties had to be replaced with contact; this was as welcome a transition as a guy could hope for. Later in the evening in the midst of all the noise of the party, Barb arose, leaned in close and said, "Let's go for a ride." Being a senior, Barb had her own car.

"A ride?" I said with a puzzled tone. "Where?"

"C'mon," she said as she grabbed me by the arm, "let's go for a ride."

Before I knew it, I was the lone passenger riding shotgun in an old Ford Falcon. Barb was slowly driving through the winding streets of Parkside. There was plenty of conversation, but I don't recall any of it. I was trying to figure out just what was happening. I couldn't figure out why no one else was going for the ride. "Why did she only ask me?" I kept pondering. "Where the heck are we going?" I wondered. She slowed and switched off the headlights as she turned onto a short dirt road with trees close on either side and a log blocking the far end. In the amber glow of parking lights, I could see we were looking directly onto the fairway of a golf course. The Chevy truck plant was in the distance, but its lights allowed me to know where we were. I could see the dark expanse of the golf course between us and the glow from the factory. She turned off the motor and the lights. As my eyes adjusted to the darkness, I felt her slide across the seat toward me, and she put one hand behind my head and the other on my knee. I could feel her face was close to mine and suddenly her lips pressed hard against my mouth. "That's why she only asked me!" was the awakening that exploded in my mind. Her breath was sweet, and it came in sharp bursts from her nose. "She wants to be with me!" was my epiphany. She was totally in control, and my head was spinning. I'm not even sure how it happened, but the next thing I knew we were in the back seat, and she was laying on top of me! I wasn't sure what I was doing, but she was. With lots of panting and clumsy hands testing the waters, I found myself wondering: "Is this second or third base?" I really wasn't sure, but I can say for certain we never made it to home plate. Neither of us was prepared to go that far. No clothes were shed, but we were close enough that I could feel her pounding heart, and her determination almost scared me. This went on for twenty minutes or so when abruptly she said, "We should get back to the party; we'll be missed."

During the ride back, we were nervously laughing like we had gotten away with something forbidden. As Barb navigated the streets back to Phil's, I looked out the window and watched familiar houses, trees, and lawns go by. I knew this area well. As a kid I had ridden my bike down these streets a thousand times-I knew every crack, every bump, and every curb. It was surreal to see them now, looking out the window of Barb's old car. I knew something new had begun, and I couldn't keep the grin off my face. How I was beginning to love high school.

TWO DEBBIES

CHAPTER 2

In the spring of 1975, I decided to compete for the assistant drum major position. The way the system worked was that a candidate would try out at the end of his sophomore year to become the assistant drum major for his upcoming junior year. This automatically would make him the head drum major his senior year. Now this may not sound like a prestigious position, but in a high school with a rich tradition of fielding an exceptional marching band, it was. The last couple weeks of my sophomore year, I entered the competition and was selected to be the drum major for the next two years. This would vault me into the spotlight where I would become one of the most recognized students in the school. It also meant that I would accompany the head drum major, Dave, to a drum major camp in Syracuse, Indiana, named Smith-Walbridge.

Dave was a very smart Jewish kid from the right side of the tracks, Parkside, and he had his own car. The first week of summer, he drove us down to Smith-Walbridge camp for our training. During the week of camp, it was extremely hot and muggy and a lot more physical than I thought it would be. We drilled for hours in the blazing sun until we were totally dripping with sweat. There were more than one hundred drum majors there from all over the Midwest and from all different sizes and types of high schools. And of course there were girls.

This was all new to me, and I was not nearly the musician that most of these people were. I was a drummer, not a percussionist, but a drummer. You may think there is not much of a difference between the two, but it is actually substantial. Being from a musical family, I had developed a wide musical appreciation, a genuine knack, and a keen ear. I was a pretty proficient drummer as well, but when it came to reading music, I was, at best, horrible. Dave had already been to Smith-Walbridge the year before, as the assistant drum major, so he knew what to expect; I was the green protégé cutting my teeth in a brand new world.

As the week progressed, there were two girls whom we began to seek out and hang around with, and they did the same to us in return. Sometimes it was with a larger group, and other times it was just the four of us. It was nothing of serious potential but more just making new friends and light flirting for a short week. Coincidentally, both of their names were Debbie. The one who seemed to like Dave was from Indiana; the one who seemed to like me was from Iowa. Interestingly enough was that our attractions were the exact opposite. We spent a great deal of time that week trying to get the girls to switch their focus, but nothing seemed to work. Iowa Deb was from a wealthy family in Bettendorf, Iowa, and seemed to be a much better match for Dave than middle class me. Indiana Deb lived on a farm deep in southern Indiana not too far from Louisville, Kentucky. She enjoyed the outdoors and much simpler pleasures; she seemed to have much more in common with me. But as these things go, the match-ups were all screwed up. I even remember asking Indiana Deb to go on walks in an effort to leave Dave and Iowa Deb alone. At first, Indiana Deb reluctantly went along, but after easy conversation and like interests, we actually began to strike up a pleasant friendship. But in spite of our efforts to correct the pairings, the two Debs would counter and strategically switch us back with maneuvers of their own. With so little time, we ultimately just went with the flow and tried not to force anything to happen that wasn't happening on its own.

Both Debbies were beautiful blondes with dark tans from the countless hours marching outside. They both were wholesome and fit with quaint accents hinting that they lived in transitional places where demarcations of North and South became blurry. I wasn't really trying to make anything serious happen other than meeting a new friend from a place far away and enjoying the moment. A big factor in reigning in any potential long distance relationship was that back in Flint, I was dating a girl named Sher.

Sher was a girl from a rival school whom I met through a friend of mine named Kevin. Kevin was a kid I met a few years earlier during the summer. He played hockey for Flint Northern High School and was dating Sher's older sister. Sher and I were the same age and she played clarinet in Northern's band. After my initiation from Barb, Sher was the first girl I really dated. We got along together wonderfully, and I didn't want to screw that up with any quick diversion from camp. In all honesty, it wasn't on account of my virtuous morality, but with Dave as a witness, I did not want anything to blow up in my face back home. Even though Sher went to a different school, news gets around. I did not want to do anything that would make me look bad. Still, flirting for the week of camp with chicks from other states was irresistible. I cautiously played the game.

In the course of trying to divert Indiana Deb's attention from Dave to me, she and I laid the foundation for a solid friendship. She had given me a folded piece of paper the final evening, gave me a hug and a kiss on the cheek, and told me to write. Still, when the time came to leave the last morning, Indiana Deb was alone with Dave, and Iowa Deb was alone with me. Iowa Deb also gave me her address and not a kiss on the cheek, but a tight embrace and a serious farewell full on the lips. For the first fifty miles on the trip back home, I was second-guessing how Dave and I had handled the week. Iowa Deb's kiss had thrown a hand grenade into my mind. "Maybe I should have been paying closer attention to her this week," I said to Dave. He just shook his head and drove without comment. I was under the impression that his farewell from Indiana Deb was not as affectionate as mine was from Iowa Deb. It took me a while to realize that the more I talked about Iowa Deb, the more aggravated Dave became; after all, I was talking about the girl *he* actually liked. At one point he suddenly asked, "Aren't you dating a girl from Northern?" The reality of the statement took me by surprise, and I just turned my head away from Dave and looked out the window. In the silence of the rebuke, I watched the unfamiliar world of northern Indiana pass by outside. I was a little embarrassed and angry that Dave had brought Sher into the conversation, but he was right. "Scott, you stupid head," I thought to myself when the picture became clear, and I avoided talking about Iowa Deb for the rest of the ride home and for the entire next year. I returned home and continued to date Sher.

For the next few years, I wrote and received letters from both Debs. The contact was sporadic and was a pleasant step out of my normal routine. To my surprise, it was Indiana Deb who proved to be a more consistent pen-pal, and over time we became fast friends and confidants via the U.S. Postal Service. I couldn't help but appreciate the irony.

JOEY

CHAPTER 3

There was a pile of kids around Joey's locker. They were buzzing with laughter from what had happened the night before. It was early in my junior year, and this was a typical Tuesday morning ritual. I was trying to avoid a mob of my friends who were religious, but not Catholic. My entire sophomore year I had successfully sidestepped every attempt they made for me to join them and their youth group. The most persistent was a kid named Joey.

Joey and I met in Zimmerman Junior High School and became fast friends. By sheer coincidence, we had many classes together and always seemed to find ourselves leading each other into trouble with the teacher. But Joey was cleverer than I was and it always seemed like I was the one to get caught, I was the one who couldn't get the best of Joey. These were the days of corporal punishment, and somehow it always ended up that I was the one in the hall receiving swats; that is, getting pounded several times by teachers or principals with their customized paddles. One class in particular in which this took place on a weekly basis, was Mr. Willie Joe Barton's history class. We called Mr. Barton 'Willie J.' and he had a wicked paddle which he jokingly named 'The Board of Education.' He was a giant black man who we could barely understand, and we feared him and loved him at he same time. Relentlessly, Joey baited me into trouble in Mr. Barton's class and relentlessly I received a beating from Willie J. The final day of class in junior high school, as we prepared to go off to high school the next year, Mr. Barton called me up in front of the class. He opened his desk drawer and pulled out his infamous paddle. He calmly signed and dated it and presented it to me: "Here, take this with you; after all, you've had it more than me." As I returned to my desk with my trophy, Joey just smiled a devious little smile.

Now that we were in high school we remained close friends. That particular morning it was hard to keep focused on one conversation as they were all talking on top of each other's stories. I would just start to zero in on one story, and the laughter from another area of the group would drown it out. One thing was for certain: They had a lot to talk about and it all sounded like great fun. Although they were some of my closest friends, I kept my distance. The fact that I was not present the night before left me totally out of the loop. I had no idea what they were yakking about and felt like an outsider. "Felt like?" nuthin', I *was* an outsider! In the midst of all the chaos, kids were gathering their books and getting ready for first-hour class. Although I already had what I needed, I tried to act occupied and uninterested in what they were saying. In reality, I was trying my hardest to focus an ear on what they were saying. I wanted to know what was so dang hilarious! Joey's back was to me, blocking much of the conversation. Suddenly there was raucous laughter, and Joey spun around. In that moment, my eaves-dropping was detected. "Crap!" I was busted being interested.

Joey took the few short steps toward me and said, "You really missed it last night."

"Sounds like you guys had a blast," I replied.

"Awe, we *ALWAYS* have fun, you know?" Joey said with a wide smile and a coaxing manner. "You know," Joey continued, "you should really come and check it out, I think you'd have a great time." I was trying to find a legitimate reason to decline, but I had already used a million excuses on a million previous invitations. I closed my locker, sighed, and stared at the floor. Joey stood in silence, very close beside me with a friendly hand on my back waiting for me to answer. I could smell the freshness of a morning shower, of toothpaste and deodorant. There was an uneasy tension. The uneasiness was broken when Joey suddenly said in a hushed gentle voice, "Don't sweat it, no pressure, you don't have to come." Joey baled me out of the moment and in relief, I simply said, "Thanks."

"But if you ever think you want to check it out," Joey added, "you're always welcome. It's a blast, and *I* would really like to see you there sometime." It was almost a whisper, but it stuck in my head all these years. A simple but sincere invitation from a friend thirty-five years ago and I can hear it in my head like it happened an hour ago. Again, "thanks" was all that I could muster in the moment.

The bell rang, and the pile broke up, headed in several different directions to different classes. Some who were headed the same way continued to talk and laugh. It slowly blended into the hum of the hallway until I couldn't hear the familiar voices any longer. As I weaved through the crowded hallway, all I could hear was my own voice talking to myself inside my head, "I'd love to see what all the ruckus was about, but those guys are such freaks," I thought. "Jesus freaks!" I had said it quietly, but out loud and a kid going the other way gave me a strange look. "I would feel SO out of place," I silently continued, "but God, they have SO much fun!" As I walked I nodded at a kid I knew but kept analyzing to myself, "I don't understand how they can have so much fun at a church meeting." Joey's words were stuck in my head: "Don't sweat it, no pressure." I was always under the impression that these people were very pushy, but Joey had never been pushy . . . persistent, but never pushy. I had appreciated that. I have to admit now in looking back, my curiosity was definitely heightened. I even remember feeling jealous of all those guys cackling on Tuesday mornings about the Monday evening before. I wanted to be "in" on the stories! Although I felt a certain amount of disdain, I was curious and envious. Not a good combination for a seventeen-year old. "'Don't sweat it, no pressure,' huh?" Maybe I would put *that* to the test; maybe I *would* go. At least that would satisfy Joey.

JESUS FREAKS

CHAPTER 4

Nearly a week had passed since Joey's latest invitation to attend the weekly Young Life meeting that many of my friends attended on Monday nights. It bugged me to be part of the popular crowd, but so much of an outcast when it came to this. Although I was reluctant, our friendship assured me that I would be in good hands if I went. I had used every excuse in the book to beg out at this point, but my curiosity was killing me! I decided I would go . . . once . . . just to stop Joey from asking me every week. I was running out of excuses, and saying "no" was becoming more difficult. After all, if I went, then I could simply say I didn't like it and everyone, Joey especially, would get off my back. It was that theory I went armed with when I approached Joey on that Monday after school.

"You guys have Young Life tonight?" I asked.

"Yeah, you wanna go?" asked Joey with eyebrows raised in disbelief.

"Yeah, I think I'll just go to check it out," I replied, keeping my defenses close.

"Cool," was Joey's simple response. "How 'bout if I give you a ride?"

"Sure . . . where is it?"

Joey excitedly answered, "It's at Davis' house in Parkside."

I immediately had visions of a large lawn capped by a huge brick house with white columns. I knew the Davis home; I had ridden my bike past it many times. I pictured the balcony and chandelier hanging from chains over an enormous front door. I recalled the immigrant servants and Mexican landscapers carefully grooming the lawn in the heat of the summer sun. A faint grin emerged when I thought of the little dirt road facing the golf course and Barb's urgent breath as she pressed her face close to mine . . . it was just around the corner from Davis'.

Parkside was the proverbial other side of the tracks. The rich of Flint lived there—doctors, lawyers, and many General Motors executives. Flint, after all, was also known as Buick Town. Parkside was the choice of many of the wealthy and a sanctuary for aristocrats in an otherwise gray industrial town. It also was the choice of residence for many of Flint's large Jewish population. Parkside was on the other side of Miller Road from where I lived in the predominantly middle-class neighborhood of Woodcroft.

Even though it was on the good side of the tracks, Parkside was in the Southwestern school district. Although I was in a different social class, I had many friends who lived there. On the other hand, the Southwestern district also included a large area that was made up of mostly middle and lower class white, black, and Hispanic households. This made for a very diverse high school of many different races, classes, cultures, and religions. Most students had come from nearly all-white or all-black junior high schools. We all learned to live together in Southwestern . . . it was ideal.

Like my family, there were many Catholics, poor and rich, who attended Southwestern. And, of course, the Jewish who lived in Parkside and other nearby neighborhoods swelled the enrollment. The Protestants, who attended many different churches, were spread throughout the school district. I never paid them much attention until I got to high school. Joey's family was Lutheran.

"I'll pick you up at seven," Joey said. I stared into oblivion. "Hey!" Joey snapped. I was daydreaming. I was imagining going into the Davis mansion in Parkside. I was remembering the soft hands on my neck, on my knee.

"Sorry, seven o'clock? OK, seven, see you then." I tried to say like I was thinking of the time and not the weird feeling of going into a rich house or the seduction by Barb. My world was about to get bigger.

Jenny, Joey's older sister, was actually driving when they picked me up a little after seven o'clock that evening. Joey's younger sister

Julie was sitting in the back seat and she beamed a giant smile when I slid into the car next to her.

Jenny, Joey, and Julie Gaus (pronounced like 'mouse') had all been encouraging me to attend Young Life with them, but it was always Joey who led the campaign. I had known them all since junior high and my brother, Jeff, worked for their father. Their house, several miles from mine, was the typical destination when I saddled up on my ten-speed. Like a lot of teenagers who latch onto surrogate families, the Gaus family was definitely mine. They were popular and a lot of kids hung out at the 'Gaus House', but it felt as if I was part of their family. Especially in the summertime, with hours of time to fill, I lazed around their house instead of mine. It was not uncommon for me to eat dinner with the Gaus family more than my own and to join them on family outings.

One summer, they left on a ten day family vacation. When they were gone I realized how much I had become attached them; I was like a lost soul looking for my refuge. I waved at them when they left, and ten days later when they returned, I was waiting for them on their porch. Now in the same family station wagon, we were all headed to a Young Life meeting . . . my first.

"We are so glad you are coming! You're gonna love this!" Jenny said when I climbed into the station wagon. "Sorry we're a bit late," she continued. I looked nervously at Joey who just grinned.

"It's going to be a good time," Joey said reassuringly. We drove the short distance across Miller Road into Parkside. When we approached the Davis house, there were cars parked solid for a couple of blocks.

"All these cars are for Young Life?" I asked.

"Oh yeah," said Joey. I was beginning to feel a little uneasy. We found a spot not too far away, and we all jumped out.

"Come on, we're late," shouted Jenny, and I, snickering the whole way, followed her, Julie, and Joey across two giant lawns. Jenny knocked and opened the huge door simultaneously. Instantly I heard the noise that reminded me of passing in Southwestern's hallways between classes. There was a mountain of shoes just inside the front door. We kicked our shoes off and walked into the house like we owned it. When we turned the corner into the room where the noise was pouring out, I was amazed to see that there was no furniture in it or in the adjacent room to the right. I could see that all the furniture was stacked neatly out of the way in the dining room to the left. Even so, there were several kids crowded in a small space there as well. The floor was a sea of students sitting with crossed legs. We stood in the back for a moment until some friends signaled us in, and they squeezed to make room for us. As I sat, a few kids I knew gestured their hellos to me and then quickly turned and spoke in the ear of those sitting around them. When those kids immediately looked my way, I knew that it was news that I was there. I felt out of place but loved the commotion I was stirring. There were five young people standing at the front of the room with their backs to the wall. I judged that they were perhaps twenty-five-years old or so. Two guys and one girl were playing guitars, and another guy and girl were clapping and singing. Everyone was singing a very different kind of song than I had ever heard. It was catchy and sort of folksy, but everyone was engaged in motions and clapping as if it had been rehearsed. I could tell they had sung it many times before. I was amazed that everyone knew the lyrics and nearly everyone knew the motions . . . except me. I stuck out like a sore thumb. I liked the rhythm, I liked the contemporary feeling, but I was reluctant to sing because something felt wrong. The words were about Jesus and God, and it just didn't seem proper. They weren't hymns. How can you sing contemporary songs about God? It just wasn't normal! I thought to myself as I looked at all the enthusiasm and energy in the room, "Jesus freaks."

At one point, the announcement was made that because there were more than 100 kids in attendance, Dale had to eat three goldfish. "What?" I thought! This is craziness!" I was enjoying it, but it was just plain goofy! Dale Moore, a little older guy . . . maybe twenty-seven or twenty-eight stepped forward cautiously and after much laughter and coaxing, swallowed three live gold fish. The place erupted with laughter. I remember thinking, "That dude is messed up!" Then there was a skit where several kids placed themselves like furniture. A story was narrated in which other kids acting like dogs or cats, and people had to sit on the "furniture" or pet the animals. Sometimes the animals climbed under "tables" and jumped on "chairs" . . . it was hilarious. I started to understand why there was such a buzz the morning after these meetings. Then after a couple more songs, toward the end of the meeting, everyone calmed down for a serious message. Much to my chagrin, Dale, the fish-eating weirdo stepped forward with a Bible opened in his hand. "Blasphemy!" I thought, "Only a priest should read from the Bible." Here was what I feared. This young, long-haired dude in a t-shirt and bell-bottoms was going to preach. I am sure my discontent was obvious by my sudden distant demeanor, clenched jaw, and folded arms. But as Dale read a short verse from the book of John and began to explain what it meant, I was pissed and awed at the same time. He totally made sense! This hippie had explained scripture in the clearest fashion I had ever heard! Amazing! Without a robe, without candles, without an altar, and with no cavernous house of God, Dale had made the passage in John seem like it was written specifically for me. One last song and we all collected our shoes and spilled out of the house, laughing and screaming at each other. The ride home was filled with recounting the events of the evening and howling with laughter.

I lay in bed that night trying to digest it all. My bedroom was a converted sunroom which had three walls of windows. In my sleeplessness, I rolled to one side and propped myself up on an elbow; I reached out and slightly raised the shade. In the faint streetlight I could barely make out the houses of my neighborhood. This was the comforting view of my childhood. It changed with the weather, seasons, or the passing years, but always made me feel safe and secure. Whenever my mind wandered or I had something deep to ponder, I usually found myself looking out windows. On many occasions I was abruptly snapped back to reality by teachers scolding me not to daydream, or friends snapping their fingers, saying, "Hey, pay attention." Even at this young age, I had always been accused of being a dreamer . . . and I was. I wanted to do big things; I wanted to see the world and be adventurous. I dreamt that someday I would settle down and live the ideal life: work a job I loved, marry the girl of my dreams, and have a family who lovingly called me "daddy." I had many vices and many virtues, but one thing was for certain; I was the dreamer everyone said I was.

But this night, as I looked out my window, I wasn't dreaming but instead found myself pondering a dilemma. For as much as I wanted to attend Young Life to prove it didn't interest me, I loved it.

For as much as I wanted to confront Dale on the irreverent manner in which he preached from the Bible, I yearned to hear him more. For as much as I wanted to attend to get Joey and others off my back, I found they had opened up a whole new world for me. I *was* interested. I couldn't wait for next Monday. "Dang it, Joey," I muttered to myself, "this is all your fault."

YOUNG LIFE

CHAPTER 5

For the rest of the year I became a regular at Monday night Young Life meetings. What I discovered was that there were plenty of Catholics beside myself who attended as well. Over time, I became more comfortable with the whole thing, learned the songs, and got to know the leaders. I was still amazed at the Biblical knowledge they possessed and how practical their teaching was. Young Life was a whole new world that I never knew existed, but got increasingly larger the more I was involved with it. It was like a sleeping giant, a secret society. I couldn't help but wonder how something so vast was so unknown.

I found that many school districts had well-established Young Life clubs. They were rarely advertised and gained numbers by word of mouth. There was no official membership or doctrine other than Scripture and having fun. It was described to me as a "non-denominational Christian organization." Kids came and went as they pleased, but mostly they came. Like any teenager from any era, we were searching for who we were and the reason for our existence. Christian or not, Young Life steered kids in a positive, responsible direction. It helped in the search for identity and if nothing else, made a kid feel like he was doing the right thing, that he was involved in something good. I think many parents were suspicious of the fun, but how could they object to a son or daughter who wanted to attend a Christian youth group meeting weekly?

During one of the Young Life meetings in the winter of 1976, there was an announcement. Dale proclaimed, "We have made our choice, and this summer we are taking a trip to Castaway Club in

Minnesota." I had no clue what he was talking about. He continued, "Not only are we taking a trip to Castaway, but we are going to bike all the way there." This definitely grabbed my attention. I couldn't believe they were planning on riding bicycles from Michigan to Minnesota. It sounded like something I wanted to be a part of, an adventure. After the meeting, I approached Dale to learn more about this bicycle trip to Castaway Club. What I found was very intriguing. Young Life was actually a national organization sponsored by big businesses with Christian ownership. They had established several camps around the United States, one of which was Castaway Club located in Detroit Lakes, Minnesota (which is actually very close to Fargo, North Dakota). Some of the other camps included Windy Gap in North Carolina, Saranac Lake in upstate New York, Frontier Ranch and Silver Cliff near Buena Vista, Colorado, and Lavita and Malibu in California. Every camp was built around a theme based on their geographic location. Castaway, which is more specifically located on Pelican Lake, is based entirely around water and water sports. If it can be done on water, you can do it at Castaway Club. The backing and support of big business make certain that all equipment, from canoes to ski boats, is top notch. According to Dale, all Young Life camps had the best of everything and existed for the sole purpose of teenagers having a great time while learning more about God. The trip was to span seven days biking from Flint, Michigan, to Pelican Lake, Minnesota, and then abandoning the bikes for a week while we enjoyed the offerings of Castaway Club. We would then use our support vehicles to drive us all the way back in about three days. Even though it would cost over $200, a hefty fee back then, I knew I had to go. I spent the rest of the winter months and the spring working to attain my camp fee. By the time the fee was due in early summer, I had raised it by means of donations from people who sponsored me, bike-a-thons, and other fund raisers that Young Life made available for its campers. I had earned my way; I was going to Castaway Club.

DIANA

CHAPTER 6

As the school year of 1975-76 ticked away toward summer, the Young Life meetings continued, and so did the typical life of a 17-year-old. My popularity continued and even grew. I got used to it but did not handle it well. Sher and I had an ugly break-up, which was totally my doing. In unbelievably bad form, I broke up with Sher on New Year's Day in order to date a girl named Martha. Perhaps it was karma, but the relationship with Martha fell apart within a month when she broke up with me in order to date drum major Dave. I'm sure he enjoyed rubbing my face in this, especially after the Iowa Deb departure from Smith-Walbridge left him feeling like he had gotten jipped. After this, I actually tried to get back together with Sher, but that was a bridge burned. She made me squirm so much in my efforts to reconcile that I finally cut bait and let her go. I knew that it had been a mistake to break up with her and felt genuinely remorseful over it. I didn't mean to hurt her, but I did. When it was all said and done, it was one of many lessons in store for me as a young man. I began to play fast and loose for the remainder of my junior year, involving myself in several brief, shallow romances. My growing popularity had an asterisk added next to it which meant "caution, girls."

Dale and the other Young Life leaders had been teaching great lessons from the Bible in an attempt to help us make good decisions, but we were still teenagers who lived for the moment and did teenage things without thinking of consequences. Even within the Young Life group, romances began and ended in a flurry. One brief romance I had was with a time bomb named Diana.

In the spring and early summer of that year, I had begun going out with Diana, whom I had met in the marching band. Diana was Latino and had thick, short, black hair and dark skin. She was thin and actually sort of tall with striking jet black eyes. She was a quiet, insecure girl with a quick streak of jealousy not far beneath her brown skin. She was hard to figure out, and any seemingly routine incident could unexpectedly blow up into a major ordeal. Dating Diana was like playing a game. This was a far cry from the effortless, direct, and to-the-point relationships I had enjoyed first with Barb and then with Sher during the fall and winter. The relationship with Barb mutually cooled and without any fanfare, we had quickly drifted away from each other and back into the dating pool. Barb was fun and easy to understand, and we remained friends until she graduated. Sher and I were a perfect match. Who knows how long we may have been a couple had I not turned into a fickle jerk? Diana, on the other hand, was a bit Jekyll and Hyde-ish.

Even though it was not smooth sailing, somehow Diana and I continued to date throughout June and the first part of July. In spite of her insecurity and jealousy, and my ego and indecision, she was a nice girl and I liked her. With our combined flaws we tried to make a go of it, but it all came to an abrupt end one summer afternoon.

I was preparing for my trip to Castaway and in spite of having a drivers' license, I biked as much as I could. I was in good enough shape for the 100-mile days that we had been warned about, but I wasn't sure how long my butt could stay in the saddle. One day, with nothing better to do and wanting to log some miles, I had ridden my bike over to Diana's house. She was not home, but her younger sister Bonnie was.

Bonnie was a year younger than Diana and possessed most of the same Hispanic features. Bonnie, however, was a bit curvier and had longer, even thicker hair than Diana. She also possessed something else that Diana did not: a pleasant personality and an easy, confident manner. When I knocked on the door that day, it was Bonnie who answered. "Hi, Scotty!" she said surprised and happy to unexpectedly see me. As we began to talk, she opened the door and came outside bare-footed. She was in a bathing suit and had a towel wrapped around her waste. Her hair had recently been combed straight back and was slowly dripping on the driveway. It was hot, in the 90s, and she had been in their swimming pool. Through dating her sister, we had actually struck up a friendship. I tried to focus on the conversation, but I clearly heard a voice in my head say, "What a fox."

"Is Diana around?" I asked.

"Nope, she had to go do something with my mom."

When she spoke, I could detect just a hint of a Mexican dialect. It was an attractive quality.

"Crap!" I murmured. "Do you know when she'll be back?"

"It shouldn't be too long; I think they just ran to the store." I stood there sweating from the ride, from the heat and released a long exhale as I contemplated what I should do.

"You can wait for her," Bonnie suggested. "We can swim!" popped out of her like a 'eureka!' Immediately I heard the same internal voice declare, "Are you nuts!? Diana would kill both of you!" At the same time, it sounded wonderful.

"Are you sure? Diana won't like it," I warned.

"Naw, c'mon," she said. "She'll get over it." I felt like she got me off the hook; it was *her* idea and after all, I was only waiting for Diana. We headed to the backyard.

As I was taking off my clothes, I heard Bonnie slip into the water. I stripped everything off except my cut-off blue jeans. They were so short that the white tips of my pockets were visible beneath the frays. This was the style in the 70s. After the last sock got tossed into the grass, I climbed to the top of the ladder and hurled myself cannon-ball fashion into the cool water. It felt marvelous. I was very tan except for the sharp line just above my ankles from rolled down socks and the perfect outline of my watch on my left wrist. Bonnie and I talked and splashed and laughed for about twenty minutes. All the while, I knew there would be hell to pay when Diana got back. But I kept trying to convince myself that this was innocent and harmless, and I was doing nothing wrong. And as long as I kept my distance from Bonnie, I felt everything would be okay. What I didn't want to happen was for Diana to show up with Bonnie and I wrestling around or something. THAT, would be trouble. I did just that: kept away from Bonnie while in the pool. Even so, I knew it would take a miracle for Diana to see nothing wrong with this.

I suddenly realized someone was at the edge of the pool . . . Diana. She had her arms folded across her chest with her elbows resting on the pool edge. She wore a light blue tank top that popped in contrast next to her dark skin. Her lips were held tight and her dark eyes blazed with anger. She had no particular expression, just the cutting stare of disapproval.

"Hey," I shouted, "It's about time. We've been swimming for hours!" I was trying to show that everything was fine, and swimming with Bonnie was no big deal, but I also knew that she would hate that joking comment. I think I was trying to make a point. I started to swim toward Diana with a big goofy grin on my face.

"I have to help my mom with the groceries," Diana said sharply, and she spun around and walked briskly into the house.

I looked back at Bonnie. "I think we're in trouble."

Trying to suppress her laughter into a whisper, she said, "I think *you're* in trouble!"

With a smile of disbelief and a crinkled up nose, I shook my head and looked at Bonnie from one eye with the other clenched tightly shut. She put both hands up to her mouth to smother her laughter. It was as if the joke was on Diana, and we were both in on it.

"Thanks for the swim," I drawled out in a long sarcastic manner. I climbed out of the pool, dried off, and put my t-shirt on. As I grabbed my shoes and socks, I looked at Bonnie. "Wish me luck."

With seriousness in her voice she said, "Sorry."

"Awe, don't sweat it," I said sullenly, realizing I had some damage control ahead. "It's not your fault."

I was sitting on the front porch steps and still putting on my shoes when Diana finally emerged from the house.

"Get all the food put away?" I asked, trying to act like there was no tension.

"Why were you swimming with my sister?" she asked straight out.

"What's wrong with that? You weren't here, Bonnie asked me to wait for you, it's hot, and you have a pool," I answered matter-of-factly. There were a few moments of silence.

"She's better than me," Diana said in a low voice.

"What?"

"She's better than me," Diana repeated a second time but a little louder. It was a strange thing to hear.

I asked for clarification. "What do you mean, 'she's better than me'?"

"You know," was all Diana said. I felt sorry for her. We sat next to each other on the step, and I held her hand. I could tell she was hurt. I acted like I didn't know what she meant, but I knew exactly what she meant.

"She's not *better* than you," I said, "whatever that's supposed to mean." I continued, "You two are just . . . different." I wasn't sure if that helped or not. She was thinking about it and all I got in reply was silence. I could tell there was some sort of history between her and Bonnie . . . maybe even a rivalry. Whatever the case one thing was for certain: Diana was insecure and a little paranoid.

We spent a few hours together that afternoon, which mostly consisted of me trying to soothe her wounded ego. During the next few days, I realized that I did not want to continue to go out with Diana. It really had nothing to do with the swim I had taken with Bonnie, but that sort of thing was typical in our relationship. It was simply too confusing and basically not very much fun. We liked each other and got along, but it just didn't seem like boyfriend-girlfriend material. We had run our course. About a week later, I broke up with Diana in her garage while rain pounded on the driveway. As I peddled home through the storm, I felt like a burden had been lifted. I decided to stay clear of any dating relationships for the rest of that summer. It had been a whirlwind of a year, and I felt like I needed a break. I spent a lot of time and emotion on several girlfriends that year at Southwestern, and I wanted to step back and get control again. Another reason to clear the slate was that I did not want to deal with any drama while on my bike trip to Castaway. I wanted to enjoy the trip without any distractions.

BOBBY

CHAPTER 7

The trip to Castaway was getting nearer, and I was riding more and more in preparation for it. One weekend a friend of mine named Bobby and I packed our bikes and headed off toward Port Huron. Bobby was a drummer in the band, a regular at Young Life meetings, and we worked together at the local Wendy's restaurant. He and I had become close friends and got into a lot of mischief together. He was also making the trip to Castaway that summer.

Once we reached Port Huron, we walked our bikes across the Blue Water Bridge to Sarnia, Ontario. After being checked through by Canadian customs, we proceeded north along the Lake Huron shore until we reached Pinery Provincial Park near Grand Bend, Ontario, Canada. It had taken us all day to reach Pinery, but we had finally made it. The going was tough as the wind off of Lake Huron was hitting us directly in the face. There was no coasting on that day. We camped there for the weekend and had a blast in the huge waves that the northwest wind was piling up against the shore.

Bobby was a small guy and couldn't have weighed more than 120 pounds. One day while we were dodging six-foot waves, the undertow dragged him away. As he went under, I could hear the panic in his voice as he unexpectedly gulped in water while yelling, "Hel . . . ." He never got the 'p' out at the end of that cry. Bobby had a t-shirt on because he had gotten badly sun burned biking. As I saw him disappear under the water, I made a desperate grab and came up with a fist full of shirtsleeve. I could feel the power of Lake Huron trying to pull him down but held on until he popped above the surf. We scrambled to shallower water and got our feet back beneath us.

Bobby was puking out water in huge burps and his eyes watered as he stood in the shallows with his hands on his knees. Eventually he straightened up, and we just stared incredulously at each other for a moment.

"God!" he cried, "You just saved my ass!"

I answered, "Holy crap, man!" We then busted out into laughter that barely hid the fear.

"That's enough of that for awhile," stated Bobby, and we trudged out of the water onto the beach.

The next day was Sunday, and we packed early to start home. The only excitement we experienced on the way home took place as we peddled south on the winding Queen's Highway. We had a tail wind that was helping us zip along at a pretty good clip. In the distance, I saw a truck hauling toward us from the south. Suddenly I heard the gurgle of a diesel engine behind us switching into the next gear as it accelerated out of a corner. I was leaned forward over my handlebars so I bent my head down and took a quick glance backward from under my armpit. A flatbed semi truck with bales of hay sticking out from both sides was coming from the north, behind us. Instantly, I realized the timing of all this was bad. I thought, "Uh oh, this could be ugly." I could see what was coming but had no alternative other than to stay as close to the gravel shoulder as I could and make sure nothing caused me to swerve into the road. There were two sharp warning blasts from the air horns behind us. As the truck began to pass me I gritted my teeth and tried to get small! Suddenly, I felt the jolt of a rough hay bale on my shoulder as it struck me hard. I never let go of my handlebars and my feet never left the toe-clips, which held them to my pedals. The first thing that touched the gravel was my opposite shoulder and my hip. The next thing I felt as the gravel ground the skin off my wrist, was Bobby's front tire plowing into my back. There was a cloud of dust and a heap consisting of two bicycles and two scraped-up bodies. We slowly got up and dusted ourselves off and checked to assess the damage: nothing but scrapes and aches. The bikes were scratched up a bit but basically undamaged. Lucky. My right knee was bleeding, and my wrist was raw. My shoulder actually had pieces of gravel imbedded in it and throbbed. Bobby had a cut knee and was hobbling around in a circle repeating the phrase, "Son-of-a-bitch, son-of-a-bitch!" I was picking the stones out of my shoulder when he finally stopped swearing and simply bent over with his hands on his knees.

"Geeeeeze!" I dragged out in disbelief, "we just got hit by a truck!" Then we nervously laughed, realizing what might have been and what a story we now had.

"We got hit by a truck!" Bobby yelled. "A stinkin' Canuck trucker rode our asses into a ditch!" he announced, solidifying the story.

"Let's get the hell outta here," I said. The small of my back had a dull pain where Bobby's front tire had hit me.

"Thanks for running me over," I said jokingly.

"Thanks for stopping me," Bobby quickly chuckled out. We took stock of our bikes and slowly got back under way. By 6:00 that evening, I was in a warm bath back home in Flint. As I cautiously washed my shoulder, I said softly aloud, "We got hit by a truck . . . how cool is *that*!"

Scott Hazel
Drum Major
1976

KEVIN

CHAPTER 8

My ride to Grand Bend with Bobby was the longest trip I took to get prepared for the adventure to Detroit Lakes, Minnesota. More typical were the rides I took to the lake. My parents, for years, had property on a lake about a half an hour from Flint. It was part of an association called the Chipper Club. The lake was named Leisure Lake and was near the railroad town of Durand, Michigan. Even though it was known as the Chipper Club of Leisure Lake, we just referred to it as "The Lake." It was about a thirty-mile trek and could be biked easily in a couple of hours.

When we first camped at the lake in 1970, I met a kid named Kevin. He was really white and muscular, with red hair and freckles. Over time, I found the girls really liked his flashing blue eyes with unusually long lashes. He was a hockey player with a short fuse. When I first met Kevin, I thought, "Irish." He was a year older than I and attended a rival school. Nevertheless, Kevin and I struck up a solid friendship. During high school, Kevin was the guy who introduced me to Sher, and eventually he and I ended up college roommates at Northern Michigan University.

But in our younger years, we spent many summers getting into trouble together at the lake. One night during the summer of my eighth grade year, Kevin and I were sitting with a bunch of summertime pals at the lake. It was dark, and we were clustered on a covered bridge, a popular teen hangout. One of the older kids produced a joint, fired it up, and began passing it around. It was the first time I tried marijuana, and I don't recall that it did anything special for me. I didn't mind sneaking my dad's beer now and then, but I felt a little uneasy about smoking pot. After that night on the covered bridge, I never touched it again until my junior year in college, nine years later.

One day in July, I made plans to ride my bike to the lake and hang out with Kevin for the weekend. As we sat around the campfire drinking our fathers' beer, we began to reminisce on goofy things we had done when we were younger.

"Remember that time we made that ridiculous go cart?" Kevin asked out of the blue. I began to laugh out loud,

"Oh man, that was a funny day!"

"Funny for you maybe; I almost got killed!" Kevin barked out.

Then together we began to recount the story play-by-play, filling in any missed details for each other. The story of the go cart begins when Kevin was a freshman in high school, and I was an eighth grader.

One Saturday in 1972 we were walking around Leisure Lake checking to see who was and who was not out for the weekend. We happened onto a pile of wood and paneling someone had thrown out from a cabin remodel, along with two old lawn mowers. We kicked it around a bit, trying to decide if there was anything we could do with it. Ultimately, we had taken some of the lumber and the wheels from the mowers. Just for kicks, we had decided to build a go-cart. We spent a couple of hours engineering and building on the fly. When we had finished, we had cobbled together what we felt was a pretty decent go-cart. It had a tapered front, which we covered with the paneling we had found. Basically, the driver sat on a board with his legs inside the paneled front and his feet on a two-by-four that stretched from one side to the other. The bottom was open, and you could see the ground only inches below your butt. We were proud of the steering. It consisted of a cut off broom handle secured through a hole in a 2x4 dashboard piece extending forward and was secured into the nose of the cart. There was a rope wrapped around it several times extending both right and left and fastened to the axel just shy of each wheel. The steering wheel itself was a mower wheel pounded onto the end of the broomstick. It would take several turns to work, but the rope would coil around the stick and pull the axel one way or the other, making the cart slowly turn. Like a couple of big kids, we took turns pushing each other up and down the road to test it out. It didn't take long for us to realize that was not too fun, especially for whoever was doing the grunt-work in the back.

About that time, Kevin's dad pulled into the lot in his red Volkswagen Beetle, which everyone called the Cherry-bomb. It was sort of comical to watch Kevin's dad roll out of the Cherry-bomb, being that he was a great big bald guy with a really hairy back and arms. He was affectionately known as "Bear." He came over to where we were still trying to tweak our new toy.

Bear kind of snickered, "What the heck is this?"

We were a little embarrassed but admitted, "A go-cart; we built it out of some crap we found," said Kevin. After studying it a bit longer, Bear slowly nodded his silent approval at our ingenuity and left to eat dinner.

Later, we were all sitting outside, just engaging in small talk. Out of nowhere Bear asked, "So why aren't you two goof balls messing around with your go-cart?"

Kevin answered, "It's fun when you're driving, but pushing that thing around kinda stinks."

"Humph," was the Bear's short reply. Nothing else was said about it. After a few minutes, Bear abruptly left, saying nothing as he went into the shed. He re-emerged a few moments later with a coil of rope in his hand: "Let's tie that go-cart to the Cherry-bomb, and I'll pull you around the lake."

Kevin and I looked at each other with our mouths hanging open and eyes popping out of our heads. "REALLY?" we asked, not believing what Bear had said.

"Let's go," he answered, as he started tying the rope to the trailer hitch on the Volkswagen. We tied the other end to the front of the go-cart and looked at Kevin's dad.

"One of you ride while the other one rides with me and watches," he said. So we took turns being the driver and the lookout while the Bear pulled around the Chipper Club grounds. We added a bent coat hanger with Saran Wrap stretched across it like a windshield. We had discovered that being dragged behind a Volkswagen Beetle on dirt roads translated into a face full of dirt. After we had weaved our way several times through the park, Bear upped the ante.

"This time," said Bear, "I'll take you around the lake." There was a dirt service road that wound around the lake. As it left the park, the road was on a high bluff with bare erosion ditches and gullies running steeply from its edge all the way down to the lake. We were extra careful on that stretch. My ride on the way around the lake was uneventful, but Kevin's return ride is what makes this story worth telling.

Kevin took his place on the board that was the driver seat. I positioned myself in the back seat of the Cherry-bomb as lookout. Bear started pulling Kevin, going all over the place and weaving in and out of trees. He then turned onto the road at the top of the eroded cliff. Bear started to go faster and faster. I could barely see Kevin through the thick dust, but at one point I noticed he was looking down and trying to do something with one hand while steering with the other. He was dangerously weaving back and forth across the road. I was just starting to say, "I think there's something wrong" when suddenly the back end of the go-cart flew up into the air! Meanwhile, Kevin's dad was pressing the accelerator, oblivious to Kevin's predicament. In a flash and to my astonishment, the go-cart pealed off the road, over the edge, and down the side of the embankment. I could see that Kevin was still driving on the side of the hill . . . his eyes were as big as saucers! I was trying to yell, "STOP!" to Bear, but it was all happening too fast, plus I was howling uncontrollably with laughter. There was a sudden jolt that made the tail of the Cherry-bomb lurch slightly into the air.

"What the hell!?" exclaimed Bear,

"He went off the road!" I finally hollered. Bear slammed on the brakes, and we scrambled out and ran back toward a cloud of dust. Kevin was grimacing and murmuring to himself as he limped around. He was totally covered in dust and had long scrapes on his arms and his legs, but looked to be okay. I began laughing when I choked out the question, "Are you okay?"

"Yessss," he said with his teeth clinched together.

"What happened? What were you doing?" I asked both questions in the same breath.

"That damned steering wheel fell off!" he yelled.

"What?" I asked.

Kevin began to retell the events as they happened. "That damned steering wheel popped right off!" He continued, "It popped off, and I dropped it right between my legs." Bear and I were listening but laughed more and more with every detail Kevin recounted. "It fell down between my legs and started rolling!"

"What do you mean 'it was rolling'?"

"The seat board," he explained, "was pushing the steering wheel along . . . it was rolling right by my crotch, and I was trying to grab it with one hand while trying to steer, holding on to the stick with the other!" I felt the tears of laughter start to well up as he told his story. "Then it went under the seat and threw the go-cart into air!" his voice cracked as he accentuated the terror of the moment. "That made me go off the road down that stinking hill!" He pointed as he finished the tale. "Then the front smashed into that giant ditch!" We looked in the direction he was pointing; there was an erosion ditch about three feet across and a couple feet deep. It was big. The front end of the go-cart had dropped into it, instantly stopping it, snapping the rope, jolting the Cherry-bomb, and sending Kevin right through the front of the cart. Kevin's scrapes were not from the ground, but from crashing through the paneling we used to form the front of the car. I suddenly realized the go-cart was literally a pile of rubble that looked amazingly like it did when we first happened onto it on the side of the road. Kevin's body had actually flown through the cart and destroyed it. He was in pain, but we were all laughing hard.

"Let's get this crap back to camp," said Bear. We picked up all the shattered material and placed it on the biggest piece of paneling that remained. We retied the rope and dragged it all back to the camp. When it was all said and done, all we had managed to achieve was moving a pile of scrap wood three lots down. It looked just as it did when we found it, except now it was our trash pile. Kevin spent the evening trying to dig out all the paneling slivers that were in his arms and legs.

As the final details of the story were completed, we both sat in silence watching the sparks from the fire drift into the night sky. We were young men now, and many of the childish escapades we had pulled off just a couple years earlier seemed decades past. In the quiet of the moment, we both knew those days were gone, that more serious matters lay ahead. The next day I rode back to Flint and continued to prepare for the Castaway trip.

THE BIKE TRIP

CHAPTER 9

The day finally arrived to depart for Castaway Club. We pulled the station wagon into the parking lot of Grand Blanc High School. It was a zoo. There were cars, bikes, baggage, and people strewn everywhere. The center of attention was the convoy of vehicles loading to accompany the bikers on their journey. It consisted of a Jeep, a Suburban, and five vans. One van had a bike rack on the front, a rack on the top, and was hauling a custom-built, long double-decker bike hauling trailer. This rig was beefed-up and looked mean. During the trip, it became known as the "Mule." It was specifically designed to carry the entire number of bicycles on the trip in case of emergency or if we fell behind schedule. That number totaled seventy-two. Another van, which became known as the "Chuck Wagon," was pulling a trailer with gas stoves fitted into it and a side-opening counter for cooking and serving meals. It also carried all the food for the bikers. The Jeep and the Suburban were the scout vehicles whose job it was to keep track of all the bikers' locations throughout each day. They both were outfitted with bike racks so in the event that they had to retrieve a biker, they could place the bike on the rack and have the rider climb in. They also carried water jugs, fruit, and first-aid supplies. We referred to these two vehicles as the "Seekers." There was also a cargo van stripped of its seats and towing a fully enclosed trailer, which carried all the baggage and tents. We called it the "Hauler." The remaining three vans were strictly designated to carry people. If we had to, the entire group of seventy-two bikers and support personnel could be picked up and transported by this menagerie of vehicles. In addition, the return trip was not going to be biked; we needed the capacity to drive everyone back to Michigan. Our convoy of seven vehicles allowed us to do that.

The parking lot was chaos, but eventually everyone was present, and his gear was stowed. We all made individual maps from a master and slid them into a clear plastic sleeve snapped to the top of a bag mounted between our handlebars. We all had six-foot fluorescent orange pennants standing at attention from the rear part of our bike frames. We were easy to see. Amazingly, bike helmets were not part of the biking culture yet, and none of us wore them for protection, as is so common today. My friend Bobby was on this trip, and he and I had personalized flags made. Just beneath the orange pennant, he and I had a second blue flag with a pelican on it and the word "Castaway" running its length. The pelican symbolized our destination—Pelican Lake, and of course Castaway being the name of the camp. When everyone was set, there were goodbyes and a prayer for safety and fun was said. Then in groups of a half a dozen or so, we were sent out at five minute intervals, orange flags rippling as they picked up speed. The seriousness of the bikers varied. Some had barely sat on their bikes until that morning. Their butts would pay the price as the trip progressed. Some had spent some time conditioning but were not driven by motivation to log miles. Bobby and I, on the other hand, and those like us, had spent many hours in the saddle and were approaching the trip as a chance to test ourselves daily. Every day there was a lunch destination and a final destination. The challenge was to reach lunch in good time to give you a better chance to reach the final destination before the Mule caught up with you and made you put your bike on the rack. When that happened, your day was over. Sometimes the Mule would pick up stragglers and take them to the front so they could slowly sift back through the groups. The idea was to keep the front group and the back group as close as possible to make it easier to monitor all seventy-two bikers. If this was not done, the Seekers might be covering strung out groups of bikers stretching more than fifteen miles to account for everyone. The five or six of us that became known as the "Trailblazers" tried to avoid being picked up by reaching the final destination everyday. The Mule began the pick-up process with those furthest back and worked its way forward. Knowing that this took some time and had a lot of starting, stopping, and loading, we pedaled as hard as we could into the evening, hoping to reach the final destination before the Mule could catch up to us. At least we wanted to be the last ones on the road, the last to be picked up. This ensured that we were at the top of the mile count. So everyday, especially after lunch, we pushed hard. But for now, we were just being sent on the road for the first time. Our pennants fluttered, and our gears clicked as we progressed through them. The trip had begun.

In less than an hour, we had worked our way to the front. We zipped along in a tight, single-file line, periodically switching who was in the lead. This drafting allowed the trailing bikers to rest a bit while the point rider did the work and broke the wind for the others. We operated in this fashion until the Mule passed us and then pulled to the side of the road a half a mile ahead of us. About fifty miles had passed since we started. The trailer behind the Mule was loaded with bikes. We were putting our bikes on the vacant racks when the convoy of vans, the Seekers, and the Chuck Wagon went whizzing past. Everyone had been picked up, and now we were the last. The day ended early because we were on a tight schedule to Ludington to get camp figured out. We needed extra time the first night to figure out how the tents set up and what needed to happen to prepare meals. It was a night of orientation intended to let the rest of the trip go as smoothly as possible. To help accomplish this, the group was divided into smaller groups, which were assigned a different chore every day of the trip.

We were awakened early the next morning in order to catch the ferry across Lake Michigan to Manitowoc, Wisconsin. After only a few miles, we all rolled into the dock area. The bikes were loaded onto the racks and trailer, and we proceeded onto the car ferry, S.S. Badger. It was a few hours of exploring the boat and lying in the sun on the foredeck while the Badger droned across the big lake. Before we arrived in Manitowoc, we copied our maps for the first leg of the ride through Wisconsin. After disembarking from the Badger, the convoy drove to a roadside park just outside the city. It was here that the bikes came off the racks, and the separate groups hit the road at regular intervals. With Lake Michigan on one side and ever-increasing farms and fields on the other, it really seemed like were starting to bike across the country now. The names were unfamiliar, and everything we saw was new. This was truly exhilarating.

It became obvious during this second day in Wisconsin that the Trailblazers created a great distance between them and the rest of the pack. Two things happened as a result of this. One result was that we were never able to leave first. The leaders would hold us until the end. This created a situation where we would overcome group after group until we finally made our way to the front. This kept us from distancing ourselves right away and helped the overall group remain closer together. I didn't mind this for the morning ride because I knew we would have to stop for lunch anyway. But they also did this to us after lunch, which hindered us from getting more miles by the end of the day. It did, however, motivate us to try and overtake everyone as fast as possible and then attempt to outrun the Mule to the final destination. We easily were biking over one hundred miles a day.

As we trekked down the back roads and secondary highways of Wisconsin and Minnesota, we were a spectacle indeed. Frequently, we would stop in small towns and roadside parks to refresh our water or take our lunch break. People on the way couldn't help but stop and find out what we were all about and where we were from. Those who were driving would honk their horns in approval of our efforts. They could see something huge was happening for us, and few short blasts of encouragement made us all feel special. The further we got from Michigan, the more people were amazed at what we were doing. Their curiosity didn't stand a chance against all those vehicles, all those kids, and all those bikes with a forest of orange standards. They couldn't resist asking the questions, "Where are you from? Where are you going?" and "How many of you are there?" The more we realized how much attention we drew, the more we loved answering the questions. Our enthusiasm was matched only by our tans.

SUZY

CHAPTER 10

The second to the last day of biking was a day that I will never forget. After lunch, the Trailblazers did something uncharacteristic from our usual quest to win the day. With little deviation, we had biked five days as a unit through Wisconsin and Minnesota and had only one full day left before reaching Castaway. We were all pretty close to each other in total miles biked, but because of breakdowns, injuries, or illness, I had about a seventy-mile edge on the others. It was going to be nearly impossible for anyone to match me with only one full day left. Also, some other friendships had started to form through the course of our journey. Many times others would ask to ride with us to test themselves or to see what it was like to ride with a team pushing as hard as it could all day. They typically would only do this for half a day and then return to a more leisurely group of riders. On this particular day, we decided to split up into other groups and ride with some of our other friends. We had proved our point, and now not driving hard sounded like fun.

I attached myself to a group with several girls in it that I thought I might want to learn more about. Although part of my motivation in breaking up with Diana was to not be involved with anyone while on this trip, flirting with new girls from different schools was certainly on the agenda. Riding with them sure seemed like a good opportunity to do this.

I immediately realized how incredibly slow they trudged along. After a week of hard-core biking, to suddenly crawl along was making me very antsy. I recall thinking, "Good Lord, I've gone from Trailblazers to 'Snailblazers'!" I could always flirt at camp, but this slug's pace was driving me crazy! Girls or not, I wanted to get going! After several miles, Dale came along side us in the Jeep and shouted, "How's everyone doin'?" Two girls immediately yelled, "We need some orange slices!" I couldn't believe it! We had only gone about seven miles, and they were getting worn out and wanted to suck on oranges! So Dale pulled ahead a little way and off the road onto a two-track entrance to a cornfield. We gathered around the Jeep, and most of the group began drinking water and eating orange slices. I was impatiently riding lazy circles in the road, trying to figure out how to get myself out of this dogged paced group. Finally, I pulled up and stopped at the edge of the road and asked, "Does anyone want to push on a little harder?"

"No way!" a couple responded in unison. "This is the pace we like." Knowing that one of the cardinal rules was no biker could be alone, my hopes of picking up the tempo seemed dashed. The line in the movie King Kong popped into my mind; "Twas beauty that killed the beast."

Then quite surprisingly, a girl in the back with a curly blonde ponytail, a rolled up bandana tied around her head, and the hint of Deep South in her voice said, "Ah'd lahk to go faster." It was Susanne. Her family had moved north from Alabama, and she was the perfect example of Southern hospitality. During the trip, we had affectionately shortened her name to Suzy. She had a gentle nature, almost shy, and rarely would start a conversation but was comfortable adding her thoughts once one was started. I liked being around her because she thought I was funny and laughed at nearly every silly thing I threw her way. She was not naïve, and she was certainly not dumb; nevertheless, she was the fuel for my ego. During the trip, we had developed a subtle fondness for each other. I think she liked my outgoing brashness, and I enjoyed that she liked me.

She walked her bike forward until she was next to me. I was trying to size her up and decide if she could handle what I had in mind. Her body was solid, and she had a few freckles that highlighted the bridge of her nose. Like many of the girls on the trip, she had abandoned any sense of conservatism and was wearing a tank top cut off so its length barely touched the top of her shorts. It was not for the style, but for the heat of biking and to avoid the dreaded farmer's tan created by shirtsleeves that modesty became a casualty. Plus, the more comfortable we got with each other, the more social barriers fell victim to function over fashion. It was impossible to ignore the cross dangling from the gold chain that hung around Suzy's neck and lay in her cleavage. Back home, she hid how well-built she was under modest clothes, but now on the trip where fashion went out the window to make room for comfort, her secret was out. At times around the campfires at night, I caught myself staring at her. She wore little or no make-up, and it was difficult to decide if she was attractive or plain. Then suddenly the light would hit her just right, or she would make a certain expression, and I realized that she was actually quite pretty. I really enjoyed her humble spirit, and her Southern accent had a peaceful quality to it.

As we stood there on the side of the road, everyone knew what was going through everyone else's minds: "Is she crazy? Who in her right mind would want to ride with *that* fanatic?" I said nothing when I looked at Dale, but my expression was easy to read. It silently begged, "What do you think?" Dale looked down and kicked at the dirt. You could tell he was trying to make certain he didn't make a mistake.

Suzy piped up, "Well, don't trah ta kill me, but ah kin keep up . . . Ah kin go faster." Dale looked at her, "Ah kin do it," she pleaded.

I looked at her with a faint grin, which meant, "Are you sure?"

"Ah kin do it," she repeated with clenched teeth as she switched her look from Dale to me. At that moment, everything that was attractive about her came to the forefront. For a brief instant as we stared at each other, biking was the furthest thing from my mind. I wondered what it would be like to kiss those determined lips, to hold her hand, to sit alone with her and have a deep conversation. Snapping back into reality, I looked at Dale and said, "I'll take care of her." Just saying those words made me feel like a prince charged with the duty of bringing the fair maiden safely home. I loved it!

"Okay," said Dale, "keep an eye on your map and follow the rules."

Much to my surprise and pleasure, Suzy sharply exclaimed, "YES!" It was uncharacteristic for her. I realized in that moment that shy, cute Suzy was also very much a gamer. I grabbed my seat with one hand and my handlebars with other, lifted, and spun my bike around so we were now facing each other, and said, "Follow me as closely as you can, and I'll break the wind. Let me know if I am going too fast," I continued, "it will make it a little easier for you." It was a serious tone. We looked at each other for a moment. Her enthusiasm changed into a bit of a worried look, like she maybe had gotten in over her head. Suddenly, she looked sort of scared and started to fidget with her water bottle. It was the perfect opportunity to score some *huge* points, and I wasted no time in doing so. I rolled forward so our bikes overlapped; and we were closer to each other. I reached out and took hold of her forearm. She looked up and we locked eyes. With a reassuring voice and a little glint in my eye I softly said, "You can do this," followed by a space of silence and then, "I'll take care of you," followed by a wink and a quick, single nod.

A soft, closed lipped smile slowly emerged across her tan face and the Alabama accent said, "Ah trust yew . . . let's go."

This was more than just biking; this was chivalry! I spun my bike back around, and off we went. As we left the group, I heard Dale holler, "You guys be careful!" and some girl yelled, "Suzy, you're nuts!" We both gave a quick wave and began progressing through our gears.

I set a moderate but pretty sporty pace, and Suzy was glued to my back tire. Occasionally, I would holler over my shoulder, "You alright?"

"Yup," came back the reply.

It was ninety degrees, and the blacktop shimmered with heat. Throughout the afternoon, we caught and passed several other groups. The other kids cheered for Suzy when they saw she was pushing herself and staying with me. I kept pressing the pace, and Suzy never faltered. It was impressive. We had several chances to connect while taking short water breaks and toilet stops. We were working hard in the hot sun but enjoying the pain. The experience belonged only to us. The farms were giving way to forests and lakes, but the heat persisted. We approached a picnic area just before a bridge at the edge of a lake, and I pointed with my right hand to indicate we were turning into it. Our bikes braked awkwardly into soft sand, and Suzy expelled a long "Whew," grateful for the rest. She leaned her bike onto a picnic table and sat down in the sand. Her face was red, and her thighs were pumped hard from the ambitious ride.

"That lake is begging us to swim," I said in the tone of a dare. Suzy wrinkled her nose and squinted up at me with one eye shut tight and a hand raised to shield the sun. She didn't say anything but was trying to decide if I was serious or not. She got her answer when I took off my gloves, peeled off my shirt, and began untying my shoes.

"Come on," I coaxed, "we have *got* to do this!" Every reason that Suzy may have had to decline went out the window when measured against the hard work she was doing and the sweat that soaked her bandana. Without a word, she rose and began taking off her shoes and socks. Before her second shoe came off, she heard me flop headlong into the water.

"Oh, does THIS feel good!" I shouted.

Without hesitation, she ran across the short beach and then stepped high through the shallow water until she could make no further headway and dove in. The water was cold and refreshing, and she surfaced, face to the sky, exclaiming, "Oh mah!" It was like a slow motion shampoo commercial as the water clung her shirt tightly to her body. I quickly looked away.

"Oh my, indeed," I said to myself. I slowly made my way over to where the lake passed under the bridge. I was testing its depth, which I determined was deep enough to jump safely off the bridge. I could tell others had done this because there was a well-worn path from the water's edge leading up to the road. Without any announcement, I followed the path to the bridge, climbed atop the railing, and cannon-balled into the lake with a huge splash.

"Oh yeah!" I declared, "c'mon!"

"Ah don't know," said Suzy with a hint of fear. I jumped two or three more times, not pressing the issue. "Okay," she finally said, and she pushed through the water toward the path. I helped her onto the railing and steadied her as she gathered her courage. Suddenly, she pinched her nose with one hand, screamed, and leapt from the railing. After the splash, she bobbed up like a cork and eagerly said, "Ah did it!" In that moment I realized that I was treating her to things that she would never dare try otherwise. She was having the adventure of her life, and I was her guide. I suddenly felt a sense of responsibility. We spent about ten more minutes just talking and letting the water soothe our aches and then returned to the business of biking. But the opportunity had been seized; the memory was in the books, and we were closer because of it.

A few miles down the road we were coasting at a pretty good clip around a blind curve with a steep hill on our left, which kept us from seeing ahead too far. As it straightened out, the hill gave way to a pasture. I was shocked to suddenly encounter three cows standing in the middle of the road! Startled, the closest one, a huge bull, spun around to face us as we were flying around the curve. We were going too fast, and the cows were too close to do anything but weave right through them. There was a narrow gap between the bull which was slightly to the right, and the other two, which stood shoulder to shoulder, more or less on the left side of the road. I turned my head and hollered over my shoulder, "DON'T STOP!" to Suzy, and began pumping my pedals as hard as I could.

She stayed right behind, and we weaved a smooth zigzag between the cattle. All I heard from Suzy was a long, drawn out, "OHHHHHHHH!" It began softly and quickly built to a loud yell fueled by fear. When we got a safe distance away, I slowed and let Suzy come along side. Both our eyes were opened wide, and we broke into nervous laughter in disbelief over what had just happened.

"That could have been ugly!" I said.

"That was scary!" replied Suzy. In a shaky voice that revealed her fear she continued, "Did yew see how *big* that bull was?"

"It was a good thing he didn't move," I answered. This was another incident in an increasingly interesting day, another story that only she and I could tell.

At one point, we entered a small Minnesota town and spotted the familiar flags of fellow bikers parked in a neat row in front of an ice cream shop.

"Yeah, Suzy!" was the cry of encouragement as we wheeled in. It was the familiar voice of Bobby. The first thing that came out of her mouth was, "Did y'all run into those stupid cows?" And she began to tell the story to whomever was close enough to hear. We got off our bikes and shook the feeling back into our rumps and tried to keep our legs loose.

"Who's ahead of you guys?" I asked.

"No one," said Bobby. Bobby looked at Suzy and then back at me with his eyebrows raised in disbelief. "How did *this* happen?" he asked.

"Long story," I answered, "but she is a trooper!" I looked at Suzy, who had found a spot on a bench. With her hands on her knees, she arched her back and tilted her face toward the sky with her eyes closed. Her face was red, and her shirt was soaked with sweat in the shape of an upside down triangle from beneath her breasts to her belly button. Looking at her, I felt she was done riding alone with me for the day.

"Hey kid," I affectionately called her as I put my hand on top her head. I could feel the heat coming off her hair: "You want some ice cream?"

"Heavens no," she answered. "That will make me sick." She stood and said, "Let's just git some fresh woter and a candy bar and keep moving. If ah sit too lowng, ah'll be finished."

I couldn't believe my own ears; she wanted to continue! "'Atta girl," I said with encouragement. She spread her feet apart, put her hands on her hips, and stretched backwards with her eyes closed and her teeth clenched in an attempt to relieve a kink in her back. The further back she stretched, the more her cut-off shirt revealed the curve of her waist and a flat tummy glistening with sweat. I could see the sweat was soaking the top of her shorts but then looked away, fearing I would get caught staring . . . too late. When I looked away, I saw Bobby had zeroed in on the same things, and he had caught me looking. He silently mouthed one word, "WOW." I just nodded in agreement.

After about fifteen or twenty minutes, someone said, "Let's get back on the road." Suzy and I, replenished with cold water and Milkyway bars, joined Bobby's group. We were with them only about five miles when, of all people, Suzy said loudly, "Do y'all care if Scotty and Ah go ahead?"

"Go for it!" Bobby replied. Suzy checked over her shoulder for cars and popped out and around the group. I settled in right behind her, and we slowly pulled away.

"See you at camp!" I yelled back as we left. Eventually, she looked back wondering why I hadn't passed her. "Yew takin' the lead?"

"Just keep pushing those pedals; you're doing great!" I yelled. I felt she would enjoy that feeling of being at the very head of not just us, but also the entire group. In that moment, she was *the* Trailblazer. She had her bike in top gear and was really trying to make sure that I didn't regret hooking up with her. She had a great pace going, and my view from behind her made my mind wander to less noble things. I was regretting nothing. The countryside was opening before us, and the views were getting better and better. From time to time, we would encounter a long decline, and we could coast for long distances as we squeezed our water bottles into our mouths and squirted them over our heads. Sometimes we would relax the pace and ride side-by-side for a couple miles and then back into our rhythm, one behind the other. It was a fabulous experience, and the road was a beautiful winding, hilly tour through alternating vast farmland and tunnels of trees that seemed to never end. Suddenly, we reached an intersection where the pavement stopped. It dawned on me that we had not seen a road sign in a long time. As I studied the map, Suzy said, "Something is wrong with mah knee." She was off her bike, flexing and massaging it.

"Are you alright?" I asked.

"Yeah, Ah think so, but Ah think Ah have to slow down a bit," she admitted reluctantly.

"That's okay. I have to figure out where we are anyway," I confessed.

"Are we lost?" I didn't say yes or no, but I responded, "Well, if we are, I'll get us back to where we're supposed to be." I was genuinely confident that I could. Another chance for the prince to score brownie points with the maiden I had pledged to take care of. I analyzed my map and tried to decide where we had gone wrong. I didn't want to waste time backtracking, but I also did not want to get us lost even more. As we had gone through a small settlement, I realized we had missed a turn. I figured that all we had to do was head north, and it would be impossible to miss the road we wanted. Sore knee and all, we took a right and began biking the dirt road that ran to the north. We made it to a stop sign, and I could tell that Suzy was struggling. As we contemplated our next move, a tractor slowly approached us, from the right. When it reached us the driver stopped and shut off the engine.

"Yous two lost?' he asked. His vowels were heavy and long, common in Minnesota.

"Yeah, I think we are," I answered, "but I think all we have to do to get back on track is keep heading north on this road." I showed him my map, indicated where we had made our mistake, and where I wanted to head.

"Oh ya," he agreed, "just keep headin' thata way until ya reach da next stop sign, eh?" He pointed in the way we were already going and said it like a question. "Take a right dair an go, oh abowt a mile or soo . . . den you'll hit anudder stop sign . . . that'll be yer road, you betcha."

"Great," I said, "thank you very much." We exchanged some short pleasantries and answered the usual questions, then headed on our way, waving as we left. I told Suzy I did not want the Seekers to miss us, so I wanted to get to the junction quickly. I told her to just keep her easy pace, and I would go ahead and wait at our road, and she agreed. I pushed down the dirt road as fast as I could make myself go. Sweat was running down my entire body when I reached the stop sign and a paved road. When I looked to my right, I was relieved to see the sign affirming I had found our road again. Even though I was far ahead, I could look back and see Suzy down the straight farm road. Eventually, she reached me at the intersection, and we sat and waited for someone to find us. I wasn't sure if we were in the back now; wondering if everyone had passed us while we were off the route. At least I had the comfort of knowing we were back on the right road. We decided we had nothing to lose by continuing in the correct direction and slowly began to pedal down the road to the west. I let Suzy set the pace. After about thirty minutes, I heard the familiar high pitched whine of Jeep tires approaching from behind.

"Thank God," I thought.

Dale pulled up and stopped right in the road next to us. "Holy cow are you guys a long way," he said, leaning toward the open passenger window. Internally, I was happy we were ahead of the pack and not behind.

"We got off the route and popped out here," I explained. "We're ahead of everyone still?" I asked.

"By about eight miles," he replied.

"Man, we must have accidently taken a short cut," I laughed a little.

"People are kinda slow today," said Dale. Then turning his attention to Suzy he said, "Wow have *you* cranked it up today!"

"Got that right!" I confirmed but then added, "But I think she's done . . . tweaked her knee." As I said this, I placed my hand on her shoulder and left it there, a flirting technique I had learned from Barb as a sophomore.

"Ah had a blast!" she beamed with accomplishment. I could tell that pairing up with her made her day, maybe even her week, but letting her lead was genius on my part.

"Ah wish Ah wooda done this more," she added and patted my hand with hers and then left it there. The non-verbal signals were subtle but obvious. From the corner of my eye, I could see that she was looking at me, but I did not turn. Not sure why, but I acted oblivious. Still, my hand remained on her shoulder and hers on top of mine. Dale said, "Let's load these bikes," and he pulled the Jeep off the road.

"How much further are we from tonight's camp?" I asked.

"I think about forty miles," he answered. I had my bike by the seat and stared down the road in the direction of camp forty miles away. The empty road beckoned, and I could not hide my desire to strike out on my own.

"You want to try and make it all the way, don't you?" Dale asked, reading my gaze.

"I would *love* to," I pleaded. Dale was securing Suzy's bike to the rack on the front of the Jeep. His silence let me realize he was thinking about letting me go alone. When he finished with Suzy's bike he stood, turned around, and peered down the highway.

"This is the final road; there are no turns until you see the sign for the campground," he said matter-of-factly.

"Are you serious!?" He continued, "Don't stop unless you have to and if you reach North Dakota, you have gone too far."

I couldn't believe he was letting me go, but I knew that based on my week, he had grown to trust my judgment. "Don't have to kick this horse twice!" I exclaimed as I hopped back on my bike. It was a saying I learned from my father that fit the situation perfectly. I was impressed at how quickly it flew from my mouth. I began to pedal away and Dale shouted, "YOU be careful!"

"Scotty!" Suzy hollered quickly, and I squeezed the brakes, dropped a foot to the pavement, and looked back.

"Thanks fer today." She said it smoothly with a little twang and a soft smile that spoke volumes.

"My pleasure," I replied. "I really had a great time." I spun around and pounded the pedals trying to make an impressive departure.

I heard the Jeep depart, and I was exhilarated knowing that I was out there on my own. My goal instantly was to bike the entire distance from camp to camp. I missed Suzy's company; it had been an interesting day, and she proved to be a capable biking partner. But this was a new feeling. I was hauling as fast as I could stand it but without exhausting myself. The road was winding through forests now with an occasional lake, wetland, or stream. A couple hours melted by and daylight was beginning to wane a bit. As I dropped into low-lying areas, I could feel the coolness of the evening settling in. I crossed one very long bridge, which spanned a wide river. The scenery was just too sublime. I stopped in the middle and simply tried to burn the view into my mind. After a couple healthy shots of water, I started up again. A few vehicles approached me from behind and each time I expected them to end my day, but they were never from the Young Life caravan and my day continued. I began to wonder why they hadn't caught me.

"Had something happened? Did I get off course again somehow?" Then I would see a road sign, "Nope, still on track."

Then I started to see campers and tents through some trees. I came to a large sign, which read "Land-O-Lakes Campground." I made it! I cooled down with a few circles in the wide driveway and then leaned by bike against a split-rail fence and perched myself on the top rail. I felt good. Not ten minutes had passed when a line of headlights rounded the corner from the east. I knew it had to be the Young Life convoy of support vehicles. Everyone was yelling and cheering out the windows as they made the turn into the campground. I was at the top of the food chain and felt like something giant had been achieved that day. Somehow in a combination of a snail's pace group, paired with Suzy, and then finally on my own, I had logged 137 miles! Most were with Suzy and then on my own.

That night, after the tents were pitched and the dinner pots were cleaned, we sat around the fire. Dale gave his nightly talk, and we prayed. Then everyone sat around and recounted the events of their day. This had become a nightly routine. Suzy and I sat next to each other and were the focus of countless questions. I let her field most of them. She was in a new element and seemingly eating it up. It was more credible for her to tell the stories than I. The others knew *she* would not exaggerate any facts or details. I enjoyed watching her bask in the moment. She was leaning forward with firelight dancing on her features as she gestured with her hands to emphasize certain points. She recounted the arduous pace we set, the soothing swim, and the jumps off the bridge. Her eyes got huge when describing the sudden sprint between the cows, then calmed to a sense of gratitude as she described the accent of the farmer who helped us find our way.

Everyone listening was fixated on her every word, and she left out no small detail. No one had heard her southern voice so much at one time with such enthusiasm and excitement. There were many things I wanted to say or add to her recollections, but there was something magical about simply letting her speak. When she had exhausted all she wanted to say and the questions were all used up, the group sat staring at the fire. In the silence, it occurred to her that she had been dominating the conversation. She looked at me with embarrassment in her eyes. I smiled, nodded my approval, and tapped my fist lightly a few times on the side of her thigh. She looked back at the fire and stated thoughtfully, "THIS . . . was a good day."

CASTAWAY CLUB

CHAPTER 11

There was an excitement in camp the morning of the last biking day. Everyone knew that no matter how the day played out, we would all be in Castaway Club that evening. We were only about fifty-five miles away, so urgency was not a top priority; packing our gear for the last time took precedent. We got a late start, and most groups rodc at a moderate, almost lazy pace. Because of this, we did not reach Castaway until after lunch. A mile or so away from the entrance to the camp, we were all herded together into one giant group. We then proceeded to parade into Castaway, riding five or six abreast and stretched across the width of the road. There were Young Life staffers and dozens of campers from other states lined along the way, clapping and cheering us on. They had arrived at Castaway via charter busses from their states and had been told about the adventurous way we came to camp. Not only did we feel special during that grand entrance into camp, but throughout, the week we were referred to as those crazy bikers from Michigan. Our convoy of vehicles followed us in, and we all stopped when we reached the main compound at the center of the camp. There were slaps on the back and hugs all around. It was a moment of congratulations and a sense of accomplishment. Then we methodically packed our bikes on the haulers and racks. They would not come off until camp was over a week later and after we had driven back to Michigan. The biking phase was over; now the actual camp phase began. In spite of our growing connection on the trip to Minnesota and the wonderful day we experienced together, Suzy and I developed no further relationship. It wasn't that we didn't talk or share any more time together, it was just that the events that would unfold during the next five days would unexpectedly steer us both in different directions. What was about to happen at Castaway Club would change many lives forever, especially mine.

We had arrived just before dinnertime and scrambled to get settled in our assigned cabins. The dining hall was a clean white building strategically located at the center of camp. The boys' cabins were located at the north end, girls' at the south. They all had nautical names like "Jib" and "Spinnaker." The reason for this was simple: The camp had a water-sports theme. The camp set on a bluff overlooking Pelican Lake. It was very large, much bigger than I imagined when locating it on the map. There were two methods to get down to the waterfront: a winding one-hundred-foot water slide or a stair system consisting of a zillion steps. Once down, you could do anything from paddling, to sailing, to skiing. You even had the opportunity to parasail if you had the guts. The amount of top-notch equipment available was overwhelming. But all this stuff was not for now; we would have to wait until later to explore all the options available to us. It was time to eat.

We filed into the dining hall, all wearing identical shirts we had printed back in Michigan. The hall was filled to capacity, and we had to find seats among people we did not know. There must have been nine hundred kids there! After dinner, there was a general meeting in a large facility named the Windjammer, which was designed to hold the entire number of campers. It was basically an orientation explaining how the activities for the week would happen and, of course, a list of "dos and don'ts." There were musicians and songs mixed in with hilarious skits and finally the featured speaker for the week. The camp staff announced that this particular week had Young Life clubs in attendance from Washington, Oregon, Kentucky, Illinois, Tennessee, Oklahoma, Texas, and of course, Michigan. As they recognized the different groups and where they were from, the group being announced would laud themselves with a giant cheer. It was interesting to take stock of each group's size and demeanor. When they recognized the group from Texas, an amazing roar of standing students exploded into the room. There were more than a hundred of them, and they were loud and proud. They would be the group that dominated the week. Because of the uniqueness of how we came to Castaway and our large number, others knew who we were as well. We were the second largest group behind the Texans and had the most interesting stories to share from our trek to camp. It was easy to talk with those from other groups because they wanted to hear about our journey. I would become the poster boy for the Michigan group because when people grilled us about our trip, who biked the most usually was asked.

Another thing that made me known to the entire camp was that I always had a soccer ball at my feet or bopping it around on my head. I had brought it along because when I returned to Flint from camp, there were Canusa Game tryouts waiting for me. Canusa Games were like junior Olympics held between Hamilton, Ontario, Canada; and Flint. I had played on the United States soccer team since I was a fifth grader. Being at Castaway was making me miss the first couple days of tryouts, and I was worried about not making the team for the first time in years. Consequently, everyone knew the tan Yankee biker who played the weird sport. Like any other situation, I loved the attention.

The atmosphere the first night was electric! It was like a Young Life meeting back home, only on steroids. By the time all the activities, introductions, and orientations had ended it, was time to go to our cabins for the night. As I a laid in my bunk and tried to hold a conversation with Bobby and the others, I realized just how whipped the days of biking had made me; and I quickly drifted off to sleep. The next day would unexpectedly begin an entirely new adventure.

"WE ARE NOT GAHS!"

CHAPTER 12

I was awake early the next morning. The days of biking had conditioned me to get up and get moving at daybreak. It felt strange to suddenly not have chores to do or tents to strike. Four of us got up and went outside: Tom Colby; who was better known as T.C.; Bobby, Matt, and me. It was nice to have the luxury of a bathroom and shower that you didn't have to walk outside to or wait your turn in line to use. As we exited the cabin, the freshness of the morning smelled good. The breaking day sent shafts of sunlight through the pines, and the dew was heavy on the grass. The coolness of Pelican Lake put a chill in the air, but the clear blue sky and sun reflecting off the water assured us that the morning would warm up soon. We were used to the chilly mornings and paid little attention to the temperature. The camp was not yet quite awake, and we took the opportunity to look around on our own.

We found ourselves standing at the top of the bluff, peering out over the lake and talking about whatever popped into our minds. I noticed a little further up there were three girls doing the same thing, except they looked cold in the morning air. The longer we stayed I noticed that we were exchanging glances in each other's direction and mumbling about each other. One girl was tall, slender, and blonde. Another was tall, slender, and had long, fairly-straight brunette hair. The third girl was petite, had shoulder length, somewhat curly, brunette hair, and a really nice shape, even at a distance. We were trying to decide whether or not to say anything to them. They were girls, for crying out loud! New girls whom we did not know; it was really not much of a decision; this *had* to be done. Slowly, we tried to close the space between them and us without looking too obvious about it. We pretended to be totally focused on the lake. The girls were rubbing their hands up and down their arms in an effort to stave off the goose bumps. Then they turned and started to walk away. It was now or never.

"Hey you guys," I hollered toward them. I got no response. Again I hailed them, but a little louder this time, "Hey you guys!" Still there was no reply. I thought, "Okay, one more time and I'm finished trying to meet these stuck up girls."

"Hey you g . . . !"

Before I could finish my sentence, the tall brunette cut me off, "We are NOT gahs!"

It stopped me in my tracks . . . I was dumbfounded. I was unprepared for what she said and had to think about it for a second. I could tell they were not from Up North and was trying to place their accent. "*Gahs*," I thought; what's that? Then I realized she meant "guys."

"Oh," I said quietly repeating what she had said with a sense of comprehension, "'We are not *guys*.'" Now it made sense. But more importantly it dawned on me that if we were going to meet *these* girls, there was some quick damage control in order. I jogged up to them before they could get away saying as I went, "Wait a minute, wait a minute."

"Do we look lahk gahs to y'all?" The blonde repeated tersely before I could say a word. Immediately I diagnosed and addressed the problem.

"We call everyone 'guys' in Michigan, it's just a figure of speech."

"Well, we don't talk that way in Texas," said the tall brunette. She was pretty and had a thin face with high cheekbones and long dark hair parted down the center of her head. Immediately, I thought she looked like an Indian. "Pocahontas!" I said silently to myself.

"WE are NOT gahs," repeated the blonde.

"Okay, okay," I said . . . I'm sorry, I won't call you that again."

"*WE* won't call you that again," chimed in Bobby. I hadn't noticed that he, T.C., and Matt had trotted up with me. They certainly weren't going to miss out on this action.

"So what should I have said?" I asked.

Again the tall brunette answered for the three, "Hey girls, or hey y'all." Her Texas drawl was wonderful and when she said "y'all" it just rolled off her tongue. It was different from the Alabama twang of Suzy. Somehow it seemed prettier. By now, all of us were in a sort of circle, cautiously checking each other out.

"Where in Texas are you from?" I asked.

"Amarilla," replied the blonde.

"Amarilla with an 'o'," added the brunette, "where the West lingers on."

I would learn later that although Amarillo ends with the letter o, they pronounce it like it ends with the letter "a". 'Where the West lingers on' is the motto of the city.

"Where's that?" asked T.C.

"In the middle of the Panhandle."

Again T.C., "Where's that?"

"Son, don't you know anything? At the top of the state," the blonde answered.

It was a funny reaction that sounded so neat in her smooth dialect, but I could tell it made T.C. embarrassed. T.C. was not dumb, but he was a very simple person. His expressions and slow manner of speaking made some people think he was not a smart guy. Once you got to know him, he was very funny, but until then, he was actually sort of shy. There was an uncomfortable silence until the tall brunette came to T.C.'s rescue.

"Where're y'all from?" she asked.

"Flint, Michigan, where we make all the cars," I said proudly as I raised my hand vertically and pointed to a particular spot on my palm.

"What are yew doin'?" she asked with a confused look.

"What?" I replied, not understanding the question.

"What in the world does your hand have to do with where ya'll are from?" asked the blonde.

"This is where Flint is," I responded in oblivion, still pointing to a spot on my hand.

She asked again while rolling her eyes, "Why are yew pointing to your hand?"

It was in that moment that I realized that the common practice in Michigan was not common knowledge elsewhere. So I began to explain, "Michigan is shaped like a mitten; we use our hand to show where in the state we are from." Then I jabbed, "Son, don't you know anything?" No one saw that coming, and T.C. laughed right out loud. Embarrassed herself, the blonde sheepishly said, "Ah guess ah deserved that."

Immediately T.C. said, "That's okay, that stuff happens to me all the time," and they smiled at each other.

"No harm, no foul," said Matt in the background, and everyone nodded in relief.

"Ah thought that was Detroit," said the blonde. Once again, she asked a question that seemed to have no relevance whatsoever.

"What?" I replied.

Getting the uneasy conversation back on track, the blonde asked more specifically, "You said Flint was where all the cars came from, ah thought that was Detroit?"

"Oh," I finally understood, then continued, "well, it's actually any decent-sized town in Michigan."

Then I realized no one had introduced themselves. "Do you g . . ." I caught myself about to make the same mistake, "Do *you all* have names?" I made a half-hearted effort to say 'y'all', but it sounded ridiculous. We all took turns going around the circle saying our names. The tall brunette was named Janet. The slender blonde's name was Megan. And the little brunette's name was Karen. When she said her name, it was the first time I had heard her voice. It was bashful and very cute. She had only spoken one word, her name, and something within me took notice. There was a quality about her that I liked right away. The others had begun to talk some more, but I hadn't a clue about what. I had looked at Karen when she introduced herself and never looked away; I had gotten stuck staring at her. She was watching and listening to the others when she noticed I was still looking at her. Slowly she looked up at me from the corner of her eye. Realizing I was caught, I quickly let my eyes fall to the ground. A couple seconds, later I raised them, and she was still looking at me, and she smiled a tender smile. There was no hiding it now; we locked eyes without apology. The others were immersed in conversation, but Karen and I were somewhere else. What seemed like an eternity was probably only the passing of a few seconds as we stood oblivious to the others and smiled at each other. In that moment, something happened; the attraction was noted and understood.

"Isn't that right, Scotty?" brought me back to reality. T.C. was asking for verification of something he had said to everyone.

"That's right," I answered, without even knowing what it was I was confirming. We continued to share small talk and little facts about our families, our homes, and ourselves. I learned that Karen and Janet were sisters. Janet was my age, and Karen was two years younger. Even though she was the younger of the two, it was Karen who caught my attention. The cultural differences we discovered were very intriguing and the general topic of our conversation. The uneasy beginning had softened into humor and the first opening of windows to new friendships. The camp was gradually awakening, and the smell of bacon mingled with a cool mist rising from the grass. I recognized an opportunity to pursue this further and asked, "You guys wanna go eat breakfast?" All three girls looked at me; Janet put her hands on her hips and shook her head with a purposely-exaggerated look of disapproval.

"What?" I asked.

"Yew did it again!"

I realized I had called them guys again. It was a tough habit to break.

"Geez, I can't help it, it's just how we talk."

"Ya know," I continued, "your 'o's' are like 'a's' and your 'i's are like 'o's. We could have some very confusing conversations!" I chuckled a little as I said this to lighten the mood a bit.

"Let's just go eat breakfast and see if we can figure some of this out."

"Alraht," Karen's sweet drawl broke the air in acceptance of the suggestion.

We all started in the direction of the dining hall. There was one last look from Megan. She squinted her eyes and said, "We're NOT gahs". Then her face softened into a smile, indicating she was not serious.

Emphasizing the long 'i' sound, I said, "You mean *guys*?" and smiled.

KAREN

CHAPTER 13

There were several individual conversations taking place as we walked to breakfast. Karen was ahead of me but then stopped, stepped aside, and half-turned until I came up next to her. She was nervously picking at the fingernails of one hand with those from the other. She looked up at me and said, "Ah'm stickin' with yew; ah don't know a soul in this place."

Her voice was like thick syrup, and I was infatuated as soon as I heard it. She had a small button-like nose and a wide smile that forced her cheeks into balls. She was tiny but well-built; a body that demanded a double-take. I did not fixate on it, but it was impossible to ignore how well she filled her t-shirt, which stretched tightly across her chest and distorted the word, "Tascosa" that was printed on it. A tiny waste that curved back out into attractive hips accented this. She had beautiful proportions and wonderful curves. She was barefoot; and I noticed she had tiny feet with toes that made them look square: that is, flat across the front, and she walked with her shoulders held back. Next to her captivating Texas drawl, the feature that most lured me in were her inviting blue eyes. What makes certain eyes attractive to certain people is difficult to describe, but the more Karen looked at me when she spoke, the more her eyes drew me in. At the breakfast table, we sat across from each other, and I studied her mannerisms, how she said certain words, and the pleasant nature of her facial expressions. The week at camp hadn't really even started, and it already had taken a surreal turn. In less than an hour, I internally confessed to myself, "I like this girl."

In that moment, for some reason, I thought of Diana and breathed a sigh of relief that we had broken up before I left for Castaway. I thought of Suzy, how just two days before we shared the most memorable ride of the trip and seemed to be cultivating some sort of relationship. But nothing had been done since then, no serious conversations, no cryptic looks, and no subtle touches. It was as if we both knew that special time was only for the duration that it lasted, and we were not looking to continue down a road to any sort of commitment. It was what it was, and we mutually let it remain as a memory. We had run our short course and were content to remain friends with a special bond and a story all our own.

"Scotty?" the small voice brought me back to the breakfast table. Karen had said my name in a way I had never heard it before. It was soft, and she kind of bent the "o" in a way that made how I normally heard it sound harsh. I had been momentarily daydreaming out the window about Diana and Suzy.

I looked at Karen: "Do you want to go look around?" I asked. The question seemed to pop out of nowhere. She looked at Janet as if asking permission. Janet shrugged her shoulders with indifference.

Karen looked back and said, "Sure," and then once again said, "ah'm stickin' with yew." For a second time that phrase struck a chord within me, and I got a strange feeling in my gut; you could have knocked me over with a feather. I picked up her tray and bused her dishes. "Chivalry," I thought, and we left the dining hall and walked around the camp for about an hour. It was then that I found that "Tascosa" was the name of her high school, and she learned why I always carried a soccer ball around. She was two years younger than I, but she didn't look it, and she didn't act it. I immediately decided that our age difference was a non-issue.

There were many planned activities that first day, broken up by meals and some free-time. If we weren't obligated to be with our own groups, Karen and I made a loose plan to meet outside the Windjammer after dinner. Neither of us knew whether or not we could, but we agreed we would try. As the day wore on, the chance of spending more time with her was always in the back of my mind. A couple times during the day we saw each other at a distance and waved. A voice inside my head counseled, "Don't get wrapped-up in this, you just want to enjoy the camp." But I think it was already too late . . . she was on my mind, and I couldn't get her out.

Dinnertime finally arrived and as I entered the dining hall, I made a quick survey in hopes I might spot Karen. The Texans were all concentrated in an area and involved with themselves. I discretely tried to locate the tiny Texan but could not pick her out of the mob. I turned my attention to those at my table, and we laughed about many of the occurrences of the day. I decided not to look too eager to meet Karen and stayed in my seat, goofing around with Bobby and T.C. I decided not to try to force anything to happen, like I might if I were back home, but to just let whatever might happen, happen on its own. In the middle of our antics, Bobby kicked me under the table. When I looked at him, he made a small gesture with is head in the direction where the Texans had been. I sneaked a peek that way and saw a line of girls filing from their table toward us. It was Janet, Megan, Karen, and a couple others I did not know. I tried to play it cool until they were passing our table at which time I heard Megan say, "Hey y'all." There were several, "Hey, how ya doings?" thrown back in a weak attempt to act as if we hadn't seen them coming.

"Hi, Karen," I said when it could be heard clearly on its own. She smiled and gave a little wave with one hand, raised her eyebrows like she was asking a question, and trying to hide her other hand close to her body pointed toward the door like it was a secret. I nodded in affirmation while holding up my index finger meaning, "I'll be there in a minute." I waited until they had all made it out of the hall and then said, "All right boys, I don't know what *you* are going to do, but I am going to walk around with that little Texan." I bussed my tray and strutted out the door, giving a peace sign toward the others with one hand and pressing my soccer ball against my hip with my other forearm.

Karen was sitting on a bench, and I went over and sat down next to her. "Hi, y'all," I said, trying to accommodate her sensitivity to being referred to as a guy.

She laughed, "Yew don't say ya'll when there is only one person . . . Y'all is plural." I felt dumb.

"It's alraht," she said, "people from the North always make that mistake, but that was nahs of yew to trah," which I quickly translated into ". . . nice of you to try." We walked around and talked until it was time for the nightly meeting, and we reluctantly separated to our own groups. The ice had been broken, and we both understood that we enjoyed being around each other. As the meeting ended and the throng of kids funneled through the bottle-neck at the door, I spotted Karen behind me with the others from Amarillo. I quickly moved off to the side when I made it outside and kept a tight watch at the door for her to emerge. The Windjammer had become stuffy with the scent of close sweating bodies, and the cool night air was a relief. When Karen came out, I reached out and grabbed her lightly by the arm and pulled her off to the side, away from the crowd. The wanton look I received from her blue eyes made it obvious that she was glad I had found her.

"I had a good time with you today," I said, and I bounced my soccer ball a couple times on the grass.

"Me too," she replied and beamed up at me with a shy smile and sparkling eyes. She seemed to be embarrassed that she had let me know too easily that she liked my company.

"Would you like to do something together tomorrow?" I asked.

"Ah would lahk that."

"Okay, I'll look for you at breakfast."

"Alraht, g'naht."

"Good night," I answered as I backed away, keeping eye contact with her and then turning away, smacked my hands together, and jogged away lightly, tapping the ball before me with my feet and trying to catch up to Bobby, T.C., and Matt.

I lay in my bunk that night staring at the ceiling. In the dark, Bobby, who was in the bunk below me, said, "That Karen's a cute girl . . . you two seem to be hitting it off pretty good." The events of the day had turned the entire trip on its head. We had only biked into camp the previous day, and already the week of biking seemed distant, almost like it had not happened.

"Yeah . . . I was NOT expecting this," I sighed. We all spoke about the day, the different things that had happened, and the people we had met. Always in the back of my thoughts was Karen. Slowly, the chatter in the cabin petered out and was replaced by the deep breathing and snoring of exhausted young men.

For a long time, I tossed and turned and kept hearing her drawl, seeing her face, and seeing her eyes. Sleep did not come easy that night, and the anxiety for the coming day would not let my mind relax. There was a small window next to my bunk, and a refreshing cool breeze sifted through its screen. A shaft of moonlight crept through the room, marking the passing of time on the floor. In the distance, I could barely make out the gentle lapping of waves on the waterfront as they slapped against the sides of canoes. It felt like I was the only person awake in the world. Although I wanted to sleep, I did not want to stop thinking about Karen. I rolled onto my side and put my head on my arm with my face close to the window. I strained to see out across the sleepy camp where so much had taken place that day. The tall trees stood like sentries guarding the open expanse that dominated the center of camp. Occasionally, the leaves made a sound in the breeze that resembled someone saying "Shhhhhhhhhhhhh." Into the night I whispered her name, "Karen," and finally drifted off to sleep.

As the week went on, Karen and I spent more and more time together. This was not like being with Barb, Diana, or Suzy. This was different. Back home, relationships came and left, and the mourning was short-lived. Someone else always seemed to be waiting to fill the void. But the closer I got to Karen, the more I felt feelings I had not tapped into before. "My God, is this love?" I asked myself one day. "How can this be, it's only been a few days?" Emotionally, I had entered a place I had not been before, even with Sher who I was quite fond of. This was something brand new that I liked and was afraid of at the same time. I felt that it was important that I didn't do anything wrong . . . I cared. At night when I thought about it, it actually physically hurt.

The more time Karen and I spent together, the more we opened up to each other. We were becoming a camp couple. Everyone became used to seeing us together, even if it was her sitting in the grass while I showed off juggling the soccer ball around. One night Karen invited me to sit with her group during the nightly meeting. I received some cold stares and some double-takes from the Texans. They were a proud people and by virtue of their sheer number, were a driving force for the activities of the week. Where the Texans were, things happened. Being an outsider and spending lots of time with one of theirs was more like being an intruder. It took a little bit of work and some forced humbleness on my part, but eventually I was allowed in by the Texans. As Karen led me into the midst of the Texans that evening, the girls who looked our way seemed jealous and leaned close to each other to whisper. This, I did not mind. But the guys were sending me signals of warning. What helped soften the tension were the girls we had met that very first morning. They came and spoke to me and showed their group I was not an intruder, but an invited guest. It was a weird feeling; I was out there in a strange land trying not to cross forbidden lines, and I didn't even know the rules. One day I sat with Karen for breakfast at a table full of Texans and got to know a few of them better. Karen returned the favor at lunch and sat with me and some of my friends from Michigan. They made Karen feel welcome, and I appreciated that they didn't scrutinize her like the Texans were me. But that was the guys. The girls, on the other hand, were not appreciating that the most outgoing group of guys were spending a lot of their time with girls from Texas and other states. It was nothing that destroyed any friendships, but you could sense that the dynamics of the trip had changed.

On Thursday, the next-to-the-last-day of the week, Karen and I went sailing. I thought I knew what I was doing but dumped us several times. It was embarrassing. Eventually I gave up, and we decided to lie on the dock in the sun. She was wearing a two-piece bathing suit and had shorts pulled over the bottoms. It was that day as we lay side by side on the dock in the sun that I reached out and took a hold of her hand. There was no other movement by either of us; we just lay there in the sun holding hands. We were facing each other as we lay on our towels, and we and just looked at each other with our fingers entwined. "You have the most beautiful eyes," I said. There were quiet smiles on both of our faces, and I knew we had moved to a different level. I looked calm, but my heart was pounding.

After a while, I noticed there was a shadow cast over me, and I felt the presence of someone standing by my side. I let go of Karen's hand to shield my eyes and saw a giant of a guy standing there on the dock next to us.

"Mah name is Kawl; ah'm from Amarilla, Texas," he stated like he was giving a speech to strangers. It took me a second to translate "Kawl" meant "Kyle". I had seen him before, and he was one of the

Texans who shot visual darts at me whenever I sat with them for a meal. He was blonde and had a firm square jaw. Everything about his appearance said, "I play football." He was built like a Greek statue and had the face of a comic book hero.

"Hey Kawl," said Karen in friendly recognition.

"Howdy," Kyle said back, softening his demeanor toward her. I remember thinking, "Good grief, they actually say 'howdy?'" But there was no act about it. This dude was the real deal.

"Hey, Yankee," he said to me.

"Yankee?" I responded, "never been called *that* before." I stood up and offered a hand. "Nice to meet you, Kyle, my name is Scotty."

He cocked his head and slowly grasped my hand. I could tell he was trying to be intimidating, and he was, but I had to at least show I had some balls. As he shook my hand, he put his other arm around my neck and steered me away from where Karen was laying. "Listen, Yank," he began, "Karen is real special t'us, and she is kahnda lahk our mascot." I thought that was a funny analogy, but I understood the meaning clearly. He continued, "She really lahks yew, and if yew hurt her ah'm gonna be very upset . . . an' yew don't wont me to git upset."

"My name is Scott."

"What?"

"My name is Scott, but my friends call me, Scotty. You keep calling me Yankee."

He took a step back and looked at me with one eye closed against the reflection of the sun on the water. "Did yew hare what ah said?" His drawl was slow and thick and had confidence behind it.

"She really likes me?" I asked.

In the midst of all the intimidation, *that* seemed to be the only thing Kyle said that registered in my mind. He looked down and shook his head, realizing he had accidentally leaked some inside information. He looked back at me, "Yeah, she lahks yew bocoups." His tone was easier now that he had blundered a little. "But ah meant what ah said; if yew hurt her, ah will break yew in two," he said sternly with his teeth clenched.

"Listen cowboy," I said in a manner that might have gotten me killed, "this was the furthest thing from my mind when I came up here. I can't even sleep because of her! The last thing I want to do is hurt her; I really like her too." I had said it sincerely and with conviction. A nasty grin spread across his face, one that was menacing but enticing at the same time, and I knew a thousand Texas high school girls must have fallen for it.

"That's the raht answer, Yank," he smirked with satisfaction, and he smacked me on my back.

"My name is, Scott." I said tersely.

"Not yet it's not," he said as he began to stroll away from us. "Bah, Little One," he said in the direction of Karen. They pronounced "bye" like "bah."

"Bah, Kawl," she beamed as she sent him off. I lay back down next to Karen and let out a long exhale.

"What was that all about?" she asked.

"You seem to have a protector."

"Yeah, he's lahk mah big brother, a real great gah."

"Great," I said flatly.

We lay on the dock for another half an hour or so and actually dozed off. Someone stepped around us, and it woke me up. I saw that Karen was also shaking the cobwebs out and had fallen asleep too. "Man!" I said, "I fell asleep."

"Me too," she replied. Then she added, "I haven't been sleeping too well at night."

"Me neither!" I wondered if her sleepless nights were from thinking about me the same way mine came from thinking about her. "That would be so cool," I thought to myself. "Well, if you can't fall asleep tonight, take a walk to the top of the waterfront steps; I'll look for you there."

"Okay," she said without hesitation. Of course, now I *knew* I wouldn't be able to sleep.

During the meeting that night, the night before the last day, there was an invitation given to anyone who had never asked Christ into his or her lives. Along with all the activities, fun, and new friendships, the speaker had done a wonderful job explaining the Gospel and what it meant to be a Christian. What he wanted us to do that evening was to silently leave the Windjammer and find a place alone and say the prayer of commitment if we felt so led. I felt like he was speaking only to me and realized I felt the need, the call to say this prayer and make this choice. As we all filed out silently, you could faintly hear the sniffles of those whose emotions, spiritual or otherwise, had surfaced beyond control. I quietly walked to the top step of the waterfront, the very place where I hoped to rendezvous with Karen later. I sat down and asked Jesus to come into my life. I wasn't sure why, but I began to sob. I knew I had done something life-changing, and it hit me hard. I sat for a short time, realizing that even though I did not understand the total magnitude, this was a pivotal moment in my life. It needed to be digested and savored. So there I sat alone and weeping.

After a while, I saw dark shapes emerge from all corners of the camp. Some who passed close by actually put an empathetic hand on my shoulder. Everyone seemed to be congregating near the compound just outside the Windjammer. Quietly, I got up and joined the emotional throng. There were many tears and lots of hugs. It was obvious I was not the only one who felt God tapping His finger on their shoulder that evening. It was powerful and unforgettable. I finally saw Karen, and we hugged.

"Are you okay?" she asked.

"I just prayed that prayer, and I feel amazing," I answered.

"Bah the look of it, ah think a lot of people prayed that prayer t'naht," she replied. We talked for a short time together and with others who saw us and joined us. Eventually, the camp counselors walked through, announcing in loud voices, "All right folks, it's late, time to head to your cabins." With that, all the groups slowly said their good nights and headed their separate ways.

As we said our goodnights, I whispered a reminder to Karen, "Remember, if you can't sleep tonight, try and meet me at the top of the waterfront stairs."

"Ah will . . . g'naht," she said with her usual soft drawl and wonderful eyes, and we walked in opposite directions.

On my way back to the cabin, I realized that at this time the next evening, we would be saying goodbye. I couldn't believe that the trip that seemed so long at the outset, now seemed to have slipped by in the blink of an eye. "Tomorrow will be the last time Karen and I will have time to spend together," I thought to myself. As I pondered that notion, I could hardly believe that time was finally upon us. I felt sick.

That night when all got quiet and I was in my usual position looking out the window at the sleeping camp, I quietly climbed down from my bunk. I silently pulled on some shorts and a t-shirt and slipped out the cabin door. I cautiously picked my way from tree to tree across the camp, hoping that no staffers would bust me. I felt like an escaping prisoner trying to avoid the watchtower. When I reached the top of the stairs, I was hoping the tiny figure of Karen would be waiting, but they were vacant. I looked around a bit and then sat down on the top step. Pelican Lake was like glass that night, and the moon was full but had a hazy ring around it. It was muggy, and the air was heavy and still. I was sitting still but felt sticky from the thick night. In my mind, I was pressing the 'rewind' button on everything that had happened to that point. The bike trip was a distant memory, and the events of Castaway were like a blur. I thought about how only a couple hours earlier, I sat on the exact same step and became a Christian. I was deep in thought, wondering about how this would change my life, when suddenly from the dark I heard my name called out in a whisper, "Scotty?"

"Here," I answered, and Karen stepped forward and sat down close next to me, wrapping both her hands around my arm. I patted her hands and we sat there quietly, staring at the yellow moon hanging over the lake. We were silent for a long while, not sure what to say, just letting the moment be.

"Tell me about Amarilla," I said, purposely exaggerating the "A" at the end. Like molasses, she slowly drawled out about the prairie wind, the canyons and the cowboys.

When she was through she countered, "Tell me about Michigan." With heavy vowels, I spoke of trees and snow and lakes like inland seas. I felt the shock of the sudden realization that soon we would have to go back to our homes and that we were from two separate worlds a thousand miles apart. I could tell by the uncomfortable silence and how she squeezed my arm tighter that she had realized it also.

"What are we gonna do?" I asked sullenly.

"Don't know," she said, and her head fell against my shoulder.

Back in my cabin later that night, I was reluctantly trying to imagine what the next day would be like. Earlier in the week, we learned that everyone in camp was leaving that Friday night right after the last meeting of the week. But because of us not arriving on a charter bus, we were going to stay until Saturday morning before leaving for home. This meant we would be the only people left in camp, besides the staff, on that final evening. As I lay awake in my bunk, I decided I had to do something. I remembered that during the bike trip, I had sent a few letters home and had some paper in my stuff. I climbed down and rummaging through my duffle bag produced a piece of stationery and a pencil. With a flashlight propped up on my pillow, I began to write a letter to Karen. As I tried to formulate the perfect words, I felt a chilly wind through the open window, and the leaves outside made a loud rushing noise. I watched as rain lightly but steadily crept across the camp. I turned back to the paper and began to write:

Karen,

While you're reading this, we're both on the road heading our separate ways. Just where you are I have no idea, and just where I am you have no idea. But you can bet wherever I am, I am daydreaming out the window about a little young lady from Amarillo I met at Y.L.'s Castaway Club. It's a difficult question to ask if we are to ever see each other again. But I'll answer it for you. Someday, under some other circumstance, in another time, we will meet again. I see you through eyes of not only friendship, but love. But right now it is difficult to see you at all through my tears.

I shall never forget Castaway,
I shall never forget Amarillo,
I shall never forget you.

Scotty

I read it over and over again to make sure it said exactly what I wanted. I began to well up with tears when I envisioned what it was going to be like the next evening when we parted. We had become the camp couple, the cute little Texan and the crazy biker from Michigan with the soccer ball. Now it would be time to go. What would happen after that seemed to be the question of the day. I neatly folded the letter into thirds and sealed it in an envelope. On the envelope I wrote: *My Dearest Karen*

I put it away and clamored back into the top bunk. It took a long time, but the rhythm of the rain on the roof finally helped me to drift off to sleep.

The next day was filled with the usual activities, but there was a somber undertone that permeated the activities. Many people had made friends that week, and beside Karen's and mind, there were several other camp romances that would end that evening.

The Friday night meeting had a somber pall hanging over it. Even though the usual songs were sung, the enthusiasm had been replaced with the dread of departing friends that, in most cases, would never see each other again. The speaker was giveing us his final thoughts when suddenly there was an unfamiliar rumbling noise from outside. "BUSES!" I thought in a panic. Slowly, another sound began to fill the Windjammer. It was the sniffles of heartbroken teenagers. Even though the musicians and the speaker tried to go on with business as usual, it was impossible to ignore the sense of sorrow that hung in the air. When we were dismissed and filed outside, I immediately saw an increasing number of buses forming into a line, idling in preparation to depart. After a short time, a pile of luggage began to build by each bus. Everyone was preparing to leave. I tried to find the Texans, but surprisingly they were nowhere to be seen. What at first was a trickle became a chaotic jumble of people loading suitcases and bags. The smell of diesel exhaust filled the night air. "This is happening way too fast!" I thought. I finally found the buses from Texas and asked if anyone had seen Karen. I was starting to panic, and then I saw Janet.

"Where's Karen?" I shouted desperately. She pointed and said, "Raht thair." I turned and there she was, right behind me, her tiny frame lugging a giant suitcase with both hands. Suddenly I realized that the letter I had written to her the night before was still back at my cabin hidden carefully in my duffle. I thought I would have time after the meeting to retrieve it. I didn't think the departure would happen so fast. I just *had* to give it to her.

"I'll be right back," I said frantically. "Don't get on this bus until I come back, okay?"

"Okay," she said, as a tear formed. Janet came close, and I looked at her with trust and said, "Don't let her get on this bus until I come back!" Janet nodded with a painful look and said, "Okay, hurry."

Janet, Scotty, and Karen

I turned and ran as fast as I could back to the cabin. Pawing through the clothes in my duffle bag I lifted up a shirt and pulled the letter out from under it. My soccer ball sat next to my bag. Without thinking, I grabbed it, and the door slammed behind me as I hustled back toward the sound of the waiting buses. When I got to the bus, everyone was on board except Karen. She nervously was fumbling with her fingers while watching for me. Panting from my run, I stopped just in front of her. I set the soccer ball down, and we hugged. It felt like a thousand eyes were glued to us as we tried to say goodbye. Some of the Texans were yelling out the windows of the bus:

"Take care of yourself, Scotty!"

"Goodbye, you crazy biker!"

"Come see us sometime, soccer star!"

Without letting go of Karen, I glanced up and nodded to them, barely keeping my emotions in check. I had become fond of many of the Texans that week. But when Kyle appeared in the doorway and said, "Hey Scotty, yew can come visit Amarilla anytime," my composure vanished. The fact that he called me by my name and not Yank or Yankee was too much, and a tear raced down my cheek. I knew I had been accepted and would indeed be welcome if I ever went to Amarillo. Karen's head was buried in my chest, and I could feel her shaking as her emotions finally let go. When we met merely five days earlier by the bluff over the lake, no one could have predicted the difficulty of this moment. I pulled away so we could look at each other and held the envelope up between us: "Don't open this until tomorrow. Here, take this to remember me by," and I picked up the soccer ball and offered it to her.

"Oh, ah couldn't," she said through the tears.

"Yes, I want you to have it," I insisted.

It was just a dumb soccer ball, but the power of the gesture was touching, and I heard a girl, maybe Megan, say, "Oh mah, this is awful."

"Okay," Karen said, and she took the ball from my hand.

Buses from all over the country had gone on their way, and only those from Texas remained. The Young Life leader from Amarillo who had been patiently waiting by the bus finally said, "We have to go, Karen." I hugged her one last time and kissed her. It was the first and only time I kissed her the entire week, and then I watched her climb onto the bus. For several agonizing minutes nothing happened. I stood there with a few others kicking at the dirt and occasionally glancing up at the windows of the bus. I felt helpless. I didn't know what to do. Nothing like this had ever happened to me before, and the drama was more than I could bear. Then I heard the motor rev a bit, and the bus slowly pulled away. One by one like a giant caravan departing on a journey, the buses pulled away until the red tail-lights disappeared down the road, and the faint sound of diesel engines faded into silence. All the noise, commotion, and smells were replaced by an eerie quiet. There was not much conversation among those who were left, and everyone quietly went his or her own way to deal with the sudden sense of solitude thrust upon him or her.

Bobby walked near me and lightly smacked me on the back with his hand as he passed, “Sorry man,” he said in a low voice. I stared at the ground and could not find any words. After a while, I walked over to the waterfront steps where just the night before I gave my life to Christ and later rendezvoused with Karen. I sat down and thought about the decision I had made and about Karen. Mostly, I thought about Karen. “What is happening?” I asked out loud. A sense of emptiness that I never knew existed began to well up within me. Out on the lake, a loon droned out its mournful call, and I remember thinking that somehow it knew my pain.

It was late when I walked back to the cabin, and everyone was in his bunk.

“This is weird,” I heard T.C. say.

“No kidding,” I replied, as I grabbed a towel and went to the showers. I turned the water on and facing the shower leaned with both hands against the wall, letting the water pour on my head. It wasn’t until the water got cold that I turned it off and went to bed. Everyone was sleeping when I climbed into the top bunk; at least I think they were. If anyone was still awake, he didn’t want to say a word to me. They had seen the closeness between Karen and me grow throughout the week, and they knew I was hurting. Like I had done nearly every night of camp, I put my face close to the small window and let my eyes adjust to the darkness outside. It was an unusually still night, as calm as it had been the entire week. Not a single leaf moved. The moon was over the lake once again, but tonight it had heavy rings of humidity encircling it. There was no lapping of waves on canoes, only the distant loon calling its lonely cry, finally lulling me to sleep.

The next day we rose early and packed our things. With the bikes in tow and everyone divided into the seven vehicles, we left Castaway Club and began our long drive back to Flint. Most of the way I sat with my arms folded across my chest and stared out the window, watching the world pass by. In my mind, I relived all the tender moments I had shared with Karen, and I wondered where she was and if she was doing the same. “Man,” I said to myself, “this changes everything.”

REBORN

CHAPTER 14

Two days later I was back home in Flint. I went to the last two days of the CANUSA soccer tryouts but did not make the team. I was told that because of my absence for the majority of the tryouts, they could not justify placing me on the team in the place of another player who had been there for the entire process. I knew under the circumstances it was long shot, but it still was disappointing being that I had been selected to play the six previous years. The head coach wrote me a thoughtful letter explaining his regret and that he felt they were leaving one of Flint's best soccer players in the United States, but there was really nothing he could do about it. For the first time in awhile, I would not be playing soccer against Canada that summer. Surprisingly, I was not as devastated as I thought I might be. The events of the Castaway trip seemed to be worth my place on the roster.

Bobby and I resumed our work at Wendy's, but for several days I was mopey and thoughtful. Oh, there were plenty of opportunities to sit with friends and family and recount the details of everything that had transpired. The excitement of the bike trip and all the cool stuff that Castaway offered was not lost in the telling. But two things rose above the rest: my decision to follow Jesus, which I learned is what Christians mean when they refer to being "saved" or being "born again," and meeting Karen. It may have been difficult to discern which relationship changed me more: my new relationship with God, or the one I had begun with Karen. In both cases, I was a young man reborn.

As a gift and memento of the trip, Dale had given everyone a street language Bible entitled Reach Out. Written on the inside of the cover were words:

> *To Scott,*
> *Young Life Castaway, 1976,*
> *Dale.*

This was the first Bible I ever owned and to this day it is close at hand for reference, study, or encouragement. I was now one of the few weird Catholics who actually carried a Bible into church and read it on my own.

In the case of my being saved, Dale had warned us before returning home that everything we left there had not changed since we had been away and would still be waiting for us when we got back. Exciting news of a spiritual transformation might not be received well. In spite of this, I enthusiastically told my parents that I had become a Christian while at camp. My mother was confused as to how I had just become a Christian considering I had been raised a Christian my whole life. It was then that the warning made sense—not everyone defines being a Christian the same way. It became evident that the fundamental differences in how Catholics and Protestants define Christianity would be a touchy subject with my family. Being raised Catholic and then making a Protestant-like salvation decision gave me insights to both sides of the issue. Basically, Catholics believe that you are a Christian through completing the rituals of the Catholic faith, beginning with baptism as an infant. Protestants, on the other hand, believe that becoming a Christian is a conscious choice to follow Christ by each individual that cannot be made for you. My impression was that Catholics believed the religion made you a Christian whereas Protestants believed religion exists to serve the personal Christian commitment. A point that I heard at camp that really stuck in my mind was when the speaker said, "Religion and Christianity are not the same thing." It was this that helped me understand that going to church, any church does not make a person a Christian. It's much more than that. To my surprise, one of the biggest points of contention was the Bible itself. In my own experience and in talking with family and friends, I concluded that Catholics down deep question the holy validity of the Bible. Protestants, although in different degrees, will always refer to Scripture as the authority of their belief. Because Catholics are unsure of Biblical authority, using it to answer tough spiritual questions, like "How does a person become a Christian?" often falls on deaf ears. The Catholic Church may have changed since the 1970s, but it seems most Catholics are not encouraged to read the Bible and therefore fear any argument using it as the basis for truth. It is ironic that one of the largest "Christian" religions in the world is scripturally illiterate; except for a handful of staple verses, they cannot delve into any of the meat and potatoes of the Bible. As proof, ask any Catholic what it takes to get to heaven and whether or not she thinks she will end up there. They will begin to recite to you the good things they do and the virtues they possess, in spite of the fact that Scripture emphatically says this is NOT the way (Ephesians 2:8). If you point that out, they will immediately begin to question the authority of the Bible.

In spite of the quandary I was in, tradition and family don't go away overnight. I tried to make the square peg of salvation fit into the round hole I had attended my whole life, St. Pius X Catholic Church. Much of what was recited in mass was beautiful and would stand up in any Protestant church. But for the first time I really paid attention to what I was reciting, and it had an entire new meaning. As I looked around, however, I felt like I was the only one who knew it! Much of the beautiful ritual is rote to the congregation and is like singing the National Anthem and not knowing the history behind it. Nevertheless, I remained a Catholic for several more years. I continued to learn and grow spiritually, but most of the growth during this time actually came from Young Life meetings, not church.

If trying to figure out what being a born-again Christian was all about caused difficulties, trying to figure out what to do with my feelings for Karen a thousand miles away was monumental. As soon as I got home, I began writing letters addressed to Amarillo. There was no Internet, no cell phones, and no texting. This was still the era of rotary phones and snail mail. Keeping in contact took some patience and some ingenuity. At first, Karen and I wrote letters and kept in touch via the U.S. Mail; it was all we had. Because it would take a letter three days to travel from Michigan to Texas and another three days for a response, we wrote several per week to keep the communication rolling. I remember actually coordinating our first phone call through letters, picking a date and time to be home for a call and waiting anxiously for it to come. That call validated for both of us that we did not want to end what had begun at Castaway. However, using "Ma Bell" for long distance phone calls cost money and always showed up on the monthly bill. We were high school kids with little money, and calls were few and far between. We developed a phone code where we would call and let the phone ring twice. Too many times, back then, people would dial a number, and the phone would ring once by the time they realized they had dialed a wrong number. So letting the phone ring twice was a simple little message that meant, "I am thinking about you" without actually talking or running up the phone bill, and we knew it wasn't a misdial. It was real time and did not cost anything, but many times I was tempted to grab the receiver before that second ring . . . and there were many times I did. Our contact was steady but left a hollow feeling of wanton. It was agony to read the letters and hear that voice and know that was as close as we could get, and there was nothing we could do about it . . . or was there?

Sometime during that autumn I decided I wanted to see her again. My senior year of high school had begun, and I was looking forward to graduation. But the events of the summer were still on my mind. I began to consider the idea of a visit. When I initially hatched the plan, it was for her to visit Flint over Christmas break. After consulting her parents, I was told it would be more proper for me to visit Amarillo first. After hearing this, I understood the etiquette, and I felt stupid for suggesting otherwise. It only made sense. I was older, and I was the guy, and this is how things were done. Even today, what parent in his or her right mind would allow a daughter to visit a boy so far away they had never met? So we switched our plan; I was to visit Amarillo from the day after Christmas until New Years Eve day . . . six days. I reserved a round trip airline ticket from Flint to Amarillo from December 26th until the 31st. I began to save my meager income from Wendy's to pay for it and made a calendar leading up until that time, religiously marking off each passing day.

Celebrating Christmas 1976 was only a sideshow to what I had really been anticipating for several months: my trip to Amarillo. My ticket was purchased, and I had accumulated plenty of money for spending while down there. Christmas night was a sleepless night; the anticipation was more than my mind could bear. Not only was seeing Karen a huge event, but I had never been as far from home as I would be in Texas; and certainly not on my own, plus I had never flown anywhere either. At the time, I could not have known that this entire trip was the start of a series of events that would ultimately form who I am today. I was just a seventeen-year-old kid on an adventure to visit a girl I met at summer camp. In retrospect, this was the first piece of a puzzle that would take years to complete.

Early the next morning, Bobby picked me up and drove me to the airport. I wore a pair of cuffed dress pants and a sport coat over an open collar shirt, as was the fashion of the day. The collar of the dress shirt was very large and pulled outside over the collar of the jacket. It was a look that had early-Jackson Five written all over it. It was cool but conservative. I had envisioned meeting Karen's parents and wanted to give a good first impression. With snow falling, the plane rolled down the runway and left the ground. I watched out the window as the gray city slowly gave way to the countryside, and I was on my way to the unknown.

THE FIRST VISIT

CHAPTER 15

As the plane descended and burst beneath the clouds, I could see for miles to the horizon. I don't recall if I could see a single tree, just a quilt-work of farms, ranches, and desert. It was immense and beautiful. The plane taxied to the terminal, and my heart pounded. One for the dramatic, I waited until I was the absolute last person on the plane before I rose to depart. Exiting the jet-way into the terminal, I scanned the unfamiliar surroundings, trying to see Karen. I could not see her; I could not find her. "Is she late?" I wondered. All around, people were hugging, and there was the buzz of reunited acquaintances in the air. I was beginning to think something had gone wrong when a tiny girl in blue jeans and sandals with a wide smile stepped alone into a small space in the middle of all the clamor. At first, I did not recognize her because she had cut her hair short like Dorothy Hammel. But the smile gave her away, and I could tell she was waiting for me to come to her. I had imagined this moment a million times but had no idea of how it would actually play out. Anything I may have planned or envisioned went out the window, and I instinctively walked up to her, and we tightly embraced. After a few seconds, I backed away enough to kiss her. "I have missed you," I said looking into those blue eyes.

"Me too," said Karen.

"I didn't recognize you at first; you cut your hair."

"Yea, do yew lahk it?" she asked in her drawl, and she raised a hand to the side of her head and touched her hair.

"I do, it looks great," I said. But inside I missed her long lazy curls and the big curl that swept like a wave across her forehead and fell over one eye down to her shoulder. Don't get me wrong, she was still as beautiful as ever, but in all our communication, she had not said a word about cutting her hair; it caught me off guard. We then walked arm in arm to the baggage claim and then out to her car. She had only been driving a year, but her parents had allowed her to come alone to the airport to pick me up. I thought that was very cool on their part, for it gave Karen and me about a half an hour to catch up by ourselves. As she drove, we talked, and I soaked in the vast country with nothing green and all the flags standing sideways in the prairie wind. I couldn't believe that I was actually in the place I heard so much about at while at Castaway with Karen . . . it felt like a dream.

Amarillo was a decent sized city with a single tall building that rose to break the flatness of the high plain. She pulled into the drive of a modest ranch-style house with a neat lawn. It was time to meet the family . . . I was nervous. The front door flew open, and Janet came out with an eager walk. "Pocahontas!" I said in my mind. I never called her that out loud, but I always thought it when I saw her or thought of her. She was really a nice girl, and we got along easily. It was good to see her, and I knew she felt the same as we hugged on the front porch. I felt tightness in my throat, and I realized that seeing her choked me up. In an instant, Janet brought the Castaway emotions to the surface.

On entering the house, I was greeted and introduced to a younger brother Mark, her parents Jack and Margarite Little, and a funny little short-haired mutt named Cowboy. We all sat down in the family room, me on a sofa with Karen next to me. I felt like I was on trial as they all basically sat in a circle around me and watched me sweat. There were uncomfortable silences, and Mr. Little tried to bale me out by asking questions about Michigan. The ice was really broken when he asked, "So what's the train lahk up there." Now this was an easy question to talk about in detail since Flint was a hub for the newly resurrected passenger train known as Amtrak.

"Oh, we have the new Amtrak train in Flint," I began. "It goes to Chicago and on to St. Louis, I think." I was on a roll, so I did not stop. "I think there are plans to continue to spread it across the country; Kansas City and Denver, and ultimately, the West Coast." When I stopped, I was confronted with a room of silence and blank stares.

It was very strange, and I began to wonder if I had said something wrong.

Finally, Mr. Little spoke up and said, "Lots of hills, huh."

I looked at him, not understanding his response but felt I needed to reply so I said, "Yes, lots of hills." Mark started to ask me some questions about something or other, I don't recall because in my mind I said, "Something just happened and I missed it." Then I asked myself, "Did I just miss something?" I repeated Mr. Little's remark, "'Lots of hills?' What does that have to do with Amtrak?"

There was a conversation continuing, but I was fixated on trying to figure out that weird conversation from moments earlier. I kept thinking "Hills . . . trains." Suddenly, I burst out, "OH, you meant TURRAIN! I thought you asked about our *train!*" There was a second of silence, and then everyone exploded into laughter.

Mr. Little said, "Ah am *so* glad yew cleared that up; Ah had no ahdea what yew were talking about!" They, too, had been trying to figure it out in their heads, and everyone seemed relieved when the clarification was finally made.

"Imagine what I was thinking when, from left field, you asked me about hills!" I said, wiping away a tear caused from the laughter. The tension was gone after that, and we all sat and learned about one another. To this day, the *train* story still gets referred to as one of life's embarrassing moments and is always good for a simple laugh.

The next morning Mr. Little took me and his three kids backpacking to the mountains near Taos, New Mexico. This was an unexpected bonus since I spent many summers roughing it in Michigan's Upper Peninsula (the U.P.). A trip like this was right up my alley. It was great fun even though it rained hard for two of the three days we were there. More importantly, the relationship not only with Karen, but also with her family, was being cultivated. It gave me a chance to show my resourcefulness when I used a rain poncho and pole-like pine trunks to make a teepee that kept our fire from being extinguished by the heavy rain. A huge item on my agenda those few days was to impress Mr. Little. After saving the fire from the rain, I recall thinking, "He has to be impressed with this!" Mark and I got to know each other better as we did some rugged climbing that Janet and Karen did not want to attempt. Whether climbing in the mountains or riding in the car, there were plenty of opportunities to have conversation. It was our first chance to get to know each other. Any chance of the romance between Karen and me encountering roadblocks from the family went out the window during this trip to the mountains. I showed that I was not a picky eater, did not have a peculiar personality, and was not particular about where I laid my head to sleep. I was normal, and I had manners and a willing spirit. My main concern was the fact that I was two years older than Karen. It's not an issue if you are in your twenties, but in high school, it can be a big deal. I certainly did not want it to be a big deal with her family; so far, so good.

The day after we returned from New Mexico, Mrs. Little drove us down to Lubbock to visit the Texas Tech campus. Janet was considering attending there after she graduated from Tascosa. The trip down was yet another opportunity to strengthen the bond that had begun with Karen and her family. The ride to Lubbock gave me an appreciation for the winds of the high plains. It didn't take me long to discover that a calm day in the Texas Panhandle is a rarity; there is *always* wind. If you think Chicago is a windy city, visit Lubbock! At one point, we stopped by the side of the road where there was a sign that read, "Caution Dangerous Winds." I grabbed a hold of the sign and hoisted myself horizontally from it, mocking that the wind was blowing me like a flag. It is a comical photo. They were amused that I got excited when I saw tumbleweeds rolling across the highway. I had only seen them in Western movies, yet here we were, dodging them in real life like we avoid deer in Michigan. I also thought it was funny that the road-kill in Texas was armadillos and roadrunners, not raccoons and possums.

My visit also included a trip to nearby Palo Duro Canyon. Overshadowed by the Grand Canyon, it is not widely known, but is nonetheless an impressive geographic site. We spent the day exploring the canyon and riding horses. There is something magical about riding horses in the canyon country of Texas. The red dirt and striped 'Spanish skirts' cascading down from the rim to the canyon floor was a perfect page out of a dime novel. Another impressive sight in the canyon was the Palo Duro portion of the Texas Longhorn State herd. Hearty cattle are bred to survive the extreme weather of the plains; they are legendary animals whose size can only really be appreciated in person. Their immense horizontal horns are their iconic feature and can reach lengths over six feet long, and their shoulders are at eye level of the average person. The climax of our day at Palo Duro was attending the historical play <u>Texas</u> in a natural amphitheater located in the heart of the canyon. If you have seen the musical <u>Oklahoma</u>, you would have an idea of what the presentation of <u>Texas</u> is like. Seeing it live in the canyon at night was quite the spectacle and as much a right of passage in Amarillo as visiting Mackinac Island is in Michigan.

There was a mandatory day of shopping included while in Amarillo. My favorite stop was a store called "Boots and Jeans." This was a massive store filled wall to wall with western wear like I had never seen before. But this stuff was the real deal, not for a Halloween costume. I had noticed while down there that boots, western shirts, boot-cut jeans, and cowboy hats were typical dress. It's not that they don't wear clothes you would find up north—shorts, t-shirts, and tennis shoes—but anyone wearing boots, jeans, and cowboy hats does not stand out like he does north of the Mason-Dixon Line. It was in the western store that I was educated on what constitutes quality boots and cowboy hats. I left "Boots and Jeans" with a top-notch pair of Tony Lama calf skin boots and a sorrel brown XXX beaver Resistol hat shaped by choice right before my eyes into the classic cattleman's cut. The jeans of choice in Texas are Wranglers, with Levi's running a distant second. Of course, all of this must include a wide leather belt with stitching along its edges, your name proudly stamped on the back, topped off by a large silver belt buckle. My belt simply said 'Scotty' on it and had a classic buckle with a bronze-long horn steer head on it. You can tell most native Texans by their belts, which typically had their first and second name emboldened on the back, just like in the movies. Sometimes their names didn't seem to flow very well, but that didn't discourage them from punching them onto their belts. Names like "Dan John" or "Bill Tom." Without going into detail of what exactly what all this means, I can tell you that the apparel I purchased that day at "Boots and Jeans" would stand up in any western town or serious western dance hall. It was authentic and, if I say so myself, I wore it well. The day of shopping concluded with some authentic Tex-Mex cuisine at a giant restaurant called

"Paradise Too." I discovered that I really enjoy the spicy offerings of Southwestern menus, and the Mexican waitresses who spoke only broken English added to the overall effect.

Karen, Janet, and some of their friends I had met at Castaway took me 'boot scootin' one evening at a place called Graham Central Station. When I saw Kyle, he just shook his head with a wide grin and said, "Boy howdy, if Ah hadn't seen it with mah own ahs Ah'd a never believed it." Then he wrapped an arm around my shoulder and continued, "SON! Yew are officially roped an' tahd!" Then he looked at Karen who just shyly grinned and shrugged her shoulders like she agreed and was complacent with the whole thing. I learned that among all the attributes possessed by cowboys, knowing how to dance was included in their cultural arsenal. It wasn't like up North where a person with some soul and a willingness to move their hips a little could be considered a good dancer. In Texas, there are specific dance steps for specific music. You cannot get by on the sheer willingness to shake your booty in public . . . you have to know what you are doing. I was impressed to see that cowboys, with their character worn as prominent as their hats, had impeccable manners and could glide across a dance floor with grace and style. I was taught the staple western dance, the "two-step." I soaked up the crash course in Texas culture, etiquette, and dress like a dry sponge. It was a whole new world being offered willingly, and I eagerly grabbed hold of and loved it.

The evening before I had to return to Michigan, Karen and I put on our best clothes and went to the top of the tallest building in Amarillo, the Amarillo National Bank building. There was an exclusive restaurant on the penthouse floor called the "Amarillo Club." Mr. Little, who was the vice-president of the First National Bank, was a member. The view from over thirty floors was spectacular. As the sun began to set, you could see for miles across the plains. The color of the waning sun against the thin clouds was like the painting of a scene that could not exist in reality. But there it was. Far in the distance, I could see a thunderhead roll across the prairie with a solid sheet of purple rain making an angled column to the ground. Jagged flashes of lightning struck randomly within the rain. "I'd hate to be in that thing right now," I said to Karen. "Yea," she said, "we have vohlent thunder-boomers here." I thought it was funny that she referred to thunderstorms as "thunder-boomers." "Up north we can never see them in their entirety like down here . . . too many trees." I continued, "The only place we can really see the entire storm like that, is when it comes across the lake," I nodded toward the storm out the window. "What lake?" Karen asked. "Well, any of the big lakes," I answered. "You know, the Great Lakes." "Ah'd lahk to see those," Karen said nonchalantly. Then and there the plan was hatched. "I think you *should* come up and see them," I said. We looked at each other, smiled, and nodded in agreement.

The next morning, I opened my eyes and realized that my stay was over. I could hear Mrs. Little quietly moving around the kitchen. The smell of coffee and eggs drifted through the room. I quickly freshened up and went out to the kitchen and leaned against the counter, "Good morning, Mrs. Little."

"Well, good morning, Scotty."

"Is there something I can help you with?"

"No, no," she said, "Ah have it awl under control."

"Thanks for letting me come down; it has been a lot of fun."

"Well, yew are welcome, we have enjoyed having yew. Sit down and have some aiggs." As I sat down, Cowboy put his nose on my thigh, begging to be petted. "He sure is a funny dog," I said.

"Yes sir, yew should feel fortunate, he doesn't lahk evrabody," she said with the standard drawl, "but he shor lahks yew."

"You have a wonderful family," I said, "I hope I can visit again someday." She turned and brought a plate of eggs-over easy, toast, and grits to the table and placed them down in front of me. "Yew can visit any tahm." It had the tone of sincerity behind it and was reminiscent of the bus scene at Castaway when Kyle said the same thing.

The realization that my visit only had a couple short hours remaining suddenly hit me, and I felt the familiar lump of emotion in my throat. I did not have the composure to answer and simply stared at my plate of food, holding a glass of orange juice in one hand and a poised fork in the other. There was an uncomfortable silence broken when she suddenly said, "They're just grits, trah 'em." I let out a shaky laugh. "It's not the grits, ma'am, I have grown fond of y'all in a short tahm." It rolled off my tongue like I had lived there for years. "Leaving is not going to be easy." Again there was a silence and

Mrs. Little had turned back and was pouring herself a cup of coffee. It touched me to realize that she was hiding a lump in her throat as well. I knew at that moment that the summertime camp romance had become something entirely different. Slowly, everyone found their way to the kitchen and in chatting over breakfast, the emotion was checked.

Mr. Little put my suitcase in the trunk and closed the lid. We were all standing in the driveway, shaking hands and giving hugs. Mr. Little and Mark were stoic, but I saw Mrs. Little clutching a tissue, and as I hugged Janet, the glassiness in her eyes could not be missed. Karen was allowed to drive me to the airport alone as she had picked me up six days earlier. There was a lot of small talk that thinly veiled the heartache that was building within us both. At the airport, I held her hand as the last call for boarding my flight rang out. We had waited until the absolute last second to say goodbye. In all the time that we had shared over the previous week, there were only a few kisses here and there, but I kissed her now. It was a simple kiss, but it was a long one that had meaning. "I am really getting tired of saying goodbye to you," I said. Karen turned her head sideways against my chest and squeezed her arms tightly around my waist. "I have to go now," I reluctantly said as I pulled away. There was one last dramatic look back from the jetway, and I disappeared into the doorway of the plane. The last vision of Karen stuck in my mind was a small wave with one hand while she bit the knuckle of the curled index finger of the other. I tried to see her in the terminal as my plane taxied to the runway, but could not pick her out of the crowd at the glass. Before I knew it, I was airborne, and the visit was over. Acting like I knew what I was doing and had ordered it a hundred times, I asked the stewardess for a "Jack and Coke." The drinking age in 1976 was eighteen, and I was only five months shy of that. Without hesitation she said, "Sure." As I passively drown my sorrows in whiskey and cola, I looked out the small window and watched the prairie gradually give way to the rivers and patchwork of the Midwest until the clouds became a thick blanket below. When I finally touched down in Flint, it was snowing hard. Bobby met me at the terminal with a fat grin, "Well," he asked, "how was it?"

"Oh, man," I answered, holding my new Resistol in my hand. "Texas is incredible, her family is incredible, *and Karen* is incredible!"

"Man," he said, "you're whipped!" I almost took offense to it except he was right. I nabbed my suitcase from the conveyor belt and put my arm around Bobby's shoulder. "She's coming up here this summer," and we walked out of the airport.

CAROLE

CHAPTER 16

The day after I returned from Amarillo, 1976 turned to 1977. I had a half a year to complete, and I would be graduating from high school and moving out into the real world. There were several harmless dating ventures and of course prom, but all the encounters I had with girls were either of a friendly nature or with no serious prospect of becoming a couple. Everyone knew about Karen in Texas and being candid about her always tempered any ideas by girls to date me exclusively. In the past, I had been less honorable in these situations, but I truly did not want to do anything to jeopardize what had begun with Karen. The tough part was that we had not really stated whether or not we were boyfriend and girlfriend. After all, it was such an unusual situation, but the sense of something special was always lingering. I was actually being faithful to a girl a thousand miles away who was not even officially my girlfriend. I wasn't sure what was going to happen between Karen and me, but I knew I didn't want any ties to mess up the possibilities.

My best friend at the time was a black girl named Carole. Carole was also a senior, and she and I had come up through the ranks of marching band together. Carole was a beautiful girl with striking features and just a slight hint of a lisp. This didn't detract from her, but was cute and only made her more attractive. Her hair was not kinky and afro-like, but long and curly and usually parted in the middle. We had a couple classes together and our lockers were close. She too, was having some sort of drama with a guy she was dating, but much the same as Karen and me, there were complications. We counseled and consoled each other and spent much time in intimate conversation. When it came time to think about a prom date, I was faced with an ethical dilemma. I knew without hesitation that if Carole were a white girl, I would ask her to prom. It was obvious to anyone that we were close friends with no real restrictions. In spite of the obvious, it was also obvious that I did not know how my parents, or more specifically, my dad, would react if I brought a black girl home. Now, not in a million years would I ever consider anyone, even my dad, in my family racist. Yet, he was from an earlier generation. Although he had some who that were black and worked with blacks, I could not be sure how this would go over. I agonized over what to do. I finally scolded myself, "If Carole were white, this would be a no brainer, you *have* to ask her." So one day when I finally got my nerve up, I pulled Carole aside in the hallway.

"Carole," I said in a serious tone, "I have to ask you something."

"What's the matter?"

"I know this might not be easy to answer, and it is difficult to ask," I started nervously, "but if you were white," I continued, "I would ask without hesitation."

Carole took a half step back, perplexed, and looked at me, "What are you asking me?"

"Will you go to prom with me?" I blurted out. Carole just stared at me for a second trying to decide if I was serious or not, then burst out laughing.

After being turned down by Carole (top right) and turning down Melissa (bottom right), Scotty finally went to prom with his friend and locker partner Linda.

"Oh my God," She said, "I would love to, but my dad would *kill* me if I brought a white boy home." I stood and stared at her for a second, totally dumbfounded. Here I was worried about my family, never even thinking it would be the same for her. One had to appreciate the irony. The only thing I could do was join in her laughter.

I finally said, "I was worried about what *my* family would think, I didn't even think about *your* family!" I continued, "Man, am I stupid."

"That's alright," she said, "I understand, and I totally get your principle and your dilemma." As she said these things, I realized I still hadn't actually received an answer.

"Well . . . so will you?" I persisted. Carole's face drew into a compassionate calm, and she took a hold of my hands and said, "Let me save both our families some trouble and say 'no'."

I was disappointed and relieved at the same time. Another black girl named Melissa, Carole's best friend, had been listening a few steps away and chimed in, "I'll go with you!"

Carole smacked her on the arm and said, "Give the guy a break!"

"No, I'm serious, I'll go with you," Melissa said again. But I did not feel the same about Melissa as I did about Carole. We were friends and all, and I actually contemplated the idea for a few moments. But as intriguing as it sounded at the moment, I turned Melissa's offer down.

Carole went to prom with a black dude who was already in college, and I went with a close friend, a girl named Linda, whom I shared a locker with out of convenience. Linda was a tall, pretty girl with straight blonde hair and blue eyes. She was also very white.

BABE

CHAPTER 17

School continued, Young Life continued, and Bobby and I continued to work at Wendy's. Early in June, we graduated, and the summer of our senior year began, the last summer before college. On the weekends, Bobby and I, with some other friends had discovered a new hangout called "The Light." It was a closed department store that had been converted into a dance club. It was during one evening out, busting moves to *Earth, Wind, and Fire*, the *Commodores*, and the *Bee Gees,* that I saw an attractive dark-haired girl sitting with friends at a table. Bobby and I were just out having a good time dancing with anyone who would say yes. I noticed she was watching me, and if she was trying to be discrete, it wasn't working. I smiled at her a couple times while dancing with someone else, and she returned the gesture.

Sitting at the table, I told Bobby, "That chick is checking me out."

"Which one?" asked Bobby.

"That dark-haired one sitting over there," I said as I casually tipped my head in her direction.

"Go ask her to dance," he said sharply.

"I'm going to . . . next good song," I replied. I thought for a second of how different this was to Graham Central Station in Amarillo. People were staking their claim on the dance floor, and there was no rhyme or reason to how anyone danced. In Texas, everything flowed; here it was every man for himself. I am ashamed to admit it, but this was disco!

"Kyle would never let me return to Amarillo if he saw me right now," I thought, "and he dang sure wouldn't let me near Karen!" It was a fleeting thought and the next thing I knew I was walking toward the girl at the table. She met me with a giant smile and was sliding off her stool before I actually asked her to dance. It was a song she really wanted to dance to, and he was eager to get on the floor. She smiled as much as she danced, and we tried to have pieces of a conversation while dancing but could barely hear each other. When the song was over, another good one came on.

"Wanna stay?" I shouted.

"Yes!" she hollered back and didn't miss a beat. After about four dances, we were both working up a sweat, and I pointed back toward her table. She nodded, and we weaved through the flailing dancers to her table.

I introduced myself. "My name is Scotty."

"My name is Therese," she replied.

"Can I sit down?"

"Sure," she said pleasantly.

We began the usual inquisition when meeting a perfect stranger at a dance club. She was short but not quite as short as Karen. She had a nice shape and beautiful thick curly hair that was cut very short. She had a dark complexion with full lips and big brown eyes. She liked my humor and was easy to make laugh, revealing large but perfect gleaming teeth. I did not stay at her table, but throughout the night, we kept dancing with each other, even to a couple slow songs. It was during the popular song, "Brick House" that I actually did the splits, a move that usually wowed anyone I was dancing with. As I hit the floor I felt my pants explode! I hopped up immediately with a look of panic on my face.

I leaned into her and shouted, "I just ripped my pants!" I was laughing as I said it because I realized how hilarious and embarrassing the moment was. Therese' eyes got huge, and then she covered her mouth, trying to hide her laughter. It was only because of the crowd and the noise that no one seemed to notice what happened. I grabbed Therese by the elbow and led her back to her table, and we sat down, absolutely laughing. We had been having a great time dancing together and I wanted to know more about her.

"I don't want this evening to end yet," I said to her "Can you take me home, and I'll change my pants?"

She shook her head, "I don't know you."

"You can bring me right back, I just want to change my pants and talk some more," I was trying to keep from laughing as I spoke to her, but it was no use.

"I drove my friends here and I don't know you," she kept saying.

About that time Bobby came over and I told him that I ripped my pants doing the splits. He howled with laughter. It was contagious and everyone began to laugh almost uncontrollably. It was a very funny situation.

"Bobby," I said in desperation, "Drive me home, so I can change my pants."

"Let's go!" he said like it was a challenge. I looked at Therese and said, "Don't leave until I come back." It was a familiar line and I flashed back to that moment standing with Karen by the bus in Castaway. In the midst of all the noise I recalled the sprint back to the cabin to retrieve the letter I had written for her. I remembered the first kiss and the painful good-bye.

"I'll try," Therese said, "but I have to take my friends home."

There were several girls around the table, all laughing of course, and I said to them all, "Don't let her leave until I come back." As I said this, I had a flashback to my urgent request to Janet. "Don't let her get on this bus until I get back." I looked at Therese, "I promise I'll be back, don't leave." Bobby and I hustled out of the club. He drove me as fast as he dare at midnight-when the traffic was light and speeders were easy to spot-until we reached my house. I ran in, changed my pants, and was back out to Bobby's car in seconds. We sped back to "The Light" just as the lights were turning on and the place was closing for the evening. It was a mob all exiting at once, and I was looking around desperately trying to spot Therese. Finally, while standing outside, I saw her waiting off to the side of the crowd.

I walked over and said, "I told you I'd be back."

"I wasn't sure you'd make it," she replied, and slipped a piece of paper into my hand. "Call me," she said, and she walked away into the parking lot. I opened the paper, and it had a phone number written on it and the name "Therese".

The next day was Saturday and although I had nothing going on, I waited until 1:00 or so before I dialed Therese's number. After some pleasantries I asked, "Do you mind if I come over?"

"That would be fine," she said in a way that made me feel like she was hoping I would ask that question. I got the address and wasted little time getting into my car. At the time, I was driving a 124 Fiat Spyder convertible, a small Italian car that resembled the popular British MG. My dad had helped me buy it, and I had spent most of my Wendy's paychecks making it look sharp. A candy-apple red convertible with white rims and black trim, it was a babe magnet.

I pulled up to the modest house on the other side of town and strolled up to the front door. Therese answered my knock and came out on the front porch. We sat on the front steps and talked. It was totally different from the night before where the conversations were basically a shouting match. Of course, we laughed over me splitting my pants. Then her mother came out and asked her, "Babe, did you tell Carrie to stop at the store and get some milk?"

"Yes," she answered. "Mom, this is Scotty," she continued.

"Hi, nice to meet you," her mom said with a smile.

"Nice to meet you, too," I said as I got to my feet. Her mother was a dark-skinned woman with distinctive Middle Eastern features.

"Okay," she said, "just wanted to make sure," and she turned and went back into the house.

Therese grinned and said, "She knew I asked Carrie to stop at the store; she just used that as an excuse to check you out."

"Funny," I said. "How come she called you 'Babe'?"

"That's what everyone calls me."

"Everyone?"

"Pretty much."

"Should I call you that? Would it be proper?" I asked.

"That would be alright," she answered, seemingly delighted that I wanted to use her nickname. From that moment on, I referred to Therese as "Babe" unless there was a serious point to be made.

"Let's go for a walk," she suggested.

"Sure," I said, and she hollered into her house that we were going for a walk and joined me on the front sidewalk. As we walked around her neighborhood, we had a pleasant conversation. I found that her family was Arab, more specifically, Palestinians, and she learned that I was an Irish Indian. When we returned to the house, we sat on the porch steps again. Carrie came home with the milk, and we were introduced. She was taller than Babe and had thick, long beautiful hair down to her waist that was stereotypically Arab. She barely said a word when we were introduced, and it only took me an instant to realize Babe had the warmer personality of the two; Carrie was stunning but simply cold. You could smell that dinner was being prepared, and her mother came out with a sample. "Would you like to try some 'cubbie'?"

"What is it?" I asked, as I took the small plate with a square of meat on it.

"It is a traditional Arab meat pie," said the mother.

"Mmm, it's delicious," I said after I cautiously tried it.

"Dinner is almost ready," she said to Babe, hinting that I should probably leave soon, and she took the empty plate and disappeared into the house again.

"I better go," I said.

"Come see me at work," Babe suggested out of the blue. She invited me to visit her at work at a park called Safetyville, where little kids could drive miniature cars on a course. I remembered going there myself as a kid and knew exactly where she was talking about. Basically, her job was sitting and making sure the kids followed the rules. She said it was okay to visit because much of the time no one was there, and she sat alone like a lifeguard on duty with no one swimming.

A couple days went by before I went down unannounced and found her helping some children into their little cars. I sat on some bleachers with some parents and quietly watched her go about her business. When the kids were done and sent on their way, she noticed me sitting alone and approached me with her bright smile.

"How long have you been here?" she asked.

"Long enough," I replied.

"You *are* an Injun aren't you . . . sneaking up like that?" she joked with a wide grin.

Following her lead with the light meaningless ethnic jab, I answered, "It was easy, *Rashid*, Arabs don't pay attention . . .

especially pretty ones." It didn't make much sense, but it surely made her blush, and she bashfully sat down next to me.

"You do nice work," I said in a half-joking manner.

"It's like babysitting," she said dryly. It was a nice sunny day, and we sat and talked. Eventually the question came up: "Are you dating anyone?" she asked.

"Well," I began, "that's not an easy question to answer." Part of me said I should say nothing about Karen, but the other part of me said, "Do this right, be honest." It was like I had a little devil standing on one shoulder and an angel on the other, whispering their counsel into my ears. Everything about my growing relationship with Karen was different than any of the other short stands I had been involved in, and I did not want to demean it by not acknowledging to Babe that it existed.

"What do you mean?" asked Babe.

Her tone had changed a little, and I could tell that my hesitation to answer meant that there were complications that she did not expect. I stood up and faced her as she remained on the bleachers and sunk my hands into my pockets. "Well," I continued, "I want to be honest with you because we get along so well, and I really like being around you." Babe looked into the distance at nothing in particular, waiting to hear what I was going to say. I exhaled heavily, gathering strength and said, "There's this girl in Texas." Now the cat was out of the bag and nothing could get it back in. It felt good to be honest, and I actually felt relieved that I had begun to tell her about Karen. As weird as it sounds, part of me just wanted to share the amazing story about meeting Karen so unexpectedly at camp and that we were still in contact. I continued, "I am not sure what is going to happen, but we really get along, and I have even gone to visit her."

Babe was nervously biting her lip and staring off into the distance. At that point, I realized that I had been on her mind a lot in the short time we had known each other. She did not like what I was telling her.

"So," she said as she switched her gaze to her feet, "are you two a couple?"

"I'm not sure. It's complicated. I live here, and she lives in Texas. I am off to college, and she still has to finish high school. We write a lot and call now and then, but obviously we don't see each other." However, I didn't want to downplay the emotion that had been kindled between Karen and me, and I continued, "But there's something there."

"Hmmm," was all Babe said.

There was a silence while everything was being digested. I broke it by saying, "She is going to visit this summer."

Again, there was a long silence. There was a weight in the air, and I felt awkward staying there. The talk after that was all small talk that felt like a diversion, a smoke screen hiding the tension. Nothing further was said or asked about Karen.

"Well, I better get going," I said.

"Okay," Babe answered, and that was it. I walked out of the park, trying to decide exactly where she and I now stood. Nothing had been said; it was just out there unresolved.

That summer, Young Life had planned yet another bike trip. This one was even bigger and farther than the one the previous year to Castaway. This year's was headed to Frontier Ranch near Buena Vista, Colorado. I was definitely on board for this monumental excursion and was training hard to be ready for it. One day, when I arrived back home after being out biking, Babe was sitting in her car in front of my house. I coasted up and stopped, balancing myself by placing a hand on the open window of her car door.

"Hey," I said, "didn't expect to see you here."

Babe smiled and said, "I didn't expect to see me here either, but here I am." She added, "I don't know what to think about you and this girl in Texas, but I know I like talking to you . . . I like being around you."

"Me, too," I said sheepishly.

"It's not like you two have a commitment, is that right?" she asked.

"No. We don't really know *what* we have. It's not a normal situation. But I want to be honest with you, we are trying to keep in touch and to visit each other. I just don't know what the future is. I think the reality for both of us is whether or not we dare tell the other one not to date. I mean we are *so* far apart!"

"I see your point," Babe replied. "Like you said before, it's complicated."

"Yes," I quietly echoed in agreement, "it's complicated."

"Can we still do things?" she asked.

Feeling like I might be opening Pandora's Box, I said, "I think we can still do things; I just want you know what is going on . . . I want all my cards on the table."

"Thanks for being honest," she said. "You could have lied to me, and I would have never known."

"Therese," I used her name so she knew the coming statement was important, "a year ago I might have, but I want to do the right thing here." We made no firm plans at that point, but I patted her arm and said, "I'll come see you at work sometime. We'll talk some more."

"I'd like that, Injun," she answered with a smirk as she turned the key and started her car. I had been sitting on my bike for the entire conversation and pushed away to let here leave.

In spite of the drama that accompanied getting acquainted with Babe, one thing was certain: we got along like two people who had known each other for years. The conversation flowed easily, and our views on most anything were identical. Our personalities gelled seamlessly. I was glad that I had told her about Karen, but now I was rolling two girls around in my mind. Babe was close, and I could see her anytime, yet my romance with Karen was straight out of a storybook. My dad had told me on many occasions, "You always do things the hard way." His words made more sense to me now than ever before.

FRONTIER RANCH

CHAPTER 18

Later that summer, Bobby and I and ninety other bikers left Flint much like we had done the year before. It was another great trip with great memories. We biked longer and much further than our trip to Castaway. We pedaled through places like the Black Hills of South Dakota, the Badlands of Wyoming, and threw ourselves against the Rocky Mountains of Colorado.

The ride through South Dakota was like riding through history. From as far away as Wisconsin, we had seen signs advertising Wall Drug, South Dakota, so we had to stop there. It was a tourist-trap town, which reminded me of Mackinaw City but without the water. Its countless souvenir shops made it worth the stop. We also made a trip to the Corn Palace in Mitchell, an entire building built from ears of corn. Strange. One of my favorite stops in South Dakota was the frontier city of legend, Deadwood. It was in Deadwood that I realized I had somehow crossed from the Midwest to the Wild West. Walking the streets of Deadwood was like stepping back 100 years. Its history oozes with gunfights, gold claims, and Indians. Eventually we made the turn southwest toward Colorado and entered the hill country of southwest South Dakota known as the Black Hills.

One beautiful day Bobby and I had been biking hard and approached the bottom of a long grade we had been coasting down for a couple of miles. It was a hot day, and the scent of pine hit me in waves as I carved my way through the sacred land of the Sioux. Before we began to ascend the next climb, I signaled to Bobby, and we pulled into a small store with a giant parking lot.

"Whew," I said to Bobby as I hopped off my bike. "This is an awesome ride!" "These turns are really cool," answered Bobby.

"I need something to drink," I said as I pulled off my sweaty gloves and headed into the store. I didn't realize until after I had gone in and bought lemonade why this small store had such a large parking lot . . . it was basically a scenic turnout. I sat down on the wooden porch that ran the length of the store and took a giant swig of cold lemonade. As I tilted my head back with the bottle to my lips, I saw the bone-white faces of four Presidents staring back at me. Bobby came out with a candy bar in his hand and saying something I could not understand because of his stuffed mouth. I just pointed and said, "Check it out."

"Whoa, Mount Rushmore," he said with his mouth full of nougat. He sat down beside me, and we tried to burn the image into our brains. It is hard to explain how incredible it is to weave your way through the granite hills, baldly exposed from pine forests, to suddenly catch a glimpse of Mount Rushmore.

On another day, I was riding with a group, including Bobby, through land that was dry, barren, and flat. In many ways it reminded me of Amarillo, but not as hot. In the distance, there were ominous clouds building into storms, and the wind was beginning to pick up. "Thunder-boomers," I thought, and as I thought it, I could hear Karen saying it that night in the Amarillo Club. Without warning, there was a sudden and drastic falling away of the land. We quickly pulled off the road into the dry dirt. There was a rim that ran beyond our sight to the horizon; the land just fell away to infinity. What lay before us was not a canyon, but a vast sea of rock formations, fissures, and craggy fractures. There was a sign that read, "You are now entering the Badlands." I had heard of these in movies and Louis Lamour novels as the place where outlaws hid themselves from the law. Now I understood why. Trying to find someone out there would be a monumental task. In our sense of awe, we had not noticed that the convoy had caught us and pulled off the road just behind us. The wind was building, and Dale seemed in a panic. "Load the bikes!" he yelled. "Hurry!" Suddenly I could feel the temperature fall, and dust was beginning to pelt us. I hopped up on the hauler, the same one we had used to get to Castaway, and Dale started handing me bikes as a pall of darkness fell over us. As I tied them down, the dirt began to sting. I yelled, "Holy crud!"

Dale answered, "Tornado watch!" I secured the last bike, double-checked all the straps and ropes, and leaped into the van, shielding my face from the first fat drops of rain. No sooner had the door been slammed that a sheet of rain hit the van with the sound of a passing semi-truck. The distinct crack of hail began to break against the vehicles as we got under way. "That was close," I said, wiping the rain from my face. The convoy descended into the protection of the Badlands, and we drove into the night. A day later we paraded into Young Life's Frontier Ranch in much the same way we had ridden into Castaway the year before.

Frontier Ranch was spectacular, nestled in the Rockies. The theme, of course, was western and heavy with riding horses and hiking. Just like Castaway, it was loaded with kids from all around the country. I made some friends there, but nothing like what happened in Minnesota. I knew there was the potential for such a thing to happen, and was even open to it, but knowing it can happen and having it unexpectedly strike you like a lightning bolt are two entirely different things.

Some of the Young Life gang at Frontier Ranch in Colorado, 1977, including 'Trailblazers' Bobby (top left), Scotty (bottom left), and T.C. (center).

My most memorable day at Frontier was the day I wandered off during an afternoon of free time. There was a road just outside of camp that was lined with signs that read, "DANGER DO NOT CLIMB." So, of course, I just had to check it out. I looked around briefly and seeing no one in the area, I quickly slipped through the pines and started the steep climb. It was not easy, and the trees had to be navigated slowly because of their close proximity to each other. I climbed for about a half an hour, and it seemed like there was no end to it. The air was thin, and I had to take frequent stops to catch my breath. Suddenly, there was brightness as the sun streamed through the thinning trees. It was a similar feeling when approaching a lake in Michigan, and I could sense the openness ahead. I took a few more steps, and I broke through the tree line, that is the altitude where the air is so thin that trees grow only sporadically and then not at all. It was as if God had drawn a line on the side of the mountain and said DON'T grow beyond here. There was an eerie silence as I climbed further, now on bare rock. The reason for the DANGER sign became suddenly very clear.

A giant chasm lay before me, and I cautiously approached the edge. It was a sheer cliff dropping straight down for a thousand feet and then rising abruptly a quarter mile away in an opposing cliff that rose even higher than that on which I stood. The view took my breath away, and it took me several minutes to adjust to the height. There was a solid rock ledge securely jutting out over the cliff. I thought, "I have to sit on that. It's been here for a thousand years, and my weight is not going to knock that loose." I was scared, but I cautiously laid on my back and crab-crawled forward. In this manner, I slowly inched my way out, let my feet drop over the edge, and sat down on the outcropping. It took some time to get comfortable, but there I was with my legs dangling over the edge of the precipice. The two opposing cliffs angled toward each other to my right, and I knew somewhere in that direction they probably merged. To my left they gradually got further apart, and the view between them blossomed out to a plateau. In the distance, I could see the endless layers of the Rockies as they ran in jagged ribbons to the horizon. I could clearly see the dominant peaks of the region, Mount Princeton and Mount Antero. In the far distance there was the faint outline of the famous Pike's Peak. Far below me I saw a hawk riding the air current rarely flapping a wing, but effortlessly gliding. It was like I was watching the lyrics of a John Denver song being played out right in front of my eyes. Suddenly, I heard a strange whistling sound come and go in an instant. "What the heck was that?" I thought. As I tried to take it all in, I kept hearing the same strange sound over and over again. It was like an arrow flying closely by. Finally I looked up, which made my head spin, and I caught sight of a small bird whizzing past. It was literally only a couple of feet from my head and seemed to be riding the edge of the cliff like a fighter plane. I discovered there were dozens of them, and they were screaming around the cliffs like a World War II dogfight. The sound I was hearing was created when their wings cut the air as they dove with unbelievable speed. It was a moment sublime, and I simply sat in silence soaking it in as the swallows, with their wings tucked close to their bodies, whistled just beyond my reach. This was nothing like looking out windows; this was indescribable and nearly more than my senses could handle. The word "awesome" is thrown around today without much thought of what it truly means, but this panorama laid out before me truly left me awestruck. I was a speck, insignificant and small. What lay before me was breath-taking, humbling . . . the entire event was epic. I closed my eyes and said out loud, "God is good."

The two-week bike ride through Wisconsin, Minnesota, South Dakota, Wyoming, and Colorado created some great memories and let me see things I otherwise may have never seen. Just riding those miles was a triumph in itself. I have memories from camp that will always stick with me. But Frontier, as incredible as it was, will always play second fiddle to Castaway. I returned from Colorado with another priceless experience under my belt, but ready to finish my last summer before college in the fall. I was anxiously awaiting the highlight of the summer; Karen was coming north.

THE SECOND VISIT

CHAPTER 19

Even before my flight from Amarillo touched down in Flint, I had begun to formulate a plan for Karen to visit Michigan during the summer of 1977. Talking her parents into a visit north had been made easier by how well my Christmas trip to Amarillo had gone. After meeting me, I think they felt comfortable letting her visit. I had been a gentleman and apparently did nothing to raise any 'red flags.' All through the winter, spring, and early summer, Karen and I had worked out all the logistics and were waiting for the day to finally arrive. We had planned a ten-day stay in order to give my family time to show her around the Great Lakes.

The night before Karen was to fly to Flint, I called her. It was late, and we talked of our anxiety to see each other again.

"Are you all packed?" I asked.

"Yes," she replied.

"I will not be able to sleep tonight, you know."

"Me neither."

It felt unreal to be able to say it, but I said, "I will see you tomorrow."

"Goodnaht, Scotty."

"Goodnight."

As I lay in bed that night, I lifted my head to see the clock; it was after 3:00 a.m. I was like an eight-year-old on Christmas Eve; I just could not sleep. I was the only one in my house who had a bedroom on the main floor. This made it easy to sneak around in the middle of the night. I quietly got up and stole one of my father's beers from the refrigerator, went outside, and sat on the front porch swing. The night was cool and still, and the can made a loud snap as I pulled back the aluminum tab. I sat silently and conjured up all the pictures of Karen I had carefully filed into my memory. I let some of the things she had said in the past play in my mind. "Ah'm stickin' with yew; ah don't know a soul." I smiled as I heard her voice say those words. I took a long slug of my dad's Black Label; it was cold and soothing as it went down my throat. I remembered the difficult goodbye at the bus at Castaway and our first kiss. I smiled as I reminisced on that very first morning on the bluff over Pelican Lake; when Janet yelled, "We are NOT gahs!" and I could barely understand her. "Five minutes later," I thought, "and we may never have met, and none of this would be happening." The possibility of that astounded me, and I began to wonder if God truly has plans for people. How easily we could have not met that first morning at Castaway. This thought began to occupy my mind. "It had to be providence," I thought. I took another long swig of beer, swallowing two or three times. I thought of the dinner at the Amarillo Club, high above the plains watching the storm move across the horizon. "Thunder-boomers," I snickered out loud. Then a thought occurred to me: "If I were to make a list of all the things that occupy my thoughts the most, Karen would have to be Number 1." The reality of how much I missed her became apparent. I counted in my head. "I have literally only seen this girl a total of eleven days of my life, and she is dominating my consciousness—unbelievable." I finished the beer and looked down the quiet street. "God, please let this go well," I prayed out loud in the dark. The Black Label had the desired effect, and for the first time I felt my eyes blink heavily with sleep. I carefully picked my way back into the house, to my room, and into bed. The next thing I knew, I startled awake. The day had finally come.

The hours between waking up and picking up Karen at the airport dragged on slower than shopping for clothes with my mother. But eventually the time came, and I drove to the airport. As people filed from the jetway, I stayed toward the back of the waiting crowd, peering over them in an attempt to catch Karen. Somehow she made it into the terminal without me seeing her. The crowd dispersed slightly, and I caught a glimpse of a lone, tiny figure holding a shoulder bag and looking lost. I did not recognize her at first, but it didn't take but a second to know it was Karen. Her hair was long again and like before, she caught me by surprise. At first she did not see me approaching, but then we met eyes, and she stepped quickly toward me. In the middle of families and others greeting each other, we hugged and kissed. In the past, it had come to me as a thought, and I acted upon it; this time the kiss seemed expected and happened unconsciously. We collected her baggage from the turnstile and left the terminal. As we drove to my house, we passed the massive Chevy truck assembly plant.

"What is this place?" she asked in amazement.

"It's the Chevy truck factory," I answered with a sense of pride.

"It's gigantic."

"Yeah, it is, and it's only one plant out of many in this town. This is what we do here."

As we got closer to my neighborhood, Karen noted, "Everything is so *green.*"

I had always thought of Flint as a gray industrial town and never really thought of it as green. But as I contemplated what she had said, I realized how much greener Flint was than Amarillo. "If you think *this* is green," I said, "wait until you see the U.P."

"The U.P., what's that?"

"It stands for the Upper Peninsula. Michigan is made up of two peninsulas," I explained, "the upper and the lower. You're going to get to see them both. I'll show you on a map. The farther north you travel, the more beautiful the state becomes." Visiting Texas was great, but I was chomping at the bit to show Karen what Michigan had to offer. "Here we are," I announced as we turned down Woodcroft Avenue. Karen noticed right away that the houses on my block were all wooden and two stories. Amarillo was dominated by low-ranch style brick homes. It was the little things like these that made comparisons interesting.

When we walked up to the house, I introduced Karen to my father, who had taken up his usual position on the front porch swing. He had a Black Label in his hand, and the ball game was playing from a radio perched in the window. Two years before he had survived a heart attack. Just when he was recovered enough to return to work, he suffered a stroke. Since then, he was unable to work. His speech and mobility had been affected, and he walked with a cane and spoke with a hint of a slur. Still, my dad was quite a character and probably drank too much, but when he met people, you could catch a glimpse of why my mother had fallen for him years ago. He was my mother's second husband; her first had died from polio, but not before giving her three children by the time she had turned twenty-one. At the age of twenty-one, my dad married a widow who already had three children. I always thought that was pretty impressive. I could tell when a connection was being made, and immediately I could see that he was fond of Karen.

"So you're the reason my monthly phone bill is so outrageous," was the very first thing he said to her. He held a stern look and squinted his eyes as he made the statement. Karen stiffened, and she had an ashen look on her face. I grinned and looked away, knowing my dad was just seeing how she would react. Upon seeing how lost Karen was, my dad's face slowly softened into a smile and he said, "But now I understand why."

Karen bashfully smiled and in relief said, "Gol-ly!" and the tension in her body relaxed.

"Nice, Dad," I said sarcastically. "Let's go in and meet my mom." Upon entering the house, I introduced her to my mother and my younger sister, Tammy. My three older sisters and brother were all married and did not live at home any longer; they would not meet Karen until later.

That evening after dinner, I drove Karen around and showed her some of the highlights of Flint. We also stopped to visit a few of the friends she knew from Castaway. Later, when we were back home, I started a fire in the fireplace. It was not that it was cold out, but more for the mood. We sat talking with my family, and my father tuned in the baseball game on the television with the volume turned down very low. As the night wore on, everyone gradually went to bed, thinly disguising that they were trying to let Karen and me have some time alone.

"Ray, it's time for bed," my mom said. He did not get the hint.

"I'll be up when the game is over."

"Rrraaayyyy," she stretched out his name so that he would understand she wanted his attention. My dad, propped in the corner of the sofa with an arm draped over his head, looked at her quizzically,

"What?" My mom just stared at him. He still did not comprehend what she was trying to get him to do.

"It's alright, Mom. Finish the game, Dad," I said. Then I could see by the look on his face that it all suddenly registered. "Watch the game, Dad . . . it's the eighth inning," I repeated in a way that assured him it was okay. Twenty minutes later when the final out of the ninth inning was tallied, he awkwardly got off the couch with a groan and turned off the television.

"Goodnight, you two," he said.

"Goodnaht, Mr. Hazel," Karen answered. Her tiny drawl was sweet, and I knew my father understood how easily it had captivated me.

"You be good," he said playfully, looking right at Karen.

She smiled in return and said, "Oh, ah will." My dad chuckled and left the room. We could hear the stairs creaking as he made his way upstairs and now after a busy day, we were finally alone.

I stoked up the fire and spread a blanket on the floor in front of it and turned off all the lights. With the firelight flickering on the ceiling, we sat facing each other with our legs crossed Indian style, our knees touching. I don't recall exactly what we said, but it was mainly catching up on news that we left out of our phone conversations and mail. As we talked, we playfully touched each other's fingers, sometimes intertwining them. The conversation eventually dwindled to silence, and as we continued the playful game with our fingers, the romantic tension built. We silently stared at each other's hands as we rolled them around each other, and then raised and locked our eyes. I reached up, and spreading my fingers apart, gently pushed my hand through her hair. Then with an open palm against her cheek, I rubbed my thumb back and forth on her cheekbone. Karen pressed her head harder against my hand and closed her eyes.

At Castaway and during my visit to Amarillo, we had opportunity but avoided quiet moments like this, partly because I did not want to do anything to screw it up. Everything was innocent and fairytale-like, and there were lines I consciously decided against crossing. But now, here in the dim light from the fire, we were confronted with the intimate situation that I knew was inevitable. "I can't believe you are finally here," I said, breaking the silence.

"Ah know," Karen answered in an exasperated manner. Then quite unexpectedly she asked, "Did you miss me?"

"Karen," I said her name to validate how poignant the thought was, "I think about you all the time."

"Ah know," Karen agreed, "me too." As she spoke, she slowly shook her head as if to say, "How can this be?"

"I'm not sure exactly what we have," I began. "It's *so* different. But whatever it is," I continued, "I like it . . . I don't want it to stop."

"What are we going to do?" she asked.

"I don't know." The silence returned.

I slid next to her, so we were now sitting side-by-side. I was still holding one hand and with the other, I lightly ran my thumb across her lips. Karen closed her eyes again and turned her face upward like an offering, and I leaned over and kissed her. At first, we kissed shortly and tenderly, but then for long periods without parting. As I pressed forward, she slowly fell back, and without separating our kiss, I followed her down until her back lay flat on the blanket. I was beside her, but our bodies were close, and I was leaning over her propped up on one elbow. I could feel the pounding of a heart, and I realized it was mine, just like on the dock at Castaway when we first held hands. My mind was doing somersaults, as this was new territory for us. It was all very cautious exploration, and I wondered how far it would go; or maybe more accurately, how far I would try to go until I heard the word "stop." As a new Christian, I knew I was operating under a new set of rules. I understood that if I did not handle this situation any differently than someone who was not born-again, then my decision to follow Christ meant nothing. I also felt a respect for Karen that, in all honesty, I had not considered with anyone I had dated before. Now, here was a moment of truth—what would I do? Our two closest legs were pressed hard against each other, and I slowly slipped mine over hers and past her knee. To my absolute amazement, I felt her heel wrap behind my calf. In an instant, our entire relationship was changing and in the midst of the passion, it scared me. We stayed like this for ten or fifteen minutes, discovering what it was like to be this close with each other. It wasn't as if we crossed any forbidden lines, but the innocence that was our relationship to that point had moved into uncharted waters.

We did not go any further. There was a time that, with our faces only inches apart, we just looked at each other without saying a word. The fire cast warm shadows on Karen's face, and I put my forehead against hers. For a long time we lay there with our eyes closed and foreheads pressed against each other. "I really care about you, Karen," I whispered. "I don't want to do anything wrong."

"Ah know," she agreed in a soft breathy voice.

"We should go to bed," I said in an effort to end the evening before it went too far.

Karen's eyes popped open, and she backed her head away. "WHAT!?"

It dawned on me what I said could be interpreted two ways. "To *sleep*!" I emphasized. We tried not to laugh too loud, but we embraced as our bodies shook together in muffled laughter.

"C'mon," I said, and I stood and offered her a hand up. We hugged tightly, and I kissed her on the forehead. "Boy, how I have missed you," I said.

"Me, too," she answered.

"Goodnight."

"Goodnaht," and she tiptoed up the creaky stairs to the room we had prepared for her. I returned to the blanket and sat down in front of the fireplace. I poked the fire a little and sat alone as the flickers slowly died into glowing embers.

In the coming days, I had plenty of events planned to make her trip to Michigan as memorable as mine was to Texas. One thing I had planned was a trip with Young Life friends to Cedar Point, Ohio, and a visit to one of the best amusement parks in the nation. I had asked Dale, and he agreed to handle the logistics for a day at the park. I was unaware that he had encountered difficulties securing the Young Life vans to transport us down to Ohio and back. Somehow our transportation ended up being a U-Haul moving van about the size of a bread truck. It was totally enclosed with a roll-down cargo door at the back. With no other option, about fifteen of us piled into the back of the U-Haul, Dale closed the door, and off we went bouncing around like packed furniture.

Cedar Point was about three hours from Flint, and we all had plenty of time to catch up as we traveled. Our day at the park was everything I hoped it would be, and we rode all the giant coasters as much as we could stand them. We stayed until the park closed and then climbed back into the enclosed moving van for the long ride home. The only difference was that now it was night, and the translucent roof let in no light. It was totally black in the back of the U-Haul, we couldn't see a thing, and had our conversations in the dark. Everything was fine, however, and Karen and I sat together, holding hands under a blanket in the dark. There was a sudden jolt, a loud noise, and the van shuttered to a stop. We could feel the rush of the traffic racing by on the expressway outside and had no idea what had happened or why we were stopped. Then Dale opened the garage-like door, and the sudden glare of oncoming headlights filled the room.

"We have a flat tire," announced Dale in frustration. "You guys get out, and I'll change it." So we all filed out like smuggled contraband and stood off to the side of the busy highway while Dale tried to find the jack and the spare. Thank goodness we had a spare, but it took a long time to figure it all out. Several motorists stopped to offer help, and we prayed that each one was not a police officer. Somehow we knew that cramming fifteen teenagers in the back of a moving van was probably not legal and certainly not safe. Dale was embarrassed and simply wanted to change the tire and get underway before anything worse happened. After about an hour, the tire was changed, and we all clamored back into the darkness of the U-Haul for what remained of the trip home. It was indeed a fun day and the crazy circumstances of traveling in the back of a U-Haul and the trip home only made the story better. It also helped me realize that Dale was a crazy dude.

The highlight of Karen's visit to Michigan was the trip we took north. My sisters, Denise and Darcy, and their husbands, Jim and Pat, came with us. It began with a must for anyone who visits Michigan: a day at the Straits of Mackinac, which include walking around Mackinaw City and a ferry trip across to Mackinac Island. For those who don't know, Mackinaw is an Indian word that is sometimes spelt with a 'c' at the end and other times with a 'w.' No matter which, it is pronounced mac-i-naw. It is also the name of a very warm winter coat, simply called a Mackinaw, named for those in the area who manufacture and wear them. Whether on the mainland or the island, this area has become well-known for the many types of fudge produced there. The island is steeped in rich history and has no motorized vehicles on it; most people ride bicycles or horses. No trip to Michigan is complete without a stop on Mackinac Island. Another major attraction of this area is the Mackinaw Bridge, which joins the Lower and Upper Peninsulas of the state. It remains one of the longest suspension bridges in the world and was an engineering marvel when it was built across the treacherous waters where Lake Huron meets Lake Michigan in the late 1950s. Since Cedar Point is located on the shore of Lake Erie, and the Straits of Mackinac are shared by Lake Huron and Lake Michigan, Karen had already been treated to seeing three of the five Great Lakes, quite a treat for someone from the dry plains of Texas. When Karen first looked across Lake Michigan she said, "I cain't see the other sahd. I knew it was big, but Ah didn't know yew couldn't see across it."

I laughed a little. "People don't realize that they are actually fresh-water seas." I continued, "If it weren't for the mosquitoes, Michigan would be more popular than Florida." The next day we crossed the bridge to the U.P. and the land of the 'Yoopers' (U.P.ers), as they were called. "God's Country," as we referred to it, is a land of vast forests, lakes, and colorful history.

After our day at Mackinaw, we continued further north to our favorite town in the U.P.-Marquette—and camped in our favorite campground, a place called Tourist Park. Located on Lake Superior, the largest and most mysterious of the Great Lakes, Marquette is also the home of Northern Michigan University, where I planned to attend the following autumn. While in Marquette, there were several places that simply had to be visited. We did the traditional hike up Sugarloaf Mountain, toting paper cups and a couple bottles of wine. Once atop Sugarloaf, the view over Lake Superior and Marquette are spectacular. Of all the Great Lakes, Superior is the most treacherous and the most unpredictable. Storms on Superior are the stuff legends are made from, and they build quickly and without warning. As recent as 1975, the sinking of the ore freighter Edmund Fitzgerald in a November storm, might be the best known testament to the power of the lake. Even in August, the water is barely above freezing and can be deadly if a person is not careful. Rivaled only by Lake Baikal in Russia, it boasts being the largest fresh-water lake in the world. The controversy with Lake Baikal is an argument of volume over area. Lake Superior is larger by area but Lake Baikal is greater by depth, and therefore volume. Which is the largest fresh-water lake in the world depends on your definition of largest—area or volume.

The day we sat on Sugarloaf was a typical chilly U.P. day with patches of fog rolling up over the summit. Sometimes you could not see a thing and within seconds, there would be a completely clear view with the warmth of the sun beating down through the mist. Superior, with an angry hint of green, was crashing against the ancient rocks that formed the jagged shore, with a sound that sounded like distant thunder. Karen and I sat side-by-side on a rock looking out over Superior.

"It sounds lahk a thunder-boomer," Karen said as she held my arm and pulled herself close for some warmth. I grinned when she said "thunder-boomer"; it was one of my favorite terms she used.

"Yeah, it's a powerful piece of water," I said. In the distance, there was a giant ore freighter plowing through the rough seas.

"Where is that ship going?" she asked, pointing out toward the horizon.

"Well, it could be headed a number of places," I began to explain.

"It might be going anywhere from Chicago, or Detroit, or even Russia."

"Russia!" she said in disbelief.

"Well, the Great Lakes are connected to the Saint Lawrence Seaway, which gives us access to the Atlantic; some of the freighters in the Great Lakes are taking iron ore, corn, or wheat from the Midwest all over the world. Mostly, though, I think it is iron ore headed to steel mills in Detroit; Gary, Indiana; Pittsburgh; and Chicago." I had to be careful when talking about the Great Lakes and Michigan. I sometimes came off like a know-it-all and was known to be long-winded and borish.

"Do other places send stuff here?" she seemed genuinely interested. I was only too eager to explain some of the aspects of living with the Great Lakes.

"Yes, mainly coal for us to operate our power plants. Without coal from other places, the U.P. would be a very dark, cold place," indicating the extremes of the northern winters. "Ah can see more water and more trees sitting raht here than there are in whole state of Texas," Karen announced. She seemed to really be enjoying the vista laid out before her, and I loved that she loved it.

We also introduced Karen to the tradition of eating pasties on the rocks. There is a park past the power plant and the ore docks called Presque Isle. To get there, you had to drive under the ore docks, which were several stories tall and ran a quarter of a mile or so out into the lake. This allowed the giant ore freighters, up to a thousand feet in length, to nestle up beside to load and off-load cargo. To give you a sense of their size, trains hauling dozens of hopper cars filled with iron ore pellets called taconite, could pull the entire length of the ore dock to unload into the freighters. It was a common scene to see trains jockeying back and forth on top of the docks, and surreal to see the massive freighters nosed right in to within a few feet of the shore. Once you passed the power plant, with its mountain of coal waiting for winter and the spectacle of the ore docks, Presque Isle lay just beyond a short bridge. It is a beautiful hump of an island that juts out into the bay with great views from nearly every little turnout. The central part of the isle is covered with dense pines, and the edges are craggy outcrops of ancient black rocks. At one location there are two opposing cliffs that run from Superior into the shore and tower fifty or sixty feet above the icy water. Between these cliffs, the water is crystal-clear and runs to the shore where a slope of natural gravel emerges like a boat launch. This is the place we called Pirate's Cove and the location for testing your nerve against the cliffs and the frigid water. Many times, stripped down to our shorts or bathing suits, we cautiously edged to a precarious point of rock ominously hanging out over the water. While standing with your toes curled over the edge gathering your courage to jump, you could see boulders the size of Volkswagens beneath the choppy water. The water is so clear that they appear to be close to the surface, but in reality, they are thirty feet or so down. Still, just seeing them plays with a person's mind. Once you finally muster the strength to leap, the sudden shock of forty-degree water nearly paralyzes a person. Most people can barely dog paddle back to the base of the cliff, only to be forced to tread water while trying to pick the handholds to pull themselves out of Superior and scale back up to the top. It is a rite of passage to anyone who visits to jump or dive off the cliffs at the black rocks.

But just as important as leaping into Lake Superior, so is enjoying the view while indulging in the local cuisine, a pasty with catsup. When we took Karen to the pasty shop, she asked the obvious question, "What is a pasty?" She pronounced it with a long "a" sound, which is a dead giveaway that you are not from anywhere near. It is actually quite humorous to hear someone say it that way, because a pasty (with a long "A") is the twirly thing strippers attach to their nipples. I laughed and had to whisper to her the difference. As we stood in line for our turn at the counter, I began to explain, "It's a meat pie invented by the Finnish immigrants to take with them into the mines."

"The mines?" she asked.

"Yeah, the iron ore that the freighters haul through the lakes . . . it's mined up here. Along with the timber industry, it's the heart of the economy of northern Michigan, Wisconsin, and Minnesota."

"And without the arn ore, we don't have any steel . . . raht?" she asked.

"You got it."

"No steel, no cars, no bridges, no buildings," she stated conclusively, "It's amazing how it all works," Karen said, like she understood something huge, that it made sense. "The Finnish?" she asked. "They make the pasties?"

"Yup, this part of the country was settled by Scandinavians, mainly Finns, because it resembled their homeland. They made up the majority of the miners," I continued to explain. "One of the things they brought to this area is pasties, these wonderful meat pies. But in order for it to be a legit pasty, it must include rutabaga." As if on cue, the woman behind the counter held a pencil over a pad of paper and with a thick Yooper accent asked, "What'll yous have?"

Ordering for everyone, I answered, "Ten pasties."

"Wid catsup or gravy?" she asked. When she said gravy, I could see Karen out of the corner of my eye look at me. It was a very long drawn out "A", so pronounced that it sounded like a fake accent.

"Holy wuh, who eats pasties wid gravy, eh?" I responded in a perfect U.P. dialect. I could see Karen's face spread into a wide grin.

"Oh yah, some people eat'em dat way now, you bet," was the answer from the lady using heavy vowels and very long "O's."

"Must be apple-knockers, eh?"

The woman chuckled, "Yah, you bet. Ten regular!" she hollered the order over her shoulder to a teenage boy feverishly working the big ovens in the back.

"You bet," came back the confirmation. I looked at Karen and smiled.

"Everything sounds like a question," she whispered. "That was pretty good."

"It grows on ya," I answered.

"Apple-knocker?" Karen asked with a raised eyebrow.

"Yeah, what we are—people from the Lower Peninsula." I continued, "It's because of all the orchards. They call us 'fudgies' and 'trolls' too."

"Fudgies because of Mackinaw, right?" she asked.

"Very good," I said, appreciating her understanding of the situation.

"Trolls? Why trolls?"

"Because we live under the bridge," I answered with a big smile.

Karen covered her mouth quickly to try and stop the spontaneous laugh. The lady handed us five white sacks with a receipt stapled to one, "Dar ya go," she said with a smile. She was old, had a leathery, worn face, and sort of hobbled when she walked around behind the counter. When she smiled, it revealed that she was missing a couple teeth. When she handed me the order, I noticed her crooked fingers and big knuckles. Everything about her was a testament of a hard existence. I thought she looked like she was seventy, but in reality, she was probably only fifty-five or so. Living in the U.P. is not for the delicate or the pampered; it is a place that will test one's resolve. "Yous goin' to da rocks?" she asked. "You betcha," I said, and we turned to leave. "Oh, it's a great day to go to da rocks wid a pasty." "Tanks, eh? I said over my shoulder." I heard Karen say under her breath with a slight grin, "Trolls." When we got in the car she asked, "Why do they say 'yous'"? I had to think a second, and then the perfect answer came to me, "It's like in Texas when you say 'y'all'. Remember how you told me that y'all is plural? Well, so is 'yous' or 'yous guys.'" I continued, "If it were only one person, they would say 'ya'." As she slid over next to me in the seat, she said, "That's kahnda funny." It was a dialect roller coaster hearing thick Yooper accents one second and a Texas drawl the next.

We proceeded to Presque Isle, the black rocks, and Pirate's Cove. We sat on the rocks and ate our pasties, holding them in one hand while squeezing catsup on them with the other and with every bite. Then we all took our turn jumping, from the cliffs into Lake Superior. Karen was a trooper and passed her initiation. As she jumped there was a moment of déjà vu that flashed through my mind. It seemed like eons ago, but it had only been a year since that wonderful day with Suzy when she jumped off the bridge into the lake somewhere in Minnesota. I snapped back to reality when I heard Karen pop back to the surface exclaiming, "Gaaawwwllllly!" in a long drawn-out expression of disbelief. Like anyone who has not experienced the cold of Lake Superior, she was nearly blue by the time she climbed back to the top. "SON!" she said as she clamored for her towel, "That is cold, cold, COLD!" Not everyone can claim that they have swum in Lake Superior, let alone dove in off the rocks at Presque Isle, but those who have belong to an exclusive club who understand what cold *really* is. Now much like I had become an accepted member of the Texas cowboy culture, Karen was earning her rights as an accepted guest Yooper.

The last morning before returning to the Lower Peninsula, I whispered through the side of Karen's tent, and I heard her say she was awake. A few seconds later the zipper of the door slowly, quietly began to slide up, and she crawled out of the tent. We had made plans to get up early and watch the sunrise from a bluff on Presque Isle. We arrived to find the park was not yet open and had a pole secured across the drive. I turned around and only a few yards away pulled into the parking lot for the massive ore dock. We grabbed what we had brought and briskly walked to the spot I had in mind where I spread out an unzipped sleeping bag. It was a typical clear but very cold U.P. morning. The lake was as calm as Lake Superior gets, with a wispy fog rolling up over the rocks from the lake. We lay facing the east with a blanket pulled over us, and I had an arm draped across Karen's back, pulling her tight to me. Below us was a hundred-foot cliff straight down to the lake. I could feel her occasionally shiver. "This bluff reminds me of Castaway," Karen said. It was unexpected, and I was slow to respond. "Yes, that was quite a morning," I finally said thoughtfully and squeezed her closer. Slowly, the sky brightened and changed from an awakening pale blue to a soft peach until a blaze of yellow sun burst across the water. "B-e-a-u-t-i-f-u-l," I heard Karen say with a sense of awe. She had said it slowly stretching out each letter in amazement. The sun climbed ever so slowly off the horizon, chasing the fog quickly away and warming our faces. "I wanted you to see this," I said. "Thanks, Scotty," was all she said in her endearing drawl. We lay there quietly for about twenty minutes until I said, "We better get back and eat; we have a long day ahead of us." I was lying on my stomach and resting with my elbows under me. Karen tucked her head against my shoulder and for a few precious moments, we lay together without saying a word, just together.

By that night, we had crossed back over the Mackinaw Bridge to the Lower Peninsula and were back home attacking a pile of laundry that reeked of campfire smoke. We had one more full day before Karen had to return to Amarillo. I took her to Leisure Lake, and we spent it laying on the beach and sailing. After my embarrassing effort at Castaway, I felt the need to prove to her that I actually knew my way around a sailboat. We did not stay at the cottage that night, but we stayed long enough to have a campfire. My parents had left earlier for Flint, so Karen and I were alone at the cottage. It was another one of those times when, had we possessed a weaker resolve, we could have pushed the physical boundaries of our relationship . . . but we did not. We both understood that crossing certain barriers changes the complexion of a relationship and can wreck it. We did not want to chance it. We did not actually speak about it much. It was almost a fear that we did not want to toy with. Oh, the desire was definitely there, but going too far would cheapen the relationship, a relationship that was increasingly feeling more like a courtship with rules and boundaries.

As much as any social norms, trying to live according to the Christian values we were learning through Young Life, church, and reading scripture for ourselves were what really helped us keep the relationship from having any regrets. Basically, we had met at a church camp, and we were both born-again Christians; this was the foundation on which we built ourselves as a couple. Approaching this relationship like that didn't matter would have sabotaged the whole thing. The entire relationship was different; *we* were different. As we had heard many times in Young Life discussions, we had to "walk the talk." We had spent time talking about 1st Corinthians, Chapter 13, in the Bible. It is known as the love chapter and is quoted at many weddings. It is filled with wonderful guidelines as to the characteristics and behaviors of true love. Our dilemma was we had no definition of our relationship! It was obvious that we got along easily and that we cared a great deal for each other, but love? That might be a little ambitious. As much as crossing any physical barriers, attaching the word love to our relationship would have been equally catastrophic. So many teenaged couples are eager to fall in love, and most of the time it is merely hormones doing the thinking. I had never told a girl that I loved her at that point in my life, but I had never felt about anyone the way I felt about Karen . . . was this love? We had become close and discovered much about each other through letters, but only seeing each other on three occasions in the course of a year made it difficult to even decide if we were a couple. Love? Still, Corinthians gave a solid basis to how a relationship should be handled, and we simply ignored that it referred to love and applied its principles to "people who like each other enough to travel across the country to see one another."

"Let's take a walk," I suggested.

"That would be nahce," Karen said. We held hands and simply began to walk without any particular destination. We walked and talked until we found ourselves on the covered bridge. I had a fleeting memory of the time Kevin, our summer friends, and I passed a joint around at this very same spot. It was a memory that I wished I did not have, and I tried to dismiss it from my mind.

"This is a nahce place," said Karen.

"Yes it is, isn't it? I have ridden my bike across here a thousand times. Kevin and I used to hang out here sometimes when we were young and dumb." We had stopped in the middle, and Karen placed her back against the lattice that enclosed the sides of the bridge. Facing her, I pressed in close, and we put our arms around each other and kissed.

"Are *we* a couple?" I asked. There was a pause.

"Ah think so," Karen replied.

"We are definitely close friends now, right?" I was trying to get a handle on exactly what we were.

"Ah think it's more than that," said Karen.

"Yeah, I know, but what?" I asked. Before that, we just let "us" be what we were and never discussed it or tried to define it. For the first time, we were addressing the tough questions about this long distance affair.

"Not exactly sure," she answered. I leaned forward and pressed my lips against her forehead.

"I can't stop thinking about you, but I think it would be asking a lot to ask you not to date anybody when we're a thousand miles apart."

Karen pulled her head back and looked up at me with a sort of hurt expression. "Do you *want* to date someone else?"

"No, no, I just was saying it in general; to say we're not going to date anyone while we are so far apart . . . ." I didn't know how to finish my thought and just left it hanging. Then I finally took a leap into unknown territory and said, "Thinking about it now, I guess I would be jealous if I knew you were dating someone."

"Me, too," she said.

"So what are we going to do?"

Karen put her forehead back against my lips, and there was a silence that filled the air with quiet contemplation at the question. After a little bit, I said, "How about this: knowing that we are going to try and see each other again, we should consider ourselves a couple. But if we want to go on a date, we are free to do so. That way we won't miss dances and stuff like that. I think that going on a date now and then is different than dating someone . . . right?"

"Yes," Karen said, thinking about what I had suggested.

"Not that I am looking to date anyone, but you get what I'm saying, right?"

"Yes, yes ah do. Ah think that is good, it makes sense," Karen said. Then she added, "But when we go on dates, we need to tell the other person, so there is no misunderstanding."

I was relieved to hear that she was thinking about us as seriously as I was. I had assumed that from the start but couldn't be certain until I actually heard it from her. Sometimes people interpret relationships differently and are heartbroken when they finally discover the other person is not thinking like they are. I knew now without question that Karen felt the same about me as I felt about her.

"Yes, from the start we need to be up front with people," I agreed.

"So, we are a couple." It was more of a statement seeking clarity than a question.

"I suppose we are . . . we *are* a couple," I confirmed. We smiled at each other with a look of satisfaction. We now had defined what we were and walked hand in hand back to the cottage.

We drove back to Flint and prepared for her to leave the next day. We sat on the front porch swing late into the night and talked with a new sense of direction. The next day, with tears at the airport, I said goodbye to Karen for the third time and watched her disappear down a jetway into the plane. I stood looking out the giant windows, watching her plane taxi out to the runway, sitting in line waiting its turn to thunder away. I waved when it passed by, but it was just a last dramatic gesture sent out like an S.O.S., hoping the right person would receive it. As I watched, I wondered what the future held for us. Each goodbye had become more difficult than the one before, and even though we planned to keep visiting each other, neither of us could really know for certain we would . . . there were so many miles and so many things that could happen. I did not leave the terminal until her plane became a small speck and vanished into the clouds.

OFF TO COLLEGE

CHAPTER 20

Between the bike trip to Frontier Ranch and Karen's visit, there were several days that I visited Safetyville and talked to Babe. We spent time just talking about whatever popped into our minds, and I told her all about my trip to Colorado. Babe and I talked very easily, but generally she was a pretty quiet person, especially when others were around. But when we were alone, she was fairly talkative and voiced her opinion on any topic. Babe was like a side-dish to my life. I was involved in a lot of things as I prepared to go the Northern Michigan University (N.M.U.), including soccer and still trying to hold down a job at Wendy's. A visit with Babe was like stepping out of it all for a while and taking a deep breath. She was my refuge. That was my perception; anyway, I think it was different for Babe. I could tell that we were looking at our involvement in two different ways, and I had to be careful not to send out the wrong signals. Unlike some of the short relationships I had before Karen, I was always honest with Babe. There were times in high school I dangled two or three girls in loose relationships, selfishly getting all I could out of all of them before they blew up in my face or simply faded away. I did not want to do that with Babe. Honestly, it wasn't that I was a playboy; I just didn't know how to handle being popular. In addition, I was fickle. I would actually get attached to everyone I was involved with and couldn't make up my mind if I really liked any one over another. Ultimately, it was a kind of a game, anyway. I never felt about any of them how I felt about Karen. It was not a game with Karen; I longed for her until it hurt. Therefore, I wanted to be true to Karen; secondly, I wanted to do the right thing, the Christian thing, where Babe was concerned. It was not easy, especially since I was still sporting the ego I developed ever since Barb had welcomed me to high school in the back seat of her Ford Falcon. In spite of the temptations, I was hanging in there. Even so, the truth did not sit well with Babe when I told her that Karen was coming to visit and that we were planning to travel around the state. But the visit came and went, and I hadn't seen Babe for a long time.

A week or so after Karen had left, I was driving past Safetyville and saw Babe's car in the parking lot. I made a u-turn and pulled in next to it. I walked down and sat on the bleachers and watched her give instructions to the miniature drivers. When she was done, she turned around and saw me sitting apart from the parents who were there watching their children drive the little cars. She smiled and gave me a little wave. When the session was over, she strolled over and sat next to me.

"It's been awhile, Injun," she said flatly.

"Yeah, I know, Rashid," I answered.

"Has your little Texan gone home?" She had a sarcastic tone that was uncharacteristic and although I understood, I did not appreciate it, and I gave her a cynical look.

"Sorry," she said and dropped her eyes to the ground.

"Hey," I said in a soothing tone, "I am being honest with you because it's the right thing to do."

"I know . . . it's just hard."

"Well, you and I don't *really* know each other that well," I said.

"I'd like us to," Babe quietly replied. "You don't *really* know her that well either, do you?" she asked, using the same emphasis I had used on her. I wanted to reply that we did know each other well, but in reality, Karen and I had actually only seen each about a month over a year's time; and that was totaling our time at Castaway and two visits. In spite of all the letters and phone calls, Babe actually had a valid argument. I looked off into the distance and didn't say anything for a long time. Finally I sighed, "Well, Karen and I talked a lot about what we are . . . I mean where exactly our relationship stands."

"And where is that?" asked Babe curtly.

"Well," there was along pause, "we want to see each other as much as possible . . . which is not that much, considering how far apart we live. But we know we are going to try to as often as we can." Babe sat leaning forward and listened with her elbows resting on her knees while she wrung her hands together. She was very tan and wore a nice pair of tennis shorts and a sharp tank top. Her skin was smooth and beautiful, and she was very fit.

"Um," I began to reveal the most awkward truth, "we basically decided that we *are* a couple."

Babe squinted and looked to the horizon. "That's great," she said dryly.

"We can still go on dates, but not *date* anyone. Does that make sense?" There was no answer. Babe was quietly deciding exactly what that meant. "Anyway," I continued, "I go to soccer training at N.M.U. in a week, and I'll be staying in Marquette until the school starts. I thought maybe we could have lunch or something before I go."

"A week?" she asked in disbelief. "Let me think on it," she continued. "Call me sometime in a day or two, and I'll let you know." Babe was unsure whether or not she wanted to get involved any deeper under these circumstances, and I didn't blame her. I wasn't even sure if I felt comfortable with it all and vowed to keep it all in terms of a friendship, nothing further.

"That's fair enough," I said. I stood up, glad to be done with that, and said as I backed away, "I'll call you."

I let several days pass before I gave Babe a call. It was two days before I left for Marquette and N.M.U. She had a full schedule that day but asked if we could meet by the stone bridge the following day. The stone bridge was a small bridge that arced over a large creek near the same golf course where Barb took me for a ride two years earlier. It was a beautiful setting with giant willows dangling their long strands over the rippling water. It was a short bike ride to the bridge from my house, and as a kid, I spent many summer days at this very same place catching tadpoles. So I met her there, and we leaned side by side with our elbows on the concrete railing, looking down at the current serpentine its way around the rocks. There was a lot of small talk about the coming year and college. Babe was going to stay at home and go to the University of Michigan at the Flint campus. Suddenly, she turned toward me and grabbed my hand, stretched up, and kissed me. It took me by surprise, but I did not resist, even returned it. In that fleeting moment, the little devil Scotty and the angelic Scotty popped up on my shoulders, vying for control of my thoughts and actions. Of course one was yelling, "Go for it!" and the other screaming, "Don't do it!" It was not a long or passionate kiss and when I backed away, I said, "Oh, Therese, this can't happen." The little white Scotty with wings had won.

"Texas," she said.

"Texas," I affirmed, and let go of her hand. In the moment, I felt tempted to let it all just take its course, but the reborn part of me kept saying in my head, "Walk the talk." As we stood there, I thought of that night at Castaway, the decision I had made on steps overlooking the lake. "If that meant anything," I thought to myself, "then you will do what is right here, you will not be ashamed tomorrow." In that moment, I recalled the counsel that Dale had given about becoming a Christian; the issues you had the day before are still issues; it's a matter of how you handle them. I knew my decision was genuine and from the heart, and I wanted to do the Christian thing, but the worldly me was putting up a pretty good fight.

"Babe," I finally said, "this would go beyond what Karen and I decided, and I just can't be untrue to her." I continued trying not to hurt her feelings more than they already were. "If we keep going, my character will be worthless."

"That's what is ironic about all this," Babe said. "That is the part of you that I like the most . . . and it's keeping us apart." I thought to myself, "yes, this is ironic because a year ago my character was very shallow. Going forward with this would not have bothered me at all."

"Do you think this relationship with this girl so far away can really last?" she asked. She wasn't being mean when she asked this; it was a serious question.

"I don't know," I answered honestly. "We really have feelings for each other, and we're just moving ahead one visit at a time."

Babe closed her eyes and slowly shook her head a couple times in disbelief and said, "You're a dreamer, Injun."

"Sorry," was all I could say.

"Can I write to you at college?" she asked. A part of me thought I should just make it easy on everyone and tell her 'no,' but I just couldn't bring myself to do it. "Yes, of course, we can write." We talked for a little while longer and eventually said our goodbye. That was the last I saw of Babe for some time.

At home later, when I was finishing up packing all the things I wanted to take to Northern, my dad said, "Can you take me to the store?"

"Sure," I said.

My dad had not driven since his stroke, and we all took him wherever he needed or wanted to go. As soon as we turned off Woodcroft Street he said, "Head to Vetchel's."

I looked at him and asked, "Really?"

He just kept staring straight ahead, "Yup, Vetchel's."

Vetchel's was the local pub that my mother had hauled my dad out of many times. He was seldom home from work right away, and if you went looking, nine times out of ten, you would find his red pick-up parked at Vetchel's. I pulled into Vetchel's parking lot, and my dad hobbled in with his cane. When we broke the dim, smoky bar with a shaft of light from the outside, I heard two voices simultaneously say, "Hey Ray!" My dad simply said, "Fellas," as he raised his cane in a sort of salute to comrades. We sat down, and he ordered two Carling Black Label beers. The bar was small, and the music from the jukebox was from a generation or two before mine. It was an old man's bar. Still, it was my dad and me, and I enjoyed the time he had set aside just for us. Even though my older two brothers and my oldest sister were from my mother's first marriage, we made no distinction, and my father raised us all like we were his blood. My brother Randy had died from leukemia just after he struggled to graduate from high school, and the loss was hard to bear for us all. Randy and I shared a room, and I was seven when he died. It is one of the earliest memories I have. When it got close to the end, my parents sent me to stay with an old friend. As clearly as if it happened yesterday, I can remember my mother's friend, Wanda, bracing herself through her tears to tell this little boy, "Scott, your brother Randy has died."

It took me many years to realize that I was actually my dad's only son. We didn't do a ton of things as father and son, and my dad was never my little league coach or anything like that. It was he, however, who introduced me to the love of being outdoors and the art of poking a campfire with a stick. He also passed on to me his love for playing the drums and how to drive a nail. He couldn't read a lick of music, but give him a pair of drumsticks and put him behind the drum set of a big band or jazz band, and he was a natural. With a cigarette loosely pinched between his lips and his thin Clark Gable mustache, he was something to behold. He was a product of the Depression, and simple things satisfied him. I think perhaps top on that simple list may have been a cooler filled with Black Label, poking a campfire, and a Tiger baseball game playing softly on a radio in the background. It was during these times of contentment that he would say the words that are burned into my memory even to this day: "I wonder what the poor people are doing?" If my mother was around, like on cue she would respond, "We *are* the poor people, Ray," and he would beam out an exaggerated grin, sometimes flipping his false teeth out from their setting and chuckle a bit. He was a man formed by his time and possessed many of the typical flaws of his generation. But under the exterior, he possessed just as many virtues. As father and son, there existed an unspoken bond between us, and I loved him dearly. I have discovered in many ways that I am him. Most recently, at a funeral for my Aunt Lorraine (who had married my dad's best friend Bob after her first husband, my dad's youngest brother, Albert, had died), my likeness to my father became even more evident.

By the time Aunt Lorraine died, my father had been passed away more than ten years and with that, my Uncle Bob (married to Aunt Lorraine) had lost his best friend. When I walked into the funeral home, filled with the Irish clan that we are, I heard my Uncle Bob exclaim loudly above the din of relatives, "Jesus Christ, it's Ray incarnate," and he came and swallowed me up with a firm handshake and the hug of a long-lost friend. His greeting reminded me of something that had always puzzled me, that is, as devout and religious as all my relatives were, how was it they so easily used the Lord's name in vain? I am not claiming that I did not curse—under certain circumstances, I could hold my own with any sailor—but using God as a swear word was strictly off limits. With both hands on my arms, Uncle Bob held me at arm's length and looked at me with a tear, "You are indeed your father's son."

I don't recall all the topics of conversation that evening in Vetchel's, but it mainly had to do with being responsible while away at college. But one piece of advice he offered that night has stuck with me all these years. It was when he looked squarely at me without any smile and said, "Son, just remember to use your big head before you use your little one." I laughed a little, but nodded knowing that vaguely masked in the humor was a serious word of advice. My dad was a gruff man, but very soft on the inside. I knew that this was his way of saying, "Goodbye, be smart, and do well." The next day when I left, he would not say much, just tear up in the background and grunt, "Take it cool."

The next day a friend of mine from Young Life named Dave was my ride to N.M.U. He was two years older than I and had already been to Northern for a couple years. Without asking, he had put my name down as a roommate choice and, having junior status, it was granted. I wasn't sure if I wanted this or not because Kevin had also been at Northern the previous year, and we had planned to room together. Dave had inadvertently messed that up. For the time being, I would be in a room with Dave on the opposite end of campus from Kevin. I packed my stuff the next day in Dave's car, said my goodbyes, kissed my mother, and drove away toward the U.P. and N.M.U. and away from the security I had known for most of my young life. I looked away from Dave out the window because I was starting to cry. Something down deep told me that the life I had known for eighteen years was over.

Eight hours and nearly four hundred miles later, we reached Marquette and settled into our dorm room. Dave was a great guy, but it didn't take long for me to realize I got along much better with Kevin and wanted to make the move. It took several weeks, but after some wrangling by Kevin's father, the Bear, I was moved up campus to share a room with Kevin. There was a bonus: my old friend Bobby, who I had shared many high school times and bike excursions with, was living on the floor above me. Most of the guys on the floor of my new dorm were from places in the U.P., mostly from Iron Mountain near the Wisconsin border, and possessed about as strong of a Yooper accent as there is in the Upper Peninsula. They liked to drink and chew tobacco, but they felt pot was something for the burnouts from downstate; that, I could tell, they did not indulge. As a freshman and a Christian, I took everything seriously: my classes, my relationship with Karen, and playing on Northern's soccer team. I would be a liar if I said I lived a straight and narrow life that Jesus would be honored by, but as things go at college, I was a pretty good guy and tried to continue to "walk the talk" as much as possible. Sometimes I was successful, others I failed. But in it all, I never forgot the commitments I had made, both to Karen and to Christ, and fought hard against the trappings of parties and girls with no parents around. The main attractions were learning more about the culture of the Yoopers, doing ridiculous antics with new friends, and drinking lots of beer.

The first organized party I went to was a Halloween party. This party required a costume, and being that most college students did not factor that in when packing their clothes for school, it became an exercise in creativity and imagination. I had some ski wear and used it to cobble together a super-hero whom I named "The Masked Avenger." The costume consisted of long underwear with soccer socks pulled over them up to my knees, a black skin-tight turtle-neck sweater with white piping, a ski mask with goggles, and gloves, all topped off by a beach towel tied around my neck as a cape. On my chest with duct tape I fashioned the letters "M-A" for Masked Avenger. It was a hot costume, but it went over well.

The Monday following the party a pile of guys were in the television room watching Monday Night Football. The Masked Avenger costume was still lying on the floor in my room. This gave me an idea. As a freshman trying to fit in, I decided to get a cheap laugh by donning the Masked Avenger suit and running through the T.V. room. I went outside and dove into the room through the open window, got to my feet, and striking a Superman-like pose, ran through the room and out the door while yelling "The Masked Avenger!" in a cartoon super-hero voice. Afterwards, while standing in the hallway, I listened to the laughter from the T.V. room and realized how funny they thought that was. "That worked out well," I thought. Reasoning that one good laugh deserves another, I did the same routine several times. What I didn't realize was how annoying I was becoming. The last time I dove through the window, stood, and started to yell, "The Masked Avenger!" I heard the window slam shut behind me and the door slam shut in front of me. When they began to fall upon me, I knew I had worn out my welcome. I prepared for some sort of beating but quickly realized they were tearing off my clothes. A sudden panic came over me because I knew that being naked was only the first step in whatever they had planned. I put up a valiant fight, but eventually I stood in the middle of a dozen guys who then grabbed me and muscled me into the hallway, closing the door behind them. I quickly darted down the hall to my room, only to find the door had been locked! In fact, every door I tried was locked! So there I stood, totally naked with nowhere to hide and a gang of hysterically laughing guys waiting to see what I would do next. What happened next was the new Resident Assistant from the floor above us, accompanied by two Night Clerks, was beginning his rounds for the evening. Both of these were positions of responsibility, and I did not want to get reported for indecent exposure. As I heard the voices getting nearer, I pleaded, "C'mon guys, somebody let me in a room!" The only response I got was harder laughter. Finally, the door by the stairs opened, and four guys walked into the hallway and stopped dead in their tracks. I decided to do a thing we called "Act Casual" whenever we found ourselves in an embarrassing or tense situation. With my hall mates literally rolling on the floor with laughter, I simple crossed my legs, leaned an elbow against the wall, and pretended to smoke a cigarette like nothing was out of the ordinary. I made no effort to conceal myself, just stood there blowing fake smoke in the air until I finally said, "Hey fellas, what's shakin'?" One clerk said, "Well, Bernie, it's your first day on the job, how do ya handle this?" He was talking to Bernie who had recently been hired to fill a vacated R.A. job on the second floor. Bernie knew me, and he asked in disbelief, "My God, Hazel, where's your clothes?"

"Not wearing any tonight," was all I said.

"You need to get into your room," was his reply.

"Door's locked," I calmly said and tilted a glance at my room.

All the while Bernie and I talked, the guys standing around and lying on the floor were beside themselves with laughter; it was a really funny scene. Then, under the circumstances, Bernie asked the most ridiculous question he could have asked. "Do you have your keys on you?"

Wide-eyed I stopped my smoking routine and put a single finger in the air which meant, "Hold on, I'll look."

"Just a second, I'll check." As I said this, I mockingly patted my hands against my nude body where pockets would normally be, as if I was searching for my keys.

"Nope, no keys," I said and shrugged.

At this time, a clerk stepped forward and saved Bernie from his first awkward confrontation. "Is this your room?" he asked. He was fumbling with a wad of keys as he indicated the door I had looked at earlier in the conversation.

"Yup," was all I said. He unlocked it with a pass key and said, "There, now get the hell outta the hallway!" A command I wasted no time in obeying. Needless to say, the Masked Avenger never flew again and I did manage to achieve my initial goal; I carved out a place in the camaraderie of the guys in my dorm. I also learned that freshmen should probably stay in the shadows and not call attention to themselves, not to do so was risky.

I played well for the soccer team that first year and made some new friends there as well. But that culture, too, was also heavy into parties and booze. In spite of my Christian convictions I consistently found myself at weekend parties with the two Scotties perched on my shoulders doing battle for my soul. Through it all I honored my commitment to Karen and was anticipating her visit at Christmas. Missing her left a giant hole in my heart and the affection I felt for her was constantly in the back of my mind. When she had visited during the previous summer one of the topics of conversation was the next visit. Even though I had gone down to Texas and she had an alternating visit to Michigan, we decided to break the pattern and have her come North during the winter. We talked her parents into it and proceeded with the plans not long after she arrived back in Amarillo from her trip to Michigan. My first semester at college was as much as an awakening as Phil's first party had been my sophomore year in high school. But now the stakes were much higher, I was at college and I was on my own and my relationship with Karen was as serious as any I had ever had.

THE THIRD VISIT

CHAPTER 21

During that first semester at N.M.U., I had Karen's picture plastered all around my desk. The focal point was a large 8x10 in a nice wooden frame. Behind it, tacked up on the corkboard, were many snapshots of Castaway, Texas, and her trip to Michigan. I took some ribbing from the guys in the dorm about my shrine, but I didn't care. They were not too hard on me for I found that many of them had shrines of their own. Amid all the directions that college life was pulling me, the relationship with Karen was getting more serious. Being a full time student with a disabled father had its perks. I received a monthly check in my name based on the cost of living. I recall it being around $200. Most of it every month went toward the ridiculous phone bill that I was racking up to Amarillo. The phone code was great, but I found it increasingly difficult to not speak to her, so on many occasions I did. Consequently, instead of having a slowly building savings account, I blew my funds on beer and phone bills and rarely had any sort of nest egg for emergencies or normal life expenses.

When Christmas break finally rolled around, I could barely stand the anticipation of Karen's visit. Her high school break was much shorter than my college break, so I had been home cooling my heels for a couple weeks waiting for Christmas day to arrive. The main reason we had decided for her to come north again, instead of me going back to Texas, was so she could experience the Michigan winter.

Her plane landed the day after Christmas and as she stepped out of the tunnel into the terminal, she appeared even more beautiful than I remembered. She looked older and more mature. I tried not to dwell too much on how young she was when we first met, but it was plain to see now that she was not a girl any longer, but a young woman. Something emotionally had changed since we parted the previous summer as well. When I caught sight of her, a flood of emotion welled up inside me that I could barely contain. We walked quickly toward each other and embraced as tightly as we ever had. It was clear that the feeling was mutual and the embrace spoke volumes about how the distance had affected us. I had ached to see her and could scarcely believe that I was actually hugging her.

It wasn't that she hadn't seen snow before; Amarillo actually receives some snow during their winter. The Panhandle geographically is not that far from Colorado. Not well known either, is the fact that many Texans, especially those from the Panhandle, are actually very good snow skiers. They don't ski as much as people from colder parts of the nation, but when they do ski, it is in the Rockies, where some of the best skiing in the country is located. Karen had been to some of the premier slopes in America. In spite of this, the bitterness of the Michigan winter was a rude slap in the face when we left the airport.

"SON, it's cold here!" she exclaimed as she nestled close under my arm walking to the car. There was not as much snow as I had hoped for her visit, but there was a few inches still hanging around from a storm that blew through a week or so earlier. I was able to take her to the local ski slope and she was able to do something she had not done in Colorado; ski under a lighted slope at night. We were able to see many of the Young Life friends she knew and even went to Young Life Christmas gathering. We also went dancing one night at "The Light" where, a year earlier, I had met Babe and ripped my pants. Even though I had been up front and honest with Babe, I was really praying that we would not bump into her at the club. What made that night even more fun was that my oldest sister, Lynn, had left me her car to drive while she was in Florida on vacation. Lynn was ten years older than me and in the process of climbing her way up the corporate ladder. She was doing quite well. A sure sign of this was that the car she left for me to use during Karen's visit was a brand new yellow Corvette. I have to admit I felt pretty full of myself driving Karen around in that thing. Looking back now, knowing how I drove that car around in the snow, I can only conclude that Lynn was out of her mind.

Karen's visit was filled with the usual planned events and we spent a great deal of time getting closer. Although being physical was becoming much more comfortable for us, there were still some pretty strict lines that we refused to cross. Being comfortable also meant not crossing the line was becoming increasingly more difficult. Certainly the milestone event of the visit happened a couple days before she had to leave. A storm had rolled in and I was finally glad she was able get a taste of what winter in Michigan was like. It snowed hard for the entire day and reached a point where the news was cautioning people to stay home and not to drive unnecessarily. It was blowing and drifting and shoveling was useless, as the wind would drift the snow over walks and driveways in no time. It was best to wait until the storm was finished and dig out in one monumental effort. We had taken up our favorite late night position after everyone had gone to bed, in front of the fireplace on a rolled out sleeping bag. With the blizzard howling outside the fire was especially cozy that night. I was sitting facing the fire and Karen was more or less lying in my lap with her back against me, and her feet toward the fire. My arms were wrapped around her and she was lightly playing with my fingers with hers. We did not feel the need to be physical or that we should be kissing or anything like that, we were simply enjoying being close. It was the simple contentment of two people meant to be together.

"Boy, it's really blowing out there," Karen said, as she watched the snow outside the window swirl spastically in every direction at once.

"Yes it is," I agreed in an ominous tone.

"Does it do this often?"

"Three or four times a winter. Usually this kinda stuff happens in January and February . . . but occasionally Christmas time can throw you a surprise . . . surprise!"

"Ah guess so," she said still looking in amazement at the white chaos outside the window.

"Maybe you'll get snowed in."

"Mah parents would NOT be happy if that happened," and we both laughed at the thought of it. There was a long satisfying silence.

Our focus switched from the storm to the fire and the magic of the moment. Slowly and unspoken, being together alone was heavy in the air. Karen still lightly rubbed her fingers through mine and there was a sense of anticipation building.

"Karen," I finally said, "I am afraid to say what is going through my head because I think it might wreck everything." There was dead silence. I began to get the feeling that she was thinking the same thing but wanted to hear what I was thinking first. Either that, or she did *not* want to hear what I was about to say. It was the moment of truth and what was about to come out of my mouth could either move this relationship to another level, or destroy it entirely. The gravity of the moment was not lost to me, and I was genuinely scared. I was glad that she was not facing me because had I looked into those eyes I may have lost my nerve.

Karen Little, 1978

"There's no other way to say this," I boldly began, "so I will just say it . . . I think that I am in love with you." Karen's fingers abruptly stopped the little pattern they had been tracing on my hands. My heart was pounding when I realized I had actually said the words out loud. I wasn't sure how to read the signal of her playful fingers being suddenly frozen. Then she took my hands in hers and squeezed them all together, but still did not say a word. I wasn't sure what that meant, so I continued, "I am, Karen." The cat was out of the bag and I came clean like a criminal making a confession. "I think about you everyday and sometimes I miss you so much I hurt. I'm in love with you and there's nothing I can do about it." Still there was nothing but silence from Karen. I was on a roll and continued to spill my emotions, "Honestly, I think I've loved you since that morning by the lake, I just didn't want to ruin everything by saying it too soon." Nothing. I pressed onward, "That last night at Castaway, when your bus pulled out of sight, I about died! I went back to the cabin and took about a two-hour shower. I didn't know if we would even *see* each other again, and that just about crushed me!" Her inactivity was starting to make me worried. "Crap," I thought, "I shouldn't have told her." But there was no stopping me now, "I have had you on my mind everyday for a year and a half."

Karen did not move, just kept squeezing my hands until finally a soft voice quietly said, "Ah'm in love with yew, too, Scotty." When she said my name, I had a quick moment of déjà vu back to Castaway, when I first heard her say it like syrup, and you might as well have hit me in the head with a two by four.

"Ah slept on your soccer ball awl the way ta Amarilla," she said. She twisted her shoulders around, turned her face upward, and kissed me. Then we sat for a long time just watching the fire and listening to it crackle and pop. We both felt the power of the moment, but also knew our time together was coming to an end. I simply held her tightly and she began to etch patterns on the back of my hands again.

That night, as we prepared to go our separate ways to bed, we embraced and I looked down at her and said, "I love you."

"Ah love yew," she answered, followed by a tender kiss and a long hug.

"Goodnight."

"Goodnaht."

I don't know if I ever really fell asleep that night. I kept repeating all the words from our fireside conversation over and over, almost not believing that I had heard what I had heard. Sometime around one o'clock, I finally could take it no longer and quietly got up and got a Black Label from the refrigerator, being careful in the dark not to step on any squeaky spots. I strategically placed a single log on the still glowing embers and watched it slowly build from smoke into a sudden 'poof' of flame. The room instantly took on a warm mellow feeling and I reveled in the joy I was feeling. I sat alone in front of the fireplace for nearly an hour contemplating what being in love with Karen meant. This was no ordinary relationship; we had some serious logistics to deal with. I also knew that the unique aspects of our relationship made it special. I didn't say anything to Karen, but I knew that this love could not continue to exist in the same way . . . something had to change. It was that night that I started to devise a plan to spend more time in Texas, *much* more. I retrieved another beer and stood in front of the large window at the front of our house. The blizzard was still whipping the snow into drifts and the trees were becoming laden and bent over with it. I smiled, replaying her small voice, "Ah'm in love with yew, too, Scotty."

Two days later was New Year's Day and we were back in an airport terminal trying to figure out how to say goodbye once again. Only this time, because of acknowledging to each other that we were in love, saying goodbye was incredibly difficult.

"This is getting really old, really fast," I said in frustration. Karen's eyes were welling up in tears and I pulled her close. "It's okay," I said in a pathetic attempt at playing the strong one, "I'll come down this summer for a long time."

"Call me when you get home."

"Ah will. Ah love yew," she said with conviction and like she had said it a thousand times before.

"I love you, too, Karen . . . more than you can possibly know." One last kiss and I watched her once again disappear down the jet-way and into the sky. I held it together pretty well until I was alone in the car, then I fought the tears all the way home.

HAIL THE KING!

CHAPTER 22

Not long after Karen returned to Texas, I was back at Northern. I was still trying to get over the emotion of saying goodbye when a timely diversion came my way.

One evening, while sitting in my dorm room being my typical mopey self, there was a knock at the door. It was a contingent of girls from West Hall, our all girl sister dorm across the courtyard. They were there to ask if I would be their representative in the competition for Winfester King.

Winfester is the winter carnival put on by the university every February. It involves all sorts of winter activities including the selection of a king and queen. It is basically a homecoming in the wintertime. I think in reality it was born out of the need to address the depression that a five month winter brings. Cabin fever in the U.P. is a serious matter. Not seeing the sun for weeks at a time, relentless snowfall, and freezing temperatures can get to a person after awhile. Winfester was a chance to combat the depression as a group united.

Out of the approximately 250 guys to choose from, I was surprised that somehow they chose me. I felt so flattered at the offer that I could not say no, even though I had no idea of what would be expected of me. I discovered later that I would have to perform in front of the student body. The weeks leading up to the selection of the king were nerve-racking. No matter how much I tried to concentrate on school work and a social-life, I was scared to death at going on stage in front of the university. Especially since they had not made it clear exactly what I was going to have to do. At a required meeting of contestants a week before the competition, I finally heard the details.

All those vying for the title of Winfester King would receive a slip of paper one minute before going on stage. The paper would give you a scenario that you would have to act out. "Improv," I cringed silently. Now my nerves would REALLY be shot! But on the positive side, I knew I didn't have to prepare anything before hand. I merely had to show up like everyone else and play the cards dealt. This might not be so bad after all. Craig, whose Gries Hall nickname was the Hulk, was also entered in the competition representing Gries Hall itself.

Hulk was a stocky muscular guy who unofficially ruled Stonehenge House, the first floor of Gries Hall where Kevin and I lived. Hulk was also the self appointed 'giver of nicknames' in the house. This process was typically tied to something a person did or something about their appearance. Somehow there was reasoning behind the given moniker and the assignment of names usually happened while under the influence of many brews. We had guys who were given names like, "Cigarette" because Denny was tall and thin, "Slash," because Steve looked like a gangster, and Kevin was called Griz, because he was a hairy dude who could grow a beard in a few short days. Plus, everyone knew his dad's nickname was Bear, so Griz, short for "Grizzly", made total sense. I became known as "Bull". Now I'd like people to believe that this was on account that I was ferocious or a physical beast, but it wasn't. It was given one night when Hulk came into my room drunk, wanting to get advice from the deer head I had hanging on the wall. It had become a house tradition to bring any girl problems to my room and consult the deer head. Even though the deer already had a name, 'Burt', Hulk referred to it as Bullwinkle because once while drunk, he thought it was a moose. Because it belonged to me, I became Bull, short for Bullwinkle. Whether I liked it or not, I was stuck with it. Many times the guys called me "Bullie", kind of a cute, sweet version of Bull, but anyone who did not know the story thought my nickname was "Bully". It gave me the mystique of being bad-tempered and nasty, and if I wasn't forced to tell what the name *really* meant, I didn't.

Hulk was a Yooper from Iron Mountain, a town located so far west in the U.P. that it was in a different time zone. Oddly enough, it was a town dominated by Italians and Hulk was no exception. He had jet black hair and when he talked he reminded me of Sylvester Stallone in Rocky. He definitely spoke with the long vowels of a Yooper, but when he really got going, the Italian was unmistakable. When he was passionate about a topic, he would even mix in a few Italian words he learned from his Grandpa and wave his hands around in the classic Italian gestures.

Gangster party in Stonehenge House. 'Slash' (front left), 'Hulk' (center), 'Griz' (front right), 'Bull' (back right).

On the way back to the dorm from the meeting he said, "I know we're competing against each other, but we *will* be drinking together the night of this thing."

"Sounds like a plan to me," I willingly agreed.

When the night of the improve show for the kingship arrived, Hulk and I did just that. We met in his room with a bunch of guys from Stonehenge and drank beer until we calmed our nerves and reached that point where whatever happened didn't matter. I believe that state was referred to as being 'comfortably numb'. Then with much fanfare from our buddies, we set out together toward Hedgecock Arena where the competition would be held.

At the arena, we were gathered with more than a dozen contenders from all over campus in a room to the side of the stage. There were several activities happening on stage, but I didn't have a clue what they were about. I could only wonder if I was about to make an ass out of myself in front of the entire university. My hopes that maybe no one cared about this, and there was only a few people attending, were dashed whenever there was applause or laughter. You could feel the attendance, and it was big. We drew numbers and the Hulk was drawn just before me. The coordinating director came over with a hat filled with small pieces of paper. One by one we reached in and picked our poison. Hulk had to do something about the 'pros and cons of armpit hair'. I only heard him say, "What the hell?" My slip only said, "You have just received a 'Dear John' letter in the mail." All the contestants silently tried to put together a quick plan and one by one we were summoned to the stage. I watched Hulk from the wings and he was funny. I thought to myself, "That's gonna be tough to beat." But when my name was finally called I delivered some amazing humor. I only know this because the place was falling down in laughter. I could feel the immense crowd, but I couldn't see a soul because of the blinding spotlights. This was probably a good thing. I don't even remember what I did, only that I started by acting like a student opening his mailbox in the dorms and receiving a Dear John letter. From there I don't know what direction I went, but I entered a zone and took no prisoners. I'm certain much of it must have been pretty saucy with no concern for political correctness or sensitivity. The college crowd ate it up, and evidently the judging panel did as well.

At the end of the performances when they announced their decision, I could hardly believe my ears, "The 1978 N.M.U. Winfester King is . . . . Scotty Hazel representing West Hall!" There was a giant applause of approval and congratulations all around and about a half an hour of pictures and interviews. It was during this time that I learned a freshman had never been crowned before. I didn't realize it was this big of a deal. Had I known I might not have said 'yes' in the first place. But now, I was gladly basking in the attention. There was also a Winfester Queen crowned that night. She was a beautiful girl named Beth from the historic Yooper town of L'Anse. In the coming weeks she and I had to make several appearances together, and our picture was splashed on the front page of the newspaper the following week.

Scotty wins Winfester King at N.M.U., 1978. He was the first freshman to win this competition and is pictured here with the queen, Beth Veker of L'Anse.

After the crowning, Hulk and I headed back to Gries Hall. "C'mon," he said, let's go get some brews." When we opened the door to his room it was filled with a bunch a guys that all fell to their knees and mockingly shouted, "Hail, the King!"

"Yea, yea, yea," I said with embarrassment. Then the beer started to flow and the laughter commenced.

It was around midnight when I staggered back to my room. Knowing there was an hour difference in the time, I called Karen . . . 11:00 Texas time. Any thought of waiting until the next day went out the window with the empty beer bottles. Karen answered the phone surprised that I would call so late. It was outside the rules of phone calls that we had established. After all, she was still a junior in high school.

"Scotty," came the small voice over the phone, "are yew alraht?"

"Karen," I said, "I got crowned King." I don't recall any more of the conversation after that.

LET'S GET NAKED!

CHAPTER 23

My freshman year in college was coming to a close but not without a final act celebrating its conclusion. The night before the final day of classes, a plan had been hatched to have a massive streak in the courtyard. The up campus, or U.C. Quad, as it was known, was actually three buildings that created a triangular courtyard. Gries Hall, the dorm in which I was housed, and the all female West Hall, bordered two sides of the courtyard. Throughout the year we combined to do many activities and we knew many of the girls housed in West. The third building actually contained the dining hall, offices, and a banquet room.

The streaking event was all set; at the designated time, guys from all three floors would disperse themselves in the rooms of Stonehenge House, the first floor, my floor, on the courtyard side. A guy nicknamed "Pup" for his small stature, was to take his megaphone out into the center of the courtyard and announce the coming streak-fest to the girls' dorm and we would all stream out the windows into the night. It was supposed to look spontaneous and take the entire quad by surprise, but when it came time for the event to begin, it was obvious the secret was out.

We removed the screens from our windows and slid them open. There were perhaps fifteen guys crammed into Kevin's and my room. Suddenly Hulk said, "There goes Pup! Strip down boys!" Without hesitation, everyone started shedding their clothes. There was no modesty or pride; throughout the year we had become shameless. Then we all donned the masks we had decided to wear so any authority present could not identify anyone. I looked over

Hulk's shoulder and noticed there was not a single light on in the girls' dorm.

"Where are all the girls?" I asked thinking this was all going to be for nothing.

"Oh, they're there," was his reply. "Someone squealed on us, the cat's out of the bag."

Breaking the night air was the obnoxious mechanical voice of Pup from the mega—phone, "Ladies and Gentlemen, Gries Hall presents," there was a dramatic pause; "LET'S GET NAKED!" and he blew a long shrill blast on a whistle. As he spoke, I noticed Hulk pull his ski mask down over his face, which reminded me to pull down the goalie mask I was wearing. At the instant Pup blew the whistle blast, someone with a hefty stereo began pounding out the song "Another Party on the Patio" by Z.Z. Top, and naked bodies streamed out of the first floor windows like paratroopers exiting planes. When a sufficient number had begun to fill the courtyard, flashbulbs began popping from the dark windows of the girls' dorm. They had been tipped off for sure, and were taking all the pictures of this spectacle as they could. There were more than one hundred naked guys spastically running around the courtyard. There were so many camera flashes it seemed like there was a giant disco ball hanging from the night sky. After what seemed like an eternity, we all climbed back through the windows laughing and yelling. As I crawled back into my room, I noticed two guys with their clothes still on laughing at us as we tumbled into the room. It was my roommate, Griz and his friend Eric from back home. They had chickened out and only watched the spectacle from our room.

Immediately, we could hear a chant from outside, "MORE! MORE! MORE!" It was the girls' dorm screaming for an encore. The word was being passed quickly, "We're going again, fellas!"

Still clothed, I heard Griz and Eric debating whether or not they would join this time. Once again Pup casually strolled to the middle of the courtyard, only this time to loud cheering from the girls' dorm. He hushed the encouragement with a 'settle down' gesture from his hands and then raised the megaphone to his mouth again. "Ladies and Gentlemen, let me introduce the next edition of LET'S GET NAKED!" and let out another whistle blast. Like before, Z.Z. Top began to blare, and naked men began to spill out of the first floor windows.

As I shuffled closer to my turn out the window, I heard Griz suddenly say to Eric, "Shit, I'm going!" and he began to tear off his clothes. With only nervous laughter, Eric started peeling off his clothes as well. The disco ball began to light up again, only this time even more intense as anyone who was not privy the first time had added her numbers to those in the know. The number of camera flashes was incredible. Also different the second time was a line of spectators sitting on a long wall next to the dining hall. They had heard the ruckus from the next quad over and had come to witness the ridiculous scene. Strategically positioned at the exits of the courtyard, I saw three police cars idling in the shadows.

In the middle of sprinting aimlessly around, I heard girls' voices yelling, "Hey Kevin (Griz)! Hey Eric!" I heard this time and time again. When I ran past them, they were yelling, "How do they know who we are!?"

Laughing in disbelief, I pointed to my head and answered them, "You don't have a mask on!"

In their last minute haste to join the fun, they had totally forgotten to hide their identities with masks. Out of all the guys running around naked that night, Griz and Eric were the only two idiots running around totally naked without anything covering their faces. There was a din of noise this time as the guests perched on the wall stood and began to clap and cheer. It seemed like there were people everywhere who had crowded into the edges of our courtyard to watch. The grapevine had worked quickly, and the word was out. "Gries Hall is running naked all over the U.C. Quad!" I started to wonder if it might get out of control or if we might get into some kind of trouble when I saw the Hulk blatantly jump onto the hood of a police cruiser and dance in all his glory facing their windshield. In my laughter of disbelief, I thought, "This could be trouble." I was in fairly close proximity when, from the passenger side, a cop suddenly opened the door and quickly emerged from the car.

Hulk leapt off the car and shouted, "EVERYBODY FOLLOW ME!" He grabbed my arm as he passed saying, "C'mon, Bull!"

Everyone within earshot obeyed, and a panic-stricken mob crowded in behind the Hulk and me. I was following closely when we passed the girls' dorm . . . or so I thought. Unexpectedly, Hulk made a quick ninety-degree turn and blazed a trail through the bottom floor of the girls' dorm.

"This is crazy!" I yelled at Hulk, but there was no stopping him now. He had pulled off his mask and was clutching it in his hand as he ran with abandon, screaming like a Civil War soldier making a charge. I couldn't help but laugh uncontrollably because with his long black hair, full beard, and stout hairy body, he looked like a caveman chasing down a mammoth! The doors were frantically opening as girls, laughing hysterically, were holding cameras at arms length into the hallway and simply snapping pictures at random. I was not blindly following Hulk because I knew waiting at the other end of the dorm was another police car. I recognized a familiar face in a doorway's of a girl I knew named Kelly. Without any warning, I darted into Kelly's room, planning to go straight into her bathroom and the security of the closest towel. As I flew past her, she screamed, having no idea who it was because of my mask. As I rushed for the bathroom, I crashed into a locked door. A bubbly voice from inside casually said, "Occupado!"

It seemed the only girl on the planet who didn't know there were a hundred naked guys running through her dorm was Kelly's roommate, Stephanie, who had taken up residency on the toilet in the one place I decided to seek refuge . . . amazing!

Kelly was screaming, "GET OUT!"

I was laughing so hard I could hardly form the words, but I was shouting, "It's Scotty, it's Scotty!" and I pulled off my goalie mask.

Kelly started laughing, as I frantically was trying to cover myself with a shoe I had grabbed off the floor.

"Get me a towel or something!" I begged. She reached into the closet and produced a bathrobe, which I quickly pulled on.

"You guys are insane!" she laughed.

"Hulk led us down here," I explained. "I know the police are waiting at the other end . . . this is a trap!" I sat down and began to laugh. "Holy wuh," I finally exhaled like a Yooper. There was a muffled flush from the bathroom, and the door opened. Out walked Stephanie in her underwear and, seeing me sitting on their couch, immediately dropped into a heap on the floor trying to cover herself with her hands.

"Is that my bathrobe?" she yelled with clenched teeth. Kelly and I burst out laughing.

"Why the hell do you have my bathrobe on?" Stephanie yelled again.

"'Cause I'm naked," I said very calmly.

"WHAT!?" cried Stephanie. "You have GOT to be kidding," she said in disgust. Kelly threw a blanket toward Stephanie and began to explain what was happening. While she spoke, she reached into her mini fridge and produced two beers, handing one to me and opening the other for herself.

"Thanks, I needed that," I said, and we filled in the details to a more relaxed, but embarrassed Stephanie.

I learned later that the police allowed most of the guys off the hook and funneled them back into Gries Hall. After about an hour, when things calmed down, and I saw the police cars drive away from the courtyard, I picked my way back to my room. I looked ridiculous in Stephanie's robe, tennis shoes, and a goalie mask, but I was home safely. I found the only people who got grilled by the police were Hulk, Griz, and Eric. But it was all harmless college fun at the end of a year, and no one got into any real trouble. I went to my final classes the next day and then left for home in the late afternoon. My freshman year was over.

THE PROMISE

CHAPTER 24

The coming summer would be different than any other before that. My days with Young Life ended the day I left for college. There would be no more Monday night meetings, no bike trip, no Frontier Ranch, no Castaway Club. The support group of friends like Joey were scattered out into the working world, and leaders like Dale had their hands full with summer camps and high-schoolers. My first year of college had been a real tester. I think leaving Dave in order to go up campus and room with Kevin may have been a mistake. I had a blast in Gries Hall, but not seeking out a support group to help strengthen my Christian commitment was asking for trouble. I had learned it was a tough task to try and grow closer to God by myself. All Christians need fellowship, people to hold them accountable. I failed to do this and my Christianity, at best, was stagnant. Scripture labels it as "faith without works" that is "dead." I had not attended church regularly, and partying with my dorm buddies was the only thing I did religiously. Although I knew better and I confessed to being a born-again Christian, I was gradually turning into someone who showed little outward sign of his faith. Now that summer had arrived, the question was whether or not I could get my Christian walk back in order, if I would continue the trend set at N.M.U., or bounce back spiritually.

Karen had traveled north for two visits in a row; it was time for me to return to Amarillo. I had blown any money I had saved on long-distance calls and beer. Any trip to Texas would have to be worked towards. So the summer of 1978 began by returning to work at Wendy's in Flint. The plan I had made with Karen was to visit her in August in order to have time to earn the money. My family was staying at the cottage at Leisure Lake, and I basically lived alone at home. It was a situation that I thoroughly enjoyed. You might think that I would have lots of parties and people over all the time, but I actually was basking in the solitude. I slowly cleaned the house to a state of spotlessness, kept the lawn quite tidy, and slept wherever I chose. Once every week or two, my parents would arrive to grocery shop and do laundry and generally mess up my house work. They easily could have shopped and done laundry in Durand, the town closest to the lake, but I think they used it as an excuse to check up on me.

I generally was a closer, so my shift at Wendy's was typically from 5:00 until midnight. Bobby still worked there, and we had become friends with the manager. Since we were now over the legal drinking age of eighteen, we frequently would all go out for drinks after work. It was nothing major, usually just an hour or less to relax and drink some of the tension away from serving fast food for six hours. It wasn't every night, but typically at the end of the week, on Fridays and Saturdays when hoards of customers really frazzled our nerves.

I had purchased a used Fiat convertible, and many of my days were spent working on it. I bought it from a guy who had stripped it down and was rebuilding it. His job had changed, and he had no more time to work on it. It was taking up space in their garage, so his wife made him get rid of it. When I bought it, it was painted with gray primer, and all the bumpers and lights were piled in the trunk. It was a neat little car and a fun project to work on, but that didn't happen until I had made breakfast and written Karen a letter.

I did not like the gap between correspondence, and I could not squander my trip money on phone bills, so I kept a constant stream of letters flowing toward Amarillo. Karen wrote a lot, but I literally wrote every day. This may have been the first glimpse of a possessiveness that began to develop in me. I would get the occasional letter from Iowa Deb, and even more from Indiana Deb, but my focus was truly on Karen. I think having those long hours every day until work time rolled around did not occupy my mind enough. Oh, the routine was great, and I had it down to the minute, but that's a lot of time to fixate on a girl halfway across the country.

I would have been smart to pick up a second job, but I did not, and I wallowed in my yearning.

Occasionally, I would visit Babe, or she would drive by unannounced, but I always kept her at arm's length. It was a strange thing because I did indeed like her, and she was right there, in the flesh and patient beyond understanding. But my heart was in Texas, and that trumped everyone and everything. In spite of this, I was riding a roller coaster ride of attention and attempting to have my cake and eat it too. It wasn't the stream of letters that I was sending to Karen, but I also wrote to the two Debs consistently. Some were lengthy and even flirtatious, but I always left them hanging like I did Babe. Eventually, Iowa Deb nearly stopped writing all together, but Indiana Deb wrote long personal letters, and the tie between us became . . . intriguing. Basically, I teased and tempted and strung these girls along just enough to keep them interested, but never totally jumped in. It was not very honest and not very wise, but with all the distance involved with everyone concerned, I didn't think it mattered. At first, Babe was the only one who knew about anyone else, and that was only Karen. She had no knowledge that I was also writing to a girl in Indiana. Eventually, I told Indiana Deb about Karen when I explained to her why I was going to visit Texas in August. Down deep, I knew it was playing a risky game and whenever I thought about my Christianity, I felt guilt and shame. Nevertheless, I continued to lead a sort of double life, that of a Christian who lived no differently than a non-believer. Over the years, I heard people refer to this as being a "secret agent Christian" because no one knows who you really are. Still, I felt like I had everything under control and would straighten out in the end. The other thing I learned was that there were an awful lot of Christians out there just like me. This only helped convince me that living this way was alright. Scripture calls this "causing your brother to stumble."

When August finally arrived, I flew to Amarillo for a ten-day visit. It was a visit different from the others, and I was anxious about what lay in store for us in the future. What became obvious to me was that we couldn't keep on like this. We had become serious, too serious to only see each other twice a year. Two nights before I flew back to Michigan, Karen and I talked over dinner at the Amarillo Club. It was raining steadily that evening, not like a thunder-boomer quickly blowing through, but a constant pour like what happens in the U.P. in October. I was transfixed on the sheets of water that flowed down the large windows when Karen said, "Castaway sure seems lahk a long tahm ago."

"Two years," I replied, without changing my gaze out the window.

Karen had just graduated from Tascosa and would be attending Texas Tech University in the fall. Janet had preceded her to Tech, and Karen was following in her footsteps. One of the things that made me nervous about this was that Janet had been in a sorority, and Karen planned to follow her lead. N.M.U., like any university, had its percentage of students who pledged Greek; that is fraternities and sororities, so I was familiar with how they operated. But it was different at Northern since the strong Residence Life program satisfied many of the reasons students pledged Greek in the first place. Sometimes there was social tension between those of us who chose not to pursue life as part of a fraternity and those who did. One thing I knew about the Greek societies was that fraternities paired up with sororities for shared social events. Many relationships were born out of these brother-sister arrangements. Even though I knew my relationship with Karen was strong and we had survived some major trials, her plan to join a sorority at Lubbock worried me.

Karen pledged to Alpha Zeta Omega sorority at Texas Tech University

"Are you excited about college?" I asked.

"Yes, of course." Karen could tell I had something on my mind and asked softly,

"What's the matter?"

After a short pause, I answered, "I don't know, college scares me a little." I was thinking about the craziness that I was involved in and couldn't see any reason that it would be any different at Texas Tech. I feared that the same things that attracted me to Karen would certainly attract someone else. And being half a continent away would hardly put me in a position to compete or protect her.

Karen patted my hand, and I looked at her. "Nuthin's gonna change, Scotty."

"I know, but things are moving along," I replied.

She had tried to reassure me, but she had no idea about college life . . . and I did. I knew a million guys would be trying to crawl all over the tiny beauty with the great curves. I knew it was impossible that she would never be approached by guys, and just the thought of it was making me crazy. It was a tense conversation, and I couldn't hide that I was wondering how strong our love really was. She was right; Castaway was a long time passed, and so was the novelty of such a romantic beginning. We were now just two people with quite an amazing story, but could we survive as a couple attending two different universities in two different states so far apart? That question was the gorilla in the room. I looked at her and sincerely said, "With you going to college, things *are* changing. What's going to happen to us?"

"We knew this day was coming," Karen spoke with a simple wisdom. "Awl we can do is keep living every day and handle thangs as they happen." I could only nod in agreement. "We'll be fahn," she stated with her usual smile and soft blue eyes.

"I know, but this . . . *this* is not enough." She knew I was referring to the bi-annual visits, phone calls, and letters.

"Ah know," she agreed.

That night, sleep did not come without a fight. Our dinner conversation kept playing through my head. It was like a riddle. I had stated that with the way we felt about each other, the current arrangement was not enough. What really made me realize we were at a milestone was that she agreed. And I wasn't just saying it to hear my own voice; with her going off the school, things *were* going to change. I felt that if we were going to survive, something new must happen, and in the middle of the night, I finally came up with the answer.

The next day we were riding horses in Palo Duro Canyon. It was the day before I was to return to Michigan. It was a typical August day in the Panhandle—in the high nineties—and we were riding in shorts and tank tops. This was weather that up north would have sent us to the beach, but down here lakes are scarce. Above the canyon rim, the wind was hot and dry and gave little relief from the heat. But down at the floor, there was no breeze, and waves of heat shimmered from the baked earth. We pulled our horses to a stop in the shade of a wall of rock that shielded us from the sun. It was a place that we had ridden to before on many occasions. The river that wound through the red dirt turned sharply and widened into a pool in front of us. It was here that we had a conversation like none before. It was here that we made a promise.

"Karen, it has been two years since we met," I stated at one point.

"Yea, it doesn't seem possible, does it?" she said. "We have overcome a lot," she added unexpectedly.

"Yes we have," I agreed. "I have to say that I can't see a day that you are not part of my life." After I said this, there was a silence.

Then after a bit, Karen replied, "Yea, ah have thought that same thang."

Suddenly, I realized I had a giant lump in my throat, and I was spontaneously headed down a trail that I had pondered a great deal on my own but hadn't shared with Karen . . . until now.

I continued, "I know this can't happen any time soon, I think we're too young still, but when the time is right, will you marry me?" When I heard the words, I couldn't believe they had come out of my mouth.

Straight out, she simply replied, "Yes, yes Ah will." At this, I reached over and took hold of her hand, and we simply looked at each other and smiled. Any concern I had about her attending college and being in a sorority with a brother fraternity melted away. There was no grand plan, no set date, no ring, just a promise.

"Also," I continued, "I am planning to move down here next summer. I need to be near you more."

"Honest?" she asked, as she pondered the idea.

"Honest." I confirmed. Then I rationalized it to her like I had done the night before to myself. "I'll be working all summer in Flint; I might as well work down here."

"That sounds wonderful," she said with a sense of total agreement.

From that moment on, I knew my future was set, that someday Karen and I would be married.

The next day was another tough airport goodbye. It was another long flight home staring out the window. But now the stakes were higher, and there was a new feeling of contentment replacing the anxiety I had arrived with.

BACK TO SCHOOL

CHAPTER 25

Stonehenge House in Gries Hall was much the same in the fall of 1978 as it was when I left it four months earlier. There were a few new faces replacing those who had either moved off campus or graduated, but the core of crazy pals were still in place. I still spent several hours daily working out on the soccer field, but I was beginning to lose my passion for the game, but not before making my mark in school history.

Northern's soccer program was in its infancy, and the team was paying its dues. Our uniforms were simple, and we did not have a set of team warm-ups. A place to practice was difficult to wrestle away from the established sports; thus, we often worked-out at the intramural fields. We traveled long distances to play a complete schedule, and not by bus, but in our own vehicles. Our closest rival was Michigan Tech, 100 miles north of Marquette. It was not unusual for us to travel as far as Green Bay, Toledo, or Chicago.

As a player, my assets were speed and great timing on head balls. Because I was ambidextrous with my feet, I typically played offense on the left side of the formation. I was not a great ball-handler, though, so most of my goals came off of long passes from Donny Leak—our captain from Chicago—which I headed into the net.

The goal I remember the most from my entire college soccer career was against a college in Harbor Springs, Michigan. We had made the five-hour trip to Harbor Springs in rotten October weather. Like many of our games, it was raining a cold steady drizzle the entire time we played. After two complete halves and deep into the second overtime, we remained tied at zero. Everyone on both sides was exhausted, and we all felt the game would end scoreless.

Then, with time waning, I saw Donny intercept a stray pass and streak down the right side of the field. As the left winger, this was my cue to dash down and cover the back post of the goal. The rain began to pound down heavier when, off of Donny's boot, I saw the ball come flying my way from the far corner of the field. It was a long airborne cross that I immediately reacted to. It caught the goalkeeper off guard, as no one had hit a ball that well the entire match. It sailed completely over the net-minder, and I was afraid I was not going to catch up to it before it skipped off the wet grass and out of play. At a full gallop, I launched myself horizontally toward the spot I felt the ball was coming down. Headlong and stretched out through the air, I never took my eye off the ball. Inches before it hit the ground, I found it with my forehead and solidly sent it forward with brain-numbing "thump!" The next moment I was face down, sliding through the mud and the wet grass; I had no idea what the result of my effort was. When I looked up, I was halfway into the goal, and the ball was spinning in place in a small puddle at the back of the net. Dazed, I slowly got to my feet, only to be knocked down by my onrushing teammates. I had scored a brilliant game-winning goal at the end of overtime to send us home victorious. My name, and a play-by-play description of my winning header, was in the next edition of N.M.U.s' newspaper, *The Lanthorn.* For a week, I was a hero.

Long before my soccer heroics, when we first returned from summer break, Griz and I had taken up residence in the exact same room as the year before, but a yearning to strive for something more would change everything.

I decided to enter the Residence Assistance (R.A.) selection program. R.A.'s lived in the dorms with the other students but were the first position of authority for the university. Theirs was an elite community within the student community. Their job was mainly keeping the peace in the dorms and protecting university property but also included facilitating a house government and enforcing the rules of the dorms. Now this may not sound like a desirable position, except it included a large room to yourself, and the cost of your room and board was your compensation. Being an R.A.

was a good thing to have on a resume, and being the guy in charge was appealing to me. I had heard that the R.A. of the floor above Stonehenge was leaving after the semester, and my plan was to try and land that position. This would keep me in Gries Hall and close to all my buddies.

I did well in the training, and several dorms wanted to interview me to fill vacant R.A. positions. Every dorm, that is, except Gries. When the interviews concluded, I was offered a job in Dakota House of Halverson Hall. Halverson was the same hall where I originally lived with Dave. This threw the proverbial monkey wrench into my plans. I wasn't sure what to do. I hadn't even considered working in a different dorm. I sat down with Brad Dillard, my R.A., and asked his advice for my predicament.

"Turn it down if you want to," he said without emotion, "but you do realize this pays half your schooling."

"Yeah, I know," I replied. I knew that this had to be a decision based on sound judgment, not what I necessarily wanted. "How can I turn it down?" I admitted. That night I called Halverson Hall and accepted their offer to be the new R.A. of Dakota House.

Dakota House of Halverson Hall was on the opposite side of campus from Gries Hall. It was a part of campus referred to as "Down Campus." This is ironic since it was actually located on the North side, a direction we normally refer to as "up." Conversely, "up campus" was at the south end, a direction usually referred to as "down." It was all backwards. I think it had to do with the topography of the land. There was a gradual rise in the campus as you walked from the north side to the south . . . thus the labels "up" and "down" campus respectfully. No matter the labels, down campus and up campus were in the state of constant feuding. Taking a job there was like going over to the enemy. It was a tougher choice than it may seem, but I made it and during Christmas break, I made the move.

An interesting event took place during the time students were home on their long Christmas Break. Legislation had been passed that changed the drinking age from eighteen to twenty one. Overnight, the university changed from a "wet" campus to a "dry" campus. New prohibitions would be enforced when the students returned. At age nineteen, I had already been legal drinking age, but now I would be too young once again. Not only would I have to enforce the new law to students who had previously been legal, I would have to do this to people whom I did not know and who wanted to test the new guy from "up" campus. This would be challenging for an R.A. who knew those around him; it was going to be monumental for me in Dakota House.

Complicating this even more, I discovered, was that the previous R.A. had been run out of his job by aggravated students whom he had busted for smoking pot. The problem for that R.A. was that when he was off duty, he had smoked with them! So when he nabbed them, they cried "foul" and he got fired. The two ring-leaders who blew the whistle on their R.A. were ex-football players who had tried, but not made the team. Needless to say, they were big, ornery, and had an ax to grind. When students were returning after break and I was trying to introduce myself, one of these disgruntled two named Pat, said with a nasty sneer, "They sent you down here from 'up' campus?"

The taller of the two said, "Hey, I recognize you, you were the Winfester King last year."

I was a little embarrassed and didn't know if that would help or hurt my rapport with anyone in the house. The shorter heavier one, at hearing this, twisted his face around and simply said, "Stupid."

At that I thought, "Not gonna help."

"Yeah, my name is Scott," I said, trying to act indifferent to his attitude.

"Well, S-C-O-T-T," he said my name in a very sarcastic way, and then continued, "we got rid of the last asshole; we'll see how long *you* last." They both snickered a sinister laugh and just turned and sauntered away, never having given their names.

"Oh my God," I thought. "What have I done?" I was wondering right away if I had made a giant mistake accepting this position. After that, I always referred to him as "Fat Pat."

The funniest, or maybe I should say the most embarrassing situation, happened the very first day students were returning from break. I was casually walking the hall, introducing myself, when I happened onto an open door with a couple guys sitting on a couch and talking about their vacation. In one motion, I knocked and entered, not waiting for permission. I took a seat on the desk and began a random conversation, just trying to break the ice. As

I spoke, I noticed they were acting very nervous. "What's wrong with these guys?" I thought. As I labored to ease the tension, I was casually looking around the room at their stuff. I happened to see an unusually long flashlight standing upright on the desk near me. It was kind of cool looking, made from shiny chrome. Nonchalantly, I picked it up to fiddle around with it and turn it on. But I couldn't figure how the switch worked and kept trying to push it on with my thumb. When I tipped it up to examine it further, disgusting brown water poured out of the end all over the papers strewn on the desk. I heard and audible gasp from the two guys. I jumped up so I wouldn't get soaked by the gross . . . whatever it was, and looked at the two who were now standing but not moving from their spot.

"What the hell is that shit!?" I asked.

"What the hell are you doing!?" the one kid responded in an incredulous tone of his own.

"I was trying to turn this flashlight on, and all that crap poured out of it." "Flashlight?!" he shouted. "You idiot, that's a bong!"

"A what?" I asked naively.

The other kid started laughing, "Oh my God, a BONG!" he answered emphatically as he stepped forward and grabbed it from my hands, placing it back on the desk. The other kid had gone to the bathroom to get something to wipe up the mess I had made.

"What's it for?" I asked the next naïve question.

"Smoking pot!" a voice from the bathroom answered.

Embarrassed and realizing I had done something very dumb, I stood there with a blank stare and finally simply said, "Sorry guys, I had no idea. Smokin' pot, huh," I processed out loud. "I better go," I said and turned and left the room. "Way to go," I said to myself, and I continued to look for people to meet.

In spite of the shaky start, I eventually settled in and had found not all the residents of Dakota House were pot-heads. However, Fat Pat and his buddies did everything they could to make my stay in Dakota miserable. The height of their delinquency happened one weekend in late February.

I was on duty, which meant that it was my turn to stay in and babysit the dorm for the weekend, when I was awakened around 2:30 a.m. by loud yelling in the hallway. I knew what it was and chose to ignore it. It was all the drunks coming home after the pubs had closed. I hoped that they would eventually tire and pass out in their rooms until the next day—no such luck. Several times I had to go ask them to turn their stereo down. They were playing it so loud that I had to kick the door for them to know I was there. They would comply, but never more than five minutes or so. Eventually, I opened up the utility room and turned the power off to their rooms. This only meant war had been declared. Around 3:30, I heard a tremendous crash in the hall. I jumped out of bed and ran into the hall as fast as I could, trying to catch the culprit. The hall was empty, but one of the glass globes at the very end had been shattered. This was only the first of almost every light in the hall that systematically got destroyed that night. I never caught them in the act, but I was reasonably certain it was Fat Pat and his pals. The hallway was pitch black. In the darkness, I began to hear a different popping noise. I discovered that door knobs were being knocked off with the sharp blow of a baseball bat, hammer, or something like that. My room became the headquarters for other R.A.'s, security clerks, and campus police officers. In spite of our combined efforts, we could never catch anyone. We would hear a loud noise and find something else destroyed. At one point while several of us were in my room discussing a course of action, a giant firework exploded just outside my open door. Even with police on the scene, these guys were bold enough to keep wrecking stuff and taunting us. Ultimately, around 5:00, we all had to stand vigil the length of the hall with flashlights to stop the methodical destruction of Dakota House. All I wanted to do was crawl into bed and get some sleep.

Finally, the sun came up, and the demons shrank in silence from the light. The ordeal was over. I sat in a rocking chair in my room, staring into oblivion. Peggy, who was the Resident Director of the dorm, was sitting at my desk. In my whole life, I have never been a smoker, but that morning I asked Peggy for a cigarette to calm my wrecked nerves. It was 7:00 on a Sunday morning, and there I sat in my R.A. room smoking a cigarette.

I remember thinking, "If this is how it's going to be, I won't have this job long." I think the only thing that made me decide to stick with it for another year was that Fat Pat and his cronies told me they were moving off campus the next year. When they left at the end of the year, they actually said, "Hazel, you were an okay R.A.

We gave you a lot of shit, but you hung in there and were a good guy about it all."

I had been baptized by fire and from the time of that long night, I vowed, "This will never happen again." When I checked-out their rooms using the beginning-year inventory, I slapped them with every room violation and fine I could: "I hope they choke on this."

PRINCE CHARMING FALTERS

CHAPTER 26

During that second year of school, the year that started out in Stonehenge House "up" campus and ended in Dakota House "down" campus, another visit over Christmas break had taken place. It would be the last trip north that Karen would make. As before, she came up between Christmas and New Years to enjoy a real winter. In spite of the promise we had made, the realization that two visits a year was not good enough was still on my mind. But at this point, we could only use the break to visit as before. It was that or nothing.

When Karen visited that winter, it was reminiscent of the previous trips. The novelty had begun to wear off, and it almost felt too cliché. We had done many of the same things but as time had passed, getting the old friends together was becoming more difficult. Oh, the trip was not a bad experience whatsoever, but time was moving along, and things were changing.

I had taken Karen to the annual New Year's Eve party at my uncle's house. It was the traditional Irish bash with all my cousins and some friends. My Uncle Bob was my dads' younger brother. The highlight of my young life was doing things with my Uncle Bob and Aunt Mary's family. Whether it was just a visit or a long camping trip, hanging out with my cousins was always great fun. I especially liked going to their house. Since they basically lived out in the country, they had more fun toys and better opportunities to get into trouble. With five boys and a girl, when our clan combined with theirs, it was always a mob of mischief and laughter. But far and away, the greatest memories I have from childhood were the summer camping trips with Uncle Bob, Aunt Mary, and the Hazel cousins.

That New Years eve, Uncle Bob had a keg of beer in the laundry room, and on the kitchen counter stood an army of liquor bottles, mainly Irish whiskey. While my parents and my aunt and uncle sat playing cards at the kitchen table, we all sat listening to the music countdown for the year and waiting for the ball to drop at midnight. I have to admit I was feeling full of myself having Karen at my elbow. My cousin David, who was exactly the same age as I, pulled me aside and said, "Man, she is everything you said she was . . . don't screw this up, dude."

"Yea, I know," I answered. "I think about that a lot." Little did I know that the first test, other than distance, of the strength of our relationship would happen before the New Year was rung in that evening.

The telephone rang about 10:30. I paid it little attention until there was a commotion, and I saw my mom and dad putting on their coats.

"What's going on?" I asked.

"Grandma called an ambulance, and they took grandpa to the hospital," was my mother's answer. I immediately felt like I should go. I wasn't sure why, as whatever was to happen was not going to change with my presence. I think in a strange way I was trying to show Karen that I was a take-charge, responsible guy. For some reason, I told her to stay with my cousins, that I would be back soon. In all honesty, I thought that would be true, but the stay in the waiting room at the hospital was lengthy, and we did not get back to my uncle's until after 1:00. Karen was sitting alone on the couch with her coat on in a room filled with my drunken relatives. She got up as soon as I came through the door and was obviously not happy. Dave slowly passed by without stopping and quietly said, "Get ready, Scott, she is *pissed*." It was the first time in over two years that I had seen her angry.

"Are you OK?" I asked.

"Let's just go," she said sharply and headed toward the door.

"What's the matter?" I pressed the question further.

"Why did yew leave me here with awl these strangers?" It was ironic that my attempt to show my sense of responsibility by going to my grandpa's side had blown up in my face. Karen was mad, and I think a little tipsy. I had never known her to be a drinker, other than an occasional glass of wine at dinner, but that night she tried to temper her anger toward me with a few drinks. Instead of seeing my error and apologizing, I tried to justify my actions.

"It was my grandfather, Karen," I stated like it should trump any need of hers.

"Yew could have taken me with yew," she burst back. "That would have been better than staying here!" She had a valid point, but I could not see it in the moment and kept defending myself all the way to the car. No one in the car said much during the twenty-minute drive home. I just stared straight ahead as I drove.

The next morning, after I processed it all, I realized that in my grandstanding, I had blundered and created our first argument. I felt horrible. When Karen came down for breakfast, I was already at the table drinking a cup of coffee. She looked a little pensive as she approached, and I stood and immediately said, "I am so sorry."

It was the right move, and she walked directly into my arms. "Me too," she said in her little voice as we hugged.

"No, it's all my fault," I said, accepting the blame . . . and it was. It was the day that she was flying back to Texas, and we both wanted to put the previous night behind us as quickly and painlessly as possible. It was a horrible way to end the visit. Even though the damage control was successful and we made our amends, neither of us forgot the incident. In retrospect, it seemed like an insignificant event, but in reality, something in the magic of our relationship changed that evening. The entire thing had not wrecked us, but it was a milestone that indicated the fairytale was over. In spite of overcoming the distance, we would have to survive or fail like any other couple.

When she boarded the plane that afternoon, we had as difficult a time as any departure before. But after she was gone, we both pondered our argument. The timing of it was unfortunate because it happened the last night of her stay, and it remained fresh on our minds. Any thought that Karen might have that I was a flawless Prince Charming was shattered by the reality that I had left her with strangers on New Year's Eve. Prince Charming had faltered, big time! While driving home from the airport, all these things were on my mind, and I was getting a headache thinking about them. "You are so dumb," I said to myself.

It was after this visit that I returned to N.M.U. and had my disastrous semester in Dakota House. One bright spot that did come out of Dakota House that first semester as an R.A. was the friendship I struck up with Jeff Krause. I hatched a plan to drive to Texas that summer, and he wanted in.

GONE TO TEXAS

CHAPTER 27

Ever since our promise the year before, the New Year's Eve debacle, and the difficult goodbye at the Flint airport on New Year's Day, I knew that my plan to live and work in Amarillo for the summer had to happen. It was bold, adventurous, and romantic and the more I thought about it, the more it felt like something that had to be done. Looking back now, I can't believe my parents let me go, but I didn't really give them much of a choice . . . I just announced what I planned to do and set about doing it. I was only home for about a week, doing laundry and packing.

I was mowing the lawn one day, and Babe drove up and parked in front of my house. She had been waiting for me to get home from college. I shut off the mower and went out to see her.

"Welcome home, Injun," she said with a big grin. She had written to me several times while I was at Northern, but I only wrote back a couple of times. I spent most of my writing efforts on Karen and occasionally sent a quick hello to Iowa Deb. But the next most consistent correspondence actually came in a fairly steady stream from Indiana Deb. Still, Babe wanted more from our relationship than I could give, and it made me very cautious. I felt badly about it, and I always told her how serious Karen and I had become. I think Babe always felt the distance would finally prove too much for Karen and me, and the relationship would fall apart. And when that happened, she would be waiting to pick up the pieces. In my letters, I had not mentioned anything of my trip to Texas for the summer, and when I told her that day in front of my house, she looked shattered. I was sitting in the passenger side of her car when she asked, "Do you want to go to the beach this weekend?"

"I can't," I said, trying not to come totally clean. "I'm going to be out of town."

"Where are you going?" There was a long silence, and I knew she was not going to like what I was about to tell her. She had been patiently waiting for me to come home for the summer. She was hoping we could spend time together, that she would have her chance to compete with Karen, and now I was going to tell her that I was leaving for the entire summer.

Finally, with no other option than lying, I just blurted it out, "I'm going to Texas."

"For how long?" Babe asked.

"I'm going down to look for work. I could be gone all summer."

"You mean you're going down to look for Karen," Babe said quickly.

"Yes, I am going to be close to Karen, but it is also true that I am trying to find summer work. I can't make enough working at Wendy's for another summer."

Looking for work was a legitimate reason to go to Texas in the 1970s. Thousands of Michiganders were doing it. The first oil crisis had put a large dent in Michigan's main product, the automobile, and for the first time people were leaving the state to find greener pastures elsewhere. The Michigan economy was in a slump, and Texas was booming. But that was not the reason *I* was leaving, and Babe knew it.

"You could still work at Wendy's," Babe argued.

"I know, but I have to do this."

"You don't *have* to do it, you *want* to do it."

"You're right, Babe, I *want* to go."

"You really like her that much?" Babe asked. I think she was surprised that a relationship started at a summer camp between two people so far away was so strong.

"Yes, I do. We have even discussed marriage. I know it seems crazy, but it's for real. I can't believe it myself, and I don't think Karen can either, but it is what it is." I was trying to be gentle and truthful, and it was very difficult.

I continued, "I have no idea how this is going work, but right now, I have to go to Texas." I was referring to the work situation, not Karen, but I don't think Babe picked up on that.

"Who knows," I continued, "it could all be a bust, and I'll be back here in two weeks." I felt a little guilty throwing out that little glimmer of hope, but I could tell she was upset, and I was searching for a comfortable exit.

"If something like that were to happen, you'd call me, right?" Babe asked.

"Yes, yes I would." I felt horrible saying it because in my heart, I had made a promise to Karen. As difficult as the situation was with Babe, I was grateful the whole time that I had not lied to her.

"Will you write me?" she asked.

I thought about it for a few dramatic seconds and finally replied, "I don't know if that would be a good idea, Babe. I'll give you a shout whenever I get back and let you know what's going on." Babe sat quietly, and I finally said, "I'm sorry, but I have to get going." We said our goodbyes, and I got out of her car, and she drove away. As I watched her drive away, I thought about her persistence. "Boy," I wondered to myself, "I hope I am not making a giant mistake here."

I was glad Jeff was going with me to Amarillo. Although I was determined to go at any cost, having company was comforting. I had told him of my plan and convinced him to come to Texas to find a summer job with me. We decided his car was a better option than my Fiat convertible, so the deal was sweetened by the fact that he was driving us to Texas. Among the things I took to Texas was my trusty bike that had carried me so many places, including Canada, Frontier Ranch, and of course, Castaway.

The day finally arrived, and after bidding farewell to my parents and little sister Tammy, Jeff pointed his Toyota toward the Southwest, and we began our trek into the unknown. We drove through Illinois, Missouri, Oklahoma, and finally Texas. We wasted no money on motels. We simply drove until we couldn't stand it any longer, pulled into rest areas, and slept in the car. It was incredible to watch the country slowly change before our eyes as we went deeper and deeper into the Southwest. Missouri was still green, but very hot and humid. Somewhere in Oklahoma, the green gave way to dry desolate stretches of sun-baked red dirt and prairie grass.

After two and a half days, we were driving the last flat miles of the Texas Panhandle toward the cap rock on which Amarillo was perched. In the hot dry waves of heat, I saw the lone silhouette of the Amarillo National Bank building, with the Amarillo Club at its top, standing alone in the distance. We made our way down familiar streets I recognized from my visit until we reached Karen's neighborhood. When we pulled up in front of Karen's house, she was sitting outside on the front porch throwing a tennis ball for Cowboy to retrieve. With a big smile, she stood and trotted up to the car as I eagerly clamored out of the passenger side, and we embraced as we met in the grass. Jeff got out and stretched, then waited patiently to meet the girl he had heard so much about.

It was early June, and our stay in Amarillo had no planned length, only that we needed to be back at N.M.U. in late August. It all depended on whether or not we could find work. If we could not find a job, we would have to leave when we ran out of money. For about a week, we displaced Mark from his room and spent leisurely mornings eating breakfasts prepared by Karen or her mother, and then we would go about looking for work. I think in all honesty it was a half-hearted effort, and we were enjoying the comfort of where we were and what we were doing.

One evening Mr. Little told us that his bank, First National, had a giant construction project in progress and that perhaps there was work to be found there. The next day Jeff and I went to the Supervisor's trailer on the site of the First National Bank construction project. After completing an interview and an application, we were told to report the next morning. We were hired.

For another week we stayed in Mark's room, got up, and went to work on the First National Bank project. Basically, we were laborers. We spent most days with a shovel in our hands for eight or more hours. The company that we were working for was Stewart and Clark Construction, headquartered in Dallas. The project consisted of a new multi-level parking structure and a tunnel connecting it under the street to the existing bank building. We were at the very bottom of the pay scale for this job, but I didn't care; I had a paycheck coming in, which meant I could continue to stay close to Karen in Amarillo.

One night Mrs. Little told us, "Y'all boys have to fahnd a place to live. We lahk y'all just fahn, but ya cain't stay here all summer." A soon as she said it, I felt embarrassed that we had overstayed our welcome. I felt like a free-loader. I began to wonder if we had taken advantage of their hospitality. But in the end, it wasn't that, it was simply time to get on with whatever was going to happen that summer . . . and Mark needed his own room back in his own house. Jeff added to the drama of the moment when he announced he was going back to Michigan. He was not fond of being a grunt at the bottom of the Stewart and Clark totem pole. This left me in a dilemma; if Jeff left, I would only have my bike to get around. I talked him into staying until I found a place to live for the summer. Knowing Jeff was going to take his car back north simplified my search. It had to be somewhere not too far away from the First National Bank work site. I finally found an apartment upstairs from the Tea Room Bar, only six blocks from work. Rent was $75 a month, and my landlord only required a month-by-month lease. It wasn't in the best part of downtown Amarillo, but it was precisely what I needed for my predicament. I had little choice; I signed on the dotted line. Jeff helped me move what little I had into the apartment, and then he left for home.

It was a strange feeling being totally on my own down in Texas. Having Jeff around had been a comfort, and now he was gone. But there was an excitement to the independence of it all. I'm sure my parents thought I might be home within a month. It was satisfying being able to call them to tell them I had found a job and a place to live. From the apartment to Karen's house was about a twenty-minute bike ride . . . nothing I couldn't handle. So the plan had been successful; I had work, I had a place to stay, and I was close to Karen. Now we would have an entire summer to see what kind of couple we really were.

AMARILLO SUMMER

CHAPTER 28

For most of that summer, I had settled into a routine. I got up early and walked the six blocks from my Tea Room apartment to the job site. Every morning, I walked past the same businesses and restaurants with a swagger. The smell of Doug's Famous Barbeque, smoking its meat early in the morning, became a welcome routine as I made my way through the sleepy streets of Amarillo to work. I usually wore an old pair of jeans, scuffed-up, dusty work boots, and a t-shirt with the sleeves tore off. I had a red hardhat that I wore backwards with my name on its front and a Stewart and Clark sticker on the side. As I walked, I toted my dad's old lunch box packed with sandwiches and a Coke for lunch . . . by Coke I mean Dr. Pepper. I had learned in Texas that 'Coke' means any and all soda pop; that when people say they want a 'Coke' the next question is 'what kind'? If you don't specify, simply request a coke, you will get a Dr. Pepper. In Texas, Dr Pepper *is* Coke.

At the job site every morning, there was a throng of workers standing outside the main gate, waiting for the foreman to unlock and swing it open. Most of them were pretty rough characters unwilling to share what was in their past. The entire site was enclosed by an eight-foot chain-link fence. The labor crew that I worked with received our instructions every day and then proceeded to the tool trailer to get what we needed to accomplish the jobs that we had been assigned. The crew was mostly made from high school dropouts, ex-convicts, Mexicans of questionable status, and me. I quickly became known by two names: "Yankee" and "college boy". I didn't mind either of them too much and tried my best to be a hard worker. Through the course of the summer, many came and went, but I was dependable and steady. I knew that if I lost my job, I would have to return to Michigan. Even though I was a grunt of the lowest status, I was enjoying learning what I could about high-rise construction. Anytime they came looking for a volunteer to do something, I jumped at the chance. Because of this, I got acquainted with carpenters, heavy equipment operators, steel workers, and those who worked the concrete. Eventually, I knew many of them by name, and they would come looking specifically for me for special projects. This willingness to work hard and try anything resulted in a pay raise after the first month. But quite accidentally, two events really helped me climb the ladder in a short time.

The first event happened one day when everything was in place to pour the concrete of the third floor. A pour day started before sun-up and lasted until the pour was complete; once it started, it could not be interrupted. An entire floor and the columns that support it must be done continuously and seamlessly, otherwise it is weak and worthless. The work every day before the pour was in preparation for this . . . it was a major undertaking. On these days, I was designated to operate what was known as a "stinger." A stinger was a long metal vibrator, about a foot-and-a-half long, at the end of long flexible hose. Its purpose was to vibrate the concrete into small places, leaving no weak honeycombs in the concrete. While stinging concrete one day, I suddenly heard my name being called. I looked around, only to find Mr. Little, some other bank executives, and Nell Robertson standing on the roof of the bank building across the street waving at me. Nell was a really sweet lady who was part of the new accounts' department at First National and a friend of Mr. Little's. She had a very strong accent and was quite an attractive middle-aged woman with long, black curly hair. When I had received my first paycheck, I walked directly across the street, and it was Nell who assisted me as I opened up my account. Through small talk, she knew I was all the way down from Michigan to date Mr. Little's daughter, and she always seemed to give me special treatment.

Suddenly, the general supervisor approached me and asked, "Hey college boy, how do yew know those people?" I was a bit embarrassed because everyone in earshot had slacked off whatever they were doing just enough to listen for my answer.

"That's Jack Little and Nell Robertson," I answered. "He's the vice president of the trust department, and Nell is the supervisor of the new accounts' department."

"Yeah, ah know *who* they are," he said impatiently, "but how do *yew* know them?" It had gone silent, and I looked around at all the faces waiting for my answer.

"Well, I'm dating his daughter, and Nell helped me open my account."

"WHAT?" he said in disbelief. "Ye'r dating the dowter of the bank vahce president, and ye'r workin' over here?"

"Yes, sir."

"Is that how yew got this job?" he asked in a stern tone and with a thick drawl.

"No, sir," I answered, "no one knew until this minute."

The supervisor's name was Hugh and whenever he was around, everyone tried not to do anything wrong. He had a set jaw and a thick western mustache that gave him an intimidating look. It was difficult to look at him because he wore mirrored sunglasses that only allowed you to see your own frightened face staring back whenever he spoke to you. Most of the carpenters and laborers were hired locally, but Hugh represented Stewart and Clark and was from Dallas. He was the guy who signed our paychecks, and he hired and fired people on the spot. You knew Hugh was important because he was the only man on the entire job who wore a white hardhat.

Hugh put his hands on his hips and looked at several foremen who were standing close by. One of them just shrugged his shoulders, and Hugh looked back at me and slowly shook his head. Without warning, he suddenly shouted, "All raht, let's get back at it; this floor ain't gonna pour itself!" With that, everyone jumped back into his tasks.

He came close to me and sternly said, "Yankee, yew an' Ah need ta have a tawk some tahm," and he walked away.

I wasn't sure what it meant, but it made me nervous. All I knew at the time was I had gotten a whole bunch of attention that I wasn't sure I wanted. "At least I still have a job," I thought. In that moment, I heard my name one last time. "Hey, Scotty!" I looked across at the roof of the bank and waved back at Nell, who was frantically waving and calling my name.

I heard the labor foreman, John Tom, say, "Yew have GOT to be kidding me." I just smiled a rye smile and plunged the stinger into the wet concrete.

The second event happened on a gloomy day when a tremendous thunder-boomer crashed through Amarillo. Work had been halted, and everyone had been told to come back in an hour. When an hour had passed, it was still pouring down rain in torrents; the returning workers were told to go home and report back the next morning. Walking back to the Tea Room apartment in a pouring thunderstorm did not seem appealing to me. I really did not have anything to do, so I went into the tool trailer and began to clean and organize everything. No one had told me to do so and as far as I knew, I was not on the clock, but it was better than getting soaked walking home. After about forty-five minutes, the storm suddenly slackened and then totally stopped. I was sweeping the dirt out of the trailer when suddenly a white hardhat poked into the door.

"What are yew still doin' here?" It was Hugh with his usual firm voice.

"I had nothing better to do, boss, just thought I'd clean for tomorrow."

"Have yew ben here awl this tahm?"

"Yes, sir."

"Anyone else around?"

"No, sir."

"Yew want to make some *real* money?" he asked.

"Why not," I replied.

Hugh pointed at a tool belt hanging on a hook with the name John Tom stamped on the back.

"Grab that tool belt and that safety belt over there, and come with me," he said with authority.

"Got it," I said. I grabbed the tool belt and the safety harness and followed Hugh out the door and through the mud on the site. He went into the foreman's trailer and emerged with a tool belt and safety harness of his own. He put his hand on my shoulder and talked as he steered me toward the vertical forms of columns standing like monoliths into the air.

"Do yew know what tools are what?" he asked. His intimidating tone was suddenly different than usual . . . almost father-like in his question.

"Yes, I know what tools are what," I replied sarcastically.

He took off his mirrors and looked at me. "Well son, ah've got to make sure this is done raht." His voice was one of confidence, revealing that what he and I were about to do was important, and he needed to know that I understood. It was one of the few times I actually saw his eyes. They were deep set and steely blue, even more intimidating than his sinister mirrors.

"I can use tools, sir . . . my dad was a carpenter, and he taught me which end of a hammer drives nails and which end pulls them out."

Hugh smiled, "You're the smartest kid Ah have out here and the hardest working laborer Ah've seen in years, but this is serious work. Ah need some help plumbing these columns, so we don't fall b'hond schedule, and it must be done raht."

"Let's go," I said confidently.

Hugh stared at me for a short moment and couldn't contain his sly smile. Slowly, he nodded his approval, placed his mirrors back over his eyes, and said, "Awl raht, then . . . let's git after it."

For the rest of the afternoon, the general supervisor, himself, and I plumbed more than a dozen columns together. He and I were the only two on the entire job site that was usually crawling with about eight hundred workers. I would climb up to the top of the column forms, hook on the safety harness, and crank the turnbuckles with a large wrench. Hugh shouted directions from below as he read the level and monitored my work. Once he felt confident I could plumb them on my own, he handed me a level, and we did them two at a time, me on one and Hugh on another not far away. When we had plumbed them all, he said, "Ah'll make sure yew get carpenter apprentice wages for awl yo work t'day."

"Thanks, boss," I said gratefully.

We were walking back to the equipment trailer when without warning, he said, "So, yew know Nell Robertson."

"Yes, sir, she helped me open my First National account."

"Well, did you know she is divorced?" I wasn't sure why he asked me that.

"I think I did," I replied.

"Well, did yew know she an' Ah have been seein' each other?" I wasn't sure what to say. I wasn't even sure I wanted to know any of this. Somehow the stern overseer had felt the need to confide his personal life to the lowly slave.

"She is a very nice lady," I finally said.

"Ya know Ah'm from Dallas, raht?" He asked.

"Yes, I did know that."

"Ah'm divorced too, and Ah don't have a house up here . . . the company puts me up in a hotel." It occurred to me that he was just a person doing his job like everyone else. There was another side to Hugh other than shouting orders and being intimidating. As he talked, I wondered if he had any friends in Amarillo at all.

"Nell told me yew came awl the way down here to be close to Jack Little's dowter, Karen." Suddenly I realized that my relationship with Karen and the uniqueness of my situation had been part of Hugh and Nell's conversations.

"That's right," I said somewhat embarrassed.

"That's pretty bold, young man," he said with a smile. "Ah've got to admahr yew fer that." He said this in a way that a father would talk to a son, and it had tenderness to it.

"It seems we both are taking chances far away from home, boss," I said.

Hugh let out a little "humph," surprised I had made us appear in the same predicament.

"This awl stays between yew, me, an' the fence post," said Hugh. "Ye'r not gettin' any special treatment from this ya know."

"I don't expect any, boss."

"Good work today," he said. He handed me a twenty-dollar bill and said, "Here, get yerself some dinner on me."

I knew in spite of what he said, he knew who I was, and he knew my story. I felt like he genuinely liked me and was impressed that I had come all this way for love. I also felt that I knew more about him than most others on the job site. I would have to kill somebody to lose this job.

"See ya tomarrah," he said.

"Tomorrow it is, boss, thanks for the grub money," I said as I gave a little two-finger salute from the rim of my hard hat. On the way home that evening, I walked into Doug's Barbecue and ordered up a marvelous Texas BBQ sandwich, courtesy of Hugh.

The next morning John Tom was putting on his tool belt. "Why is this adjusted so damn small!" he murmured as he tried to figure out who was playing tricks on him. I kept a perfect poker face as I tied my boots and said, "Not sure, boss, (I called everyone boss who out-ranked me, which was everyone, because I knew they liked hearing it) but I think Travis has been pulling some practical jokes on a bunch of the hands around here."

"Ah ain't no hand," grumbled John Tom through clenched teeth as he re-adjusted his belt, "Ah'm a boss-man!" Travis was one of the carpenters who called me "Damn Yankee" all the time. This was an easy way to cause him some grief. I only hoped it wouldn't come back to haunt me later. As John Tom continued to swear at Travis under his breath, I grabbed a shovel and left the trailer with a hint of a smile. Fifty yards from the trailer Travis passed me and greeted me with the usual disdain, "Howdy, ya damned Yankee."

"Mornin' boss," I answered with a sharp nod. At that moment from the door of the tool trailer I heard John Tom bellow, "Travis, yew ass-hole, Ah want ta tahk to yew, boy!" With a wide grin I quickly put as much distance between me and them as I could.

Not only did the summer in Amarillo turn a page of independence for me, but Karen and I grew even closer. We saw each other nearly every night and usually did something special on the weekends. It was a summer filled with dinners at the Amarillo Club, riding horses in Palo Duro Canyon, and country-western dancing. Our favorite place to eat dinner was a little place called Gardsky's Loft. It was a quaint little restaurant-bar that featured a band called "Tejas" that performed there for most of the summer. The motto for Tejas was "Put the J back in Texas." They played a pleasant mix of classic rock, country, and thoughtful, romantic music that Karen and I liked to listen to. Our favorite that summer was a wonderful rendition of the Eagles' song "Desperado." We didn't dance at Gardsky's, but this was the place where we sat and held hands and talked about the future. The only glitch in the entire summer was, that without a car, Karen always had to drive us on our dates. It just didn't seem quite right, but it was all we had. Most evenings, after a hard day working for Stewart and Clark, I rode my bike to Karen's house, and we watched television together, took walks, or sat and talked on the front porch. Most of the time, I would make the long ride back to the Tea Room, even after dark, but occasionally Karen's parents would let me put my bike in the trunk, and she would drive me home. We had plenty of opportunity to be alone that summer but always remained careful not to let the physical go too far. There was always a respect there that, in spite of the temptation, we honored, fearing getting too physical would jeopardize the relationship. We became more serious, and the love grew stronger.

Together with all the good stuff, there were a couple of bumps in the road that happened that summer. I didn't realize it until years later, but this summer may have been the turning point for Karen and me. I treated my summer in Amarillo as if I were in college. I lived selfishly for the moment and really got wrapped up in the culture. Looking back now, I think I was just too young and definitely not as mature as I thought I was, and did not understand the 'big picture.'

The giant missing piece was the lack of leading a Christian lifestyle. I had slowly taken my focus away from God and was living how I wanted to live, no matter what the consequences might be. I should have been strengthening my spiritual life and going to church with Karen and her family every Sunday. Not only would this have paid dividends in the relationship with Karen and the trustworthiness of her parents, but it was simply the right thing to do. I had fallen into the trap of many; things were going great, and God had gotten placed on a shelf in my life. I had my moments of self-reflection and there were times that I went to church with Karen, but this should have been a major aspect of our lives, not an occasional exception to the norm. I was drifting away from the decision I had made at Castaway three years earlier.

Instead, I reveled in my independence and gobbled up the western lifestyle. The first bump in the road happened one Friday when Karen and I had made plans to go out for dinner. It was payday, and we had made the date earlier in the week. Since I had no car, she was going to pick me up. I arrived home from work an hour before she was due to pick me up, so I went straight into the Tea Room Bar for a couple quick "end of the week" brews. The next thing I knew, Karen was standing next to me in casual, but nice clothes. It was a rough bar filled with rednecks, roughnecks, and Mexicans.

A blind man could tell Karen was out of place, and I was ashamed that she had found me there. She had been upstairs knocking on my door and when I did not answer, she found me downstairs in the bar. I wasn't drunk, but several beers over the course of an hour had made me comfortably numb. There I was, perched on a barstool in a thick conversation with the bartender, still in filthy work clothes and boots with my hardhat cocked lazily on my head. In the middle of some story, I noticed the barkeep was not looking at me, but at someone beside me.

"It seems ya got company," he drawled. I was shocked to turn and see Karen standing there. I took a quick glance at the clock: 6:10. I was supposed to be waiting for her at 6:00. I couldn't believe the time had gotten away from me.

"Karen!" I exclaimed in surprise. "I am so sorry . . . I totally lost track of the time."

"That's OK," she said. "We can do this another tahm." She didn't seem angry, but I could see in her eyes the hurt and disappointment that I had let this happen. I was embarrassed and quickly threw some cash on the bar to cover my tab.

"Keep it, T.J.," I said to the bartender, referring to any change I might have coming. "No, c'mon," I insisted. "This won't take me but a minute." I grabbed Karen by the arm and escorted her out of the Tea Room. It seemed as if there were fifty sets of eyes on us as we left, all who knew I had messed up. I'm sure many of them were wondering how I was with such a nice young lady. I suddenly realized that this was exactly what my mother had to do with my father on many occasions. Although it was different from my angry mother dragging my dad out of Vetchel's, the scenario was too close for comfort. I had told myself that I would never be like that, yet here I was, a chip off the ol' block.

We went upstairs, and I quickly washed and got ready to go out on our date. I can only wonder now if in that moment Karen started to see someone different than the guy she met at Castaway, the guy she had promised to someday marry. But nothing seemed to overshadow that I had actually come all this way to be together, to be close, even forgetting a date for a couple of drafts. I think above all my faults, Karen knew my love for her had brought me across the country, and that trumped most shortcomings.

The second gaff happened early in August when the Little family was going on vacation. They did not invite me along, and I actually could understand this. Just because I had come all that way did not make me automatically part of all their family plans. Even though I understood this, to my dismay, Karen did not. Unknown to me until later, Karen had lobbied hard for me to be included in their trip. But it was not to be. She was worried about me being alone in Amarillo, especially without a car. She had always felt badly that I had to ride a bike around. Feeling bad about me being alone, Karen had made plans with Megan to keep me company while she was gone to New Mexico with her family.

I was at their house as they prepared to leave. A smarter guy would have stayed away because it made the atmosphere very uncomfortable, and I'm sure it heightened the tension between Karen and her parents. Finally sensing this, I said, "Well, I'll get out of your hair, have a great time y'all." After collecting the various goodbyes from Mr. and Mrs. Little, Janet and Mark, Karen led me to the garage where my bike awaited me. As we said our goodbyes, she slipped a set of keys into my hand. They were to the house and the Chevy Nova that she and Janet shared.

"Here," she said, "just so yew can watch T.V. or in case yew need to drahv somewhere." I couldn't believe it; this was more like something *I* would do. She continued in a low voice, "This one will get you into the house and this one is to the car." I felt uneasy about the whole thing, but never objected. I thought about the millions of things that could go wrong and brushed them all aside in bad judgment. Karen then reminded me, "Megan is supposed to give yew a call so yew two can go out and do something. Come back later tonight, and wait for her call." She trusted Megan totally, and rightfully so. I had no scheming plans or ulterior motives in hanging out with Megan other than catching up on old news and passing the time. I said my goodbye to Karen and took the keys.

I returned a few hours later and let myself into the Little's house. It felt strange to be there alone, and I basically made myself comfortable, watching television as I waited for Megan's call. Finally, the phone rang and when I answered it, the voice on the other end was not Megan asking for me, but Karen's Grandma asking for Margarite. I should have just said, "Sorry, wrong number," and hung up, but foolishly I said, "No, they're gone on vacation; I am here watching T.V." Instantly, I knew I created a mountain of trouble to deal with when the Littles returned. My gut churned with the reckoning that I knew would one day come. For the rest of their vacation, I never re-entered the Little home and didn't dream of using the car . . . but it was too late; the damage had been done.

Two weeks later, when they had returned from their vacation, I was sitting with Karen in their front yard. "There is something I have to tell you," I reluctantly told Karen. "The day you left I was here waiting for Megan's call. I accidentally had a short conversation with your grandmother." At hearing this, Karen's face went flush, understanding that sooner or later what we had done, what *she* had done behind her parents' backs, would come out. She knew there would be hell to pay. I felt sick. "I am so sorry," I said in a low voice.

"This will not be good," she answered.

"Well, I'm the one who was here, I'm the one who answered the phone . . . the heat will be on me," I tried to console her.

"Yea, but *Ah* gave yew the keys," said Karen. "This is going to come down on me."

"Well, maybe your grandma will forget; it was a long time ago," I said, grasping at the possibility that we might get out of this unscathed.

"Ah sure hope so," said Karen in a solemn tone.

The thought of what might or might not happen hung over us like a dark cloud. A few days had passed, and we started to think maybe nothing would become of it. We were not that lucky. One night while I was at their house, Karen answered the phone. She had a short conversation that I could not hear and then laid the phone down on the counter. She walked across the living room, headed to her parents' bedroom, where they liked to watch their own T.V. and have a glass of wine. As she walked, she looked at me and mouthed the words, "It's my grandmother." Instantly, my stomach turned into a knot. She came back out and sat with me, and we waited for our uncertain future.

After about ten minutes, Mr. Little came out and said, "Karen, can you come back here, please?"

Even though it was a question, it was not asked; it was a demand. I knew in the tone of his voice we were sunk. About five minutes later, Mr. Little emerged once again from the hallway and said, "Scotty, can you join us, please?"

Again his tone was not a request, but a demand. When I cowed into their room, Karen was sitting on the edge of the bed with a tear-stained face. I felt as low as a guy could feel in that moment, knowing this was all my fault. Not that I had botched being deceptive on the phone with the grandmother, but that I hadn't led us on a good path as a couple. In that moment, I realized I had done as much harm that summer as I had done good. Mrs. Little was lying in bed with a pillow propped up behind her head. Very directly in a stern voice, she looked at me and asked, "Can yew tell me how it is that yew were in this house wahl we were gown?" I was standing next to Karen as she sat at the foot of the bed.

"Mrs. Little," I started uneasily, "this is all my fault; I just came in to watch T.V."

"Yes, but how did yew git in?" she asked again. I was hanging my head, and I put my hand on Karen's shoulder. I knew what Mrs. Little already knew, but she wanted to hear from me.

"Karen gave me a house key," I confessed. Karen put her hand on top of mine.

Mr. Little then piped up, "Mah mother called here the naht that we left. What did yew do, just leave and turn around and come back?" When he said it out loud, it sounded ridiculous, but it was true.

"Yes, sir," I said straight out. "I peddled my bike around and got bored and came back here." I tried to soften the blow by explaining that Megan was supposed to contact me, and I had no phone at my apartment, but I don't think it helped.

Mrs. Little then said, "How are we ever gonna trust yew again?" The question was actually directed toward Karen. "It's just lahk eighth grade all over again." At this, Karen began to cry. She had gone through a phase when she was in eighth grade during which she had gotten caught sneaking out of her window at night. It had been a tough stretch for her, but she had slowly regained her parents' trust . . . until now.

"Oh, Mrs. Little, that's just not fair." I couldn't believe I was actually speaking to her in this way, but I was trying to defend Karen. I added, "She was just trying to be nice to me."

Mrs. Little glared at me and said, "Yew two get out of here until we figure out what to do with yew." Karen stood up, and we left the room.

As we went out, I tried to deflect the blow. "I apologize, this is all my fault." Mr. Little gave a faint nod and motioned with his hand for me to leave. Mrs. Little had her arms folded across her chest and staring at the wall away from me, said nothing. We went and sat on the front porch, pondering what our punishment might be.

To our surprise, they were sensitive to the fact that I was leaving in a few weeks and thought it too harsh to keep us from seeing each other. They knew we were genuinely sorry, and the conversation in the bedroom was agony. Even so, I lay low for awhile. But even though they had been lenient, something had been lost between Karen and her parents that would take time to rebuild again. As far as for me, this incident tarnished a good rapport that I had built with the Littles since the first time I nervously sat on their couch and mistakenly talked about trains. It was certainly a character-damaging event and certainly changed how they viewed me.

The last month of the summer, Hugh had dragged me out of a hole I was backfilling with a mountain of sand and told me I was being promoted as a carpenter's apprentice. This was a major jump in pay and learning skills more meaningful than the menial tasks of a laborer. I was required to purchase my own basic tools and tool belt and was assigned to assist a carpenter the entire day. I was even taught the basics of being a rigger. This is the guy who directs the crane operator, or picker, with hand signals to pick and drop loads all over the job site. I enjoyed learning the trade of a carpenter under the watchful eye of a seasoned veteran, but I really enjoyed the time I spent rigging for the picker. My last day on the job, I got ribbed by a bunch of guys I came to know by working next to them everyday for three months. Hugh handed me my last paycheck and said, "Mah number is written on th' pay stub; yew cowl me when yew come back ta Texas. You'll awlways have a job waitin'."

I actually had to fight back a tear, "Thanks, boss," I said as I shook his outstretched hand. In a reminiscent flash, it reminded me of Kyle's goodbye at the bus that difficult last night at Castaway.

In spite of a couple stupid mistakes, it was a summer I had only dreamed could happen. Who would have thought on that morning three summers earlier, when a bunch of guys from Michigan mistakenly called three Texas girls "guys," that I would be living and working in Texas and in love with one of them. It was better than any Hollywood script. But August was fading, and I knew I had to return to Marquette. To ship my bike home on the plane, I purchased a bicycle box from the airport and built a wooden frame inside of it to help protect it. The day finally came, and we loaded my bike into Karen's car, and she drove me to the airport. Once again, we replayed the tearful departure, but it was clear now that, in spite of our promise, in spite of how serious we were about each other, there were some issues emerging that would have to be rectified. We had survived some drama that summer; the question now was whether it weakened or strengthened us. We both clung to the providential way we met and the love we truly felt.

At the airport, we both said, "I love you," kissed, and I got on that jet and flew home. I stared out the window and watched the country pass below. As the country rolled past, the future seemed certain and uncertain at the same time. In my mind, I had envisioned that when college was over, Karen and I would be close, and a new phase of life together would begin. I also understood that time was far away. We had made our vow and had a loose concept of the future; I just wasn't sure how it was all going to happen. By the time I laid over in Kansas City, I already missed her and felt heartbroken. This was going to be a difficult year.

THE NEW DAKOTA

CHAPTER 29

In the short time I was home before I returned to N.M.U., I kept my word and visited Babe. She was happy to see me but could not hide how disappointed she was that I had spent the entire summer in Texas. It always amazed me that during all the time I had held her at bay, she was waiting to see if anything had changed. I have no idea if she dated at all during all that time, and I never pressed her to find that out. She just always seemed to show up the day I got home, and I could never figure out how she knew. Nothing different took place than what had happened previously between Babe and me. We had a couple nice conversations, I dashed her hope that maybe Karen and I were through, and then I quickly left for Northern when I finished with my laundry.

When I got back to Dakota House, I also kept the promise I made to myself after the endless night of vandalism drove me to smoke cigarettes; that it would never happen again. I was diligently welcoming all the new residents as they moved their possessions into their rooms. I paced the hallway in my boot-cut Wranglers, Tony Lamas, and Resistol cowboy hat. I'm not sure what they thought of me, but I didn't care; I had embraced the Panhandle culture and brought it with me to N.M.U. In reality I was not just trying to be the welcome committee, I was on a mission to find some enforcers. There was one guy who caught my attention right away.

When things settled down and everyone seemed to be moved in and relaxing, I pulled him into my room and shut the door. Mike was a mountain of a man and went by his last name: Sharkey. He was a giant presence as he stood in the middle of the room. He wore a broke-in Stetson and a pair of well-worn Justin boots, and I could see he packed a giant wad of Skoal in his cheek. It was easy for me to gravitate to him as he looked no different than many of the hands I had just left in Texas a couple weeks earlier. He stood cocked to one side with all his weight on one leg and his arms dangling free from the width of his shoulders. The chip on his shoulder was as big as his hat, and he carried himself with pride. Sharkey was a big man . . . he was perfect.

"Listen, Sharkey," I began. "Ah want this to be a good year for everybody. Last year there were some real jackasses in here and Ah vowed Ah would not let it be that way agin." Sharkey stood without expression, just listening and not saying a word. So I continued, "Ah want it to be clear that you are gonna be on mah sahd."

Sharkey looked at the floor for a second and said, "What's in it for me?"

"A place where you can live without a bunch of pot-heads making it miserable."

"I'm listening," he said flatly with a tone of interest.

"If Ah have any major trouble, Ah'll tip you off and make myself scarce for a few minutes. You can deal with it however you wish. Ah'll be very . . . grateful. This place will not be the zoo it was last year . . . ye'r gonna be on *mah* side."

"Let me think about it," he said, and he shook my hand and turned to leave. Then he stopped and turned around and asked, "Where are you from?"

"What?"

Sharkey asked again, "You have a southern accent; where are you from?"

"Oh," I said, "Ah'm actually from Flint, but Ah live in Texas during the summers . . . must've picked it up down there."

"Cool," was all he said, and he turned and left.

A little later I was sitting in my room thinking of the conversation I had with Sharkey. It was weird that he thought I was from the South, but I must admit I embraced the whole idea. I had developed a bit of the Texas dialect—not strong—but certain words just came out like I was talking with Hugh. It dawned on me as I thought, that in the previous two years, I actually had spent more time in Amarillo than at home in Flint. From that point on, I began to consider myself both a Michigander and a Texan. There came a knock at my door. It was Sharkey, and he had another giant dude with him.

"This is Art," he said. "Tell him what you told me earlier." Art wasn't as muscular as Sharkey, but he was a very big guy. Art stepped forward and shook my hand. He had blond hair and a red beard and spoke with a simple rural dialect of his own. He confessed proudly as being a farmer from Mount Clemens and a Pollack. Listening to him and looking at him, it all fit perfectly. Because he spoke a little bit like Gomer Pyle, he was not as menacing as Sharkey, but his size was impressive, and his eagerness to have some power made him a perfect candidate for what I had in mind. The instant I saw this, I grinned because I knew that Sharkey was on board. Not only was he on board, but he was recruiting. Before I knew it, I had established a regime charged with rebuilding Dakota House according to my vision; and so the new era began. Others who were part of this group of insiders included four guys from Chicago—Pete, Ed, John, and Tommy—and a guy named Steve from Detroit.

Every Friday, Art and his roommate, John, who was known as "Stats," (because of his immense knowledge of sports statistics) hosted a kegger in their suite. I had used my R.A. position to secure them the rooms closest to the stairs. This allowed them to sneak beer kegs into the dorm easier, minimizing the risk of getting caught. Usually, they would call me so I would know to steer clear while they hustled the contraband up the stairwell. Occasionally, Stats would come to my room to keep me occupied while the deed was being done, usually by one of the two gorillas, Art or Sharkey. When they arrived at my room, everyone knew the coast was clear. We spoke in a loose code to protect each other; we all knew that this could be major trouble for me and for them if we were ever caught. The weekends that I was on duty, I gave them a head's up when rounds were about to begin. They understood that if no one had a reason to stop at their rooms, the keggers would go undetected . . . so they partied in near silence until I gave them the all clear. Most of the time when I returned from making my rounds, I would find a pitcher of beer waiting for me in my mini fridge. It was sneaky, and it was wrong, but it worked like a charm. Knowing the consequences of getting caught, I never let it get beyond control or get too risky; there were only a handful of occasions that I actually drank with them in their rooms. I did not want to make the same mistake as the guy I replaced.

Dakota was perhaps the most traditional house on campus and had a rich history of pulling off events that no other house could. We had jackets and hats made with the distinctive Dakota Sioux Warrior emblazoned on them. On campus and around Marquette, people knew who we were. It was much like being in a fraternity but without all the hoopla. The year before I arrived, Dakota had gotten off track and I decided I would be the one to bring it back into prominence. Fat Pat and his cronies had moved off campus, and this made the task of re-building Dakota a lot easier. The few newcomers who tried to fill their shoes were no match for Sharkey and Art, and frankly the majority of the house. In addition to being the Godfather of the Dakota House Mafia, I also put together a pretty respectable house government, which participated and planned many activities at Northern. It was a good thing that we were so successful at the positive things because it helped us when we pulled off the other things we were known for: trouble and mischief. We also became known for holding some of the most legendary parties, on and off campus. Over the next couple years Sharkey, Art, and I became good friends. With their help and the help of other residents, Dakota House became legendary once more. For two years we ran a tight ship.

The downside of all this was that we embodied the college devil-take-care drinking stereotype . . . and loved it! I was drifting further away from my Christian faith and deeper into a hedonistic lifestyle. I always held the belief that at some point, I would pull the plug and return to a Godly life. I felt that there would be an obvious end point at which time I would put all this behind me and turn on a dime to live right. I developed a fraternal love for many of the guys I met in Dakota House, but I rarely stood my ground as a Christian. I seldom walked the talk. Many times I felt the guilt of forsaking what I knew was in my heart, but without conviction or fellowship, I fell short just as many times. But life was fun, my grades were good, and Karen was waiting for me in Texas. I felt like it was all under control and I was living on the clouds, when in reality I was beginning to plummet toward earth.

Scotty outside Dakota House in the Payne/Halverson Hall courtyard at N.M.U., 1979-80.

Christmas break of that year was business as usual: a trip down to Amarillo and a difficult airport departure. Now that Karen was attending Texas Tech, I noticed right away there had been a change in our correspondence and our discussions during that winter visit. She was discovering, like I had, that life was much bigger than what she knew during high school. Since she had begun a new, exciting phase of her life, the conversations between us had changed to new topics. I could tell by the passion with which she spoke of her classes and her sorority that she was fitting right in and loving college life. As she spoke, I remembered how cool it felt to finally be on my own, to not have my parents monitoring my daily activities. In our relationship to that point, I had always been the one paving the way, the older one living in the big world. Now she had stories of her own. She had changed from the bashful young girl I met that fateful morning at Castaway. She was a young woman now, not a girl who hung on my every word or action. After three years of me talking apples and she talking oranges, we were both now speaking apples to apples. As we shared about our college lives, hers was understandably filled with stories of her sorority. I was beginning to realize that I was not the biggest thing in her life anymore, and as much as I knew she had to live her own life, I was feeling threatened. What I tried to ignore was that something different was happening. I was totally immersed in my role as Dakota's R.A., in school, and in the guys who had become my friends. At the same time, Karen was just as committed to her life at Texas Tech and to her sorority. There was nothing wrong with that, except we were in deed drifting a little. I tried to suppress that feeling, but deep down I could feel it.

With the exception of a couple hiccups along the way, Karen and I had plans for the future, and we were making our difficult situation work. Everyone on my end knew about her, and everyone on her end knew about me. We both felt that no matter what happened, our relationship was a constant. We would survive in the end.

LLOYD

CHAPTER 30

The summer of 1980 arrived, and I returned to Amarillo to work. It had been four years since Karen and I had met. I had recruited three buddies from Dakota to go with me: Parker; Kevin whom we called Deek; and Jim. Parker and Deek were younger than I, but Jim and I were the same age. He was an adventurer who had spent time working in Alaska. A trip to Texas and into the unknown was right up his alley. We drove Parker's car down, and Jim followed closely on his motorcycle. While passing through Oklahoma, we rode headlong into a tornado. We all took refuge in Parker's car, holed up in a self-serve carwash. In the morning, Jim discovered during the night someone had stolen the saddlebags off his motorcycle. It was an auspicious start to our summer. When we arrived in Amarillo, we all piled into an apartment I had secured beforehand in a complex called Casa de Warren. It was not far from Karen's house. It was a tight fit, but our objective was to save some money, so cramming into a single apartment was not a big deal. Parker might have thought differently since he drew the short straw and was sleeping in a walk-in closet.

The next day I went back to the First National Bank project I had worked on the summer before and tracked down Hugh. When I walked into the foreman's trailer, he looked up, started to look away, and then took a double take. Hugh stood and walked toward me with an extended hand. "If Ah hadn't seen it fer mahself, Ah wouldn't have believed it." He seemed genuinely happy to see me and added with a sly smile, "But Ah know why yer REALLY here."

"You said to come calling if I ever came back and needed a job," I started. "Well, I'm callin'." Hugh slowly shook his head. "Boy, Ah'm really sorry, but there's nuthin' here, Scotty." He continued, "We're nearly done here, and Ah'm headed back to Dallas next week. Ah could probably git yew some work down there, but Ah don't believe yew'd be interested in leavin' Amarilla . . . raht?"

I nodded slowly and answered, "Right, boss." We did some catching up for about twenty minutes. Then Hugh looked at his watch and said, "Ah have a meeting in ten minutes across the street; Ah gotta run." He put one hand on my shoulder and shook my hand with the other and said, "Good luck to yew, boy. Call me if yew ever fahnd yer way to Dallas."

"I will do that; thanks, boss," and I left the trailer. It was the last time I ever saw or spoke to Hugh.

The next day Parker, Deek, Jim, and I all drove around to large commercial construction sites looking for work. We discovered that the building market was in a slump, and no one was hiring. In the days and weeks that followed, we switched our focus to smaller residential construction sites, but with the same result. Three weeks had passed, and we were getting short on cash. If we could find no work within a few days, we would be forced to return home. Mr. Little had pointed me in the direction of several projects that he knew of, but with no luck. Our fortunes changed one morning while talking to a guy whose crew was building a house not far from Casa de Warren. He pointed across a field to a place where you could see stacks of lumber, piles of dirt, and heavy equipment. It was the obvious site of construction in its early phases. "Y'all maht fahnd work over thar," he said with a very heavy drawl.

When we pulled up and piled out of Parker's car, we encountered several guys going about their business with a purpose.

I asked, "Any of y'all the boss?" Only one man looked up to respond. He didn't say a word but only pointed toward a tall, well-built guy pouring over a set of blueprints stretched across the hood of a pick-up truck. When we approached I asked outright,

"We're looking for work. Are you hiring?" He didn't look up right away, trying to finish the calculation he was fixed upon. When he finally straightened up, and looked at us I was taken aback . . . he looked remarkably like my brother, Jeff. He was quickly sizing us up and finally spoke, "Any of y'all worked residential construction before?"

Everyone reluctantly murmured, "No."

Then I chimed in, "I worked commercial construction for Stewart and Clark last summer on the First National Bank building."

"What was yer job?

"I was a laborer most of the summer but ended as a carpenter's apprentice."

"Do yew have yer own tools?"

"Yes, sir."

"What about the rest of yew?"

Jim said, "I've logged in Oregon and worked on a fishing boat in Alaska."

Parker said, "I'll do anything." It came out desperate and pathetic.

Deek just shook his head.

Turning back toward his blueprint, the tall Texan didn't speak for a couple of anxious seconds, then said, "Ah can only hahr two hands, not all four of yew." Then he looked up and pointed at me and said, "Yew and one other hand."

It took a few seconds to process what he meant by "hands." "Like a cow-hand," I thought. "He just means a person, a worker." I had no clue as to who else might be interested because faster than lightning Parker said, "I'll do it."

We both stepped forward and introduced ourselves:

"My name is Scotty."

"My name is Parker."

When I shook his hand, I couldn't help but notice how large it was. "This dude has been pounding nails for a long time," I thought to myself.

"Mah name is Lloyd Cunningham; Ah own this company." Then he added, "How soon can y'all start?"

"How soon do you want us?"

"How about an hour?"

"How about a half 'n hour?" I quickly countered.

Lloyd smiled with satisfaction and said, "Ah'll see y'all in a half an hour," turned and refocused on his blueprint.

When Parker and I returned, Lloyd introduced us to three other hands: Kenneth, his foreman and lead carpenter; and Frankie and Earl, who were brothers and both carpenters. Kenneth was a stout guy with a full beard and huge arms covered with heavy blonde hair, bleached almost white from the Texas sun.

Frankie was very short with a long braided pony tail, arms covered with tattoos, and missing his two front teeth. He sort of reminded me of Willie Nelson. Earl was a scrawny guy who spoke with such a thick accent and a mush mouth that, at times, it was nearly impossible to understand him. He and Frankie both spoke with the same dialect, but it wasn't the Texas drawl. It was different; it was even slower and thicker. I learned later that they were from deep in the hills of North Carolina. Earl wore a floppy cowboy hat with the front tied into a point. It reminded me of a Robin Hood hat. He was like Frankie's sidekick. They dressed, spoke, and acted like men who had a rough past . . . and they did. Working for Lloyd was their chance to pull themselves out of destructive lives.

Lloyd and Kenneth, on the other hand, were men who seemed to have it all together. They certainly knew their way around a building. They both had wives and children and came to work clean with fresh clothes. This did not always happen on a construction job. Lord knows it did not happen with Frankie and Earl. I think there were weeks that those two never changed their clothes, and I could tell when they had a tough night of drinking or smoking dope. Lloyd and Kenneth always figured out the plan of attack for each day and gave us all our assignments. I discovered that being a mere carpenter's apprentice for a short month did not prepare one for swinging a hammer on a residential construction site. Parker was mainly a grunt, doing all the odd jobs that were beneath everyone else. He carried a lot of lumber and dug a lot of holes. I mainly assisted the carpenters, and they taught me as we proceeded along. Ultimately, we proved that we were good hands, and Lloyd did not regret hiring us.

In the meantime, Jim and Deek continued to look for work. Deek landed an entry-level job on a survey team for an oil company. After another week of fruitless searching, Jim decided Colorado was calling him, and he packed his motorcycle and headed north. Although we were sorry to see him go, Parker was happy to finally move out of the closet and onto the couch that Jim had claimed for a bed, but it didn't last long. A few weeks later, Parker also packed his things and headed back north. He felt he could be a grunt at home just as easily as he was in Texas and would rather live at home without the bills. So for the remainder of the summer, Deek and I worked hard and lived together. We pooled our money and bought a car that we shared.

Lloyd had taken me under his wing and taught me how to read a blueprint and build a house. I was making decent money working for Lloyd, but I wanted to make more. I don't know where I got the idea, but the next thing I knew I had landed a second job at night as a waiter . . . in The Amarillo Club of all places. It was quite a dramatic change to go from pounding nails and manhandling lumber to being polite and pouring wine. It also took some concentration not to slip at the Amarillo Club and speak as if I was talking with Frankie and Earl. As with Hugh the summer before, Lloyd and the crew found that I was in Texas to be near Karen. They were in disbelief when I told them that we had managed a long-distance relationship for four years. Karen was busy with her own job, so the summer had a little different feel than those before, but still we persisted.

When the time came to head back north, Lloyd told me to keep in touch, and if I needed a job the next summer, he'd try to hire me back. He was a great boss, and I did my best to work hard for him that summer. I was beginning to establish many friends beyond Karen. You might say I was starting to plant my first roots in Amarillo. Returning to school was getting more difficult, but I stuck to my plan, and Deek and I drove the long way home in late August.

BECKY

CHAPTER 31

I was now a senior at N.M.U., still an R.A. in Dakota House, and in my last year of eligibility on the soccer team. Karen was a sophomore at Texas Tech, and the romance continued as before, or so I thought. I sat in the cafeteria one day and caught sight of a girl carrying her food to a table. We all had a tendency to sit with people from our own dorms, and I could tell by where she sat she was not from Halverson, but Payne Hall, which was across the courtyard. I had noticed this girl before, but today something made me fixate on her. I studied her as she strolled across the cafeteria. She was average height, taller than Karen, and walked very slowly with a very straight posture. She had striking, long wavy red hair with subtle light streaks through it. Unlike today, these streaks and curls were natural and free of charge. Then and now, girls would pay big bucks to have this girl's hair. She had it parted on one side but was flung over to the other in a very seductive manner. It was thick, like a lion's mane, and it cascaded over her shoulders down to the middle of her back. She carried herself almost with an air of arrogance, but something told me she was not. Another girl who looked vaguely familiar sat with her, and I periodically would steal a glance their way. Her mannerisms looked very pleasant, and I caught myself being intrigued. Sharkey was sitting across from me talking when he noticed my attention was elsewhere. He braced the table with both hands for leverage and labored to turn his large body to investigate. He saw the red-haired beauty and turned back to his lunch. He looked down at his plate and began to eat again and without expression, said, "What about Texas?"

"What?" I said, trying to act oblivious.

"I see what you're staring at . . . what about Texas?"

Sharkey had become one of my best friends, and he knew everything about Karen. I felt embarrassed. "I'm just looking; Texas will always be there."

Sharkey shook his head a little. "Don't screw it up."

"I'm not going to screw anything up," I shot back. "I don't even know who that is."

"Yeah, but I'll bet you ten bucks within two weeks time you will," he said with a little grin. During the entire conversation, he never looked up from his plate; he just talked with his head down while shoveling in the food.

"You're on," I said, and reached across the table and grasped his huge hand. "I don't even care about that girl." I tried to brush it off like it was meaningless, but silently, I felt compelled to find a way to meet the girl with the red hair.

A few days later I was sitting alone eating breakfast in the exact same seat when the red-haired girl walked to her usual table. I watched her take a seat at a table with the familiar girl I thought I knew somehow. Then it dawned on me that she was in one of my classes. Without much thought, I picked up my tray and headed toward their table.

"Excuse me," I said as I stood holding my breakfast, "you have Professor Neilson, right?"

"Oh yea," she said in recognition. "You're in there, right?"

"Yes, Ah'm Scotty."

"That's right, I remember now . . . I'm Darcy."

I had literally paid zero attention to the red-haired girl.

"Yea, Darcy, how can Ah forget that? It's mah sister's name," I said.

I knew exactly what the assignment was for the next class period, but I acted like I had missed something and asked her to clarify it for me. As she started to fill me in with the information that I already knew, she stopped mid-sentence and asked if I wanted to join them.

"Would you like to sit down?" she asked.

"Sure, if you don't mahnd." I acted spontaneously and directed the question toward the red-haired girl.

She simply shook her head and said, "No, have a seat."

As I sat down, Darcy introduced her. "This is Becky," and opened her hand in a gesture toward the girl with the thick red hair.

"Hi, how are you?" I said as I smiled and nodded in her direction. "Hope Ah'm not intruding."

"No, not at all," they both answered together.

I don't remember any of the rest of the conversation that morning; it was all a ruse to get introduced to the red-haired girl, to Becky. Except at one point she placed her fingertips over her mouth to politely cover the swallow of some tiny morsel and asked, "Where are you from?"

Without missing a beat I answered, "Amarilla, miss, where the West lingers on."

When I got back to my room, I sat on my bed and looked at the picture of Karen on my desk. I asked myself aloud, "What are you doing?" The promise Karen and I had made two summers earlier was still in place; there was no reason to even think about girls. It was reminiscent of my fickleness in high school except that was before I knew Karen. Ever since Castaway, I had kept Babe and Indiana Deb at a distance and stayed faithful to Karen. Now here I was, making moves to meet a total stranger like a man without commitment. I felt guilty, yet I continued my efforts to get to know Becky.

A couple days later I was having a late lunch. Nearly everyone had already come and gone, and only a few late stragglers were ducking into the café before they closed the doors. When I came out of the line with my lunch, I saw Becky sitting alone. Without hesitation, I walked close to her but like I was headed to a different table. I was hoping she would stop me, but when that didn't happen, I quickly activated plan "B." I had all but passed but stopped and backed up a couple steps.

"Becky, right?" I asked like I hadn't paid close attention when we were introduced before. In reality, I had burned that name into my mind; I knew exactly what it was. Then I continued, "Do you mind if Ah sit with you?"

"No, not at all, have a seat."

I sat down and began a trivial conversation of discovery with Becky. Aside from her wonderful hair, Becky had striking blue eyes, lips like rose petals, and lots of freckles. In addition to the freckles, her skin was slightly pale but beautiful. I remember thinking, "Oh, peaches and cream." I heard that expression before, and it dawned on me in that moment that it was sitting right in front of me. Everything she did seemed calculated. She spoke cleanly and in a very measured way. She handled her silverware with precision, slowly and neatly cutting delicate portions as she ate her lunch. Immediately, I could tell she was very smart. A voice in my head said, "This girl is WAY out of your league." Still, she had captured my attention, and I had skillfully managed the introduction.

I didn't try to make too much out of it, as I was merely testing the waters; why, I don't know. I looked over to where I normally sat, and to my surprise, Sharkey was sitting alone, with his back to the wall. Eating a late lunch as well, he was fixated on Becky and me, waiting for the moment when I saw him. With his elbow resting on the table, he held his hand in the air and rubbed his fingers against his thumb. Instantly, I realized I owed him ten dollars.

After that day, Becky and I shared several meals together with no apparent planning nor direction. Just casual meals when we happened to see each other and nearly every time only if *I* made the effort. Of course, I wouldn't have expected it to be any different; being forward was not her style. During the course of these meals, we gradually learned more about each other but in the end, Becky always seemed a little guarded. After a month or so of this, I decided to pay her a visit at her room. By means of a little cloak and dagger, I found out her room number and showed up in Payne Hall unannounced. The door was open, and Becky was sitting at her desk in plain view when I rapped on the door. She did not expect to see me and was clearly surprised that I was standing there. She invited me in, offered me a seat, and we began a pleasant conversation.

In the short time we had become acquaintances, one thing was clear: I was very brash and outgoing, and she was under control, focused, and proper. It made sense when I saw the neat condition of her room. It was spotless with everything in its place, including inspirational posters and a Bible on her bed.

"Are you a Christian?" I brazenly asked at one point of the visit.

"Yes, I am," was her direct answer.

I am sure Becky must have thought that this would surely be the end of the growing attention she was receiving from me. She must have felt that the next thing to happen was me trying to find a way to gracefully excuse myself from her room. It totally shocked her when I said, "I am too . . . I was saved a few summers ago."

She just stared at me for a second, wide-eyed, with a look of total disbelief, and her mouth actually hanging open a little. She finally admitted, "I had no idea." This was an indicator that college life was not doing my spiritual growth any favors, or should I say I was not carrying that special air of difference that Becky possessed. Becky's demeanor totally changed after she learned that I was a Christian. It occurred to me that this was the reason she always seemed distant and guarded: self-protection . . . she was not interested in anyone who was not a Christian. Now that she learned that I was, it was a whole new ballgame. It was obvious from the start, however, that she had been a Christian much longer than I. Nevertheless, our conversation turned deeper and more personal. Suddenly, there was an interest, and there was definitely chemistry.

However, through it all, I had kept one major detail out of the conversation: Karen. I wasn't sure what I thought would happen, but I thought I could keep these two worlds separated. I convinced myself that I was doing nothing wrong, but I doubt if Karen would have agreed, and had she been doing the same sort of thing at Tech, I would have come unglued! Even though I had many battles with my guilty conscience, I continued to have meals with Becky and have the occasional visits. Ironically, it was my Christianity that opened up the lock Becky had put on her feelings, yet not being totally forthcoming was deceptive, not very Christian. "What's the harm?" I thought. "I have everything under control."

To my amazement, one evening I was studying in my room when there was a knock at the door, which as usual, was wide open. Thinking it was one of my guys, I said, "C'min," without turning to see who it was.

"Hi there. I brought you something." It was the pleasant voice of the red-haired beauty. I spun around in total surprise to see Becky cautiously entering my room with a plate piled with cookies. Luckily, my room was clean, but I was completely taken aback that *she* had paid *me* a visit. Without having to survey, I knew pictures of Karen were where they could not be missed. I invited Becky to sit down and nervously talked and ate cookies that had been sent by her mother. Eventually, she asked the question that I knew was coming. "Who is that?" she asked, looking at the 8x10 picture of Karen on my desk.

"That is Karen," I answered. There were other pictures pinned up of Karen and me together, and I could tell Becky knew Karen was not my sister.

"So, who is she?"

I let out a long sigh and said, "She's a girl from Texas I met when I was in high school."

I commenced to tell her the whole story. In the seriousness of the moment, I lost any drawl that I brought back with me from the Panhandle. It was plain to see by her fallen countenance that this news hurt her. I felt badly because I had made this whole thing happen. Deep down I knew I had been leading her on, but I didn't think it would develop into much. Evidently, I was wrong. I wasn't sure what would happen, but Becky became interested in me, and now here we were in this awkward moment. Becky and I had not done anything but share some time together and some meals, but in my thoughts and actions toward her, I knew I had cheated on Karen and been dishonest to both girls.

"You should have told me about her," was the soft, hurt statement Becky, said looking at me perplexed.

"I'm sorry," was all I could think of to say. But then I said something that I never thought I would say in a million years. "I didn't want to scare you away."

Becky looked around my room, which was filled with items from Texas. There were boots and cowboy hats, steer horns and photos. But the most convicting item was a cheap rug I bought at a Cracker Barrel restaurant in Amarillo displayed in front of my rocking chair. It had the silhouette of the state of Texas on it and in giant letters read, "Texas Is For Lovers."

"How serious are you two?" she asked.

Without actually answering the question, I replied, "I go down every summer."

As she was trying to digest all this new information, she nervously was biting her bottom lip and picking at a tiny flaw on the knee of her blue jeans. She looked puzzled and hurt, and I wanted to hug her, but in that thought, it hit me that I was as confused as she was. I experienced a pain in my stomach that until then I had only experienced with Karen. I realized I liked her! Becky suddenly stood up and said, “I have to go.”

Not wanting it to end right there and then, I asked, “Can we talk about this some more . . . another time?”

“I don’t know,” she said. “Maybe,” and she turned and headed toward the door. As she left, she bumped smack into Sharkey, who had turned the corner and was coming into my room. She tried to hide the emotion that had welled up inside her, but Sharkey saw it. He watched her hurry down the hallway and disappear into the stairwell before he turned and stepped into my room.

“I told you you would screw things up,” Sharkey declared with an open palm extended toward me. I opened my desk drawer and rummaged through some papers until I found what I was looking for—a ten dollar bill. I slapped it into Sharkey’s hand then walked across my room to look out the window. It was a pleasant evening, perhaps one of the last before the long dreary rains came, pulling months of snow close behind. Becky appeared in the courtyard, and I watched her walk to a bench and sit down in heavy thought.

All I could say to Sharkey was, “I have a problem.”

IRONY

CHAPTER 32

What had happened with Becky was like a wake-up call. Not only did I have to decide what course of action, if any, to take with Becky, but I also had a drawer full of letters from Babe and from Indiana Deb. I realized that the distance between me and Karen that I loathed so much had allowed me to live several different lives. I had been honest with Babe, but still strung her along. Indiana Deb had been sending me pages of letters filled with emotion, and I responded in kind. Now I had manipulated Becky to the brink of fondness, only to hurt her. All the while, I was never going to let any of these interfere with my love for Karen and the vow we had made. I realized I was a jack-ass, playing with people's hearts. I had to make it all right.

Sharkey and I went to the pub that Friday, and I used him as a sounding board for my predicament. After a few hours, we stumbled home. I had made a decision that night to discontinue any contact with Babe and Indiana Deb and to not try and create anything further with Becky. Having secrets was no way to be faithful; I decided to come clean and tell Karen about Becky. I hadn't really felt like I was cheating on Karen, but the accidental discovery by Becky let me see it for what it was. Even though Karen did not even know Becky existed, I wanted to tell her what happened and that I was sorry. I felt a burden lifted that I didn't even know I was carrying.

When I got back to Dakota, I had to talk to Karen. Now that she was away from home, I didn't have to worry about her parents, about how late it was. I didn't do it often, but there were times I called her late at night, especially if I had too much to drink. It was after midnight in Texas when I called and much to my surprise, there was no answer. Now why I thought she should be in her room on a Friday night is beyond reason. But the beers were doing the thinking, and I continued to call, and I continued to get no answer. The deeper into the night it got, the angrier I was becoming. When it finally reached 2:00, I was livid. "Where is she? What could she be doing?" When Karen finally answered the phone at 2:45, the worst part of me spilled out. I kept asking her questions that only backed her into a corner. And the more persistent I was, the more I cut my own throat.

"Where have you been!?" I began. "I've been calling you for hours!"

"C'mon, Scotty, it's Frahday naht . . . that's not fair," she replied.

"Were you out with guys?" I persisted.

"Yes, Scotty, we had a mixer with our brother fraternity."

"You didn't have a date did you?" I couldn't believe I had the audacity to ask that question, knowing what I had been up to, but I did. I was expecting her to say "no," I mean, we had made a promise. How could she go out on a date? But there was silence on the other end of the line that gave me my answer.

"You were on a date!?" I asked incredulously. I was shouting into the phone. If there is such a thing as a good drunk, I was not that guy, and I was making it easy for Karen to tell me what was on her mind. Still, there was no answer to my question. But in the silence, I knew the answer, and my world was suddenly smashed.

"Yes, Scotty, Ah've been seeing someone," was the soft, shaky answer that finally broke the quiet.

Her answer actually stunned me. I knew she was going to have to admit she was on a date, but that was not what she said; she said she had "been seeing someone." I wanted to fix this, but being so far away I was helpless. It was the same voice that captured my heart over four years ago, but now it was turning everything upside down . . . it was now the voice of hurt and emotional carnage. In the anguish of the moment, I declared, "I need to see you! We need to talk . . . I'm coming down there!"

"NO, Scotty!" she said emphatically. "Do NOT come down here. It will only make things worse."

There was much more back and forth to the conversation, but eventually the call was over, and I sat in the dark, wondering how we had gotten to that point. I rummaged around in my mini fridge and produced a beer and cracked open the top. I sat on the edge of my bed and stared out the open window into the dark courtyard. It was late October, and the wind was blowing the leaves off the trees and swirling them down the sidewalks. They made a sound like someone saying, "Shhhhhhhhhhhhhh." I couldn't help but reminisce about Castaway, how the leaves made the same sound as I looked out the tiny window by my bunk and heard Karen's molasses voice in my head. I thought about the original reason I had called Karen that night and let out a short sarcastic chuckle.

"Now that's ironic," I said aloud. I finished the beer and washed my tear-stained face with water and lay on my bed fully clothed. Just like that first night at Castaway, I spoke her name, "Karen," out loud and drifted off into a reluctant sleep.

THE FALL

CHAPTER 33

I woke up late the next morning to pounding on my door. The door was not locked, and Art and Stats entered before I had a chance to say anything. They came in like they owned the place, and Art plopped down on my bed with me still laying in it.

"What's this, bankers' hours?" he asked in reference to the late time.

"I guess," I said in a worn-out voice. About that time, a parade of guys streamed into my room. Before I knew it, Sharkey, Pete, Tommy, and Ed had piled into my room and jumped on the bed.

"It's almost lunchtime, man; you gonna come down with us?" asked Sharkey.

"Get off of me you fat asses!" I groaned from under the combined weight of four men. After messing around with me more and laughing up the moment, they all got up and were standing, waiting for me to get up.

"C'mon, let's go get some lunch," said Pete impatiently. Pete was a good looking guy with red hair and an athletic build. He was a hockey player from Chicago, and he sort of reminded me of Griz. I swung my feet over the edge of the bed and sat with my elbows on my knees and my head in my hands, trying to collect my thoughts. I was hoping that what was in my head was a dream, but I knew the conversation between Karen and I had really happened; it was reality. I was waking up to a whole new world.

"What's the matter with you?" asked Tommy. Tommy was Pete's roommate. They had come to Northern together from Chicago. He had a really gruff voice, and sometimes we called him Froggy, after the Little Rascals character with the raspy voice.

Ed chimed in, "Looks like somebody shot your dog." Ed, also from Chicago, was a very tall guy with poor posture who dressed in Bermuda shorts and flowered shirts all the time and usually had a cigar stuck in his mouth. He always reminded me of a tourist. These guys had become my closest friends over the two years I had been in Dakota. They were like brothers, and they all knew about Karen.

Finally, I told them, "Karen is seeing another guy."

"WHAT?!" exclaimed Tommy in his gravel voice. "Why, *that* wench!"

"No," I interrupted. "It's my fault."

Pete was standing by my shrine, looking at the collage of photographs of Karen pinned to the cork board: "That stinks, man . . . I'm sorry."

Pete knew what it was like to have a girlfriend far away. He had a shrine in his room filled with pictures of his long-time girlfriend, Patty, who was attending college back home in Chicago. Once, Patty came to visit for the weekend when, typical for the time, someone pulled a fire alarm in the middle of the night. My chief duty was to immediately clear Dakota House, whether the alarm was false or real. A shortcut to opening every door was to go into a room and then cut through the bathroom to the connected room. When I checked Pete and Tommy's room, it was empty, and I took the shortcut through the bathroom. As I passed through, I noticed the shower curtain drawn completely across the shower door. Many students tried to hide during fire alarms and avoid congregating in the lobby with an entire dorm population in the middle of the night, waiting for the all-clear. The shower was a typical hiding place and having the curtain drawn during a fire alarm looked suspicious. I backed up, grabbed the edge of the curtain, and whipped it to one side in a swift, single motion. Quite unexpectedly, I encountered a totally nude Pete vainly attempting to shield a totally nude Patty.

"What the . . . !" was all that came out of my mouth. Then as Pete was grabbing at the curtain, which I would not allow to be drawn, I burst out laughing, "Fire alarm, Pete!"

"C'mon Hazel, get the hell outta here, and let us stay!" he pleaded as we fought for control of the curtain.

"Alright," I finally agreed while Patty continued to cower behind Pete. "Just don't make a sound." Then I let loose of the curtain and finished clearing the hall.

The next morning, we were all sitting at the Dakota table having breakfast when Pete and Patty took the seats directly across the table from me. Patty had arrived late the night before and had yet to be introduced to anyone so Pete began to dole out the names. He finally turned his attention to me, whom he left until last, hoping something would interrupt the process. No luck—the introduction would have to happen.

"This is my R.A., Scotty," he finally said.

I reached forward and politely shook her hand. Then with Pete glaring at me, I said, "I think I've *seen* you somewhere before."

Her eyes darted down with embarrassment, and she covered a faint laugh with her other hand. Pete just closed his eyes as he took his seat and said, "Oh, man."

But that was weeks earlier, and now I think my predicament was making him wonder what it would be like if Patty began seeing someone else back in Chicago.

Stats eased the moment. "Forget her for now; let's go eat."

"Yea, you're right, Stats," agreed Art. "Let's eat."

They all could tell I was hurting and were doing their best to help me out. Sharkey finally came over and grabbed me under one armpit and lifted me up. "Let's go, chief, you gotta go eat something." He put a large arm around my neck and basically led me out of my room. Then he added, "It'll be alright." We all went to the cafeteria and ate a long Saturday lunch. At one point, I saw Becky stroll in, and I felt another dose of guilt. Part of me wanted to run over and tell her what happened, but even *I* knew that would not be good form. Plus, I was worried more about what I was losing with Karen than what I might gain with Becky. She purposely sat with her back toward the Dakota table, and we never spoke. As we left the cafeteria, Sharkey put his arm around me again and said, "I know this just happened, but you got to get over it and move on." I did not answer. I did not want to move on; I wanted to fix it. I wanted to go back in time, figure out where I went wrong, and get a second chance. But as difficult as it was, I knew Sharkey was right. When I got back to my room, I rolled up the Texas rug and put it in the back of my closet.

I took down all the pictures of Karen, except one small photo of me and her at Castaway. That week, when she and I met, was still the milestone of my life, and I did not want to ever forget the feeling I had there. I had gained my salvation there and even though Karen left me, I knew that God had not. There were still many items from Texas in my room, as I was not prepared to abandon the culture I had grown to love, but Karen, with the one small exception, had disappeared from sight.

For the rest of that semester, I fell further away from my faith. I began to party harder, and my grades started to slip. My focus was simply not there, and studying was nearly impossible. I was floundering in a sea of despair, shame, and pity, but I couldn't seem to get it together. I even dropped courses that I knew I would fail in order to rescue my G.P.A. I was so thankful to my buddies in Dakota House. They recognized what I was going through and kept me out of trouble for the most part. It was during this low time when I had thrown many of my responsibilities to the wind that Dakota pulled off one of the most remembered antics of debauchery in its history.

THE LAST PANTY RAID

CHAPTER 34

I read in the Dakota House History, a file left in the desk in R.A.'s room, that Dakota traditionally decorated the house Christmas tree with panties stolen from girls in raids. In my first full year as the R.A., only a couple old timers still around brought it up, but nothing became of it, and the tradition seemed to die. This was a welcome loss for the university and especially the girls of "down" campus. But after Thanksgiving of 1980, I decided to resurrect the tradition. I wasn't sure how much longer I was going to stay in Dakota House, but I felt this might be my last year. If this were true, then I wanted to leave something to remember me and this group of guys by. It didn't take much work to convince the rest of the regime that this was something that had to be attempted. We decided right away that if we were going to pull this off, it must be masterful. It all began with a planning meeting of the house government, which coincidentally consisted of Art, Stats, Sharkey, Steve, Ed, Pete, and Tommy. These guys all knew that they were definitely moving out of the dorms after this school year; they also wanted to go out with a bang.

The great Dakota panty raid of 1980 began with the dilemma of trying to plan something without drawing attention that would nip the whole plan in the bud. There were still people around that knew of the tradition and might become suspicious if we handled the planning wrong. The scheme was to join with a girls' house to go Christmas caroling at the local old folks' home. Dakota House had done enough legitimate activities that this was actually a believable diversion. We targeted three girl floors—the two that were below us on the second floor of Halverson Hall and one located on the other side of the quad in Spalding Hall. This would spread them out and minimize the chance that they would discover what was happening by the mere proximity. We had contacted each girls' house and set up a meeting with each of them to discuss the details of caroling together. Each meeting was scheduled twenty minutes apart to give us ample time to ransack their rooms and flee with the goods to the next house. We had scheduled the meetings to take place in the television room of each house. Television rooms were all located at the outside corner of the L-shaped dorms. The closest student room to the T.V. room was at a ninety-degree angle, and the door knobs between the two rooms were only about sixteen inches apart. Both doors opened into their respective rooms, away from each other. We made short ropes with a loop tied in each end, just long enough to reach from one door knob to the other. When attached, neither room could be opened from the inside. We actually had meetings in Dakota House during which we rehearsed how the raid would proceed and warned not to stay in any one room too long, don't be identified, and at any cost, don't get caught!

The night of the raid arrived, and the members of Dakota House crammed into the television room wearing masks and all sorts of ridiculous clothes. We did our last-second reminders then Art, Sharkey, and I went to Déjà Vu House, the floor directly under Dakota, for our scheduled meeting. We were the only ones not wearing masks, but I have to admit I was dressed like General MacArthur, with a captain's hat, mirrored sunglasses, a corn-cob pipe, and a riding crop tucked under my arm. The girls just thought I was being weird and were never suspicious. Art and Sharkey stood by the door. When all the girls were gathered in the room, I began to speak about Christmas caroling together. As I spoke, I slowly moved toward the door. Without warning, I leapt out of the room, Sharkey pulled the door close, Art produced the double-looped rope, and quickly secured the television room door to the first room door. The girls at first were clueless and stood watching through the lengthwise plexi-glass of the door. When I blew the long shrill of a whistle, the men of Dakota streamed into Déjà vu simultaneously from both ends. Because the meeting took place in their own house, most girls came to the meeting and left their rooms unlocked and even open. The mob of raiders efficiently ransacked the underwear drawers of nearly every room in plain view of the girls who were locked in the T.V. room. The cat was out of the bag now, and there was an angry mass of women's faces, swearing . . . mostly at me, plastered against the glass door. The R.A. from Deja Vu was yelling, "Hazel, you bastard, I'm gonna have you fired for this!" I only smiled at her contorted, reddened face and shrugged. We made our way back up the stairs to Dakota and deposited the contraband into our individual rooms and proceeded to successfully repeat the performance in Maggie Mae House. In both cases we left, leaving the screaming girls locked in their T.V. rooms to keep them from sounding the alarm.

It was at this point that the plan began to unravel slightly. After raiding Maggie Mae, we did not return to Dakota, but instead made our way down near the cafeteria and hid behind a giant partition. It was quite a scene. Fifty guys in masks and bathrobes with girls' underwear on their heads and bras hanging from around their necks. We were trying to suppress our laughter to avoid being detected, and were thus far successful. The problem was that we were *too* efficient; we were way ahead of schedule. We had about twenty minutes to wait before heading to our meeting in Spalding Hall.

"Hazel," Sharkey said, "we cannot stay here for twenty minutes; we'll get caught."

"I know."

"What are we going to do?" asked Art.

After a few moments, I hatched a quick amendment to our plan: "We'll go to Quad Two; we'll raid Magers Hall." I said it like a challenge.

Indeed, raiding Magers Hall would be a challenge. Magers was across a large snow-covered field. But that was the least of our challenges. Quad Two hated Quad One, where we were from, and invading Magers would certainly unleash the dogs of war with the entire quad. But Magers was the closest Quad Two dorm and was an all-girl athletic dorm. It was bold, and it was daring, and it was perfect for leaving our mark stamped in the annuls of Dakota House. At the suggestion, there were a couple moments of contemplation, and then we all looked at each other with sinister smiles and Sharkey said, "Let's do it."

Quickly and quietly, I gathered everyone as close as possible and gave these instructions:

"Ok guys, we're WAY ahead of schedule. If we stay here, we'll surely get caught. We're gonna go to Magers and then head over to Spalding for our scheduled meeting." There was the sound of muffled laughter, and everyone knew that this was going to be unprecedented. I continued, "I'll let you in the end door, go up to the second floor, raid the first house, and then go down the middle laundry stairwell and hit the first floor house as you head back toward me." It sounded. simple, a blitzkrieg on two unsuspecting houses deep in unfriendly territory and then a hasty retreat back to safe ground.

I continued, "Everyone got it?" I canvassed the mob of anxious eyes and devious sneers for any questions; there were none. Then finally I said, "Let's go!"

"Follow Hazel!" yelled Art, and we fell into a ragged line headed toward Magers Hall.

As we filed past the double doors of the cafeteria, I noticed they were propped open. This was unusual at night, and I threw a glance into the cafeteria. I saw my Resident Director and several R.A.'s in some sort of meeting. I had the unsettling thought, "Am I supposed to be in there?" What I didn't know until later was that they immediately recognized that Dakota was up to no good, adjourned their meeting, and put a general call out to the campus that "Dakota is on the rampage!"

As we approached Magers Hall, I ran forward and opened the end door, and the rabble scrambled up the stairs toward the second floor. Knowing that if I got caught leading a panty raid in Quad Two would probably cost me my job, I stopped at the door into the second floor and watched the boys go about their business. As I watched, I noticed the door of the closest room was partially open. I could clearly see the dim lights of a stereo playing soft music. I was overcome by temptation and darted into the room and began rifling through the top dresser drawers, where most girls kept their underwear. Suddenly, I heard the voice of a girl shout, "What the hell are you doing?" And then a male voice, "Hey you . . ." I didn't hear the rest of his sentence as I laughed, "Don't be alarmed! I'm just stealing your underwear." I had stumbled into a romantic moment between a couple and wasted no time to see if I knew them. I grabbed handfuls of undergarments and bolted out the way I came and down the stairs to the exit.

Time dragged by, and I started to feel like something had gone wrong. I could hear the muffled thunder of feet running on the second floor and then eventually sprinting, men laden with more apparel racing toward me. The first guys were laughing uncontrollably, but those who followed looked more panic-stricken and even angry.

"What happened? Why did it take so long?" were the questions I was shouting at passing raiders.

Someone hollered back, "There's no middle stairwell in this building; we all got bottled up in the middle of the second floor, and then they started to come out after us!" As he spoke, I saw the last stragglers hustling my way with a mob of angry women close behind. Now these weren't your average girls. These were field hockey players, basketballers, and softballers. It seemed to an individual they all carried a bat, a stick, or a broom as they tackled the laggers one by one.

"Poor bastards," I said aloud, watching these rough girls engulf them like a swarm of angry ants. But then I saw more were still coming with their sights set on those of us watching near the exit.

"Holy crap," I exclaimed, "let's blow this pop stand!" We ran out into the middle of the snow-covered field we had just traversed ten minutes earlier. The entire Dakota raiding party was gathered together when the doors of Magers Hall flew open, and a stream of angry women, with whatever weapon they had grabbed, came right out in the snow after us. Most had on nothing more than slippers, robes, and twisted angry faces. It was an understatement to say they were pissed! When I realized we were not safe, I yelled, "Head for the woods!" We all trudged through two feet of unbroken snow toward a small clump of trees that separated the quad from a parking lot. When we reached the safety of the woods and looked back, the irate women were still in hot pursuit. As impressive as it was, I was not prepared to be caught or beaten by a bunch by women in slippers. Suddenly, I realized everyone was looking at me.

"What now, chief," I heard Tommy's rough voice ask from the mob.

"Every man for himself!" I hollered. I continued as we started to disperse in every direction. "Hide the underwear, don't get caught . . . and get back to your rooms!" I purposely did not yell out Dakota House for obvious reasons. I knew exactly the route I planned to take. It was a long, round-about trek, but I knew I could avoid getting caught if I made it happen quickly. As I took off, I heard a kid named Scott, one of the nicest guys in the house, say, "Follow, Hazel, he's not gonna let himself get caught!" And he was right. Three guys fell in behind me as I headed the long way around the four dorms of Quad One, through a parking lot, and eventually toward the middle stairwell in the back of Halverson Hall. These were the stairs whose non-existence in Magers Hall spoiled our lightning attack and the same ones that Art and Sharkey used to smuggle kegs to their room every Friday. I had to round one last corner before I would be in shot of the stairwell, and just before making that turn, I stopped and took a deep breath and calmed myself. Then slowly and casually, I walked around the corner as if on a nightly stroll. As soon as I cleared the corner I saw three figures walking toward me: a Quad Two director and two R.A.'s from Magers.

I learned later that one of these R.A.'s, a small girl named Nissett, tried to stop the Magers raid. They were having a meeting in a conference room and had not been reached with the alarm. At hearing all the commotion in the hallway, they all emerged from their meeting. Nissett, seeing the hoards of masked men pillaging her house, took a stance in the middle of the hallway, raised her hand like a policeman halting traffic, and yelled "STOP!" at the onrushing young men. She was unceremoniously run down. Needless to say, Nissett was angry and motivated to catch the perpetrators of her insult.

I hesitated and looked at the door, only several feet away. They looked at me, puzzled, and I realized they did not recognize me because I still donned my MacArthur costume. We stood and stared at each other for a moment, wondering what was next. What was next was three idiots running full tilt around the corner and smashing into the back of me like the three stooges. At this, I wasted no time and bolted for the door. I heard Nissett yell, "Get 'em!" It was too late for them to get me, and I scrambled like a ninja up the three flights of stairs to Dakota House. I learned later that of the three behind me, two retreated back around the corner and into the night, but Scott had fallen and was nabbed.

As I opened the door to Dakota, Ed was standing by his room, the first room, looking like a casual tourist and sporting his trademark cigar. Without a single word, I blew past him and into his room. He followed me in and closed the door. I was stuffing all the loot I was carrying into the cushions of his couch while nervously laughing, "That was close!"

Ed handed me a beer and said, "You can lay low here for as long as you need to." Getting into Dakota House and into Ed's room was a relief, but this room was the absolute furthest from mine, and I knew eventually I would have to make the attempt to get there.

After about forty-five minutes, I told Ed, "OK, you get the door, I am just gonna zip down the hall as quickly as I can."

"OK, chief," he said.

"I put you in charge of that contraband; I never had it, and you never saw me with it," I instructed.

"Right," he answered. I nodded, and Ed opened the door. I walked out and made the turn into the long hallway toward my room. Immediately, I ran into the director of Meyland Hall who was calmly walking the length of Dakota House with an R.A. from the first floor of Magers. Meyland was another Quad Two dorm and shared a close relationship to Magers. Suddenly, I realized I still had a captain's hat on and was holding the horse crop.

I passed them and nonchalantly asked, "Come to see how the better half lives?"

He only said, "Busy night, Hazel?"

"What?" I asked, trying my best to act innocent.

"Where are all your guys? It's like a ghost town up here." the R.A. said.

"I don't know," I answered quizzically. "I was just asking Ed that same question; he doesn't know either."

They continued to grill me as I slowly kept walking backwards away from them, like I was going somewhere with a purpose,

"Have you been in Magers tonight?" they inquired. Sarcastically I answered,

"Who in their right mind would ever go to Magers Hall?" With this, I turned and wasted no time getting into my room. My phone was ringing and when I answered it, I received an immediate scolding by the R.A. from Déjà Vu. I simply hung up on her. Straight away, the phone rang again. This time it was the R.A from Spalding, "What happened to you guys tonight? Did you forget we had a meeting?"

"Sorry, can we reschedule?"

"Not on your life!" came the unexpected response. "I got a warning call from Wally about you guys, and we locked our doors." She continued, "You're in deep shit, Hazel."

Wally was the Halverson director, my director, and he was in the cafeteria when we passed the doors headed out to raid Magers. He had been around a few years and recognized instantly what was happening and who was doing it; and he sounded the alarm. I found later that the ONLY building they couldn't reach on thc entire campus was Magers Hall! Magers was having a staff meeting in a conference room that did not have a phone! When I learned of this later, I just laughed to myself and thought, "What are the odds of that?"

For the rest of the night, my phone kept ringing with angry women on the other end. Dakota was eerily quiet. Every so often, I would hear the door by the stairs squeak open, followed by the sound of heavy feet running to a room, the jingle of keys, and the slam of safe refuge. Then, silence once again.

The next week was filled with hilarious stories of young men escaping the clutches of angry women and the authorities sent out to stop them. Poor Scott, perhaps the least mischievous guy in the entire house, took the fall for the rest of us after he got caught ten feet from the laundry room door. When it was all said and done, he was the only member of Dakota who actually had any written report attached to his record. The last slow guys who did not make it out of Magers paid in beaten bodies. They were the objects of ridicule for the rest of the year, but truth be told, none of us wanted those amazons to get a hold of us. Most of the men from Dakota were not caught with any items stolen from any girls' houses and so denied any participation in the raid and escaped any sort of punishment. Sharkey, Pete, and Tommy were even confronted by Wally as they casually walked through the commons area by the cafeteria.

"Where are you guys coming from," asked Wally.

"The library," said Sharkey, as he patted his backpack of stolen underwear like it was filled with books.

"Then why are you sweating?" Wally challenged.

"Studying makes me nervous," he said, and they boldly walked on.

"Riiiiigghhtt," said Wally in a drawn out tone of disbelief, "you don't even know where the library is," but he let them go.

Every night for two weeks, groups of girls paraded through Dakota House to see if their underwear were draped on Dakota's Christmas tree. But the tree remained conspicuously bare. Very smartly as I made my run to avoid capture, Art had rallied most of the guys, and they stashed all the stolen loot in the back of his pick-up, which had a topper over the bed.

A faction of the panty-raiders: Ed (back left), Pete (center with fist raised), Sharkey (center right with fist raised), Tommy (far right), Scotty (back right). Front row left to right: Kurt, Darren, 'Stats', Jim, and Art.

During the weekly staff meeting, there was an uncomfortable silence in the conference room. As I perused the agenda, item #10, the last item on the list, simply read, "Panty Raid . . . SCOTTY !!" When we reached that place in the meeting, the two R.A.'s from Maggie Mae and Déjà Vu exploded on me for not only participating in the raid, but apparently leading it! At this, I offered my defense: "The guys were going to do the panty raid with or without me; I was only there to make sure it didn't get out of hand." In spite of the fact that my colleagues cried hogwash, that slim defense actually made some sense and probably saved my job, but not in Dakota House. I got reprimanded and had a blemish on my record as an R.A., but we all stuck steadfast to that story, and I lived to serve another day. At the end of the year, that is spring 1981, I was informed that the following year I would be an R.A., not in Dakota, but "up" campus in Carey Hall. Carey Hall was the oldest building on campus and essentially the "old folks" home of dorms. It was filled with seniors and foreign students who did not want the distractions of lower classmen dorms; they were serious about finishing their programs and graduating. This relocation was surely the result of the panty raid, and I had no choice but to accept it or resign my position as an R.A. Being an R.A. had its dilemmas and sleepless nights, but it paid for the majority of my schooling and had nice perks; I did not want to give that up. I decided to take the university up on its offer to put me out to pasture in Carey Hall.

The week before Christmas break, we decided it was finally time to decorate our poor naked tree. Everyone dispersed and retrieved the loot they had stolen nearly two weeks earlier, and we strung them all over our tree, fulfilling the tradition. Just one night later I was up very late with Scott, of all people, watching M.A.S.H. Suddenly, the T.V. room door burst open, and about a dozen enraged girls rushed in. Several jumped on me and Scott and held us down while the others grabbed all the underwear off the tree and stuffed it into garbage bags. Then they systematically wrecked our T.V. room and stuffed the tree out the third-floor window before leaving. After they left, Scott and I both lay on the floor, laughing. I finally got up and looked out the window. It was snowing hard, and three floors down I saw our broken Christmas tree lying in the deep snow. The final chapter of the last panty raid was in the history books, and I slid the window closed.

COMPASSION

CHAPTER 35

With the exception of the panty raid and a few other antics, I was in a state of constant depression. The bombshell Karen had dropped on me was taking its toll. Karen and I had several conversations, but it was plain to see that things had changed. To myself, I reasoned, "She's just dating a guy." I decided that dating wasn't necessarily the death knell of our relationship. Perhaps it was just an obstacle, and I still felt confident that in the end, our love would win out, and our promise would be fulfilled. I was not going to give up; I just needed to hang in there. But for the moment, I was a wreck, and close pals like Sharkey knew it, and he decided to take some action.

Unknown to me, one day Sharkey approached Becky in the cafeteria and asked, "Do you mind if I sit down?" Becky was surprised but courteous and answered, "Sure." Becky and I had only spoken a little since her visit with the cookies. Mostly, the conversations were meaningless pleasantries, and Becky had rebuilt her wall of protection. As big and menacing as Sharkey appeared, down deep he was a softy and a guy who could be counted upon. He also possessed incredible manners and debonair when speaking with women. Becky was unsure why he wanted to sit with her but was suspicious that perhaps I had sent him. She soon found out that was not the case.

"How can I help you?" she asked with a hint of sarcasm.

"Did you know Karen broke up with Scotty?" Sharkey replied plainly.

There was silence and a sudden look of contemplation on Becky's face. She was not expecting to hear this and had stopped abruptly, staring at her plate without saying a word.

"No, no I didn't," she finally acknowledged.

"Yeah," Sharkey continued, "about a month ago; the night he decided to tell her about you."

Becky looked stunned and then biting her lower lip, stared at her food for a few seconds more. "That's crazy," she said quietly, like she was talking to herself, and Sharkey was not there.

"Yeah," Sharkey continued, "it changed him . . . he's puttin' up a good front, but he's havin' a hard time." Sharkey said everything matter-of-factly while calmly eating his lunch.

Becky said, "You know I saw him one night, and he looked totally out of control." She continued to confide in Sharkey: "I know he's a little rough around the edges, but it seemed so uncharacteristic." Becky was putting everything together, like lost puzzle pieces finally found. "Why didn't *he* tell me?" she asked.

Sharkey responded, "How could he? Think about his predicament; Karen breaks up with him, and then he comes runnin' to you?" Sharkey added, "How would you have felt about that?"

"I see your point," she said. "Did he send you to tell me this?" she suddenly asked with suspicion.

Sharkey leaned back in his chair and placed his hand flat on his heart. "No ma'am, I am here on my own."

"I heard about the panty raid," Becky added. "That's going to get him into trouble for sure."

Sharkey smiled, "We protected him; he'll be ok." There was a long silence while Becky tapped the handle of a spoon on the table and bit her lower lip in deep thought. Sharkey, feeling like he accomplished his mission, picked up his tray of food and said, "I just thought you should know," and he walked away.

That same evening, I was in my room, with the door hanging wide open as usual. I was sitting in my rocking chair listening to the stereo. It was dimly lit by lamps, not the harsh overhead globe. I always liked it a little moody, a thoughtful atmosphere I liked to call it. There was nothing out of the ordinary when the knock came at the door. "It's open," I said loudly over the music. When I looked up, I was shocked to see Becky with a plate of cookies.

"May I come in?" she asked with a soft voice of compassion.

I stood up awkwardly and answered, "Sure."

My room was not a mess, but you could sure tell someone was living there. I quickly grabbed the loose clothes that were lying around and tossed them into the bathroom.

"Don't worry about that," Becky said.

I pulled the chair away from the cluttered desk and offered it to her. "Here, have a seat," after which I turned down the music and sat back down in the rocking chair. Becky had set the plate of cookies on the desk and really didn't even offer them. I realized she was here for something other than sharing cookies.

"How *are* you?" I asked.

"I'm fine," she answered. How are *you*?" she bounced the question right back.

"Oh, I'm OK . . . got myself into a little hot water, but I think it'll pass."

"Yes, I heard about that . . . panty raid, huh?" She had a faint smile on her face when she asked. "I didn't think those existed any more."

"Yeah, well . . ." I left the thought unresolved.

There was an uncomfortable silence, and I was wondering when all the small talk would end and the real reason for her visit would come out. Becky looked around the room silently for a few moments, then asked, "Where are all your pictures?" I did not answer. "Your picture of Karen is gone," she said flatly. She continued to look around and finally asked, "Where's your rug?"

All I could do was look at her. Eventually, she returned my stare, and we sat there pondering what each other was thinking. At last I said, "I put it all away." I did not want to admit to her what had happened; I did not know that Sharkey had already filled her in on the details.

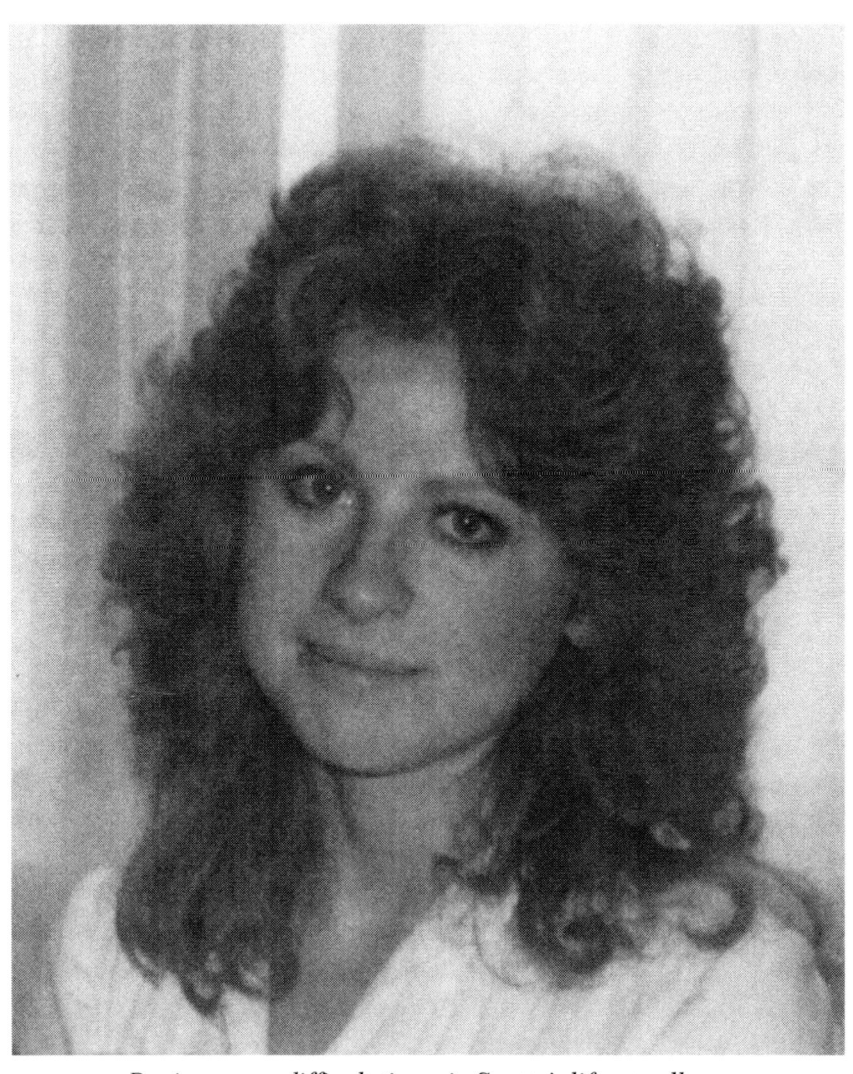

During many difficult times in Scotty's life at college, Becky became a close friend, romantic interest, and a constant example of living a virtuous life.

Becky kept up the leading questions: "Why did you put them all away?"

Then something clicked, and I realized that somehow she knew. There was no sense in tap dancing around it now. I let out a long, drawn out, exasperating exhale as if I were blowing out candles on a birthday cake and answered, "Karen is seeing someone else." I was looking at the floor when I said it.

After a few moments, Becky confessed, "I know. Sharkey told me."

I shook my head, "Man, *that* guy."

"He's just looking out for you."

"Yeah," I said with little smile, "he does that."

"I'm sorry about Karen," Becky said unexpectedly. It was strange because Becky's accidental discovery of Karen put the skids on any feelings she might have had for me, yet now she was sorry that Karen had broken off our relationship. It wasn't that Becky was catching me on the rebound, but the true compassion of her Christianity and her genuine feelings, hurt as they were, was why she was sitting there. I was ashamed and humbled at the same time.

"*This* is what walking the talk is," I thought. When I finally looked up from the floor, Becky was biting her lip and looking at me with sympathy and forgiveness. I squinted my eyes and smiled at her and said, "You're quite a piece of work, Becky." She smiled, knowing that as unpolished as that phrase was, it was a compliment of the highest order.

"Well," she said with a new sense of ease, "you're a nice guy; I hate to see you down."

"I don't know about *that,*" I replied.

"Well, you *are* a bit of a stinker, but your heart is in the right place," she said. I laughed that she used the word "stinker."

"Stinker!?" I joked, "how old are you?"

"Now that's not very nice," she said with a smile. The conversation had eased the tension, and I was grateful she had paid me a visit. We talked for a while, and eventually she got up to leave.

"Don't forget your cookies."

"No," she said, "those are for you."

I walked her to the end door of Payne Hall and parting, said, "Thanks, Becky, that was very nice of you."

She pulled the hair back that had fallen across her face, looked up with her blazing blue eyes, and bashfully bit her bottom lip and then replied, "Oh, that's alright, it's what friends do."

As we stood staring at each other, nothing further was said, but a strange tension filled the air.

"I had better go," she finally said.

"Okay," was all I said as I slowly nodded.

Then as she was leaving, she turned her head over her left shoulder and said, "You can visit me if you'd like," and walked down the hallway with her stately posture. I think as I watched her walk away, I actually scratched my head in puzzlement. This was an interesting turn of events. "God," I thought, "what are you up to?"

I went back to my room and sat on the edge of my bed, digesting everything that had just happened. I looked out my window into the courtyard. It was beginning to snow, and the lights illuminated white whirlwinds of snow. It reminded me of the storm that almost snowed Karen in during her visit a couple years earlier. But those memories were painful now; the wounds were fresh and the future uncertain. My world had changed. But it didn't matter, for that evening when I looked out the window, it wasn't Karen I was dreaming about: it was Becky! I wondered if God had placed her in my life to save me from myself. One thing was for certain: Becky was an amazing young lady.

LIMBO

CHAPTER 36

My family was surprised that, for the first time in years, there was no visit to Texas and no visitor coming from Texas over the long winter break. Instead, I made the forty minute drive to South Lyon to visit Becky several times. Having Becky in my life was like rubbing salve on a wound. We were not in a relationship per se, but we found that we really enjoyed each other's company. I got the feeling that she was sort of a home body with few friends and little, if any, romantic interests. This was surprising because without a doubt she was beautiful, and her hair was like a magnet for attention. What typically happened was once a guy talked to her long enough to discover she was unwavering in her Christian walk, he was unwilling to try and cross the moat she built around herself. Especially if after all their efforts, they discovered a self-imposed chastity belt. A lot of guys in college do not want to spend any time with a girl who is saving herself; they want a bad girl, and that was certainly not Becky. Her isolation was because of her reputation . . . her good reputation. In spite of her caution and defensive walls, I had managed to get close to Becky. I was not scared off by Godly women; in fact, I knew they were exactly what I needed. But I was in a state of rebellion and if Becky was going to turn me around, she had her work cut out for her.

I had come to understand that aside from God, family, and school, I was the only excitement Becky had. She was content with that, but when I forced myself into her awareness, I became a firework in her calculated life, and she liked it. She understood the depth of the relationship that Karen and I had developed and was not about to get tangled up in my chaos. Nevertheless, she spent a lot of time helping me understand what it meant to live as a Christian. At times, I almost felt like she had taken me on as a project to fix, and as hard a nut as I was to crack, I was grateful that she cared.

She was a very pleasant person to spend time with and possessed a surprising sense of humor to balance her serious side. I jokingly called her a prude whenever we differed in opinion on something, and she would smack my arm and say, "I am NOT a prude!" We were so different, but somehow very compatible. Everything she did was beyond reproach and always seemed to be the correct thing to do at the time. When she heard of some of my adventures, she just shook her head in amazement and said, "I could never do that." She enjoyed it when I encouraged her. "Yes you can, Becky, you might surprise yourself." Whenever talk flirted with her feelings or if I complimented her to a point of embarrassment, she would bite her bottom lip. It was an endearing little quality and cute beyond words. Once I told her, "Do you know how beautiful you are?" It wasn't really a question, but pointing out a fact, a fact that somehow eluded her. She just looked down and modestly bit her lower lip.

"Do you know you do that?" I asked.

"Do what?"

"Bite your lip when you're nervous or embarrassed."

"I guess I do, don't I?" she said in a manner like it was a flaw.

"It's one of the little things I like about you, Becky," I said. "Don't ever stop doing that . . . it's very cute." It was one of those times I had visited, and we were sitting on the hearth in front of the fireplace in her living room. There was a silence and that sense of connection in the air. "You're a dreamer," she said. It was a statement that came out of the blue.

"Yeah, I've been accused of that many times," I agreed thoughtfully.

"It's what I like about you . . . and what scares me about you the most."

"I can understand that."

"What are you going to do?"

"What do you mean?" I asked.

"With your life—what are you going to do?"

It was a tough question that forced me to think beyond a few weeks or months. "That's a good question," I responded. Then I began to say what I felt down deep, things I had not even shared with Sharkey. "I feel like my life is in limbo . . . so many things seem unresolved. I have to resolve all the questions before I can move on . . . I'm in limbo," I stated again.

"You need to resolve your life with God," said Becky with no hesitation. She continued, "I know you have Him in your heart, but you don't live like it."

"I know," I agreed. Then I added, "First, I have to go back to Texas."

Becky turned and was looking at the fire. "I know . . . you're a dreamer."

She silently watched the flames and began to bite her lip. In that moment, I could tell she was wishing Karen was not an issue, that we could concentrate on whether or not there was anything to "us." I broke the silence: "What are you thinking, Becky?"

She let out a heavy sigh, then drew her lips tightly together, as if she wasn't sure she wanted to say what she was thinking.

"What?" I persisted.

Then without looking away from the fire, she said, "I wish you didn't have to go to Texas."

I didn't know how to respond, there was just awkward silence hanging in the air. I wasn't sure if she would let me, but I reached out and took hold of her hand. Neither of us spoke. She just continued to stare into the fire, and I looked at some random spot on the rock hearth while I held her hand. Eventually and reluctantly, I said, "I have to go get this figured out."

"I know," she said in frustration. "That's why I am so mad at myself for letting myself like you so much." As she spoke, I saw a single tear glide down her cheek. This caught me off guard, and I had no reply. We simply sat together quietly in emotional agony.

The rest of that year Becky and I continued our conversations and muddled through our unrequited relationship. When summer came around, I said the difficult farewell and headed down to Amarillo. I also had bid farewell to Dakota House and mentally prepared to move to Carey Hall when I returned the next autumn. Before I left Flint, there was the annual emotional visit from Babe. The status there remained unchanged. I told her everything that was going on and as usual, she was miffed that I was giving another entire summer to Texas. Her devotion scared me a little, but now that Karen and I were unsettled, I wondered if I should consider learning more about Babe. Between Karen, Becky, Babe, and Indiana Deb, life had turned into a ball of confusion. But the overriding truth was that I wanted to find a way to get Karen back. That hope took precedent over anything and everyone.

Once again, I holed up a few blocks away from Karen in the Casa de Warren apartments. Once again, I found Lloyd and continued to learn the trade of building houses. I was learning what it took to be a carpenter. Once again, I continued to give God very little leverage in my life. Becky, however, had me thinking . . . hard.

LaVisa

Chapter 37

The summer was moving along as planned. Karen and I bumped into each other a few times, and I had even stopped by her house to visit her family on occasion. It was difficult to see them now that the romance with Karen was on the rocks. Still, my presence alone was testament that I had not given up hope, and I always made sure they knew I was there. Karen and I met several times to talk, but there was no reconciliation. The conversations were difficult for both of us, and even Karen had second thoughts about giving up on five years invested into us. It wasn't just Karen who had touched *me* so profoundly, but I had done the same to her. I put on a determined face but always left broken-hearted. It all made me realize that I had not been a very good boyfriend, even from across the country. I never thought the different worlds in my life—Flint, N.M.U., Indiana, and Amarillo—would ever meet each other. Not only did they meet—they collided with each other, crashed, in fact—like a giant car accident with hurt people strewn everywhere. I was always under the impression that the novelty of our romance alone was enough, but in that misconception, I neglected the little everyday things that make or break a couple. In this case, this arrogant attitude and unfaithfulness broke us. Still, what we had was powerful and sincere; I couldn't imagine how this guy, whoever he was, captured Karen's heart from me. I had also neglected my faith but still had the audacity to think God would not let this romance end. I was holding out hope, waiting, living in limbo.

Early in the summer, I was getting my hair cut and, of all places, I noticed a poster taped to the mirror of the girl cutting my hair. It was a flyer advertising tryouts for a local semi-professional team for anyone who had played soccer.

"Why is that flyer in here?" I asked.

"Oh, the owner of the salon is putting a soccer team together," she said smartly as she continued to snip away. She could see I was rolling the information around and asked, "Are you a soccer player?"

"Actually, I am."

"Would you like to meet Antonio?" she asked as she poised the scissors.

"Who is Antonio?"

"He is the owner; he's the guy putting the team together . . . he's in the back right now; I can go get him." I thought about it for a second and finally said, "Why not."

The girl walked through the maze of chairs of people getting haircuts and perms and stuff and shortly returned, leading a sharp looking guy with shoulder length hair.

"Hello, my name iza Antonio," he said as he extended a hand. He had a thick, unmistakable Italian accent.

"My name is Scotty," I replied, and shook his hand.

"Are you a footballer?" he inquired right away. Knowing that every place else in the world except the United States, football was soccer.

I answered with a hint of pride, "Played all my life, including college in Michigan."

"Well, I gotta tryouts in a couple weeks; why don'ta you come and we see ifa you can play?" When he said this, he handed me his business card and a flyer from a stack on the counter.

"Okay, I'll see you there." He smiled and turned to leave, saying, "Chao," as he walked away.

Two weeks later, I went to the tryouts for the Amarillo Challengers. Antonio's dream was to form a team that would become a farm-club for the Dallas Tornado. The Tornado was one of the teams making up the young North American Soccer League. This was America's first attempt at a professional league that might, ultimately, compete internationally and be the catalyst for players to participate in the World Cup. These were huge ambitions, but at the time, playing soccer at this level interested me.

There were hoards of people at the tryouts, and I have to admit, I was intimidated. It didn't take long for me to realize that I was the only American present. Most of those showing their soccer skills that day were Mexican, African, Vietnamese, and a handful of Europeans, including Antonio. It seemed the only language not being spoken was English. I was in my own country and felt like the outsider.

In spite of the stiff competition, I was selected to play for the Challengers. It was an interesting team to play for, and Antonio made sure we had the best of everything: uniforms, food, transportation, and groupies, mainly from his hair salon. On the field, we were, at best, a mediocre team. The only whites on the team were Antonio, who was a great goalkeeper; Johannes Verkampt, a stunning Dutch scorer who looked like a Norse god; and me, the speedy left-winger with dangerous headers. The bulk of the squad were Mexicans, who always seemed to end up fighting with each other, and Africans, who also squabbled among themselves. It became really interesting when the Africans and Mexicans argued with each other; no one could understand a thing! Antonio, Johannes, and I would simply stand back and let the chaos play itself out.

My best memory as an Amarillo Challenger came in a game versus the Dallas Sidewinders. At this time, the soccer rules allowed players to pass backwards to their own goalkeeper's hands to relieve any threat by the opposition. I recognized this play developing during our match and sniped it; that is, I waited until just the right moment, when the defenseman was making this pass to his keeper, and I cut between them, collecting the ball as I went. This allowed me to calmly tap the ball into an empty net just before it rolled out of bounds. Later in the game, I scored a second goal with a crackerjack shot from twenty yards out. We lost the game 4-2, but I proved to all the foreigners on our team that this American could play the game. Perhaps the best part of the whole day was that Karen was in attendance. She had heard that I was on the Challengers, and at my invitation, she came with some friends to watch. I only played two years for Antonio, but in the coming years, it was a nice addition to my resume. The North American Soccer League only lasted a few years, and with no team to feed, the Challengers folded.

In the meantime, the friendship with my boss, Lloyd, was growing. One day, quite unexpectedly, Lloyd told the crew that we needed to find something else to do for the coming week. He was going to Mexico with a crew to do some work in a remote village. Right away, Frankie and Earl began to devise plans involving drinking, smoking, and carousing around. Watching their gears turn about the coming week made me wonder what I was going to do for a week without responsibilities. I thought about Lloyd's announcement for the rest of that day. I knew that if I stayed in Amarillo for a week with nothing to do and feeling like life had dealt me a poor hand, I would blow a ton of money and probably end up in jail. At the end of the day as we finished picking up all the tools, I lingered until everyone else had gone. Then I approached Lloyd. "What is it you are doing in Mexico?"

"We're working on a school in a very remote village."

"Do y'all need any help?" I asked with the faint Panhandle dialect I was developing.

"Why, would yew lahk to go?"

"Ah was thinking about it. Could you use another hand?"

"Sure," said Lloyd, "but it's quaht a trip . . . it takes two days hard drahvin' just t'git thar. And Ah cain't pay ya; this is a mission trip."

He seemed a little puzzled why I would give up a week's vacation to go work in the Mexican desert for no pay. I could see he was trying to understand it, so I spelled it out for him plainly, "Listen, if Ah stay up here with nothin' to do, Ah will surely end up in trouble. Besides, Ah've never been to Mexico . . . it sounds lahk an adventure."

"Oh, it's an adventure alraht . . . OK, pack yer tools and a small bag and Ah'll pick yew up Saturday morning at 7:00."

"Thanks, boss, Ah'll be ready."

When Saturday arrived, I was ready and waiting when Lloyd pulled his diesel work truck into the apartment parking lot and picked me up. I wasn't even sure of all the details, but I was looking forward to the unknown. Silently, I wondered what Becky would think of this. I remember her poignant words, "You're a dreamer." I started to wonder who else would be going with us. I had envisioned ten or twelve carpenters, cement workers, plumbers, and electricians.

Eventually I asked, "Who's going with us?"

Without really answering the question, Lloyd just said, "We're pickin' 'em up just up here." After a few more blocks Lloyd turned the truck into the parking lot of a giant church.

The named carved above the Romanesque pillars read, "San Jacinto Baptist Church." I was shocked to see dozens of vehicles and mobs of people all buzzing around. I wondered what all the activity was until I spied a line of six or eight very rugged looking vehicles receiving most of the attention. One big truck was attached to a long flatbed trailer stacked with lumber. Another enclosed trailer was being loaded with tools of all kinds. I saw women loading food and clothes in yet another trailer. Two men were struggling to load what appeared to be a dentist chair into the back of a truck. I didn't know what all these folks were doing, but I was looking for Lloyd's work crew. It dawned on me suddenly that all these people *were* the work crew.

I looked at Lloyd, "Are all these people going to Mexico!?"

He had a wry smile pasted on his face and only said, "Yup."

I looked back out my window and said, "Oh, God, Baptists . . . what have I gotten myself into?"

Up North, I had very little interaction with Baptists. I had only gotten to know any Protestants at all through Young Life, and most of those were non-denominational or Lutheran, like Joey. As an Irish Catholic who liked his beer and to shake it on the dance floor, Baptists were the epitome of religious people too strict for their own good. Lloyd pulled his truck into line behind the others. Immediately a bubbly girl about my age ran up to the window and greeted Lloyd with one of the thickest drawls I had ever heard come out of a young girl: "Boy howdy, Lloyd, how are yew?!"

They exchanged some pleasantries before Lloyd directed her attention toward me and introduced us. "LaVisa, this is Scotty. He is one of mah hands, and he asked to come along."

"Son, it is so nahce to meet yew," she said with unbridled enthusiasm. "Mah name is LaVisa." Before I could even get a word out, she continued, "We're gonna have a big tahm in Ol' Mexico!" and she turned and ran off.

"Good grief," I said to Lloyd, "she makes me tired."

"Yea, she's a little fahrball, but she has a heart of gold."

When everything was packed and a prayer was said, the convoy rolled out from San Jacinto. At the last second, LaVisa came running up and asked, “Can Ah ride with y’all nail drahvers?”

Lloyd said, “C’mon, hop in.” I opened the door, stepped out, and let LaVisa ride between us. During the long ride, LaVisa did most of the talking. She was a short, cute girl with a face full of freckles, even more than what Becky had. She was exactly my age and had a wide grin and piercing green eyes that sparkled when she spoke. She sported a pony tail, had a solid athletic body, and was a tom-boy through and through. But more than anything, her love for Jesus was blatant and undeniable. Without apology, she brought into focus anything that was not worthy of a Christian. Not thinking twice about it, Lloyd and I put in a tape of music we listened to while on the job. I don’t recall what it was, but ten seconds into the first song LaVisa said, “Good honk, d’y’all actually listen to this!?”

“Yea, what’s wrong with it?”

“It’s garbage, that’s what’s wrong with it,” she said straight out. She rummaged around in a bag she had brought with her and produced a tape of her own. “We cain’t listen to this junk,” she said, and without asking just ejected Lloyd’s tape and popped in hers. It was the first time I heard Keith Green’s amazing contemporary Christian music. I looked out the window and thought, “If Becky could see this, she’d be laughing herself silly right now.” LaVisa used the hours of driving to share what she knew about striving to live a life worthy of being called a Christian. She was what believers called a person who is “on fire.” During the long ride, she and I also learned a great deal about each other. One thing I discovered about LaVisa was that she had a giant sense of humor. Mingled in with serious conversation about spirituality was a great deal of laughter.

The time in Mexico was a humbling, eye-opening experience. We did not drive the convoy through customs at any border check, but directly through the Rio Grande at the back of an enormous ranch. The closest border crossing was about seventy-five miles further west at El Paso, so the “River Ministry,” as it was known, had special permission to cross at this point. We drove for miles into the mountains of the Chihuahua frontier until we reached the tiny village of Corrales. There was no water or electricity, and all the work we did was done by hand. I drew a lot of attention as that young hand who came with Lloyd. I was twenty-three, strong, and in the Mexican sun, my Indian skin was as dark as the Mexicans'. No one knew from where I had come, but they appreciated the help, and they made me feel welcome. Through the course of the week, they showed me that there was a giant world beyond what I knew. My problems seemed insignificant, especially compared to what these poor misplaced villagers endured every day. In watching these Baptists work selflessly for people they did not even know, it revealed to me that I had placed God in a box and had not done much in His name. I felt humbled.

Lloyd (right) in the village of Corrales, Mexico with a village elder.

By the time we returned to Amarillo, I had made many friends with people who, frankly, I had avoided before. LaVisa and I had made a connection, not romantic or anything of that nature, but as friends. At her invitation, I began to attend San Jacinto Baptist Church. Had my Catholic family known this, they may have come down to Texas to try to rescue me. I remember the first time I entered San Jacinto; it was like violating a taboo. It was a cavernous building with white pillars and sky-blue walls. There was no crucifix and no altar, just a barren cross and a platform with several chairs and a podium. I felt like a fish out of water, but LaVisa and a few others from the River trip sat by me for support. When service began, they sang uplifting praise choruses combined with a couple of hymns. The men who occupied the chairs on the stage were dressed in slick suits, not robes like a priest, and were surprisingly fairly young. I wasn't sure who they were or what their role with the service was until a sharp young guy in a neat suit arose and began to deliver the sermon. I was shocked and uncomfortable at the lack of decorum. Suddenly, I had a flashback to my first Young Life meeting. It was so similar in experience that I almost laughed out loud. I recalled how Joey sat next to me as LaVisa did now, and how this young guy, Reverend David Walker, began to preach a message much the same as Dale Moore had done years before. It was uncanny in similarity. The spiritual doors that were opened by attending San Jacinto were as unexpected and timely as those opened through Young Life. It was like pouring water on a parched plant, and I slowly began to reverse my fall from grace.

BOTTOM OF THE BARREL

CHAPTER 38

I returned to Northern and took up my new residence in Carey Hall. Although we were scattered around the N.M.U. campus and city of Marquette, the Dakota boys still made time to hang out. Becky and I had regular conversations and occasionally would go out together. It was obvious that there was something special there, but until I could resolve my relationship with Karen, a more serious relationship with Becky was not possible. I still felt like I was Becky's project, but I also understood that she was not just trying to lift me out of my gutter to feel good. She had developed feelings for me, and she was cautiously investing her heart in my spiritual reclamation. She was making headway, but admittedly I was a reluctant student of the truth. My life was enigmatic; on one hand, I was a Christian and genuinely understood that God was there for me, whether I sought Him out or not. On the other hand, I was rebelling against God for allowing my fairytale relationship with Karen to implode.

In the middle of my emotional acrobatics, I was trying to carry out my duties as an R.A. and hold down a full load of classes. Truthfully, neither were going very well. The greatest casualty was my art degree. Trying to hit due dates on art projects was a monumental task that I rarely achieved. I was within a single semester of completing a degree in art and could not close the deal. I was adrift in emotional turmoil.

In the meantime, I had managed to bring a taste of college delinquency from Dakota House to the upper classmen of Carey

Hall. I discovered that age had no monopoly on acting immature. There were many, like me, in Carey who were also sorting out their lives and were perfectly willing to drink hard in vain attempts to ease their dilemmas. In fact, it may have been easier to drink our problems away at Carey than in Dakota since everyone was an upper classman; therefore, everyone was of legal drinking age. We became known as the "Carey-holics"; a moniker we embraced. Also, it became common knowledge that this was the last year Carey would house students; it was to be converted into offices the next school year. The university had been very clever in figuring out how to get rid of me without making it a scandal. No other dorm would want to hire me after my antics in Gries Hall, Dakota House, and with Carey Hall closing down, I would have nowhere to go. When it came time to retire Carey Hall from service, it then would be time for me to go. I was always given credit for the good things I had done in Dakota, mainly bringing it back into prominence on campus. I also was praised for breathing life one last time into Carey Hall, but it was obvious I had run my course as an effective R.A.

All was not negative; however, I managed to leave a legacy at Northern. In the five years I attended N.M.U., I never lived off campus, and three-and-a-half years of that time was spent as an R.A. At least five guys who I know of from my time in Dakota House became R.A.'s in dorms around the campus. I'd like to feel that my example as their leader was a factor in their decision to pursue these positions. The names of these Dakota born R.A.s that I remember include Art Miller, John Hopkins, Jim Anderson, Clint Burnette, and Steve Auger. Through the course of the last couple years in Dakota and Carey, Steve and I became fast friends. The night he was informed that he had been hired, we all celebrated with a kegger . . . in his room. Stupid. It was supposed to be a quiet affair, but in the end, the party was discovered and before he even started his new job, he almost got fired. Thankfully, and in the spirit of Dakota brotherhood, a suite-mate took the rap and saved the day and Steve's job.

I also knew my academic days at N.M.U. were numbered. So, much like resurrecting the traditions of Dakota House, I decided Carey Hall also had to go out with a bang. It was from these thoughts that I decided to sponsor a road trip to watch the Northern football team play North Dakota State in North Dakota.

On the Friday before the game in North Dakota, we skipped our classes and boarded an R.V. we had rented from a local dealership. The passenger list included students from Dakota, Carey, and Gries Hall. Pizza Joint, the pub we frequented the most, donated a full keg of beer for the trip. This was because we hung a giant sign on the side of the R.V. which read:

N.M.U. Carey-holics
North Dakota or Bust!
Sponsored by: Pizza Joint

I volunteered to drive first because I knew after a couple of hours I would be in no shape to drive. This turned out to be the wisest decision I had made the entire weekend as the keg was empty by the time we hit the Wisconsin border. When Sharkey announced that the keg was empty in such a ridiculously short time, I remember thinking, "There are some serious drinkers on this bus!"

At one point while driving, I looked in the rearview mirror and saw Art go into the bathroom. In my head, I calculated the time it would take to go through the motions of him standing in there relieving himself. When I was satisfied that I had him at a disadvantage, I began to swerve widely back and forth across the two-lane highway. Everyone could clearly hear Art yelling, "STOP IT! STOP IT!" and could also hear him crashing against the walls and door of the bathroom. Without warning, the door exploded off its hinges, and Art tumbled out with his pants down. In the midst of the uncontrolled laughter, it was determined my time of driving was over.

I took a seat in the back of the bus and proceeded to drink from the cases of beer we had brought in addition to the Pizza Joint keg. The next thing I knew, we were causing trouble in a pool hall in Duluth, Minnesota. The barkeep told us he had called the police and that if we knew what was good for us, we'd get out of his bar. At this, we wasted no time in scurrying to the R.V. and racing out of town.

I'm not sure who got us there safely, but when we grudgingly awoke in the morning, we were in the parking lot of the North Dakota State University football stadium. When I rummaged around to find something to eat, all I found were cases of cheap Schmidt beer that someone bought when we passed through Fargo. So at 9:00 a.m., we all began to drink on empty stomachs. We managed to drive around and find some breakfast at McDonald's, but it was too late to effectively counter the early drunk we had begun. We were the first fans in the stadium and took up a prominent position in the first row of seats behind the North Dakota bench. We were obnoxious beyond reason and increasingly built the rage of the N.D. State faithful who had filled the stadium seats behind us. When N.M.U. won a close game just before the time on the clock expired, we were approached by a security guard, who said, "If I were you guys, I would hop the wall and leave here with your team; you may not make it out of here alive if you try to go through the crowd." As he spoke, I looked behind us and saw throngs of North Dakota fans staring at us—the unruly drunks from N.M.U. who taunted their players the entire game and insulted their school. You could tell by their demeanor that they were probably going to jump us on the way out.

"Thanks for the head's-up," said Sharkey, "We'll take you up on that offer." We all quickly hopped over the wall and ran out to meet our team as they headed toward the locker room. This got us close enough to the parking lot to make our escape.

We followed the football bus until it arrived at the Holiday Inn in St Cloud, Minnesota. We found a remote corner of the parking lot and set up to spend the night. We had several friends on the football team who came out and drank, smoked cigars, and played cards with us. Later in the evening when we realized we were hungry, we went into the hotel and ordered pizzas to be delivered from the room of Chip Shezpansky.

Chip was a giant middle linebacker whom we all knew from Halverson Hall. He reminded me a lot of Kyle from Amarillo; they even looked remarkably alike. The main difference was that in place of Kyle's thick Texas drawl, Chip had the heavy vowels of a Pollack from Eau Claire, Wisconsin. When the pizza arrived, Chip opened the door, shoved the delivery boy away from the cart that held six or seven pizzas, grabbed the pizzas, and slammed the door. The kid began banging heavily on the door and we began to devour the pizzas.

"We *are* gonna pay that kid, right?" I asked.

"Ignore him," Chip said calmly as he crammed another piece of pizza into his mouth.

"Oh, c'mon, really?" I asked again.

I could see that this was raising the ire of Chip. He finally said, "Fine, I'll pay him!" He rose with purpose and quickly opened the door that was still being pounded on by the delivery boy. He grabbed the flimsy cart, smashed it against the wall, and threw it over the railing into the swimming pool below. All this happened while he was holding the delivery boy at an arm's length with a single outstretched paw. Chip then calmly turned back into the room and slammed the door and said, "There, the bill has been paid." I felt bad for the kid, but I was not prepared to confront Chip on the matter any further. He was in an ugly mood.

This old photo was taken just before the 'Carey-holics' boarded a rented R.V. bound for North Dakota. Back row: Art, Gina, 'Stats', Mark, Sharkey, Scotty, and Brett Kneeling: Darcy and Mike. On roof: Tom

The next day as we pointed the bus toward Michigan, I found myself in the familiar position with my arms folded, looking out the window and watching the country pass by. I was reviewing the road trip and the life that was waiting for me back at N.M.U., neither of which were very positive. It was a melancholy trip with the autumn of the North Country assisting me into the foreboding mood. Weighing heavily on my mind were my classes, Becky, and Karen. None of these situations had an easy solution. One thing I knew for sure was that there were some tough decisions ahead. I also knew that pulling my Christian walk together would have been the best first step—Becky reminded me of this constantly—but I simply could not make myself do it. I think I was upset with God, and like many, I decided to take matters into my own hands. This is a typical mistake that only leaves God with no choice but to make you need Him more. Things were only going to get worse.

That afternoon, when we arrived back in Marquette, we had to clean and repair the rented R.V. in order to get our deposit back. Generally, the entire bus smelled of spilled beer and nasty cigar smoke. There was a torn cushion and a missing screen. The biggest job was re-attaching the bathroom door that Art had crashed through while I was driving. Art and Stats did most of the work and returned it to the dealership; we did not get our deposit back.

That Christmas, I returned home as a young man whose life was in a state of chaos. Most people did not realize how much emotional baggage I was carrying around. Outwardly, I just seemed to be a typical rowdy college kid who liked to have fun. On the inside I was barely hanging on. I was like a captain navigating dangerous seas, hoping to come through unscathed in the end. But I always felt a foreboding that if I didn't do something soon to get my life on an even keel, something would do it for me. Even though I knew this, I persisted to sail near the rocks with my life listing perilously close to disaster.

One night I took my parents' van, so my sister Tammy and I could go out to the Light to dance. On the way, we picked up several of Tammy's high school friends. I was the cool college guy, and I reveled in the attention I was getting from all these young girls. We stayed until the club closed at 2:00, and I drove them all home. Being the only one old enough to drink, I was probably the last person who should have been driving that evening. After all the girls had been dropped at their homes, Tammy and I headed for home. Suddenly, I opened my eyes and realized we were going to crash into the guard-rail. I tried to brake and steer away, but it was too late. I had passed out behind the wheel and crashed my parents van on the expressway. Tammy hit her head hard on the dash board and was bleeding badly. Somehow, all of this had instantly sobered me up, and no one at the scene, bystanders or police, ever accused me of driving while intoxicated. I waited at the hospital as the doctors attended to Tammy until my mother and father arrived in a panic. I had called home and said, "Dad, I got into a wreck, but we are all right."

"Where are you?" he asked calmly.

"At the hospital . . . Tammy is getting stitches."

"We'll be right there."

When they arrived, my dad simply asked, "Are you OK?"

"Yeah," I said ashamed, "sorry."

"What about Tammy?" my mother quickly interjected.

"She cut her head on the dash board. She's okay, but she needs some stitches."

Now that they knew we were okay, and they relaxed a bit, my dad asked, "What about the van?"

I sat down and stared at the floor. "It's totaled, a complete loss."

"I knew this call would come someday," said my dad while slowly shaking his head. "You've been asking for trouble for a long time."

At this, I had no reply; he was right.

My dad drew in a heavy sigh and said, "Well, we can replace the van; we can't replace kids." I looked away as tears welled up in my eyes. I did not want them to see me cry. Then in true Ray Hazel style he added an old saying that perfectly fit the moment, "Sooner or later you gotta pay the fiddler for all that dancin'".

I looked out the window and thought about how lucky we were, how lucky *I* was! I wondered how horrible this might have been had the crash happened before I dropped off all of Tammy's friends. I thought about what might have happened if I hadn't awakened and steered away at the last moment; what might have been the result if we had slammed directly into the guardrail without any last second attempt to slow and avoid the crash? "I could have killed my little sister," I agonized.

The accident was on my mind for the rest of my vacation and after I returned to Northern. The first morning I awoke at N.M.U. I lay in bed staring at the ceiling, contemplating all the possibilities. I took a long shower and let the water run on my head. I had a brief recollection of that last night at Castaway, how utterly lost I felt after Karen had left, and I let the shower pour on my head until the water got cold. The memory was bitter-sweet, and I did not dwell on it long; I had more serious issues at hand. The school year had been a disaster. Although it was quite an experience, the trip to North Dakota was nothing to be proud of, I was struggling with my classes, and I narrowly averted tragedy while home for Christmas. As a young Christian, I had de-railed. "What are you doing to yourself?" I asked out loud. I knew I had reached the bottom of the barrel and lectured myself, "You cannot go on this way . . . something *HAS* to change." This was the moment I decided to take a year off from school, return to Texas to work, and find a way to mend my relationship with Karen. This moment was a fork in the road, and I knew I had to choose wisely.

I don't think I ever told Becky about the accident; I was too ashamed. It was difficult to keep hidden, since the accident had resulted in my losing my license for ninety days, but somehow I managed to conceal it. I had accumulated a pile of points on my driving record from speeding tickets; the accident put me over the limit. My license was returned to me just in time for my summer trek to Texas.

Becky knew I was once again heading to Amarillo, and she kept encouraging me to get my life straightened out. Being around Becky was, perhaps, the best thing I had going for me at this point in my life. She was always there to remind me what was *really* important. In spite of my fall from grace, she never gave up on me. She was my constant reminder that, good or bad, Christianity is about living by faith; a person has to continue to be faithful, even when things are not going well. Even though we had found an obvious fondness for each other, Becky understood the issues which I needed to resolve and patiently, without conditions, gave me the space to deal with them. I don't think she was too happy about it all, but she understood it was necessary. She was resolving an issue in her life as well: what to do about me. Only her faithfulness allowed her to let me go, so that, God willing, I would someday return. It was an interesting irony that I was hoping Karen and I could reconcile, while Becky was praying we would fail. Perhaps even more interesting, both she and I knew what was on each other's minds, yet we managed to stay connected until events played themselves out.

When June rolled around, Deek and I set sail for the Panhandle, only this time I drove my Fiat, and he was the passenger. Only time and the will of God would tell if I would return or stay in Texas. Knowing that I did not plan to return to N.M.U. gave the departure an entirely different feel. The future was uncertain and no one—Becky, my family, or even me—knew when I would be back. It was an open-ended venture with no guarantees. When Deek and I drove down my street, I sighed a giant breath of uncertainty and proclaimed, "Well, here comes the rest of my life," and the trip began.

THE FARMERS' DAUGHTER

CHAPTER 39

Deek and I decided to make our journey a memorable one. I had been in contact with Indiana Deb, and together we had made plans to stop and pay her a visit on the way to Texas. We had kept in contact since we met at Smith-Walbridge nearly six years earlier but had never seen each other since then. She lived deep in southern Indiana, a trip that took an entire day. On the way down, Deek and I took back roads and stopped at every small-town hardware store, collecting painter hats which displayed local names and logos. It was a cheap way to keep track of our trip, create memories, and see the Midwest off the beaten path. It took us a while, but we finally tracked down the rural route address in Brookeville, Indiana, where Deb's family farm, the Stenaker farm, was located. We drove up the long, ascending driveway until the farm house came into sight. A blonde figure sitting on a porch swing arose, and with a beaming smile, met us in the drive. It was Deb, the friend from years gone by who had never stopped writing letters to me. It was like a reunion of friends who had a lengthy history; in reality, we had only seen each other for a five-day stretch at summer camp. More accurately, we were more like pen-pals. Our correspondence had helped us know each other far beyond our short introduction, and we greeted each other with a giant hug and unexpectedly, a tender kiss on the cheek.

"I like this," she said as she placed an open palm on my closely cropped beard stubble and rubbed it up and down.

"You look fantastic," I replied, and she did. She was tan and even prettier than the day we said goodbye at Smith-Walbridge; the years had, indeed, been very kind to her. Seeing her in her own element, everything she had tried to describe to me in letters suddenly made sense; she was truly a farm girl from a part of America I had only read about in history texts.

I introduced her to Deek, first by his real name and then his nickname. She introduced us to her mother and younger sister, Sharon, who had emerged from the house to meet these crazy boys from up north. After spending time catching up, Deb and her sister gave us the tour of the farm. It was large, much larger than I had imagined from descriptions in her letters. Even though it was a working farm, her father had a job working at the local hydro-electric plant. Times had gotten tough for farmers, and he had been forced to work off his land to make ends meet.

We were shown a guest room, which had been prepared for us to stay the night, and then told to relax while the three women began to fix dinner. While sitting on the front porch discussing our day, a pick-up lumbered up the drive, and Deb's dad slid out of the cab. Deb came from the house and greeted her father with a hug and a kiss on his cheek, then led him over and introduced him to us. "Daddy, this is Scotty. We met years ago at Smith-Walbridge Camp, and this is his friend Kevin." I hadn't heard anyone use Deek's real name in a long time, and I could tell since she used it, that Mr. Stenaker was a no-nonsense man. Deek and I took turns stepping forward and shook hands with Mr. Stenaker. Although he was mildly gruff, Mr. Stenaker was also very cordial. As he made his way for the front door, he pleasantly said, "You boys are staying for dinner, right? The Mrs. and my girls are wonderful cooks; you'll not want to miss their meal."

"Yes, sir," I answered. "If you've got a couple extra chairs, we'll stay."

"Daddy," Deb chimed in, "they are spending the night with us."

"Good," he said as he disappeared through the door, "It will be good to hear another male voice around this place for a change."

"That went well," I turned and said to Deb. "I was a little nervous about meeting your dad."

"Yes," she said, "I was a little nervous too. I can tell he already likes you; that doesn't always happen." Then she continued, "We'll be calling you in shortly; dinner is almost ready," and she went into the house.

"She really likes you," Deek said suddenly with a bit of a laugh.

"Well, of course she likes me; we've been writing each other for years."

"No," Deek rephrased it, "she *likes* you, likes you."

"Naw," I disagreed, "she and I are just good friends. I really only know her through letters."

"No," Deek said emphatically, "I'm telling you, she *likes* you!"

The debate ended when Deb cracked open the front door and hollered, "Dinnertime!"

Dinner was like going back in time; the men all sat while the three women, mainly Deb and Mrs. Stenaker, waited hand-and-foot on us. There was a lot of pleasant conversation and questions for me and Deek to answer. I found myself doing most of the talking. Occasionally, I flashed a look at Deb and noticed she was hanging on every word. A couple of times we locked eyes for a few moments and she sent me a gentle smile from across the table. It was one of those looks that could not be mistaken. Internally, I said, "Good grief, Deek is right . . . she *likes* me, likes me!" Instantly, the evening had an entirely different potential than I had ever considered. For that night, everything in the rest of my life was put on hold and was barely in my consciousness. At Deb's farm, I felt as if I had been plucked out of reality and landed in this surreal slice of past Americana.

After dinner, Deb, Sharon, Deek, and I were sitting on the front porch enjoying sharing stories and having laughs. One thing was for certain: Deb loved my sense of humor, and it took little work on my part to make her crack-up. It was good to hear the mild southern dialect of southern Indiana, and Deb spoke it with a subtle allure. While we shared time on the porch, Sharon suddenly rose and said to Deek, "Would you like to see the pond; it's really pretty out there at sunset?"

Deek promptly got to his feet and answered, "Sure, let's go," and they walked off together talking.

It was a suspicious departure that suddenly left me alone with Deb on the porch swing. The conversation became more thoughtful, and that old familiar romantic tension hung in the air. To my surprise, neither the little Scotty with wings nor the little one with a pitchfork appeared on my shoulders; I was on my own. If my struggling Christian convictions were sending me warning signs, I was ignoring them. That evening, Karen and Becky were relegated to another planet while I spent time with Deb. It was actually a relief to step out of my many dilemmas and let Deb and her corner of the world soothe my troubled life. I did nothing to keep it in check; I let the night flow as it willed.

Deb drew both her legs up and crossed them Indian style as she turned and sat sideways in the swing, facing me. At this point, the conversation turned personal.

"Are you still going to Texas to see that girl?" I had told Deb about Karen several years earlier in a letter, and occasionally the topic would surface in our conversations. She knew Karen's name, but she always referred to her as "that girl in Texas." This always indicated that she did not like hearing about the girls in my life; I think she liked to feel exclusive, which made me feel special. In the same way, I never asked her about the guys in her life; ours was a relationship that existed all by itself in its own little world. I don't think either of us ever thought it would develop into anything other than the faithful writing of letters. So, I was taken aback that she brought up Karen so abruptly.

"Well," I started, "sort of."

"Sort of?" she asked. "That doesn't sound very convincing."

"It's not," I agreed, "it's gotten complicated."

"Can I ask how so?" she persisted in a sincere tone.

"Well," I slowly began, "she has been dating someone else for a while now."

"Let me get this straight," she said in disbelief. "She's seeing someone else, and you're still going down there?"

"I know it sounds stupid, but I have to know if she and I are *really* through; we had quite an amazing relationship, ya know," I said defensively.

"I didn't mean to offend you," Deb said apologetically.

"No, no, I didn't take it that way; I didn't mean to be so short with you. It's just been a difficult year," I breathed out in an exasperated manner. There was a silence until she asked, "So what have you been doing; I mean have *you* been dating too?" It was a fair question that I wasn't sure how to answer.

"Well, I've gotten sort of close with this girl named Becky," I admitted. "We're not really dating, just kinda hanging out with each other."

"Does she know about Texas?"

"Of course she knows; I wouldn't lie about something that big." I felt a little insulted that she thought I would lie about it but was flush with guilt since I did, in fact, try to keep Karen a secret from Becky in the beginning. "I told *you*, didn't I?" I wasn't sure why I added that, but I did.

"What does *she* think about you going down there?" she asked.

"She actually has been encouraging me to get it all figured out, so she knows where she stands."

"What!?" Deb blurted out spontaneously. "Let me get this straight: You're going to see a girl in Texas, who is dating someone else, while there is a girl waiting back home to see how it all plays out?" The simplification of the complicated situation made it all sound ridiculous; I felt embarrassed at how stupid it sounded. I looked at Deb and said, "I guess that is correct; sounds kind of stupid, doesn't it?" She smiled a little smile and shook her head and simply looked at me and said, "You are either a hopeless romantic or the biggest flirt I have ever known."

"Yeah, my dad says I always do things the hard way. I think he might be right,"

"Mr. Hazel, sir," she said with an animated tone of properness, "you are some kind of dreamer."

"Hah," I chuckled, "that's what Becky says scares her the most about me."

"She must be quite a girl," Deb added. She said it in a way that left me unsure if she was being sarcastic or actually paying a sincere compliment.

"Actually," I replied, "she *is* quite an amazing young woman."

Then after a few moments passed, she said, "And yet, here you sit with me." It shouldn't have surprised me, but it did. One thing I had learned over the years from all my correspondence with Deb was that she could be counted upon to be brutally honest and pragmatic about any topic.

"Yes," I finally answered.

"What?" she asked, not understanding the meaning of what I said.

"Yes," I repeated, "and now here I sit with you."

As I said this I turned, and we smiled at one another. Then without warning, she reached forward and took hold of my hand and said, "Well, I'm glad you are." Then much like Barb had said, "Let's go for a ride," in 1974, Deb stood, still holding my hand, and said, "Let's go for a walk."

Deb slowly steered us around the farm, and we continued to catch up on the lost years. Eventually, we ended up in the barn, and she showed me the different cattle in their stalls. As she showed me her favorite horse, she stepped up on the bottom rail of the wooden gate and leaned over the top rail, coaxing the animal to come closer. I stood behind her and put my hands on the top rail, one on each side of her and snuggled up close. I leaned my face forward on her left side, and our cheeks neatly pressed together. Based on the signals I was receiving throughout the evening, I felt confident that she would not resist this, but still there was that moment of excited uncertainty. My heart was racing, wondering what would happen next. My answer came when she reached back and wrapped her arm around my neck and squeezed our cheeks firmly together. There was only silence and two hearts pounding. After a few minutes like this, Deb twisted her head sideways, and I met her halfway; we kissed while I was still standing behind her, and she still stood on the gate. It was a magical fit, like we had done it a thousand times. Eventually, she turned herself around, slid down off the bottom rail and faced me. I still had both hands on the rail, and she stood between them with her back against the stall, and we continued to kiss. My head was spinning, and I felt much the same as I did with Barb: totally mystified by the developments as they unfolded, but totally happy to be experiencing them.

Suddenly we had company; Deb's horse had quietly joined us and pushed a large wet nose into the middle of our embrace.

"Maggie!" Deb yelled at the pretty sorrel-colored mare, and then we both began to laugh nervously at the interruption.

"That's alright, girl," I said to the horse as I ran my hand up and down the top of her long nose.

Deb grabbed my hand and said, "Let's go over here," and she led me several stalls down to one which was empty except for stacked bales of hay. Apparently, she was not finished with what we had begun. She unlatched the gate and pulled it open far enough for us to enter. She turned and kept stepping backwards, pulling me by both hands until we fell together into a cushion of hay. As she lay looking up at me, I could barely see her face in the dim light of the barn. Orange shafts of sunlight sifted through cracks in the old barn that created vivid stripes on the wall. For another half an hour, we continued our roll in the hay. Then I broke the mood when I began to laugh.

"What is so funny?" asked Deb as she pushed me away.

"So, are you the farmer's daughter?"

"What?"

"You know, like in all the stories and jokes—the farmer's daughter! This is *exactly* like the stories! Your dad is not going to come out here and kill me with a pitch fork, is he?"

Realizing how long we had been missing, Deb answered, "He might if we don't show ourselves soon . . . we had better at least go sit on the porch."

We straightened our disheveled appearance before walking out. When we emerged from the barn, we saw Sharon, Deek and both Mr. and Mrs. Stenaker sitting on the porch!

"Oh crap," I said under my breath, "they're gonna know we've been messin' around."

"Just relax and act like we've been walking the back lot."

"Yeah, but if you're wrong, your dad is gonna stick me with a pitchfork," I joked. Deb laughed, "Stop that!" and smacked my arm. We didn't go directly there, but let everyone see us strolling around. Eventually, we made our way to the porch and joined the others. The sun had just gone down in a fiery orange ball, and a purple haze hung in the twilight sky. It was a very pleasant evening. With all the seats taken, we sat next to each other on the step.

"How do you like the farm?" her mother asked.

"I really love it; I had no idea how beautiful it was going to be down here," I answered. Then in an attempt to quell any suspicion, I added, "We've been walking out in the back lot." I had no idea what the back lot was, but Deb had mentioned it, and I prayed that it was, in fact, beautiful. I felt relieved that they did not ask where we had been or what we were doing. As the conversation went on, I stole a peek at Deb and gave her a quick wink. She smiled and pressed her knee hard against mine.

"Well, we'll leave you kids to catch up," announced Mrs. Stenaker, as she and Mr. Stenaker rose simultaneously and headed for the front door. Goodnights were said all around, and Mrs. Stenaker said, "Don't stay up all night."

"We won't, mom," said Sharon.

Mr. Stenaker held the door open for Mrs. Stenaker, and she stepped into the house. He started to go in himself, then stopped short and turned back, "Debbie?"

"Yes, daddy?"

"You've got hay in your hair." No one said a word, and no one moved; that is until Deek coughed out a loud laugh he had been struggling to suppress. I felt numb with fear and turned and looked cautiously at Mr. Stenaker as Deb pulled at the hay stuck in her hair. He didn't seem mad, but I could clearly read the message in his eyes. Then, without another word he, turned and melted into the house.

"I'm a dead man," I said as I leaned forward and covered my face with my hands.

Laughing, Deb said, "If he were truly mad, you'd be runnin' for your life right now! I'm tellin' you, he likes you!"

We all had a good laugh, and I was hoping that her father would be gone for work before I got up the next morning. Against her mother's wishes, we did stay up nearly the entire night, all four of us. Before Deek and I drifted off to sleep, he said, "She made us leave you alone on the porch."

"Who did what?" I asked, not understanding what he was telling me.

He explained, "Remember when Sharon and I went for a walk?"

"Yeah."

"Deb gave us a nod; a silent signal to leave."

"Are you kidding me?" I exclaimed.

"Nope, she wanted to be alone with you."

"Well," I smirked in the dark, "she got her wish. That was a crazy night."

Deek replied with satisfaction, "I told you she liked you."

We managed to get a couple hours of sleep, long enough for Mr. Stenaker to leave for the power plant, but getting back on the road the next day was very difficult. Deek drove my car, and I rode with Deb to her apartment in Louisville. We did this to have a couple more hours to talk together. But finally the time came, and we said goodbye, uncertain if we ever would see each other again.

By that evening, Deek and I had made it as far as Henrietta, Oklahoma. We decided to find a bar and have a couple beers. Much to our dismay, we were in a dry county, where alcohol is not sold. I had encountered this before in Texas but had forgotten how common dry counties were in the South. It had been a long day, and we were intent on having a drink somewhere, so we kept asking around. Finally, a hand we asked at the gas station said, "I know where y'all can fahnd a beer, so folla me; Ah'm headed there mahself."

"Thanks, we'll be raht behind yew," I drawled out. Even though he was an Okie, it was good to hear what sounded like a Texas drawl, and I immediately began to assimilate back to Scotty Ray of Amarilla. He led us to a building adjacent to what appeared, at first glance, to be a racetrack. He was a tall dude with a cowboy mustache and wore an impressive gray Stetson. As we followed him toward the mysterious building, I thought about the disdain that existed between Texans and Oklahomans. Once, on a very windy day in Amarillo, I was trying to shag down some papers that were blowing across the job site. Franky yelled at me, "Don't worry about that! Tomorrow it will be in Oklahoma . . . with rest of the trash!" Everyone in earshot guffawed, and the ridicule was obvious.

The Okie knocked on the door and after a few moments, it cracked slightly open. There was some sort of quiet conversation taking place which ended with a woman, wearing heavy make-up and a long pony tail, peeking at Deek and me from around the door. Deek said, "I don't know about this, Scotty, it seems kinda shady."

"No," I whispered, "I think we're alright here."

There were a few more words between the Okie and the woman behind the door, and then he gave us a nod, and we followed him into the dark room. When our eyes adjusted to the dimly-lit saloon, it looked no different than any western dance club I had been in before. It was nearly empty, but you could tell by its immense size that it was a popular place. Deek and I sat down and started to drink cans of Lone Star. We thanked the hand that helped us gain entrance by sending him a drink. When he received it and the barmaid told him who sent it, he turned on the barstool and simply held the short glass in the air and subtly dipped his Stetson in our direction. It was a scene right out of a Louis L'Amour novel, and I said, "Deek, we are officially out West," and we tapped our beer cans together.

We stayed around for a couple hours, mixing it up with a few locals who curiously, but politely, tried to find out who we were and where we were from. Without warning, the door flew open, and an older cow-hand walked in trailing a rope behind him. On the other end of the rope, he led a giant bull into the room. There was a combination of laughter and people yelling. Deek and I couldn't believe our eyes, and we laughed uncontrollably at the absurdity of the scene. Everyone cleared the way as this guy slowly escorted the massive animal, all the while being yelled at by the pony-tailed woman who allowed us to come in. "Git that stinkin' animal outta here!" she kept yelling, but at the same time, she was trying not to laugh. We had taken a position next to the tall cowboy and I asked, "Who is that dude?"

"He ain't no dude; that's Jim Shoulders."

"Jim Shoulders, who's that?"

"Good Lord, y'all ARE Yankees, aren't you?" Then he told us, "Jim Shoulders was a world champion bull-rider, and he owns this place." Others who were close by took the liberty of telling us all the exploits and accomplishments of the famous Jim Shoulders. They were amazed that we had no idea who he was. One drunken cowboy kept repeating, "Jim Shoulders is a LEGEND . . . a LEGEND!"

This fuzzy old Polaroid captures the moment Scotty and 'Deek' posed on a bull in Henrietta, Oklahoma. Bull-riding champion Jim Shoulders is in the background on the left.

After a while, he was invited over to meet us. He was gray-haired with a set jaw and a mischievous grin. He had character in the lines of his face as he began to explain that we were in the bull-riding capital of the world. These people were full of pride, and they were insistent that we understood the importance of their world. At one point, Jim Shoulders said, "Let me show yew somethin'." He brought us behind the bar and threw several large switches. Giant banks of lights, like those at a football stadium, illuminated a rodeo arena right outside the windows of the saloon. It was what I initially thought was a racetrack. An endless stream of glory flowed from his memory. Then he quietly stared out the windows at the arena. He was a man reveling in his past, wishing he was twenty-five years younger.

Before we left, Jim asked if we wanted to sit on the big bull, which was still standing in the bar. "What?" I asked.

"Do y'all want to sit on the bull? He won't hurt you, he's docile . . . we'll take y'all's picture."

"Why not," I finally exclaimed after a few moments of self-convincing; and a cheer rose throughout the room. Jim pulled a chair over next to the bull and helped both Deek and me on the bull at the same time. Jim stood and posed next to us, and the barmaid snapped a picture. After a while, Jim finally heeded the urging of the pony-tailed lady and led the bull outside, but not before it deposited a massive pile of stinky, wet crap in the middle of the floor. The lady with the pony-tail was not happy. Not long after this, Deek and I left and found a rest area to sleep in until the morning.

I awoke early the next morning and began to drive. As I left Oklahoma in the rear-view mirror, Deek was still balled up, sleeping against the passenger door. I looked out the window and watched the grass-lands of the high plains roll by. In the silent ride, my mind was taking stock of everything that had happened. Most dominant in my mind was the reunion with Indiana Deb and the unexpected tour of her barn. In my head, I replayed every little detail I had experienced with Deb, especially the surprise romp in the hay, and smiled. I wondered if there were possibilities of something in the future with her if we chose to pursue it or if she was just enjoying the moment as I did. I knew the answer to my own question was to stay focused on why I was really returning to Texas: to reconcile with Karen. Thinking about Deb in any other way than I had for the previous six years would only throw a giant monkey wrench into the gears of my already messed-up life. "Don't even *think* about it," I scolded myself aloud.

"Think about what?" Deek's eyes were still closed, but he was awake.

"The farmer's daughter," I answered.

"I told you she *likes* you, likes you," Deek mumbled in a sleepy voice as he tried to reposition himself against the door.

As I closed the distance toward Amarillo, I could only wonder what lay ahead for me. Deek woke up, and we traded places. As he drove, I looked out the window and watched the prairie slowly give way to the scraggly mesquite trees and the yellow dirt of the Panhandle and drifted off to sleep.

FINALLY, RECONCILIATION

CHAPTER 40

Deek and I arrived in Amarillo and took up residence at the Casa de Warren apartments once again. Deek went back to work surveying for the oil company he had worked for the previous summer. I hunted down Lloyd, and he hired me back as a framing carpenter. The housing market had slumped since I left, and building houses with Lloyd was not going to be the same. I looked up some of my old friends, and the word quickly spread that Scotty was back in town.

The next Sunday I went to service at San Jacinto, and it was like a reunion. Perhaps the person most excited to see me back was the excitable, green-eyed LaVisa. I began attending a Sunday school class of young single people. In spite of all the poor decisions I had made in the last year, one thing I always managed to do right was place myself in the right company. Hanging out with these folks was a good way to try and get my Christian walk back on track; they would definitely be good medicine for my fractured life. The guys I befriended included Paul Wooden, a big, muscular guy; Jim Wier, a bull-rider from East Texas; Kevin Gambrel, a student at Texas Tech in Lubbock; and of course my boss, Lloyd Cunningham.

It was during this summer that I made the decision to get baptized. I had been baptized as an infant in the Catholic Church, as is expected of every Catholic. But baptism after, not before, a decision to accept Christ into your life is the hallmark of the Baptist Religion. It is one of several major points of contention that drive a wedge between Catholicism and Protestants. One Sunday, San Jacinto held an outside service at Sam Houston Park, just down the street a short distance. The main reason for this outside service was to perform several baptisms in the park swimming pool. My baptism was one of these. I finally had taken this step years after I had made my decision at Castaway. According to Baptists, it is the next necessary spiritual step but is only done at the request of the individual. It is the symbolism of the act of baptism that is so important to Protestants; that is the outward sign of an inward choice in front of witnesses. In Catholicism, baptism is one of seven sacraments expected and offered to Catholics. Baptism itself for them adds you to the membership of the church and into God's family; as a baby there is no choice involved. These are two very different perspectives on exactly what the act of baptism is. My family would surely wonder why I felt I had to do it a second time. Those in attendance celebrating my baptism that hot Texas day included Lloyd, LaVisa, Paul, Jim, and Kevin Gambrel.

I had immense respect for Kevin, and his counsel was something I always valued, plus he was simply a fun guy to hang out with. It was not long after my baptism that Kevin made a life-changing choice to join an organization called "Y.W.A.M." which people pronounced 'Why-wham' and stands for Youth With A Mission. After signing on the dotted line and completing a rigorous orientation, Kevin left for China to secretly evangelize under the watchful eye of the communist government. The next time I saw Kevin, he introduced me to another American he had met on the mission field in China named Barb. He was only home for a visit and was then headed back to China indefinitely with Barb. He tried, but in vain, to get me to get on board with Y.W.A.M., but I just did not feel "the call" as Christians say, to commit to that life. Don't misunderstand me; I contemplated it seriously. If nothing else, it sounded just like the type of adventure Becky always associated with me. And the dreamer part of me that scared her most was envisioning myself strolling down the Great Wall. I am not ashamed or guilty at not going into the mission field; it was something I did not feel was in my future. I felt that I would make my difference somewhere else. Within a few years, Kevin and Barb would return to the United States and be married. Kevin finished school at Texas Tech and became a teacher at, of all places, Tascosa High School.

In addition to Kevin and these other guys, I also found a friend in another young carpenter working for Lloyd named Chuck Irwin. Chuck spent much of his time working on and racing stock cars. He was a very funny guy who looked an awful lot like the rock singer, Billy Idol. I also paid a cordial visit to Karen and her family. It was good to see everyone, but the strange discomfort that filled the air was like greeting people at a funeral. My ulterior motive for the visit was to let Karen know that I was still willing to travel to Texas; I had not given up.

I also paid Antonio a visit, and he immediately invited me to fill a place on the roster of the Challengers. But more fulfilling than that was his invitation to assist him in coaching a local high school boy's soccer team. This was my first involvement in the world of coaching—the assistant varsity coach for Amarillo High School. I discovered I had a lot to offer and was good at developing positive rapports with teenagers. In addition, one of my major contributions to the team was translating Antonio's heavy Italian accent to the drawl laden high-schoolers.

Chuck and I were out country-western dancing with the local cowgirls one night at Graham Central Station, when I saw Karen at a table with a group of friends. I went over and asked her, "Excuse me miss, would you like to dance?" The guy seated next to her started to say something, and Karen put a hand on his arm and said, "It's okay," and she got up to dance with me. As I took her hand to escort her to the dance floor, the guy gave me a disapproving glare, and I shot back a sarcastic smirk and a wink. The dance I had with Karen was just that, a dance; I didn't try to bring up any serious topic or even act hurt, we just danced. Internally, it felt amazing to be holding her, and it was difficult not to feel like we were together as before. After the dance, I escorted her back to her table and never looked at her date, but I knew this had to be my competition from Texas Tech. The fact that she accepted and danced with me was a good sign; she just as easily could have declined and sent me back the way I came.

As the summer played out, I did many of the things I had done before: rode horses in Palo Duro Canyon, went on the River Ministry trip to Old Mexico with Lloyd and LaVisa, and swatted nails in the hot sun. I had also met a guy named David Roy who installed fireplaces and woodstoves; he was basically a stone-mason. His brother, Dan, was the youth pastor at San Jacinto, and they both played a mean guitar as part of the praise band. It was through David Roy and his brother that I first began to sing in front of the congregation and help out with the church youth group. When Dan asked for help from anyone brave enough to assist with high-school aged kids, I jumped at the opportunity; it was reminiscent of Young Life, and I wanted to be a part of it. David Roy often encountered carpentry problems with his work and was looking for someone to help him out. Since Lloyd's house contracts were dwindling, I began to work with David Roy. We eventually became partners, and I had a desk in the building he rented. Outside the sign read:

Fireplaces by Roy
&
Hazel Building Services

I had established myself enough to secure a business loan and purchased everything I needed to build on my own. It was exciting to be working for myself but also nerve-racking to be accountable for so much debt. Helping David Roy broadened the region in which I worked; it was not unusual to travel to Kansas, Oklahoma, Colorado, and New Mexico to work. Most of our work was still in Texas, but more and more we found ourselves installing fireplaces and doing building projects in New Mexico. We spent a great deal of time working on new houses in a developing ski resort named Angel Fire.

I spent the next year going back and forth between projects for Lloyd in the Panhandle and jobs for myself and David Roy in New Mexico. There was still building going on, but the market had slid downward, and the competition for construction work was intense. I was doing a little bit of everything and was forced to travel to pay my share of the bills with Deek. I spent the year becoming a better carpenter and even more adopting the lifestyle and culture of a Texan. Deek had also taken time off of college to save money and continued to work long hours surveying prospective oil fields.

As Becky continued to pursue her degree at N.M.U., she kept in constant contact with me. It was a relationship that, despite the complications and uncertainty of the "Karen dilemma," grew. During the Christmas break of 1983, she even paid me a visit in Texas. I was working on a house in Amarillo at the time but took time off, and we drove to Angel Fire to ski. The three-hour drive from Amarillo through Cimarron, New Mexico, and on to Angel Fire gave us ample time to catch up. There was little talk about Karen; she was the giant gorilla in the room of which we did not speak. We actually just enjoyed our time together and, for better or worse, grew closer. On the way home from our ski trip, I was surprised when Becky slid across the seat and nestled up next to me. I drove through a Rocky Mountain blizzard and where the mountains spilled out onto the plains, her head fell against my shoulder. I watched through the windshield as the dancing white chaos took me back to the night when Karen visited me in Flint. Silently, I shook my head and thought, "Man, I've got a serious problem, here."

Becky and Scotty skiing at Angel Fire, New Mexico

Being that I remained in Texas spoke volumes about my priorities, and Becky was skeptical as to whether or not there was any future for me and her. Nevertheless, she remained patient, hopeful, and above all, faithful. A few days after our ski trip, Becky boarded a plane and flew back to Michigan. Her visit was wonderful but only confirmed to me that I had some huge decisions in my future. Something had to give. She went back to school, and I went back to pounding nails. I finished the house in Amarillo in early spring and prepared to start a new job in Angel Fire.

Angel Fire, New Mexico, was a planned ski resort owned mainly by wealthy Texans. The closest established towns were Eagle's Nest in the valley to the west, the old ski resort town of Red River through the mountain pass to the north, and to the south, the cultural and art Mecca of Taos. In late April of 1984, I moved all my gear to a job site in Angel Fire and used a borrowed pop-up camper as home. I had purchased a work truck to haul everything and a motorcycle to zip around the mountains easily. I hired LaVisa's little brother, Lawrence, to be my helper. We were shocked the first morning in Angel Fire when we awoke to six inches of fresh snow and were surrounded by a herd of elk, which had come down to feed in the night. Angel Fire was a vast change from the Panhandle; it was mountainous, green, and smelled like sun-baked pine. The people were a strange mix of rich Texans, Native Americans, Mexican-Americans, and Vietnam veterans trying to get as far away from civilization as possible. In the midst of all this intrigue, Lawrence and I set about building a large cabin on the side of a mountain for a wealthy restaurant owner from Dallas named Bobby Dean.

One weekend, Bobby Dean, who flew his own small plane in an out of Angel Fire, offered to drop us in Amarillo on his way back to Dallas. It had been a few weeks since we had been home, so we accepted. While I was in Amarillo, I got an unexpected call from Karen.

"Hey, Scotty," she began, "it's Karen." I was shocked to hear her familiar drawl on the other end of the line. I covered the phone with my hand and mouthed to Deek, "It's Karen!" He silently flashed a double thumbs up sign to me with a giant, cheesy grin.

"Hey," I replied, unable to disguise my surprise, "how are you?"

"Ah'm fahn," she said in that same voice that captivated me at Castaway. I was hanging with anticipation on what she might say next.

"Can Ah come and see yew? Ah'd lahk to tawk to ya." I couldn't believe my ears.

"Certainly, Ah'd love to have a chat," I answered enthusiastically. "When?"

"Well, if yer not busy, can Ah come over now?" Again, I couldn't believe how fast this was all happening.

"Sure, do you know where Ah live?"

"Casa de Warren, raht?" she asked. I was impressed that she knew.

"Yeah, that's raht, apartment 243."

"Alraht, Ah'll be there in ten minutes."

"Great, Ah'll see ya then."

"Okay, g'bye," she said, and hung up.

After we hung up, I quickly began to straighten up the apartment while telling Deek, "Oh good gravy, that was Karen, and she wants to talk!"

"About what?" asked Deek.

"Ah don't know. She just said she'd like to tahk to me." I could hardly contain my excitement. "Ah knew if Ah hung around long enough she would finally come to her senses." I was frantically buzzing around picking up clothes and empty cans while narrating to Deek what was bouncing around in my mind. "We had been through too much," I reasoned, "and we had made a promise to each other!" I stopped suddenly like a soldier coming to attention and stared at Deek, "Maybe this is finally reconciliation!" It was half statement half question; at any rate it was hopeful.

When I was satisfied the place was presentable, I simply sat down and fidgeted with my fingers until a knock came at the door. I opened the door, and there stood Karen, no different than any time when we were together.

"Hey, c'mon in," I said, and she stepped into the apartment. "Can Ah get you something to drink?" I asked.

"No thanks, Ah'm fahn," she said softly.

"This is Kevin, my roommate from Michigan, but everyone calls him Deek."

"Howdy," was Karen's short acknowledgement, along with a little wave. We sat down and began a measured conversation about trivial things. There was an uncertainty in the air, but I knew it would be that way. I had no expectations of simply picking up where we had left off without some awkward moments, and this was surely one of them. After catching up on small talk for a half an hour or so, she said, "Well, Ah have to go, but Ah just wanted to see how yew were getting along."

When she said these words, I almost wanted to cry. I held my composure and calmly said, "Aw, Ah'm holdin' my own," and smiled.

Then, just to make me even crazier, she asked, "Can yew walk me down to mah car?"

"Oh, sure," and I walked out of the apartment with her.

I don't remember what we talked about on the way through the apartment complex, but I know we had a nice conversation all the way to the parking lot. It was here that she abruptly stopped walking and said, "Ah have to tell yew somethin'."

We happened to be standing in front of my car, and I backed up and leaned on the fender and replied, "Sure, what's on yer mind?"

There was a long pause, and I couldn't wait to hear how she was going to broach the topic of reconciliation. Finally I said, "Karen, it's OK, it's me; yew can say whatever is on your mind."

She was looking at the pavement, building up her nerve, when she finally took a deep breath and looked up at me: "Ah'm getting married."

My countenance suddenly changed, and my whole world seemed to spin out of orbit. She looked at me with the saddest face I had ever seen on her, and my eyes began to well up. I could not find any words, just stood there staring at some random spot in the distance. Eventually, a tear streamed down my face. Seeing this, she stepped forward, reached out and put her hand on my folded arms and said, "Ah'm sorry to tell yew lahk this, but Ah didn't want yew to hear it from anyone but me." I hopped up and sat on the hood of my car and tried to gather my emotions.

"Ah didn't see *that* comin'," I finally struggled to say. "But Ah do appreciate that yew thought enough to tell me yerself . . . thanks."

"That's alraht," she said with a sad smile, "yew at least deserved to hear it from me." Then she continued, "Ah will never forget what yew and Ah had; it was very special." Her attempt to soothe my heart only forced another tear to race down my cheek; I was really struggling to take the news with dignity. Suddenly, I had a flash of reality explode in my mind. "What am I *doing* down here!?" I posed to myself.

I finally gained control and said, "We really have some kahnd of story, don't we?"

"Yes, yes we do," she agreed with a tender smile.

"This gah better treat you raht; he'll have to deal with me," I said forcing a smile.

Karen grinned at hearing me use the word 'guy' with a Texas accent. "Remember when y'all called us 'gahs' at Castaway?"

"Yew have no idea," I said flatly, implying how much I had thought about that day in 1976.

She was glad that I had tried to lighten the mood and responded to my original statement, "Don't worry about me; he treats me well."

There was an uncomfortable pause until Karen said, "Ah'm sorry, Scotty, but Ah have to go. We're having a gathering of friends at Graham Central Station t'naht; Ah have to get ready."

"That's OK, Ah have things to do, too," I vainly said, trying to show I wasn't as hurt as I was. I slipped down off the hood of my car, and with no apologies, hugged her tightly. Once again, the finality of what was happening struck me, and tears ran down my face. As I backed away to leave, I tried to hide how emotionally wrecked I was and saw that she, too, had a tear ready to fall from the edge of her eye.

"Goodbye, Karen," I said with a trembling voice. "No matter what happens, Ah will always love yew." At this, her tear let go and dropped straight down, making an instant dark stain on the pavement. I stepped forward and kissed her on the forehead.

"Goodbah, Scotty. Ah will never forget yew." I let her go and walked away.

I entered the apartment and Deek asked, "Well?"

"She's getting married," I answered with gritted teeth and slammed my bedroom door behind me.

For the rest of the afternoon, I sulked and tried to get a handle on what had happened and what it meant for me. One instant question was whether or not I was going to remain in Texas. As much as I had assimilated to the culture and had established friends and work, the foundation of my living in Texas was to be near Karen. Her pending marriage left no room for hope, no reason not to go home. Still, I had found a church that was good for me, friends who offered solid Christian fellowship, and was basically running my own building company. Maybe there was more to living in Texas than being near to Karen. Right away, it was obvious that I had a difficult decision ahead of me.

As I digested Karen's visit, I decided to accept it with my usual flair for the absurd. Much like I had masterminded legendary exits in both Dakota House and Carey Hall, I decided the end of the amazing relationship that Karen and I had forged was valid cause to go out with a bang. Inadvertently, Karen had told me her plans to meet with friends that evening at Graham Central Station. I decided I would also be there and leave Karen's life on my own terms.

I waited until I felt the time was right and went alone to Graham Central Station. Like most patrons of Graham Central, I was decked out in my boots, jeans, and cowboy hat. This was a place to country-western dance, and whether or not you were a cowhand, dressing the part was almost required. In the dim dance hall, I strolled around until I spotted Karen and her party of friends. All of the sudden, I heard a familiar voice, "Scotty, what are yew doin' here?" It was my friend from Sunday school class, Kevin Gambrel. Kevin and I were exactly the same age and had shared many serious conversations about many topics, including Karen. He was one of the guys living a faithful Christian life whom I tried to hang around as much as possible. I was hoping that being near him, and others like him, that their faithfulness might rub off on me.

"Ah don't think you'd understand," I replied in a loud voice, trying to be heard over the music. Through our conversations, he knew the entire story about me and Karen. He knew how we met, how we fell in love, the promise, and finally about the split.

"Well, actually Ah maht," he said.

"What do you mean?"

"Are yew here because of Karen?"

"How do you know that?" I asked, puzzled that he knew before I had told him.

"C'mere," he said, while steering me to a corner where we could hear each other better. "Ah haven't been totally honest with yew," he started. "Karen's fiancé is my best friend; he and Ah were roommates at Texas Tech."

"You can't be serious!" I bawled out. "You mean you have known all about this saga from the other side too?"

"Yeah, Ah'm afraid Ah have. Ah'm sorry, but Ah did not know how to tell yew."

I thought about it all for a few seconds, "That must have been killing you, having friends on both sides of the same drama."

"Yeah, it wasn't much fun, Ah gotta confess."

"Don't sweat it, Ah understand . . . no harm, no foul," I said, and patted him on the shoulder.

I started to walk away and Kevin asked, "Where are yew going?"

"To dance with Karen," I said, with a mischievous grin.

"WHAT? Yew cain't do that!"

I kept on walking, not giving up on my devilish grin. "You just watch me!"

I walked straight over to the booth with Karen and all her friends and slid right in next to her. Her jaw visibly dropped open a little, and everyone who knew who I was stopped in mid-sentence to see if I was toting trouble with me. It was obvious who the fiancé was, and I recognized him from dancing with Karen before. I extended a hand in his direction and said, "Howdy, Ah'm Scotty."

"I know who you are," he said cautiously as he shook my hand.

Karen, who was sitting between us, jumped into the conversation and said, "Scotty, this is Ross."

"Nahce to meet yew, Ross," my adopted accent kicked in at full throttle: "Congratulations, yer gonna marry a wonderful woman."

"Thank you," was all he said. Ross was from Indiana and even though he had attended Texas Tech, he had not picked up the drawl like I had.

Karen leaned in close and trying not to be obvious, quietly asked, "Scotty, what are yew doin' here?"

"It's alraht, Ah'm not here to cause any trouble. Yer new beginning is mah ending; Ah just couldn't let it all end in a parking lot." As I said this, I looked at Ross. "This is congratulations for yew two, but it is also mah farewell." Everyone at the table was hearing everything, and the scene was surreal. I slowly canvassed everyone's eyes—some I knew, and some I did not. Then I looked back at Ross, and we shared a stare. Just then, one of the favorite songs of Texas, "Amarillo by Morning," blared out and broke the tension.

"Ross, can Ah dance with yer fiancé?" I asked in a humble way, so he knew that I recognized Karen as his woman and was requesting his permission. Ross blinked slowly and gave a very shallow nod. Then I looked to Karen and asked, "Miss, would yew lahk ta dance?" Without waiting for an answer, I stood and offered a hand, and she took it and rose to her feet. I led her to the crowded dance floor, and we began to two-step.

"This is so strange," Karen said with a grin, shaking her head in disbelief. "Are yew alraht?" she continued.

"Ah'm as good as Ah can be, under the circumstances, but Ah *do* wish yew well."

"Thank yew," she said. "That does mean a lot to me."

"It'll be tough, and it'll take awahl, but Ah'll get over yew," I said with conviction. "Ah'll be alraht."

"But yew won't forget me, raht?" she asked, and looked up at me with her blue eyes. She asked in a tone that immediately sent my mind back to Castaway when she said, "Ah'm stickin' with yew." The brief vision from the past made my head whirl, and I knew if I kept doing that, I would probably crumble, so right away I shook it out of my mind.

Her simple question took me off guard, and I looked down at her as we glided across the floor. "Not a chance," and I actually tightened my hold on her enough that she could sense my sincerity and know my anguish. The song ended, and I led her back to her friends, who by now were buzzing at the audacity of this transplanted Yankee.

"Thank yew," I said to Karen. Then I turned my attention to Ross. "Thank yew," as I took a vacant seat across from him.

To everyone's astonishment, we began to talk a little. I don't recall about what, but at one point he said, "I was in the car at the parking lot today."

"Ah didn't know that," I replied.

"Well, we weren't sure how you were going to react; shoot, I thought I might have to defend myself!"

At hearing this, I chuckled. "That must have been an anxious thing to watch," I added, trying to imagine him sitting in the car witnessing Karen giving me the news that crushed my heart.

Then quite compassionately he said, "You took it well; I could tell it was not easy."

I didn't say anything. I didn't want to think about that moment; it was too much to bear. I was saved by the waitress, who came and stood by the table and asked if anyone needed anything. "The next round's on me," I perked up. "Congratulations to Ross and Karen." I reached over and shook his hand one more time and looked intently at him. "Yer a lucky man! Take care of her."

Ross shook my hand and said, "I know; you take care of yourself."

"Brother Kevin," I said as I clasped Kevin Gambrel's hand and put my other hand on his shoulder, "let's stay in touch."

"We'll have to," he replied with a grin, "How else will Ah keep yew outta trouble?" and he pulled me into a hug without letting go of the handshake.

Even though there had been no talk about leaving Texas, there was a finality hanging in the good-byes of that moment. Everyone knew this was a milestone; that a giant page was being turned in the lives of all who knew Karen and me and the journey we had shared since 1976. At the very least they understood that it was a monumental moment for Karen and me.

Then I looked at Karen and took a hold of her hand. "Yew have a wonderful life."

"Thank yew," she said and stood up and hugged me tightly. I think she knew, as I did, that we might never see each other again.

I kissed her on the cheek and said, "Good-bye, dear heart," and I turned and walked away. It was the last time I saw Karen.

Two days later, I was back in New Mexico working on Bobby Dean's mountain house. We had reached a point where the plumbers and electricians had to take over for awhile, and I saw an opportunity to visit home. My family had planned a massive family camping trip at a remote lake in the U.P. We all knew where it was and were supposed to rendezvous there at our earliest convenience. Being as far away as New Mexico, I was the only one who was not expected to make it. But, with all that had happened, I needed some serious thinking time to myself; this was a perfect chance. Not only did I decide to surprise my family at the campout, but I planned to get there by means of my motorcycle. I plotted my course the long way: straight north through Colorado and Wyoming, then east through South Dakota, Minnesota, and Wisconsin; this would surely give me the thinking time that I needed.

Taking this route, I retraced some of the same roads I had ridden when I bicycled to Frontier Ranch and Castaway Club. As I slipped into western Minnesota, I deviated slightly from my course and pulled into Castaway. Being a Sunday in the middle of summer, there was a lull in the camp while they reorganized between the session that ended the day before and the one arriving the following day. I stopped in the parking lot and dropped my feet down on opposite sides of my motorcycle, wondering if I really wanted to continue. Just seeing the familiar cabins and the bluff overlooking the lake, I felt the emotion start to build within me. I killed the motor and leaned the bike onto its kick-stand. I stood and ground the heel of one heavy riding boot into the gravel. I laid my gloves on the seat, carefully placed my helmet on top of them, and unzipped my leather jacket. I scanned the view before me, drew in a heavy breath, and spoke out loud like someone was with me, "Well, let's go see what's goin' on."

Slowly, I strolled around the camp, remembering the events of those timeless days in the summer of 1976. I recalled the places where Karen and I had sat together and grinned when I remembered my encounters with big ol' Kyle. Inevitably, I stood at the top step of the waterfront, recalling the night I gave my life to Christ. A flush of guilt washed over me as I thought about how I had been living. As I made my way back toward my bike, I paid a visit to the bluff where we had called the girls from Texas "guys," and they got so upset.

The weight of the memories was almost unbearable. I couldn't help but contemplate how a few moments of time; shorter or longer, and that fateful meeting may have never happened. It baffled me to think how close it was, that the previous seven years of knowing Karen were only seconds from never happening at all, that the agony I was wrestling with I could have never felt. Everything I had experienced; everyone I knew that were related to Karen or Texas would be non-existent had Bobby, T.C., Matt, and I dozed in our bunks three minutes longer. And all those I kept at arms length because of Karen . . . well . . . who knows. It was mind-boggling and although I was thinking of the heartache it would have saved, I also realized how many loving memories, precious people, and great things I would have missed; it was a double-edged sword. I decided I had punished myself long enough and quickly turned and left the bluff. I stopped briefly by my cabin and stared at the tiny window I had looked out from my bunk every night. It had been many years, but I remembered everything like it had happened the day before, and the nostalgia was overwhelming, the melancholy; oppressive. I returned to my bike and left Castaway in my rear view mirrors.

It was nighttime when I reached Marinette-Menominee and crossed into the western U.P. of Michigan. I was exhausted but pressed on until I made the north shore of Lake Michigan and pulled into a rest area. I unrolled my sleeping bag and stretched out on a picnic table; I was fast asleep within five minutes. In the middle of the night, I awoke to flashes of lightning and thunder echoing across the lake. The waves were crashing against the shore, competing ominously with the approaching storm. Before I could think about how much time I might have, a wall of driving rain swept in from the lake. I scrambled to cram my sleeping bag into its stuff-sack and climbed back on my bike. I figured if I was going to get soaked, I might as well be putting some miles behind me. When it began to get light, I shivered into a restaurant cold and drenched to get some breakfast and a cup of hot coffee. After I warmed up and wrung myself out a little, I turned my motorcycle north and headed for the campsite at Triangle Lake, thirty miles away.

I negotiated the muddy two-tracks by memory and slogged my way into the campsite. It was still very early, and no one was stirring. I stopped in the middle of the clustered tents and revved the motor until I saw a head peek out from under a tent flap; it was my sister, Tammy, who exclaimed, "Oh my God, it's Scott!"

It wasn't long before everyone lumbered out into the gray morning to greet the prodigal son. It felt great to know how overjoyed they were to see me. After all, I was the renegade who chased a girl all the way to Texas and was building houses in the Rockies. I enjoyed a week of hanging out with my family and lazing in the water of Triangle Lake. I wasn't sure if I was going to tell them about Karen and Ross, but when they asked questions, it forced the issue. They knew then that, like an Aborigine on a 'walk-about', I had made this trip to find myself . . . to try and discover what to do with my life now that Karen was not part of it.

When it came time to return, the long trip back to New Mexico was a marathon I did not want to make. If it weren't for all the unfinished business I left and the debt I owed, I would have stayed in Michigan. But I had no choice in the matter; I had to return. The motorcycle I had ridden all those miles was only a small Honda 450; a definite chain driven bone-rattler. On the way back to Texas and New Mexico, I was forced to stop at nearly every rest stop in Missouri to give my butt a break. It was on this return trip that I made up my mind to return home to Michigan. The plan included returning to N.M.U. to finish the Art degree I had begun.

After three days of hard riding, I finally arrived back in Amarillo. I needed to get back to the job in Angel Fire, but my heart just wasn't in it. I spent some time visiting my friends and paying the bills that stacked up in my absence. After several days, I called Bobby Dean to see how the house in Angel Fire was coming along. I tried to act like everything was normal, but in reality, I knew that I had been out of touch way too long. Bobby was upset and to the point. "Ah have someone else finishing mah house; come and git yo tools and yo camper off the site. Ye'r done."

"Can Ah get the balance of pay for the work Ah've already done?" I boldly asked. I desperately needed the money to help settle my debts in Amarillo. I decided to do everything I could to cut my ties with Texas, so I could return to Michigan. It was now or never.

"No, yew made a mistake with the door sizes, and it cost me more than I owe yew to have them fixed," he said with a hint of anger. I didn't realize I had made a mistake, but I had no reason to think he was not telling me the truth; he had always been a fair man. I felt badly that I messed this up; Bobby Dean was a good guy to be connected with, and he had aspirations of building more mountain homes in Angel Fire. Once, he told me of his plans and hinted that he wanted me to do the work for him. This had been a great opportunity, but now it was a bridge burned, and I had no recourse other than to do as he asked.

I made one last trip to Angel Fire and collected all my equipment, took a final glance at the magnificent chalet I had built with my own hands, and then drove out of the mountains. I was glad that Bobby Dean was not there, and I didn't have to see him face to face, but the fact that I had been fired was difficult to swallow. I was at a critical point in my life, and things were beginning to unravel. I knew if I didn't handle things right, I could end up in a bad way, a very bad way.

When I got back to Amarillo, everything was in disarray. Deek had left to attend N.M.U. again, and I was under pressure to vacate the apartment. The rent and the phone bill were past due, and creditors were looking for payment. I owed a lot of money to the bank for the business loan to *Hazel Building Services,* and without the money from Bobby Dean, I began to liquidate everything in order to pay those debts. I even sold my motorcycle and a Jeep that I had bought for transportation. I decided to keep my work truck and small tools so I could earn a living if I had to. When I was finished and squared up with everyone, I had a meager $150 to my name. The question became, "Should I try and make it home on this, or do I work somewhere until I know I can make it?" I decided if I didn't try to make it home at that moment, I might be stuck in Texas for awhile. Considering all that had happened, I did not want to be there any longer; it was time to take the chance and go—it was time to go home.

THE PRODIGAL SON

CHAPTER 41

It was a Sunday in late August when I finally chose to make a break for Michigan. I was hoping that if it went smoothly, I might be able to reach Marquette in time to register for some classes. I attended service at San Jacinto Baptist and said goodbye to everyone who had been so kind to me, especially Lloyd, LaVisa, and Kevin. It was tough; we had all truly become friends, and saying farewell was emotional. Before service was even complete, I slipped out and began to drive toward Oklahoma; I did not want to face any more difficult goodbyes. I would be a liar if I said there were no tears shed in the cab that morning.

The few things I kept were stored in garbage bags and tied down on the exposed flatbed of my truck. My water pump had been acting up a little, so, as a precaution, I had a half dozen plastic milk jugs on board filled with water. It wasn't long until I noticed the temperature gauge climbing dangerously high. I pulled off to the side of the expressway and saw water pouring out of the engine and onto the road. I hadn't even made it to Oklahoma, and my water pump was failing. Returning to Amarillo would have been the wise thing to do, but I chose to try and nurse the truck the remaining nine hundred miles. In spite of the risk, I wanted to keep moving forward. I had finally left Amarillo and did not want anything to force me to return. At regular intervals, I exited the freeway and filled my radiator with fresh water, always keeping my milk jugs full in case of emergency. It was an agonizingly slow trip.

When I was getting close to Norman, Oklahoma, the weather began to turn menacingly dark. It was early evening, but it became as black as midnight. The lightning gave way to giant hail, and I immediately understood the implications; this was tornado weather. I was concerned about everything on the bed of my truck becoming drenched and ruined by the rain. I was in the process of seeking cover when my temperature gauge indicated the engine could seize up at any moment.

Just when I began to think that it couldn't get any worse, a flash of lightning revealed the unmistakable "V" shape of a giant cyclone cutting a path of destruction through the field to my left. I could only see it clearly when the lightning flashed. After this happened several times, I could see it was not going away, but actually bearing down in my direction. It almost seemed to have the mind of a predator that was trying to catch me. My wipers were slapping back and forth as fast as they could with little effect on the torrent; I could barely see the road as I raced forward as fast as I dared. The rain was blowing horizontal across the road, and I leaned forward and squinted, trying to see better. The wind made a high-pitched whistling noise as it forced a breach in the window seal. I couldn't tell what they were, but all sorts of objects were flying across the road. Like a ghost in the night, I finally spied an overpass in the distance. When I reached it, I pulled off the road, around a retaining wall, and cozied in behind the concrete supports. At first, I sat there with the engine idling and my lights on. Then, I shut the truck off and lay down across the seat. I could hear the rage of the funnel as it passed over the bridge, and I felt its power as the truck shuttered in the blackness. In that bleak moment, lying in a crippled vehicle with everything I owned in garbage bags, I realized that I had reached the lowest place in my life. I barely had a hundred dollars in my pocket and was hiding from a storm that resembled the finger of God. I have always felt that having all my possessions in garbage bags was somehow symbolic.

"What are you doing?" I asked myself out loud. "It's time to ask for help." I lay there while the storm still raged and decided that the next day I would call home for money to fix my truck. It occurred to me in my despair that I was exactly like the young man in the Bible; I had left home to sow my oats and was returning home broke and ashamed. "It can't get any worse than this," I acknowledged to myself. "You ARE the prodigal son."

I awoke to traffic speeding down the freeway. I sat up and looked out the window. The storm had passed, and it was a perfectly clear morning. There was standing water in the fields, and people were canvassing debris that the tornado had strewn across the land. I rubbed my hands over my face in an attempt to wake myself from my slumber. I slid in behind the wheel, closed my eyes, and tilted my head back. "Lord, please let this thing start." I turned the key, and the engine came to life. I maneuvered around the retaining wall and merged back onto the expressway. Five miles down the road I came to an exit with a truck stop. I knew that truck stops had a little bit of everything, including a mechanic and a Western Union office. The mechanic told me what I already knew. "Yer water pump needs ta be replaced."

"How much?" I asked.

"'Bout seventy-five bucks," he replied.

"Hold on, Ah'll be right back."

I called my mother and told her of my predicament. She was thrilled that I was on my way home and wasted no time in wiring me the money. I had only asked for the seventy-five dollars I needed to fix my truck, but when the cash came in, she had wired me one hundred. With some of the extra, I went in and ate a hot breakfast while the mechanic went to work on my water pump.

A couple hours later, the truck was repaired, and I got back under way. During breakfast I recounted how, in July of that summer, my world crumbled to a point of mental, emotional, and financial exhaustion. I vowed then and there, that I would never let that happen again. As a reminder, I wrote, "7/84" on a small piece of paper and taped it to the ceiling, just above the driver's side visor. In bad times, this would remind me of how much worse it could be. The peace of mind I had, knowing that with a repaired truck I would make it home, was a feeling of relief beyond description. Now my only worry was whether or not I had enough money to make it to Marquette.

It was after midnight when I crossed the border at Michigan City, Indiana, into southern Michigan. I glanced at my fuel gauge and saw it was reading well under a quarter tank of gas. I fumbled around and looked into my wallet; I had seven dollars. It didn't take much calculation to understand that making Marquette, over 400 miles away, was out of the question. My older sister Darcy and her family lived just north of Grand Rapids, only 150 miles away; that became my new objective. But, with only seven dollars, even making that seemed unlikely. Then, on the other side of the road, I saw a Citgo gas station. Something about Citgo registered in my mind. It was a common gas station in the North, but they were nearly non-existent in the south, I hadn't seen one in a long, long time.

"Citgo," I mumbled to myself, and I pulled off the side of the road. I rummaged through my wallet and hidden deep in its pockets, I produced a Citgo credit card. It was a card my father had given me years earlier to use in case I needed gas in an emergency. I had totally forgotten that I had it until that sign in the middle of the night sparked my memory. I wasn't sure if it was still a valid card or not. In those days, expiration dates were not embossed on credit cards. I shrugged like someone else was present. "Oh well, I got nuthin' to lose."

I wheeled around in a giant u-turn and pulled into the Citgo station. I filled my tank before inquiring whether or not the card was any good. "If they want their gas back, they'll have to suck it out themselves," I said to myself as I topped off the tank. I was nervous when I went inside and handed the attendant the Citgo card. He punched the numbers into the machine, and we both waited for the outcome. I was mentally preparing myself for the confrontation that I knew *must* be coming, when he slid a receipt before me and said, "Sign here, please."

"It worked!" I thought. Walking out to my truck, I once again felt the stress leave me. I hurried to get out of there, just in case something were to happen and the guy came running out to stop me. As I sped through the cool night, it felt wonderful to be in my home state. The moon was full, and I could see the alternating silhouettes of irrigation pivots and stands of woods. Looking out the window, I read road signs with familiar names and felt the comfort of getting closer to home. "Thanks, Dad," I said aloud, and drove toward Grand Rapids and the sanctuary of my sister's house.

Trying to digest the last few years as I drove into the night, I simply shook my head and said, "The prodigal son returns."

NOWHERE, BUT UP

CHAPTER 42

I had only been to my sister Darcy's house once or twice before, and that had been several years earlier. It was in a suburb north of Grand Rapids called Comstock Park. Somehow, I was able to dig into my memory and find it like I had been there only the week before. When I arrived, I was basically flat broke, with under a half a tank of gas left in my truck, and all I possessed in life was in soaked garbage bags. I was, in a word, pathetic. They were glad to see me and let me stay with them while I tried to get back on my feet. It became obvious that I was in no shape to make it to Marquette in time to register for classes, not to mention I had no money to do so. My brother-in-law, Jim, was part of a family business that had just completed a new building that they were preparing to move into. The exterior of this new facility was complete, but the interior still needed a ton of work. My timing couldn't have been better; there I sat with my building experience and a truck full of tools, and Jim needed his warehouse finished. So, I began to live and work with my sister and brother-in-law.

In September, I made the two-hour trip to Flint to visit my parents. During the drive, I thought about how persistent Babe had been during all those years I was running all over the country.

"Perhaps," I thought, "I should give her a call and let her know the 'Texas' chapter in my life was over." I had not forgotten about how good Becky had been to me, either, but I was headed to Flint and thought I might pay Babe a visit. When I pulled down Woodcroft

Street, the street of my youth, I couldn't wait to see my folks and the old house again. As I parked in the driveway, a yellow MG convertible pulled in front and parked by the curb. To this day, I have no clue how she knew, but there sat Babe, arriving as if on cue. I approached the car with a different attitude, one that might open the door for something more with Babe. She turned off the engine but did not get out of the car. I walked up to the door, leaned in, and hugged her. This was uncharacteristic behavior on my part, and I think it caught her a little off guard.

"Wow," she said, a little startled, "how have you been?"

"Pretty good Ah guess; Ah had to dodge a tornada in Oklahoma, but Ah'm still alahv."

"You've picked up a little twang, I hear," she said with smile. She wore mirrored sunglasses and was the perfect fit in her sports car.

"Yeah, it comes an' goes," I replied. Now that she had me thinking about it, I did my best to talk like a Michigander again.

After some small talk, I finally broke the news that I was anxious to share, "Karen and Ah are through; she's getting married." Babe suddenly looked serious, not what I expected her reaction to be, so I continued, "Ah'm back; Ah'm not going to Texas any more."

"I am, too," Babe said.

"You are too, what?" I asked.

"Getting married." She took off her sun glasses and watched my reaction.

"Man," I said, taken by surprise, "that's great, Therese." I seldom used her name, but at such news, I automatically defaulted to it. I tried to act happy for her, but I think the stunned look on my face made it obvious that this was not what I wanted to hear. Then she said something that really took me off guard.

"Unless you tell me not to."

"What?"

"I won't get married if you tell me not to."

I initially laughed when I heard her say it but then sobered up when I realized she was not joking. Again, irony slapped me in the face. I had to wonder if God was getting a chuckle out of watching me get handed my walking papers every time I thought someone was re-entering my life. Babe and I had connected easily and had somehow fostered a bond through all my years of running around. It had always been effortless with her and we were very like people. Many couples who are very similar clash, they are too similar, but that had never happened with Babe and me, it always flowed. She always referred to us as 'soul mates', and considering our connection, I couldn't disagree. But to think it was of a caliber to allow me to cancel her wedding plans was absurd.

"Therese, I can't do that. Honestly, I am actually a little sad to hear that you are getting married, especially when I just thought we might be able to sort things out, but to ask you not to would mean I would be committing myself to something I cannot." I was amazed that she was putting that decision in my hands. "You know, Therese," I began in a serious tone, "if you are willing to let me stop your wedding, this might not be the right guy."

"Just tell me to call it off, and I will," she said again, almost pleading for me to intervene.

Down deep I was rolling the idea around. "Should I tell her not to get married?" I wondered. I tried to imagine if I did, what it would mean. To be in the condition I was and still have someone care so much about me made this situation very tempting, but also very scary. Finally I said in earnest, "I just can't *tell* you that, Therese, it would be giving you a promise that I just can't keep; this is something that *you* have to decide." We had reached an impasse, and I got the feeling she was hoping I would bail her out of a situation that she wasn't sure she wanted to be in, but I just couldn't do it. After some further conversation, we said an awkward goodbye, and she drove away. I stood in the street for a few moments with my hands in my pockets and kicking at some stones. As her little car turned the corner and whined away out of sight, I wondered if I would ever see Babe again . . . most likely not. I tried to get my head wrapped around what had just happened. Had God just thrown me a life-ring and I threw it back? As I went into the house to see my parents, I had to act normal, but internally my head was spinning.

Being back home gave me some time to continue to think about how my life was moving along. Both Karen and Babe were out of the picture, and Indiana Deb was a surreal encounter committed to my memory. She had accepted a job and moved to Virginia Beach. It seemed that everyone was moving forward with their lives except me. I had reached the bottom of the barrel and had nowhere to go but up. I had little money, and the college life had done me no favors. It was time to grow up; it was time to get right with God.

One evening while visiting my parents, I sat on the front porch watching a new crop of youngsters play on the street that held so many childhood memories for me. I was in the process of taking stock of all that had happened since high school began. It seemed like that was when life started to move faster than I could manage. Ever since Barb took me for a ride, the pace was out of control; I was in a current that swept me along. For the most part, I was a willing participant, but I knew now I needed a foothold, a foundation on which to stand. Suddenly, much of the council I had been given by people like LaVisa and Kevin Gambrel made sense. Then, almost without a thought, I stood, walked into the house, and picked up the phone. I dialed a number I knew by heart and heard the familiar voice answer, "Hello?" There was a short pause before I said, "Hey, Red, how are you?" I affectionally called Becky "Red" for her fiery hair.

"Well, if it isn't the dreamer; this is a pleasant surprise. I was not expecting *you* to be on the other end of the line; what's the occasion?"

"Oh, Ah felt the urge to hear your voice," I answered.

"Oh, you did, did you? What's the matter, you usually call when something's wrong?"

"Ah guess Ah deserve that," I said. "You *have* always been there to pick up the pieces."

"I hear you still have a bit of that drawl thing happening," she joked.

"Yeah, it kinda comes and goes, but Ah think it will be going more than coming."

"Oh yeah, why is that?" Becky asked. I could tell that she knew I had led her into the question.

"Ah don't live in Texas anymore," was all I said.

"Really . . . so where are you now?" she asked with peaked interest.

"By Grand Rapids," I answered in anticipation of her reaction.

"Grand Rapids, Michigan?" she asked in disbelief.

"Yes, ma'm."

"Are you coming to Marquette?"

"Not right away, but it *would* be nahce to see yew; we have a lot to talk about."

"Like what?" she pried.

"Oh, Ah'll leave all the details for when we can talk in person. Ah will tell yew this, though, Ah am not goin' back to Texas."

"Okaayyy," she said in a long curious manner, "I can't wait to hear this."

We talked some more, but nothing about the details of why I was back or of my situation in Comstock Park. I never managed to make the trip to Marquette, but we talked many times over the phone and wrote back and forth several times. We did not see each other until she came south over Christmas break.

It was mid-December when I made the trip to see Becky. I had driven to my parents' house and then made the short trip to South Lyon from there. By this time, nearly eight months had passed since Karen dropped the bomb on me in the parking lot in Amarillo. I had taken advantage of this time to get Karen out of my system. I had not seen Becky since she visited me in Texas the Christmas before when we skied at Angel Fire. When she boarded the plane in Amarillo to return to Michigan, neither of us knew what the future held. But now, all that had changed.

When she answered the door, she stepped out of the house, and we hugged. I could tell by the embrace that she felt something between us was about to change for the better. It was surely a hug by two people who longed to see each other.

"Boy howdy," I said with a drawl. "It sure is good to see yew."

"It's good to see you, too," Becky replied, and we savored the embrace a bit longer. We entered her house and, after greeting everyone, sat down on the hearth in front of a fire and began to catch up. Her family conspicuously disappeared to unknown corners of the house, so Becky and I could have some time together alone. As usual, she looked stunning; her red hair was parted in the middle and the firelight danced on her freckles. Her blue eyes were fixated on me as I spoke, eager to hear what news I brought with me. After a lot of small talk, Becky finally asked the question that she had been waiting to ask: "Why are you here; I mean, why did you leave Texas?"

As soon as she asked the question, she nervously bit her lower lip. I smiled a little smile and said, "I really miss that."

"Miss what?"

"That whole lip biting thing you do."

She lightly smacked me on the arm and released the bite she had on her lip.

"Come on, what is going on?" she persisted.

I looked at her and finally answered, "Karen is getting married; hell, she might already be married." At my cursing, Becky gave me a look of disapproval.

"Sorry," I said. But that was the end of it. She was too anxious to hear what else I had to say to worry about my language. "Yeah," I confirmed, "Karen came by one day and told me she was getting married. I guess after that, I realized there was no reason to stay."

"I'm sorry," Becky said, "that must have been difficult." She was trying to act sincere about it, but she could not hide that she was overjoyed at hearing this news.

"Well, it's been awhile. Ah'm over it."

"Awhile?" she asked, taken aback. "When did she tell you this?"

"Ummm, early last summer," was my matter of fact reply.

"WHAT?!" Becky snapped with widened eyes as she leaned backwards to get a better look at me. At that moment I realized that, perhaps, I might have told her sooner.

"This happened months ago, and you're telling me now?!"

A look of panic slowly spread across my face as I sensed her anger. "Becky," I began, "I needed time."

Becky looked at me halfway smiling and halfway clenching her teeth, "Dang you, Scott, you know how I feel about you, and you let me tread water all this time?"

"Becky," I began with a serious tone, "Ah had a lot to take care of, and Ah honestly needed time."

"I am *so* mad at you right now," she answered.

"How *do* you feel?" I asked.

"What?"

"You said, 'I know how you feel about me' . . . how *do* you feel about me?"

When she realized what she had said, she was embarrassed. "You know," she said in a quiet voice.

"I think I do," I answered with no drawl, and I slid my fingers over her hand.

It became silent, and she leaned forward and put her forehead on my shoulder and whispered, "You make me crazy."

I stayed late, and we talked into the night. There was a new atmosphere around us now; all the obstacles that previously existed were gone. When I finally stood to leave, Becky led me by the hand toward the back door. We stood in the dimly-lit kitchen and kissed. Then with her head held sideways against my chest, we held each other, and I whispered, "You are too good for me, Becky."

"I'm afraid you're still a dreamer," she said quietly, "but I'd like to think I'm part of the dream now."

As I drove U.S. 23 back to my parents that night, the snow began to fall. I looked out the window at the dark, frozen land, feeling like everything finally made sense. I had not known that peace of mind for a long time, and I smiled in my contentment. I couldn't help but wonder if Becky was God's plan for me. She certainly was a godly woman, and Lord knows, I needed that in my life.

"God?" I asked aloud, "please don't let me mess this up."

MOVING AHEAD

CHAPTER 43

Many things happened in the year of 1985. I was working for my brother-in-law in his boat business, *Olson's American Marine*. I had completed all the building projects he needed done on his new facility in Rockford and continued to work in the business. Mostly, I loaded boats and boat trailers on semi-trucks to haul all over the Midwest. Eventually, I became a truck driver myself, then finally a foreman over the workers.

Driving for Jim and his father, Gene, was a stressful endeavor. Neither of them could say "no" to a client and as a consequence, we were constantly delivering what we called "ten pounds of shit on a five pound truck." But the hours were long, and the paycheck was steady. Before I knew it, I was slowly building up some savings.

It was at this time that Jim and Darcy decided to move from Comstock Park to Rockford to be closer to the business and into a larger house for their growing family. I helped with the move and instantly took up residence in their new basement. I was not quite ready to go out on my own, so I imposed my presence on them a little longer. Eventually, I was able to move into my own apartment in Rockford, and I bought a used motorcycle to get around.

At the age of twenty-seven, I was eager to get on with life. I had many dreams when I was younger, and I was becoming increasingly anxious to pursue them. One of my dreams was to find the right girl, marry, and have several children. There was no reason to think Becky was not that girl. We visited each other several times, and I began to dance around the subject of our future together. Ironically, after all her patience with me and Karen, it was Becky who was unsure if we were ready to broach the subject of marriage, and she warned me about moving too fast. Her largest concern was my spiritual life, and she was justified in it. Personally, I understood that my avoidance of God had gone on long enough. With her encouragement, I searched for a church to attend. I finally settled on Rockford Baptist, a small church in the center of town. It was here that many good things began to happen for me.

Rockford was a very charming little town with a river, the Rogue River, running right through the heart of it. It was also the headquarters for the company Wolverine Worldwide, and its shoe factory dominated a prominent place on the riverfront. As I slowly gained a fondness for the town, I began to feel like it was a place to stay; Marquette, as much as I loved it, might only lead to another fall from grace. My plan to return to Marquette was put on hold while I began a comfortable existence in Rockford. I decided that I needed to find something to do besides work and pay my rent. The best place to do this and stay out of trouble was church.

I began to help with R.B.C.'s (Rockford Baptist Church) high school youth group. In no time, there was a buzz around the church as to who this new guy with the faint drawl was and where he had come from. R.B.C. also gave me opportunity to sing again, and occasionally I added my voice to the choir and praise group. It was a very conservative church, and being raised as a Catholic with a sense of soul acquired from Southwestern High School and San Jacinto made many very leery about me. Nevertheless, I started to feel my roll at R.B.C. might be to introduce them to contemporary Christian music and to loosen their ties a little. Most Baptists, I discovered, especially the conservative ones, tend to separate everything into secular and Christian pigeonholes. In my struggle to adapt from my Catholic upbringing to my understanding of being reborn, I believed that, in many ways, this categorizing only distanced conservative Baptists from those they sought to evangelize . . . it made many of them intolerant and stuffy. Nevertheless, they were Godly people who tried to live right . . . being around them surely would not be a bad thing for me.

As much as I loved the big church atmosphere of San Jacinto, I came to believe God called me to R.B.C. for a purpose, and I rejected any notion of attending other cutting-edge large churches in the area. I was going to reacquaint myself with God through Rockford Baptist.

Another attempt to make Rockford my home was made by a casual visit I paid to the high school. Out of the blue, I walked into the athletic director's office and inquired as to the condition of their soccer program. "Do you need any help with your soccer team?" I asked.

"That's funny you should ask," said the large, loud man. "We just started one; this will be our first year." Then he asked, "Why, do you know something about soccer?"

"You might say that," I replied with a smile, "Ah've played my whole life, including college and a semi-pro team, and Ah was an assistant coach at a hah school."

"Where are you from?" he asked at hearing my drawl start to spill out.

"Oh, Ah spent the last few years in Amarilla, Texas . . . that's where Ah coached."

"Well, this is great," he said. "We have a parent trying to put a team together. Why don't you go out and talk to him; I'm sure he'd welcome the help."

I found the team practicing in a local park and introduced myself. Before I knew it, I was an assistant coach for the very first Rockford High School boys' soccer team. Little did I know at the time, but this would be the beginning of a passion that continues to this day. The following year I was named the head coach and within several years, I would also be coaching Rockford's new girls' team.

Even though I had moved back into the state, as far as seeing Becky, it was not much different than when I lived in Texas. She had switched from N.M.U. to Moody Bible Institute in Chicago, which is actually closer to Grand Rapids than Marquette, but I was working long hours, and she was studying hard to finish her degree. I will admit it was much cheaper to visit than when I lived in Amarillo, and it was comforting to know we were closer, but we still were only able to see each other when our schedules allowed.

The busy schedule kept me out of trouble and slowly life, though hectic, was taking on a sense of normalcy.

From my involvement with the San Jacinto youth group and coaching, I began to realize I had a talent for working with young people. I approached the youth pastor at R.B.C. and asked if I could help in any way with the teenagers. Being that I dropped out of the sky and no one knew much about me, it took a couple weeks to answer me. It was after they learned I was the high school soccer coach that they gave me the nod. I also was singing more during services and was attending a young adult Sunday school class. My active schedule left me little time to party or to even consider going out dancing, which was a good thing. Even though I was increasingly involved with church, I was still an outsider and an odd duck in the middle of the small conservative Baptist church.

The more Becky and I met, it became evident that, aside from our differences, we were falling in love. From that moment in Becky's dorm room when she learned that I was a struggling young Christian, she had never given up on me. Now, several years later, and post-Karen, I was finally coming around. I was doing everything that Becky was praying I would do.

It also became obvious that, in spite of our growing closeness, we were living in two vastly different worlds. Moody is one of the premier Christian universities in the nation, if not the world. Those who attend it are aspiring to work in some faith-based profession. I, on the other hand, was gaining nothing academically. The only education I was pursuing was how to better build, load, and deliver boats on time. Her conversations were about the magnitude of God's power in the world, and mine were about making good time to Toledo and back. I was independent and slowly getting back on my feet, financially and spiritually. As long as this continued, I started to think more about setting up housekeeping than finishing my degree. This is where Becky and I differed the most.

On most everything else, we saw things eye-to-eye, but on planning for the future, we were galaxies apart. Oh, the attraction was there, the thought of a future together was realistic to both of us, but the timing was a major point of contention. Even so, I persisted with a hard-headed plan to marry and begin a family. "If I propose," I reasoned, "how could she refuse?" I had hinted several times about my intentions, so my thoughts were not a mystery to Becky. On more than one occasion, she told me, "Do not ask me to marry you, Scotty. We are not ready yet." When she told me this, she might as well have been speaking to a rock; I dismissed it and decided to pop the question anyway.

Christmas 1985 was the time I chose to propose to Becky. She would be home from Moody, and I would be at my parents' in Flint. She and I had made plans to meet anyway, and the timing seemed romantic and perfect, at least from my perspective.

I used all the tools available to me and made a simple but beautiful jewelry box as a present for Becky. It was dark walnut with an inlayed ash heart on the top. Inside, I placed a modest diamond ring with a note which read: "*Will you marry me?*" The plan was set.

Christmas afternoon I drove down and spent some time with Becky and her family. Then I took her back with me to Flint, and we spent time with mine. Late in the evening, when everyone had gone to bed and we were alone, I said, "I have something for you." I had already given her several gifts, and this extra gift came as a surprise to her. I went and retrieved the jewelry box, wrapped like any other Christmas present. We sat side-by-side on the sofa in the same living room where I first gathered the nerve to tell Karen that I loved her. It had been a long time, but sometimes those memories haunted me like a ghost. But on this night, there were no lingering memories; with the fire crackling, it was all about Becky.

As was typical Becky, she carefully unwrapped the gift, being cautious not to tear the paper. As she did this, my heart began to pound. When she finally pulled out the jewelry box, in a whisper she said, "Oh Scott, this is beautiful."

"I made it just for you," I said, making sure she understood that the design and the craftsmanship were mine and made specifically for her.

Becky ran her hands over the smooth, glossy box and traced the outline of the inlayed heart with her fingers. "It's beautiful," she said again.

"Open it," I said in a shaky voice.

My nervousness tipped Becky off that something bigger was yet to come. She cocked her head, squinted her eyes, and looked at me suspiciously. "What have you done?" She unlatched the catch and slowly opened the lid. When she saw the ring and read the note, she quickly snapped it closed. She stared ahead at the fire and did not say a word for several tense moments.

Finally, I said, “Well?”

Becky looked at me and said, “I asked you not to do this . . . we are not ready.”

When she said this, the entire mood changed.

“When is ready?” I asked. Even though she had asked me not to propose, I was surprised that she did not say “yes.” Instead of a magical moment, we were locked in a tense debate.

“I don’t know,” answered Becky, “but I don’t believe *now* is the right time.”

I stared at the fire and slowly nodded. “I see,” was all I could manage to say.

After some uncomfortable silence, I felt the emotion well up within me, and I got up and left the room. I walked down the dark hallway to the back door. I slumped down on the cool floor with my back against the door. It was a snowy night, and the backyard light was sending a dreamlike illumination through the window. I was processing everything, and a tear streamed down my face. Briefly, my mind flashed back to the parking lot when Karen unleashed the lightning bolt that made me leave Texas. All I could do then, as now, was stare at a random place in the distance.

“Ah’m gettin’ real tarred of this feeling,” I said to myself with a drawl.

At this moment, Becky quietly appeared in the shaft of winter light. When she saw the broken man that I was, she tenderly said, “Oh, Scotty,” and sat down on the floor next to me and began to speak. “I’m sorry, but I just can’t say ‘yes’ right now. I want to, but I don’t believe it’s God’s will right now. *You* might be ready, but *I’m* not.” When she said this, I realized it was more than just her not wanting to; she did, but it was more to do with what she felt God wanted.

“Man,” I said, gaining some composure, “how can I argue with that?” In the midst of my dejection, I was amazed and in awe at her obedience to her walk with God. I knew we were “unequally yoked,” as the Bible puts it, but I went ahead anyway. Becky’s faithfulness would not allow her to act according to her own desire; as always, she was definitely walking her talk. In spite of the gains I had made, this was still the major difference between our Christian walks. I was still making my own decisions, even when I knew they were not done prayerfully or in God's timing. Once again, God was teaching me a tough lesson.

Becky took my hand, and we began to have a soft conversation, interrupted by the occasional sniffle and random tears.

"I love this jewelry box," she said as she cradled it, "but you must keep the ring." As she said this, she placed the ring in the palm of my hand and closed my fingers around it. Even in the dim light, I could see that every now and then, she would bite her lip. I could tell that this was not easy for her, either. I began to feel guilty that I had put her into this position, that I had tested her faith instead of supporting her wish to not rush things. She continued to speak in a quiet, gentle voice, "Our time will come, but it's not right now." There was a comfort in that she was not dismissing the idea, just asking me to be patient. In the time Becky and I had been together, I had always felt that I was driving our relationship, that everything depended upon me. That evening, I discovered that was not the case; it was Becky and her faith in God.

We had plenty more time to talk that evening when I drove her back home to South Lyon. Even though Becky had made it clear that this did not mean we were through, I was emotionally exasperated. In less than two years, Karen and Babe had gotten engaged, Indiana Deb moved to Virginia, and now Becky had said, "No." I felt like just stepping back from everything and everybody and giving my heart and brain a rest. It was reminiscent of the feeling I had back in high school when I broke up with Diana just to get an emotional break, but now the stakes were much higher.

Becky and I kept in touch as before, but it became obvious that since that Christmas night, the relationship had changed. It was frustrating to know that she loved me but reigned in my hope for us to be married. There was no animosity or no official time when we mutually decided we were through, but the passion began to wane, and the romance began to fade. The slowly deteriorating relationship was more because of me than Becky. There were still a lot of feelings between us, but there was also a wounded heart, and I withdrew and became guarded. One had to appreciate the irony; she was the guarded one when we first met at N.M.U., and now *I* was the one protecting myself. We both returned to our hectic lives, she in Chicago and me in Rockford, and time rolled on.

It was during this time that Kevin Gambrel called me from Amarillo. He was coming north to Indiana and wanted to try to get together for a visit. He wrote me a letter explaining what he was doing in Indiana and added that there was a girl he wanted me to meet in Goshen. Evidently he and Barb had a friend that they both felt was perfect for me. Kevin knew more about me than most people, because he had been close to my situation in Texas from every perspective. He always was looking out for me. It was intriguing to wonder who he thought was right for me, but internally I knew the last thing I needed was another girl thrown into the mix.

Kevin made his way to Michigan and we spent a couple days catching up with each other. He had never seen Lake Michigan, so when it came time to take him to Goshen, he hopped on the back of my motorcycle and I took him on the most indirect route to Indiana that any normal person would have considered. True to my love for the state, we diverted first to the shore at Holland and then through all the winding back roads of West Michigan. It turned a routine three hour trip into a sight-seeing adventure of five bumpy hours. When we finally reached Goshen that evening, we were two very sore men. I was used to riding my cycle, but Kevin, especially riding on the back, took the worst of it. He basically fell off the bike in Goshen and was bent over like an old man for awhile. It made for a wonderful journey and we certainly used the trip to catch up on old times. Nothing ever came from meeting the perfect girl in Goshen, and unknown to me at the time; this was the last I would see Kevin Gambrel.

WHAT'S YOUR SISTER'S NAME?

CHAPTER 44

The spring of 1986 found me planting deeper roots in the quaint town of Rockford. I was fully engaged with the youth group at R.B.C. and, as a chaperone, attended a winter retreat to a camp called Spring Hill. It reminded me of Castaway and Frontier and only fueled my interest to become more involved with youth ministry. The great music during the Spring Hill weekend awakened a desire in me to do something more with my passion for music. The exposure to contemporary Christian rock had really caught my attention. It had begun with LaVisa, who showed me there was a lot more to this genre than "Kumbaya." I put an ad in the local paper looking for Christian musicians who might be interested in starting a band. The next thing I knew, I was the lead singer in a Christian rock band named *"2nd Chance,"* a name that fit the five-member group perfectly. Like me, all the guys in the band had come from troubled pasts and were trying to get right with God. After loads of practice, we began playing at festivals and school assemblies, usually as a warm-up for a featured speaker. Eventually, we were asked to play at Spring Hill Camp for winter retreats. Playing for retreats at Spring Hill were my favorite performances. But perhaps the biggest event we played was as a warm-up band for a popular Christian group *"De Garmo & Key"* when they played a concert at DeVos Hall in Grand Rapids.

2nd Chance Band. Left to right: Brian Schilling (guitar), John Bove (drums), Rick Sieracki (keyboard), Scotty (lead vocals), and Gary Raterink (bass) kneeling

It was during this time that I was trying to get better acquainted with those who were in the young single's Sunday school class at R.B.C. It was not easy since these people had grown up in the church, and they all knew each other and their families. They were all polite and friendly, but as the mysterious outsider with a shady past, I was on the outside looking in. Even in a group, I felt like a third wheel. Attempting to be a part of a church was much different than the welcoming spirit that I found at Young Life in 1976. The walls of caution were different than the defensive bastions that Catholics erect, but they were walls, just the same. In all fairness, they were being cautious and protective.

One Saturday, they planned a class trip to Versluis Park, a beach on a lake close to Rockford. The party had already begun when I glided in on my motorcycle and parked beneath the shade of a tree. They did not know who it was until I removed my helmet; then the whispering began. I could not detect if it was good or bad whispers, but whatever it was, I could tell it was about me. I felt a little awkward strolling up to the group, but several, who remembered my name, welcomed me. I'd be a fibber if I said I wasn't taking notice of the girls who were present that afternoon. Baptists are very conservative but are not ashamed to wear bathing suits where bathing suits are necessary, and I was taking mental notes on everyone there, especially these sheltered Baptist girls. Being a bad boy seemed to perk their interests, and I did not mind a bit being that guy. At one point, everyone was laying in a long line sunning him—or herself. I plopped down next to a girl and struck up a conversation. Her name was Beth and she had two other sisters there. Even though I was talking with Beth, the girl who caught my eye was several people away from me. When I asked Beth to point out her sisters, the girl I noticed was one of them. Her name was Susan.

Susan was a petite brunette with pretty hazel eyes. There was no rhyme or reason to it, but some people called her Susan, and others called her Sue. At the time of introductions, I didn't really hear her name, only that she was Beth's sister. There were plenty of conversations that day, but she did not take part in most of them. Susan was a quiet young woman who seemed a little unsure of herself. I didn't get much of a chance to talk to her, but she had grabbed my attention; something about her timidity was attractive.

Becky and I had entered a strange place in our relationship where we were actually giving each other some space. We were adrift in indecision and frustration. For as much as we knew how fond we were of each other, we simply could not agree on the timing of things. Our dreams were the same, but our timetables were different. Whether we could last until we both arrived at the same place was the big question. In the middle of this uncertainty, Susan entered the picture.

A few days after the Sunday school gathering at Versluis Park, I decided to give Susan a call. I had thought about her on and off since that weekend at the beach, but I was struggling to decide if I should, being that Becky was still very much involved in my life. Right or wrong, I decided it was okay to give a call. The problem was, I could not remember her name. I had no trouble remembering Beth's first and last names, but for the life of me, I could not conjure up the name of the girl with the pretty hazel eyes. Finally, I just took a chance, looked up Beth's number, and called. I wasn't sure what the plan was; I was just going to muddle through it as it happened.

"Is this Beth?' I asked when I finally dialed the number and got an answer.

"Yes, this is Beth. Who is this?"

"Scotty, the gah from Texas," I began. "We met at the beach last weekend."

"Yeah, I remember," she answered politely.

Beth and I had about a five-minute conversation about what, I don't recall. At one point I just flat out asked, "What's your sister's name?"

"Who, Linda?" she replied. I couldn't remember the name of the girl I really wanted to talk with, but I knew one thing for sure, it wasn't Linda.

"No, no," I quickly responded, "the other one."

"Susan?" As soon as she said it, I recognized it was the one I couldn't remember. It was an awkward conversation at this point, but ultimately I didn't care how. I just knew I wanted to talk to the hazel-eyed girl.

"Yeah!" I said like it was a eureka moment, "that's the one! Is she around?" Very slowly, politely, and in disbelief at my nerve, Beth said, "Yes, she's here . . . would you like to speak with *her*?"

"As a matter of fact, Ah would," I said, embarrassed that I had not remembered.

Susan got on the phone, and we began a conversation. After a bunch of small talk, I finally got around to asking what was on my mind in the first place. "Would you like to do something sometime?" I asked.

"Sure," was all she said.

"I don't know what, but I'll figure out something."

Then, quite unexpectedly, she said, "How about a ride on your motorcycle?"

"We can do that," I answered.

The next day I was rolling through the countryside, down a road I had never been on before, watching the numbers on the mailboxes flash by. I was looking for the address Susan had given me the day before. Suddenly, I saw the address and quickly braked, down-shifted my gears, and cut hard into the driveway. It had come quicker than expected, and it was all I could do not to go flying past. Riding past and turning around may have been a wiser choice, however, for when I whipped into the drive, the pavement changed to gravel. As soon as my tires hit the gravel, I dumped my bike right there at the entrance to her house. I got up as quickly as I could and was dusting myself off when I noticed a man, Susan's father, sitting on the porch. He had witnessed the whole thing. I grunted my bike back onto its tires, started it, and rode the last twenty yards from the road to the front of the house. I turned off the motor and removed my helmet and said, "Howdy, Ah'm Scotty. Ah'm here to see Susan."

"Are you alright?' he asked.

"Yeah, wasn't expecting that gravel," I said in an embarrassed tone while continuing to pat the dirt off my pants. Then Susan emerged from the front door.

"Here she is," he said.

"Hi, are you okay?" she asked.

"Heh, heh, yeah," I was feeling really embarrassed, "didn't see the gravel 'til it was too late."

Then quietly she asked, "You're not going to do that with me on there, are you?"

"Let's hope not," her dad chimed in.

I grinned and said, "Ah'm not plannin' on it." I handed Susan a helmet, and she climbed on the seat behind me, and I cautiously steered down the drive and onto the road.

Being in the same church, the same Sunday school class, I saw Susan frequently without much effort. In addition to that, we started to go on rides and occasionally had time together when there was some sort of church event. We had dinner a couple times but, since I was working long hours at Olson's and she was working at D&W, a local grocery store, it wasn't often. I wasn't sure what to think about Susan at first; it was nice just to have a friend, someone to do things with. I had told her about Becky, but I was very cryptic about it, and truthfully, I downplayed the seriousness of the relationship. I didn't lie about anything; I just wasn't very forthcoming.

In the class, I met a guy named Doug who had started dating Beth. Doug had a nice BMW motorcycle, and we began to take rides together on the weekends—Beth on the back of his, Susan on the back of mine. Doug even began to work with me at Olson's, so it was easy to make plans that included the sisters.

Susan's family had all grown up in Rockford, attended R.B.C. their entire lives, and the three sisters all graduated from a Baptist high school. Many times I felt like a fish out of water, like I had that morning when Lloyd turned his truck into San Jacinto's parking lot, and I found myself knee-deep in Baptists. But after a couple of months of this, I became more comfortable with it all, and a subtle fondness began to develop between Sue and me.

The roots I was planting in Rockford went a little deeper when I began to play soccer in a men's' league in Grand Rapids. The team I played for was sponsored by a local sporting goods store called "Bill and Paul's." They may not have had the lofty goals as Antonio and the Amarillo Challengers, but they played the game just as seriously. Once again, like with the Challengers, it was a bit of a process to arrive out of the blue and develop a playing relationship with total strangers. Again, I was not a star on the team, but the others recognized that I possessed some attributes that could benefit the team, mainly speed and dangerous headers. They also came to realize that I was a very accurate passer of the ball. I don't know if in the three years which I played for Bill and Paul's if I ever scored a goal, but I racked up a ton of assists.

There were not many spectators at these games—mainly wives and girlfriends—but one fan I began to see more and more was Sue. I remember the first time it dawned on me that she was one of the few fans in the stands; it took me off guard. After the game, I casually walked across the field and with a drawl and in the words of LaVisa, asked, "Good honk, what are yew doin' here?"

"Well," she began, "you mentioned you had a game here today; I thought I would come and watch."

"So, how'd yew lahk it?"

"You're pretty fast."

"Yeah," I smirked a little, "Ah can run."

"It took me a while to find you, though," she added.

"Why's that?" I wondered.

"'Cause you're as dark as the Mexicans on your team," she joked.

I took it as a compliment and replied, "Yeah, my grandma, on my dad's side, was an Indian; it doesn't take much for me to get dark."

The field was next to the Grand River, and we took a leisurely stroll by the waterfront. Maybe an hour passed before I had to leave to go to work a few hours at Olson's. Before we separated, we made tentative plans for a motorcycle ride that evening.

After dinnertime, the four of us met at Sue and Beth's house. It was a beautiful, cool Michigan evening, so we decided to ride out to the Grand Haven pier on Lake Michigan. After zipping down forty miles of West Michigan back roads, we popped out near the Grand Haven pier just in time to see the sunset.

Grand Haven was gorgeous that night, and the sun hung like a giant orange in the cool haze that hung over the great lake. Like with many things, this picturesque view hurled me back into my past. Several memories unexpectedly popped into my consciousness: sitting at the waterfront at Castaway, lying on the bluff overlooking Lake Superior with Karen, and sitting on Indiana Deb's front porch. Now I had another melancholy vision to add to my mental slideshow. In that moment, I knew that I had to tell Susan more about Becky before things got too serious. Until then, she had been a casual acquaintance, a new friend I knew from church, similar to the friendship I had with LaVisa at San Jacinto. But after she began to show up at my soccer games and she, Doug, Beth, and I were basically going on rides that felt like double-dates, it was time to disclose more information about myself.

After the return ride from Grand Haven to Rockford, Sue and I found ourselves at the dam in Rockford. The Rockford dam was a common place for people to gather. It was right in the center of town and had a park surrounding it. As we sat there watching the Rogue River gently pour over the spillways, I gathered the courage and began to spill the beans.

"Ah think there is something you need to know," I began. Sue didn't say anything, just waited for me to continue. "There is more to Becky that you should know."

"Yeah, what?" Sue asked quietly.

"She's a girl Ah met in college, and we still see each other."

"Is she from around here?" Sue asked, trying to get the picture straight.

"No, she is at Moody Bible College in Chicago."

"Is she from Chicago?"

"No, she is from South Lyon, near Brighton," I continued to answer Sue's questions.

"How much do you see her?"

"Well, we actually don't see each other that much; our schedules don't allow it. We try to whenever we can, but right now we mainly talk on the phone and write letters."

Then she finally started to get to the questions that I think she *really* wanted answered. "How serious are you two?"

There was a pause as I formulated the words in my mind. I didn't want to say it in a way that would discourage Sue, but I also didn't want to give her the wrong idea; I had to tell her the truth. Even though Becky and I had our friction, she was still a woman I had proposed to, and even though distant, we remained a couple. Now that I had laid all my cards on the table, any future Becky and I might have together was in her hands; in many ways, I felt like I was waiting to see what Becky was going to do.

"We're going through a tough time right now," I started, "but the relationship is serious." I did not want to tell her about the refused proposal; I did not think it was worth bringing up; so it remained unmentioned. "Ah think you and Ah are okay right now, I continued, "but Ah just thought it was tahm to tell you about this." I could tell she was thinking hard about it all, but being the quiet girl that she was, Sue did not say anything further. Our stay at the dam ended, and I took her home.

THE GIRL OF MY DREAMS

CHAPTER 45

Sue and I continued to do things via Sunday school class, we took more rides, and she watched me play soccer. For a couple months, everything went on this way until one weekend, Becky came for a visit.

I had to tell Sue she was coming, so there would not be any accidental, uncomfortable meetings. She was not thrilled about it, but since I had been honest with her about Becky, she knew one day this was inevitable. I think she felt as long as Becky was in Chicago, she had me as a captive audience, and life rolled on comfortably. As much as she did not want it, she knew this day would come, and so she stayed away.

It was autumn and threatening snow the weekend that Becky drove north to see me. It had been a couple months since I had seen her, and it was good to see that red hair pull into my driveway and climb out of her car that chilly Friday afternoon. Knowing she was coming, I had worked hard that week to free my weekend from working at Olson's. I think both of us knew some sort of decision had to be made during this weekend; we had to shit or get off the pot, as my father used to say.

It was a wonderful visit, and Becky seemed to arrive with a fresh attitude about our situation. Our time was spent in deep conversation about many things but usually steered its way back to the topic of "us." We sat quietly talking and enjoying each other's company that night, when quite unexpectedly she said, "I would like to take you up on your proposal now." It was so out of context from what we had been discussing, that its meaning didn't register.

"What proposal?" I asked with a furrowed brow, trying to understand what she had said.

She looked at me intently, so I would know that it was something monumental,

"Your Christmas proposal," she said very deliberately and with a faint smile. Then it hit me like a cold wave. I was dumbstruck and just stared at her with a goofy grin pasted on my face.

Finally, I asked, "Really?" I wanted to be sure I was actually hearing her correctly.

"Really," she confirmed with a tender look. "Let's get married."

We embraced and began to talk about what this meant. Keeping in character, I was thinking in overdrive, and she was only in first gear. I was advocating for a wedding as soon as the following spring; she wanted to aim for a date two or three years away. Now that she accepted, at age twenty-seven, I wanted this to move forward promptly; but age had no bearing in her thoughts for marriage at all.

I even went so far as to mention how soon I wanted to have children and how many. Neither of my plans matched hers. I wanted several kids, like my own Catholic family, and I wanted to start as soon as we said "I do." She wanted to wait, finish school, and land a decent job before considering bearing children. Becky also wanted a family similar to her own—three children or less. We had barely decided on marriage, and we were already discovering that our vision of a future together was vastly different. Just like our personalities, her dreams were calculated, intelligent, and quite wise. Mine were spontaneous, impetuous, and impatient.

Now in the world of "opposites attract," this might not always be a problem, but for Becky and me, it was. Of the things we had in common, one was certainly stubbornness in our ways. The joy of the moment got lost as we continued to haggle over the timing of the wedding and starting a family and the number of children we would try and bear together. These topics popped up many times the following day, and it was clear that we were both steadfast in our desires.

The evening before she returned to Chicago, we were once again locked in a debate as to when the wedding should take place. That night, she stayed with me in my apartment. We actually slept in the same bed and, being that we were eventually to wed, I would have gone all the way with her . . . if she would have allowed it. When it came to the physical aspects of our relationship, it was a good thing that she was a mature Christian of unquestionable moral standing, because I was not. I have always respected her for that and wish that I had been as strong as she was. Becky had a firm line drawn on what was physically acceptable, and what was not. I was like a pouting child who had just been told he couldn't have any cookies. Reluctantly, I never crossed Becky's line. In total honesty, I was a frustrated man, but I also admired her beyond words for her Godly stance. What gnawed at me was that, according to her timetable, this abstinence might continue for two or three years! It became a point of contention between us that night and the following morning. This, along with my impatient attitude about everything from the wedding date to when we should have our first child, turned a joyful evening into a tearful break-up. In a short twenty-four hour period, we went from wonderful to woeful. I recall the callus words I spoke to Becky the morning she left: "Well, if we can't come to terms about these things now, we have no business getting married." When I heard myself say this, I could hardly believe it. I was basically laying down an ultimatum that I knew she could not meet. I felt that after taking so long to decide she wanted to marry me, and driving all the way from Chicago to tell me, that she would relent on these issues . . . I was wrong. Even though I knew what a Godly woman Becky was, I learned something else about her that day; no matter what the leverage, she was uncompromising in every aspect in her life with Christ. I also learned that, in spite of the gains I had made as a Christian, I was miles away from living right.

Everything within me that Sunday morning told me to backup and make amends, to find some compromise in my plans, but my pride would not let me. I allowed Becky, whom I loved deeply at the time, to tearfully pack her things and walk out of my life. It was not a time I like to remember; I was unwavering and mean. We hugged a cold hug and said goodbye, and I didn't even walk her to her vehicle. From the window, I watched Becky walk through freshly fallen snow to her car, which she had left parked in the street. When she reached it, she found a parking ticket on it. In one of the few times I ever saw Becky angry, she snatched the ticket from under her wiper, looked at it, crumpled it up, and threw it down. I could tell she was in pain, yet I did not move from the window. It took her a few minutes to clean and defrost her windshield, and I was given every opportunity to go down and make it right, but I was frozen in my obstinance. Then, after what seemed an eternity, she slowly drove down the street and out of sight.

I continued to look out the window long after she had gone. I focused on the tire tracks left in the snow and wondered if I had made a mistake letting her go, if I would ever see her again. I chastised myself at how mean I had been, how unforgiving and uncompromising. It made no sense, yet there I stood a victim of my own pride while the girl of my dreams drove out of my life. In the days and weeks that followed, Becky and I did not talk, not even once. Days went by, weeks passed, and then months. The damage was done; we were finished. The red-headed beauty who caught my attention walking across the cafeteria floor at N.M.U. years prior had agreed to marry me, and I made that impossible by my stubbornness. Now it all had disintegrated into heart-wrenching silence.

Only a couple days after Becky left, Sue called. "Is your friend from Chicago gone?"

"Yes, she's gone," I somberly replied.

"Can I come over?" she asked.

I wasn't sure if I wanted to talk with Sue, or anyone for that matter, but told her, "Sure, Ah'm not doin' anything. C'mon over."

For a couple days in my apartment, I had been stewing over the swift change of fortune for me and Becky; I was hoping Sue wasn't going to force me to discuss it. When she arrived, we talked over a cup of coffee and to my relief, there was no mention of Becky.

For the winter months that followed, Sue and I spent more and more time together. The topic of Becky was seldom brought up but lingered like a ghost hiding in the corner of a room. Slowly, as it became clearer that Becky was a chapter in my life that had passed, Sue and I became closer, and we began to focus on each other. We were opposites; I was loud, outgoing, and egotistical, while Sue was quiet, unpretentious, and humble. Ironically, she was very similar to Becky, except she approached me in a different way. We turned out to be the stereotypical "opposites attract" couple. I was involved with many things: the church youth group, *2nd Chance Band*, high school soccer, and working for Olson's American Marine. On many occasions, Sue brought me dinner at Olson's. In much the same way as Indiana Deb waited hand-and-foot on Deek and me, Sue was very servile in her actions. I would be a liar if I claimed this didn't have an attractive quality.

It became obvious that something special was brewing between Sue and me. As time went on, we saw more and more of each other. Slowly, Becky faded into a memory, but not totally. Occasionally, I wondered if she was a chapter in my life whose final sentence had been read; to be honest I wasn't quite sure. As Sue and I grew closer, Becky became the final hurdle, a festering issue that wouldn't quite die and kept us from moving forward as a couple. It was common for us to become embroiled in conversations about our relationship, only to trip across Becky like a tree root stretched across our path. Sue knew about Becky, but had no clue as to our history, that our relationship spanned several years and of how close we had come to getting married. It was information that I did not willingly share and Sue was unaware of how good Becky had been for me. It didn't matter, to Sue she was just a girl I needed to forget.

There was a sense of finality in the silence that followed Becky's departure the previous winter. As I relegated her to the past, I slowly fell in love with the sweet Baptist girl with the pretty eyes. I had come to the realization that Sue, not Becky, was the girl of my dreams and I wanted to marry her. One evening in May I invited Sue to my apartment and like many times before, we strolled down to the dam over the Rogue River. As we sat holding hands she sensed my anxiety and asked, "Are you alright? You seem nervous." She had no idea what was on my mind and that in my pocket was an engagement ring. It had not been an easy road, but it had become clear that Susan was God's plan for me and I stoked up my nerve to pop the question.

Several months earlier I had invited Sue to my apartment and I told her, "Maybe we should cool it until I resolve my relationship with Becky."

Much to my surprise, the normally passive Susan said, "No, I don't think I want to do that." Then she continued, "You told me you two haven't spoken in months; you need to let her go and think about what you have right here."

"Yeah, but Becky and I have been through a lot . . ."

I didn't finish the sentence when Sue interrupted me. "Becky's in the past." She spoke with such clarity and determination that it seemed to snap me out of my stupor. But more than that, what she said was true: Becky *was* in the past, and Sue and I fit like a hand in a glove.

"Wake up, stupid," I thought to myself, "What more do you want?" We sat down, and I held her hand and said, "You know, you're right." Then I went one step further, "If we're talking like this, and you're already telling me what to do, we might as well be married . . . don't you think?"

There was a hint of humor in what I had asked, but the seed had been planted. In the heart of the discussion, it indeed felt like we were a married couple solving a situation. With hardly any reaction she said, "I don't know, you worry me sometimes."

I knew what she meant. I understood that with my crazy history any girl should be worried, nevertheless I asked as if I just arrived in town from a seminary, "Worried . . . worried about what?"

Sue rolled her pretty eyes, smiled, and then looked at me intently, "You're a dreamer," she began, "you don't seem to like to stay in one place too long."

"Huh," I laughed a little, "If I had a dime for every time I've heard that, I wouldn't be livin' in this tiny rat-hole."

"Do you deny it . . . dreamer?" she said with a bit of playfulness.

"Naw, I don't think I can; the proof is in the pudding, as they say."

"Yeah, but I think you're right," she replied. It seemed to be a comment out of context.

"Right about what?" I asked a little puzzled.

"Maybe we should be married."

As unexpectedly as I had bumped into Karen at Castaway, the evening had spun on itself and delivered the unimaginable. It had been several months since I delivered my dogmatic ultimatum to

Becky, and she drove out of my life. Now there I sat with Susan and we began the first conversations about a life together.

Now months later, after what seemed like a saga of biblical proportion, I was sitting with the girl of my dreams, and it wasn't Karen, Babe, Indiana Deb, or even Becky, but a quiet Baptist girl from a small town in West Michigan. Once again, it was plain to see that God's plan was different from anything I tried to force. It was a cool summer evening and the water spilled gently over the dam with a low, muffled sound that you could feel in your feet. Finally I reached into my pocket and produced the ring and holding it out to Sue asked, "Will you marry me?" Softly and without hesitation she beamed up at me and answered, "I would love to." I slipped the ring on her finger, we kissed, and the next phase of my life began.

A NEW CHAPTER

CHAPTER 46

Saturday, October 17, 1987, was a cool, overcast fall day. It was trying to rain as the soccer game began. It was a make-up game that had been canceled earlier in the season because of inclement weather. It was against a team that could easily dominate us, but my mind was elsewhere. I wasn't concerned at all about the outcome. Later that afternoon, Sue and I would be married. People thought I was nuts for coaching a soccer match the morning of my wedding, but in reality, it helped keep my mind off of things and calmed my nerves. After the game I went home, showered, put on my tux, and drove to the church only a few blocks away.

Not long before the ceremony started, I realized that I had not eaten anything all morning, and I was beginning to feel light-headed. My buddy Steve, from college, was one of my groomsmen and at the last minute, I asked him if he would drive down to the Corner Bar and bring me back a hotdog. He looked at me like I was an idiot at first, but then realized that I really needed to eat something, so he obliged my request. My wedding party included my first-year college roommate and childhood pal Kevin from Leisure Lake; my brother, Jeff; my cousin, Dave; and Art, Pete, and Steve, from Dakota House. When Steve arrived with my hotdog and an order of fries, he was drenched in his tuxedo. During his trip to the Corner Bar, it had begun to rain, and he got caught in it as he stood outside and waited at the take-out window.

On Sue's side, she had Kelly, her friend from high school; her sisters, Beth and Linda; and a friend from Rockford Baptist named Heather standing up for her. The wedding was simple and modest in number of guests invited. My sisters, Tammy and Darcy, sang, and at one point, Sue and I sang to each other. The ceremony went off with no major glitches except for the piano player, Rick, from the *Second Chance Band*. It is safe to say that most who knew him would consider Rick as aloof and were not surprised when he added some drama to the ceremony.

The groomsmen from left to right: Pete (from Dakota), Dave Hazel (cousin), Jeff Morey (brother), Scotty, Kevin ('Griz'-childhood friend and roommate from Stonehenge House), Steve (from Dakota), and Art (from Dakota). Nephew Steve Morey in front center

The song that my sisters were singing was right at the top of their range. It had a key change in the middle that made it even trickier, but they had figured out how to handle it. At the time when Rick was supposed to step up to the piano to play, Sue and I were facing each other, holding hands. Sue had her back to him and could not see what was happening, but I could see him out of the corner of my eye. He was still comfortably seated in the front row with his legs crossed, smiling and nodding his head at the beauty of the moment. With her teeth gritted tightly together, Sue tried not to let people see there was something amiss and without moving her jaw asked me quietly, "What is going on?"

"Rick is still sitting down," I mumbled. Finally, my sister Denise leaned forward and flicked Rick in the back. It dawned on him that the uncomfortable dead space in the ceremony was because he was supposed to already be at the piano. He hastily bungled up to the piano and, flustered with his gaff, quickly dove into the music. When he began to play, he started in the higher key change, the change that wasn't supposed to occur until the middle of the song. Consequently, when the key change came, it was even higher than what had been practiced. My poor sisters struggled to make it work, but it was obvious it was beyond their capability. It was not a major meltdown, but Tammy and Darcy felt horrible. Rick seemed oblivious to the fact that he had messed things up and that Sue and I wanted to brain him. I'm sure my sisters wanted to take him out back and give a good old Irish thumping.

I think my side of the family was a little taken aback when they realized the reception afterwards was dry—that is, no booze. Being sensitive to my new Baptist in-laws, relatives, friends, and wife, I didn't push my desire to have alcohol at the party. We also had made no arrangements for dancing. This was unheard of for my family and my college friends. Basically, our reception was a nice dinner, with social time. Oh, there were the customary speeches and a few standards like the throwing of the garter and bouquet, but it was very mild in comparison to the Catholic receptions from weddings on my side of the family. I was fearful of stepping out of bounds at the start, so the thought of a conservative dinner was fine with me. My dad and brother's-in-law remedied that with a kegger party at my sister Darcy's house late into the evening after the reception had ended. Sue and I stopped in, and I had a few. It might have been the first time she saw my side of the family in action. She was probably wondering in that moment what she had gotten herself into.

The marriage of Scotty and Sue Hazel, October 17, 1987. The morning of the wedding Scotty coached a soccer game.

That night, we stayed in the honeymoon suite in the Amway Grand Plaza Hotel in downtown Grand Rapids. The next morning we boarded a plane to Boston where we rented a car. We had made plans ahead of time and rendezvoused with my Aunt Betty, who lived there. We spent two days with my aunt. My cousin Wendy met us there and gave us a quick tour of the sights of Boston. After Boston, we drove up the coast road to Bar Harbor, Maine, where we stayed in a hotel virtually looking out over the Atlantic. For several days, we saw the sights and sounds of Maine and daily ate cheap lobster. Eventually, we made our way back to Boston and flew home to Michigan.

We set up housekeeping in my apartment and began our life as husband and wife. Being that I was twenty-eight at the time of our marriage, we did not want to wait too long to start our family. Sue was younger than I—twenty four—but did not want to wait for children either. Our plan was to spend three years settling in and getting to know each other before trying to have our first child. It was during these three years that Sue was the bread-winner. While she worked a steady job, first at D&W food store, then as a law clerk for the firm *Wheeler, Upham, and Bryant* in Grand Rapids, I was working for *Olson's American Marine,* coaching soccer at Rockford High School, and eventually re-entered college to earn a teaching degree.

Six months after our wedding, Sue and I were sitting and talking over dinner when the phone rang.

"Hello," I answered in a typical monotone manner. There was only silence on the other end, but a cracking sound that I instantly identified as a long distance call coming in.

"Hello?" I said again, only this time it sounded like a question.

I was about to hang up when a familiar voice finally answered. "Hello, dreamer." Immediately, a vision of red hair flashed into my mind: "Becky?"

"Yes, it's li'l ol' me," she acknowledged, trying to hide her nervousness with a cute answer. I was excited to hear her voice, but I was nervous in my own right. The last time I had seen or heard from Becky, it was in this very same apartment. I wanted to hear everything that she had to say; I wanted to know what prompted her to call after all the months that had passed since she drove away in anger. I wanted to tell her how sorry I was about how I had acted that last weekend we spent together before the relationship crumbled. I wanted to do all these things, but with Sue still sitting at the table eating dinner a few feet away, I didn't know if I should. I cautiously listened and spoke with Becky for several tense minutes before she finally dropped the bomb.

"Scott," she began, "I'm sorry how we parted last winter. I know we have some major differences, but I can't get you out of my mind." As she spoke, I didn't utter a single word, but just sat with the receiver pressed against my ear in silence. Becky continued, "I was hoping that maybe I could come and see you again." I was stunned. "Do you think I could come and visit?" she added.

One minute I was happily eating dinner with Sue, and the next minute the red-haired girl from my past was asking to visit. I knew the answer had to be "no" but at the same time, I missed the friendship I had with Becky. She was more than a romantic acquaintance; she and I had a history born through fire. Becky was the person who pulled me out of my funk when Karen started dating Ross. She was the one who let me go to Texas, only praying that I would return to her. And she was the steadfast Christian who showed me what it meant to walk the talk. I had always felt Becky was a person God put into my life to save me from myself. She was important, significant, and I wanted to see her; I wanted to talk. All the while that these thoughts raced through my mind, there was a silence. Finally, I picked up the phone and trailing the long cord behind me, walked with it over to the window. As I looked out into the evening, I could vividly remember Becky crumpling up her parking ticket and driving away in the snow. I wasn't sure how to say it, but when I finally answered her question, what came out once again sounded mean. "I don't think my wife would appreciate that." I didn't mean for it to, but my tone almost sounded like I was saying, "Sorry, too late. You had your chance, and I have moved on." There was a brief hesitation of shock before Becky responded.

"Oh," she said, "I'm sorry. I didn't know." I could hear the shock in her voice, and I wanted to comfort her and tell her how it all came about, but then again, "Why," I thought, "what good could come from that?"

"Congratulations," she added. "I should let you go."

"Thanks for calling," I said, trying to soften the tone from before. "It was nice to hear from you."

"Goodbye, Scott," she said.

"Goodbye, Becky," I answered, and I heard the phone go quickly dead. I hung up the phone and stood looking out the window, trying to digest what had just happened.

"Who was that?" Sue asked with a hint of suspicion.

"Just an old friend," I answered without any further explanation.

About a month later, I received a package in the mail with no return address on it. Inside, I found the jewelry box I had made for Becky when I proposed marriage to her. With the jewelry box was a short note that only read, "Scott, I thought you should have this back." It was the last I ever heard from Becky, the beautiful red-haired girl who had done so much for me. A new chapter had begun in my life.

SUSAN

CHAPTER 47

From the day we met on the beach at Versluis Park Susan had quietly found her way into my heart and we had fallen in love. I came to realize in a short time, that she possessed the best qualities of all those girls rolled into one wonderful woman, she was the complete package. She was pretty, patient, athletic, kind, and when the time was right, passionate. But perhaps what captivated me the most was that she was Godly and tolerant. The love Sue had for me was in spite of myself; a forgiving love like that which God offers man. I think in many cases, that is what men need. Like I counsel many teenage girls today, "men are just big, dumb animals; you need to be prepared to accept some past demons." Not that there aren't some great guys out there with no ghosts in their past, there are, unfortunately for Sue, I was not one of them. Fortunately for me, she saw deeper than that and falling in love with her was the best thing to happen to me.

But I'm not letting girls off the hook either. There are certainly girls out there with just as saucy a past as mine, but I think typically men are trading up; they usually get the better end of the deal when they marry. I knew that this was my saga and a man like me needed a woman like Susan. My manic past needed someone to come along and say, "Stop the nonsense." She was easy to fall in love with and unlike the roster of girls who appeared and disappeared over many years; Susan and I had courted for only six months.

After we wed, our plan was to wait three years until we had children. In those three years, like many couples, we got to know each other. That may sound like a ridiculous statement for a man and woman who have married, but in reality sleeping in the same bed every night and sharing a bathroom every morning can teach people more about each other than many are prepared for. Guys are exceptionally good at hiding nasty habits until the knot is tied and it is too late for the poor bride to reconsider or remedy. In many cases the first big test for newlyweds is the initial time when the young wife's head is held beneath the covers after her caveman has dropped some horrible fart in bed. After that, the education comes in waves of, "You are so gross!" events. For some reason guys think stuff like that is hilarious and as years roll by there is no shortage of immature revelations of men on their wives. Sue and I were no different . . . poor girl.

In those first years of marriage, when Sue was learning that my family was heavy drinkers, that I gag when I brush my teeth, and that I can complete an entire crossword puzzle while sitting on the pot, we took advantage of not having any children. One of my favorite memories from that time was when Sue and I biked from Petoskey to Wilderness State Park and then to Mackinaw Island.

We had made Sue's car, a little Dodge Omni, our good car and I was driving a beat up old Crown Victoria as a work car. We packed our camping gear and loaded our bikes on the Omni and headed north. We left the car by the State Police station in Petoskey and loaded our gear onto our bikes. I had the same small tent that Bobby and I had used thirteen years earlier when we rode to Pinery Park in Ontario and got driven into the ditch by the hay truck on the Queen's Highway. We packed as light as possible bringing only a hobo pie maker in which to prepare all our food. To keep the bread for the pies protected, we packed it in coffee cans. The most cumbersome items bungied to our bicycle frames, were two identical sleeping bags. It was one of our first big purchases as a money strapped young couple, but items we knew we would use for years.

We rode County Road 119 from Petoskey to the outskirts of Mackinaw City, which is also known as the "Tunnel Through the Trees." It is a beautiful twisting two-lane that parallels Lake Michigan through small villages and thick forests. In a word it is scenic. Many times over the miles I reminisced about my trips to Canada, Castaway, and Frontier Ranch, but this time was different, this time I was with my wife. When we stopped at Cross Village for a splash to drink, Susan sat down on a bench to soothe her muscles. It was a hot day but the breeze off of Lake Michigan made it a perfect summer day. Sue was sweating and her face was beat red. I put my hand on her head and said, "Good job, kid." I could feel the heat coming from Susan's hair and the sweat soaked her tank top and shorts. Instantly I flashed back to that wonderful day when Alabama Suzy and I went for our epic ride in Minnesota. "You are finally livin' the dream," I thought silently. Sue looked up with her wonderful hazel eyes and smiled. She had no idea what I was hoping would happen that night in the tent. But for now, we had some miles to put behind us and I said, "Let's get back at it."

Scotty and Sue biking near Cross Village, Michigan on County Road 119

The scenic road descended after Cross Village for an amazing three miles and spilled out into the sand dunes at lake level. We pulled off at a beach and took a glorious swim in the cold water. Unlike my swim with Alabama Suzy years before, I pulled Susan close and we embraced while the waves lapped at our waists. Eventually we stumbled back to the beach and onto our laden bikes. We finished the trek to Wilderness and set up the small tent. We zipped our sleeping bags together like one giant bag and nestled in. I suddenly realized that the day of biking had worked up some pretty powerful gas. I knew our love was solid when in the midst of rounding third base I slowly released a silent odor into the bag. As soon as I got the least little hint of the raunchy scent, I pulled the bag closed over the top of Sue's head. As she wrestled trying to find a way out, in a muffled voice she pleaded, "Good lord, let me out of here!" I just laughed like a fifth grade boy.

"Oh my lord, that is disgusting!" she gasped as she panicked to escape.

It wasn't what I had in mind when my hormones were scheming at Cross Village, and when I finally released her it did not stop the ballgame we had started earlier. This let me know we were the perfect match.

For the next few days we made trips to Mackinaw City and the island. We roughed it and loved it. It was one of many great memories Susan and I would make in the years to come. We peddled the road back to Petoskey, packed our campfire smelling gear into the Omni, and made the four hour drive home to Rockford. It was in times like these that the mountainous journey I had taken was eased into peace of mind. The love that Sue and I shared allowed me to relax and realize what a gift God had given me; contentment. Together we began to forge a life together; the conservative Baptist girl and the wild Catholic boy.

THE OTHER ME

CHAPTER 48

It was the spring of 1991, and my life was a hectic hodge-podge of activity that kept me on the go. Among other things, I was still the varsity soccer coach at Rockford High School, for both the boys and girls. It was March, and as usual, the pre-season practices for the girls' season had begun. I had also undertaken the role as the Youth Director at Rockford Baptist while the church was between Youth Pastors. I didn't have the proper education to be a youth pastor, nor was my character faithful enough to warrant such a title, but the elders in the church had seen how easily I built rapport with young people and how proficient I was at programming activities; that was good enough for them. To fill the niche, they re-named the title of the position and hired me as a director.

Sue and I shared a passion for bicycling, and she and I had already been an integral part of previous bike trips for the church. We had not only taken them biking to the U.P. but had also facilitated wilderness canoe trips at Big Island Wilderness Area near the settlement of Steuben. Our most ambitious ventures were the rugged backpacking and canoe trips to Isle Royale National Park in Lake Superior. We had purchased a bus, brought several hauling trailers, and built a chuck wagon. Together, Sue and I recreated our own version of the Young Life trips I had taken in high school that steered me to Christ and changed my life. I had come full-circle and was attempting to give back to teenagers a taste of what I experienced at their age. We called the company T.E.S.T. Camp, which stood for *To Examine Self Totally.* We were overjoyed that a couple of churches had hired us to plan their trips, and by February several excursions for the coming summer were already in the beginning stages of planning. T.E.S.T Camp had potential, and I had grand visions for it.

Meanwhile, I had quit singing with the *2nd Chance Band* to pursue my education. My studies at Grand Valley State University were nearly finished, and my teaching degree was within reach. Sue and I had been married nearly four years, and she was four months pregnant with our first child. I was thirty-one years old, and many of the dreams I had for my life were beginning to become realities. Life was good.

The only drawback to all these activities was how poorly I slept. My mind was torn in several different directions and as a result, I was beginning to physically break down. The most annoying side-effect to my insomnia was constant pain in my lower back, and I was a regular at the chiropractor's office. I had tried a number of different things to relieve chronic lower back pains, but none seemed to really do the trick. Sometimes the pain got so severe that I would lay flat on my back on the floor with my feet propped up on the couch. This was usually in the middle of the night and was the only way I could find enough relief to sleep. You would think that something like this would be a warning sign to see a doctor, but I didn't.

Another weird ailment I was experiencing at the time was a misshaped testicle. It was not information that I was willing to share, even to a doctor. It wasn't painful at all but kind of felt like a piece of cauliflower. I just figured it was a soccer injury and waited for it to cure itself. After all, getting kneed, kicked, or drilled in the "man-berries" (as Frank Romano calls them) is a common occurrence in soccer, and I played and practiced hard. I was confident that eventually these little nuisances would pass, and I continued to soldier through my schedule.

Rockford's basketball team was playing in the state tournament, and one Friday evening Sue and I went to watch them in a game being played at Ferris State University. Driving home that evening, I experienced some sort of a spasm or attack that almost forced me to pull off the road.

"That's it," I finally said, "I'm going to see a doctor."

The next day I made an appointment. Like many young couples, we had not established a family physician, so I simply called the closest doctor's office to our apartment. Amazingly when I saw the doctor, I was reluctant to discuss my testicle; I intended only to discuss my back problems with him. I had thought about mentioning it, but when he politely knocked on the exam-room door and entered, he was a she. Not only was the doctor a woman, but a surprisingly young, attractive woman. Suddenly, the exam had a new dynamic. "She *has* to be a nurse," I reasoned. But a quick peek at the name tag on her white coat revealed the title, "Dr. Young." She smiled and introduced herself, "Hi, I'm Doctor Young."

When I heard this, I joked silently to myself, "Young, alright, too damn young!"

As she looked at my chart, she glanced up and asked, "Are you the soccer coach at the high school?"

The question caught me off guard, but I answered, "Yeah, how'd you know that?"

"My little sister played for you last year; I saw a couple games."

"Uh oh," I thought, "this is not good." I had a sudden flashback of the time I came home from N.M.U. to have my wisdom teeth removed. Because they had become impacted, I had to have oral surgery. My mother accompanied me, so I had someone to drive me home. It turned out that the assisting nurse was a girl named Cheryl I knew from high school. She was very attractive and in high school many guys, myself included, secretly drooled over her. Throughout the preparation, she and I had a very pleasant conversation, catching up on all the news since we graduated. Eventually, I was given gas and instructed to count backwards from 100. The last number I remember was 98. In what seemed like only seconds, I awoke with a mouth filled with soggy, bloody gauze. What happened next is still mentioned from time to time when my mother tells of embarrassing things her children have done.

I was still groggy when the three of us entered the elevator. With my mother holding one arm and Cheryl holding the other, I began to tell Cheryl in detail all the raunchy things I wanted to do to her in high school. My mom started yelling, "Shut up!" at me, but it did no good. Erupting from some deep, subliminal black hole, I could not stop the spew of explicit perversion pouring out of my mouth. Cheryl only laughed and said, "It's OK, this happens all the time . . .

it's the drug we use; it's like truth serum. Whatever you are thinking, you are saying." It didn't seem to bother her one iota.

"Oh great," my mother exhaled in embarrassment. The entire time they spoke, I continued the torrent from my dark side. The moment that burned into my brain the most was my mother finally slapping my stitched up mouth and yelling, "You shut your filthy mouth!"

When we exited the elevator and Cheryl held the door for us, she sweetly smiled and un-phased said, "It was nice to see you again."

These were the visions occupying my mind as my exam with the pretty Dr. Young progressed. I thought to myself, "There is no way I'm letting her touch my business!" I continued to have a conversation in my head. "Who knows what might happen if she touches me there! This could be the most embarrassing day of my life!" In fact, I was becoming increasingly un-nerved as the examination proceeded through the normal paces, getting closer and closer to that awkward moment when THOSE infamous words are spoken.

When she opened her mouth to say, "Drop your pants," I was preparing to counter with, "Not for you, girlie!"

But instead she said, "Dr. Kitts will be right in."

At this, I think I audibly "whewed" a sigh of deliverance.

It was with reluctance and only as a side bar that I later said to Dr. Kitts, "By the way, while I'm here can I show you something else?"

This was the ridiculous manner in which I told the doctor about my abnormal testicle. At this point, I had known about it for several months and was now finally telling a doctor as an after-thought! Stupid.

The visit with Dr. Kitts was going along more or less like I expected, and I was waiting for him to prescribe something to cure my pain and fix my testicle. Toward the end of the visit, he said, "Let's take an x-ray of your chest."

I recall thinking, "I wonder what my chest has to do with my back pains and my testicle?" After the x-rays were taken, he told me he wanted me to see another doctor, and he could set up an appointment for the next day.

The following day I found myself seated in a waiting room filled with pregnant women! I was beginning to think a mistake had been made when a nurse opened the door and, looking at a chart, called, "Hazel Scott?" Embarrassed, I rose and corrected her, "That's Scott Hazel." She looked up and said, "Oh, I'm sorry, I was . . ." I knew what she was going to say but didn't let her finish the sentence,

"I'm wondering what I'm doing here, too," I said as I answered her summons and walked through the waiting room, I could feel the eyes of all the other women who surely must have also been wondering why I was there.

It wasn't long until I realized the reason Dr. Kitts arranged this strange visit. It was to undergo an absolutely humiliating, fun little test called a "scrotal ultrasound." Lying flat on my back in a room with several people I had never seen before in my life, I had on no pants. I was worried more about shrinkage or an uncontrolled boner than what might be wrong with my testicle. Of the two, I quickly decided shrinkage was the lesser of two evils. With a tightly twisted towel cinched up under my man-berries, I was asked to hold them as best as I could. While I did this, they spread gel all over them and methodically ran an ultrasound camera on me. I completely understood the process as I had recently sat next to Sue several times while they checked her pregnancy.

"Have you found the heartbeat, doc?" I asked in uncomfortable humor.

But it did not have the desired affect; they all were highly focused on whatever was showing on the monitor. Finally, without blinking his gaze at the screen, the doctor slowly said, "No, no heartbeat, yet." His voice had no humor in it, just serious contemplation. To my amazement, it was about this time that there were two quick knocks on the door and without anyone responding, Dr. Kitts entered the room. I was twenty miles from Rockford and I recall thinking, "Wow, what a great doctor," I thought, "to check in on me at 2:00 on a Wednesday. I thought most doctors golfed on Wednesdays."

He said "hello," then quickly joined the rest studying the ultrasound images on the monitor.

When the examination ended, I was sent back to run the visual gauntlet of pregnant women in the waiting room. It was at this moment I started to think something unusual was up.

After about twenty minutes, it was Dr. Kitts who called me back into a vacant examination room. I hopped up on the examination table, and he rolled a chair from a desk directly in front of me and sat down. The words he spoke at that moment have been burned into my memory ever since. Without hesitation, he looked straight into my eyes and said, "You have cancer, and it doesn't look good."

I laughed out loud a little until I realized it was not a joke. Suddenly, all the unusual attention made sense. A numbness began to fill my mind. "I can't have cancer," I reasoned. "I have too much to do." Then the impact of what he actually said started to sink in; what does ". . . and it doesn't look good" mean? Dr. Kitts continued to fill me in on some of the details as he showed me the results of the x-rays and ultrasound, but I vaguely remember. My mind had already drifted away, and I was thinking about what this would mean for my family, school, church kids, and soccer team. Telling all these people was going to be devastating. "Why me, why now?" was the stunned repetition in my mind.

Looking through the windshield, I watched the scenery pass by as I drove the twenty miles back to Rockford. I tried to take it all in, not miss any detail, wondering if it was the last time I would look on the random things that scrolled by as I drove. The song "Forever Young" played on the radio. "How cruel of God," I thought, and I began to openly weep. This was going to affect a lot of people, and I wondered if I would live long enough to hear my child call me "daddy"; I agonized over Sue raising our child alone. But true to form, I was also battling a giant case of self-pity. I couldn't believe that this could happen to me! But then I realized everyone who receives this news probably asks themselves the same question. In reality, why *shouldn't* it happen to me? I was no different than anyone else.

So urgent was my situation that Dr. Kitts had tried to get me into surgery the next day. I talked him into waiting until Friday, so I could have a chance to inform the church, the youth group, my professors, my soccer team, and my family. "This is going to be a nightmare!" I thought.

Being that all this happened on a Wednesday, youth night at church, the timing of Dr. Kitts's crushing information was convenient. After telling my pastor and Sue, it was all I could do to control my emotions while informing the wide-eyed church kids. After the initial shock, I began to get a better grip on the situation and realized that

I needed to be stoic in order to bring a sense of ease and calmness to those closest to me. The more people I told, the easier it got for me, but my familiarity with each announcement didn't soften the blow to those who were hearing it for the first time. It was always difficult. One thing that became crystal clear to me as I muddled through this process was the lesson in faith I was receiving. There was nothing I could do for myself; it was all up to the doctors and to God. I gained a new understanding of what it meant to have my life in God's hands. Suddenly, I became aware of scripture that made more sense now than ever before. The Bible verse that rose above all the others was 1Peter 4:12-13: *"Beloved, do not be surprised at the fiery ordeal that is upon you, as if some strange thing were happening; it comes upon you as a test, but to the degree that you share the sufferings of Christ, keep on rejoicing . . . ,"* and a sense of peace began to take hold.

I spent the next day making calls to my professors at Grand Valley, informing the principal and athletic director at Rockford High School, and attempting to contact my parents in Flint . . . which I continuously failed to do. Telling Sue was the most difficult, and there were lots of shed tears. But perhaps equally as traumatic was telling the girls on the soccer team.

I handled the Thursday practice like any other, and I was hoping that no one had let the cat out of the bag. But there were no pre-empted confrontations by distraught teenagers, and I was able to tell them in my own way. It was tough because in the back of mind throughout practice, I knew what I had to do before I dismissed them for the day. I had emotionally invested a great deal into the program and developed a precious rapport with these girls. The program and the players were my "babies." I agonized over how they were going to get along without me. This egocentric attitude was only matched by how much I wore my heart on my sleeve, and it took an enormous effort to keep myself under control.

Toward the end of practice, I huddled all the girls in a corner of the soccer field.

"There's something I have to tell you," I started, "and unfortunately it's not good news." In dead silence with giant eyes staring at me, I told them I had cancer, and I had to leave the team immediately to have it treated.

Among the growing sniffles and shocked faces, one tiny girl named Mandi asked, "What kind of cancer?

I pretended I didn't hear her because I did not want to suffer the embarrassment of telling sixteen-year-old girls about my testicles. We basically collected into a team cry during which Mandi persisted, "Coach, what kind of cancer?"

After ignoring her several times, I eventually had to answer her. It was the first of many times in the next year that I would have to decide whether or not to be candid about my condition or flat out lie. In this case, I decided I better come clean, and I finally answered her. "I have testicular cancer."

A puzzled look washed over Mandi's face, and she asked for clarification.

"What kind?"

"This is cruel," I thought. "Testicular cancer," I repeated.

I could tell by the look on her face that she still did not understand. She wrinkled her brow as her eyes roamed the ground, trying to gain an understanding of what I had said. Several of the other girls looked at her as if to say, "Mandi, let it go." I could tell *they* knew what I was referring to.

Finally, I pointed awkwardly toward my crotch and said, "Testicular, you know, as in testicles?"

Suddenly, her eyes got huge, and she covered her mouth, but not before blurting out, "Oh, my God, your balls!?"

There was only silence, and then we all burst out laughing. She was embarrassed beyond imagination, but her timing was perfect, and it broke the emotional quagmire in which we had been stuck. It is a moment I both cherish and loathe to this day.

The next day, Friday, I was about to go into surgery, and I still not been able to contact my parents. I made one last attempt from a pay phone in the hospital lobby, and my father answered the phone. It took me by surprise since it was my mother who usually answered the phone. Although it was only a few measured words, I could hardly choke them out. "Dad, I don't have much time, but I have to tell you some bad news . . . I have cancer." My voice faltered, and I wasn't sure if he was able to understand what I had said.

After a couple of seconds, I barely heard him say, "Mmmm, how bad?"

"I'm heading into surgery right now."

Over the years our family, especially my dad, had been riddled with various cancers, heart attacks, and strokes. Now at thirty-one, it appeared I would die before my father. In the silence and measured words, I could feel the anguish over the phone. Without asking for any details, he simply said, "We'll be right there."

About that time, a nurse trolling through the lobby approached me and asked, "Are you Scott?" With the phone still pressed against my ear, I nodded.

"It's time," was all she said.

"I have to go, Dad," I said matter-of-factly.

"Alright, take it cool," was all I heard, and the conversation ended abruptly.

The surgery was to remove the source of my disease: my cancerous testicle. As in the past, I decided to go about this operation on my own terms; I decided to add a little humor to the dire situation. As I prepared that morning for the surgery, I took a felt tipped marker and drew two arrows on my stomach pointing toward my testicles. One arrow was labeled "good," and the other one labeled "bad," to indicate which one to take and which one to leave. I was hesitant at first to do this, thinking it might raise the ire of my doctor, but thought, "What can he do to me, cut off a nut?" When I awoke in "post op," the crew of doctors and nurses expressed the chuckle I had given them and assured me they had removed the correct testicle. A few weeks later, I began my chemotherapy treatments.

My oncologist, Dr. Zakem, had given it to me with both barrels. "We're either going to kill this cancer, or it will kill you." I was told my chances were, at best, 50-50, and I had no choice—the treatment had to be aggressive. I later realized that Dr. Zakem's no-nonsense aggressive approach saved my life. The alternative was a coffin. I received three different chemos intravenously over a five-day period, four times during the summer of 1991. Dr. Zakem allowed seventeen days to recover between treatments. In the simplest of explanations, it was a controlled death wherein the hope is that the cancer dies before the patient. In his explanation about my chemotherapy, Dr. Zakem had told me, "It will probably start out ok, but gradually get worse." What he also stated was how fickle chemotherapy can be . . . that in spite of trends, different people react differently to it. As it turned out, I was one of those people.

Metropolitan Hospital was full of activity and foreign sounds. My mother had come to sit with me and comfort me through my first chemotherapy treatment. She had been through this herself with lung and ovarian cancer. She knew an awful lot about cancer and cancer treatment; it was comforting to have her there.

I lay in my bed while a nurse went about rearranging the room, placing everything exactly where she wanted it. She was methodical, and I could tell she had done this many times before. Although she made small talk to help put me at ease, I was anxious and nervous. She put a port in the vein of my left arm and taped it into place. "You have wonderful veins," she marveled. "My nurses are going to love you." As she prepared a shot, she explained, "This is Decadron; it is an anti-nausea drug; it will keep you from vomiting from the chemo." With that statement, she put the needle into the port and pushed the Decadron into my veins. Almost immediately, I felt a sensation—like my scalp shrank on my head, like when you accidentally eat too much ripe horseradish. In an instant, I could tell I was going to puke.

"I'm going to throw up," I said in a panic. I was looking for a waste basket, but there didn't seem to be any around.

The nurse looked surprised, "That can't be so, that's anti-nausea medicine."

"I'm telling you I'm gonna hurl!" I said this time with conviction.

"Are you sure?" she asked in disbelief once again.

I was scanning the room for anything to catch what I knew was coming, but there wasn't a receptacle of any kind in sight. "Lady," I said tersely, "if you don't get me a bucket, you're gonna have a giant mess to clean up in about two seconds!"

Without stirring a bit, my mother said, "You better listen to him; he's going to puke."

At this, the nurse began to move with a purpose. Just in the nick of time, she emerged from the bathroom with a brisk step and a trash can in her hand. As she reached the edge of the bed, I grabbed it from her hands and began to unload my guts into it. When I finished,

I wiped my mouth with a tissue and said with a hint of Panhandle, "Ah told you Ah was gonna puke."

"I don't understand," she said a bit bewildered. "It's supposed to *stop* you from vomiting."

Casually, my mothered interjected, "You'll have to give it to him slowly. If you inject it quickly, all at once, he'll puke every time." The nurse seemed to ignore her advice until my mother added, "I've been through this; you just have to give it to him slowly."

"I'd listen to her," I said. "She's had cancer twice, and she's been to Vietnam." The nurse looked at me, wondering why I had mentioned my mother's trip to Vietnam.

"This lady," I began, nodding in the direction of my mother, "has had a husband die of polio, given birth to seven children, had a son die from leukemia, been through cancer twice, had one lung removed, and rescued my brother from a prison in Vietnam; she knows a lot of stuff." The nurse looked at her, and my mother, sitting calmly with her hands folded in her lap and looking like Eleanor Roosevelt, just nodded and smiled.

After some thought, the nurse calmly prepared another vile of Decadron and very slowly pushed it into my body over the course of about five long minutes. I had no reaction, no shrunken scalp, no vomit.

"That's amazing, thank you," she said, looking at my mom, who simply grinned and shrugged.

Then she prepared and hung a bag of clear liquid from the stainless-steel hook next to my bed, stuck the needle into the port, and then regulated the flow from the valve near the bottom of the bag.

"Is that the chemo?" I asked.

"Yup, that's the Sisplatinum, the heavy metal. This is the stuff that does all the damage, but it's also the stuff that's gonna save your life." When she said this, she raised her eyebrows as if to say, "This has to be done."

She knew what lay ahead was going to be tough. As she spoke, I felt a warm wave flush through my body. I could feel the chemicals spread through me. My head began to swim a little, and I slowly fell into a stupor, and I suddenly felt tired. I started to drift off to sleep and breathed out, "This is some serious stuff."

When my treatment was complete, I was only a shadow of the man who signed into the hospital a mere five days earlier. The chemo had wreaked havoc on my stomach, and I could barely keep a bite of anything down. I was physically so depleted and weak that they kept me in the hospital for three extra days. After regaining some strength, they finally released me. My father-in-law, Charles, who saw me spill my motorcycle in his driveway years before, took me home after my first treatment. I asked him to stop by the soccer field, so I could see the team.

When we drove the van down close to the field and I emerged, the practice lost its regimen, and the girls ran en masse and gathered around me. I didn't really comprehend how feeble and weak I was, and as I spoke to the team, I suddenly felt faint. As I began to feel light-headed I knew I had to get back into the van. I recall putting one hand on the side-view mirror, and the next thing I remember is awaking to a crowd of horrified teenage faces staring down at me. I had passed out and collapsed right in front of them. Charles helped me into the van, but the incident frightened everyone.

"Maybe we should have skipped that," I said as we drove away from the field.

Before we got to my apartment, I asked Charles to take me by the dam in Rockford. It was a sunny spring day, and I was elated to finally be out of the hospital. I wanted to see a few things before I planted myself on the sofa that I knew was waiting for me. At the dam, I got out of the van to watch the steelhead leap into the falling water. The sun felt good on my face, and I wondered how many more times, if any, I would see this sight. Suddenly, the same sensation I had felt at the soccer field began to overtake me.

"Oh, oh," I said out loud, "here we go again," and I tried to get back into the van before I fell down in the parking lot. I had opened the door and began to lift my leg in when everything began to go dark. My father-in-law had already gone around and was seated in the driver's seat and grabbed my arm to keep me from falling back out of the vehicle and onto the pavement. For several anxious moments, I lay crumpled and unconscious, half in and half out of the van while Charles held tightly onto my arm. Then, as before, I slowly came back into consciousness and finished getting into the van. I could tell my father-in-law was shaken up, and he said with a hint of humor and concern, "You have to stop doing that to me." He took me to the apartment, helped me up the stairs, and I collapsed, exhausted on the couch. I would not leave it much for the next week.

My first morning home, I sat up on the couch and waited a moment for my head to clear. Slowly, I rose and shuffled to the bathroom holding onto walls, doors, and furniture the whole way. I had lost an incredible fifteen pounds during my treatment the week before, and my right calf had become atrophied and weak. I had encamped on the couch, doubled up with constant stomach pains, mustering all my strength for trips to the bathroom or to get a drink in the kitchen. When I staggered into the bathroom, I grasped both sides of the sink and stared at myself in the mirror. It was as if someone else was staring back. My face was thin, and my complexion was a pasty white. The sunken eyes surrounded by heavy dark circles brought visions of holocaust victims I had seen in documentaries. I thought of the words the doctor had said: "Keep in mind, your chemotherapies will probably start out okay, but they will gradually get worse." "Worse than this!?" I thought. This was only my first treatment, and I could barely walk. The words ". . . gradually get worse" were stuck in my head. As I peered at the other me in the mirror, I spoke aloud, "Buddy, you're a dead man." And that is exactly what I thought my future held.

One of the most poignant events that happened after my first chemo-therapy came at a soccer game in Holland. After that initial treatment when it seemed death was inevitable, I wanted to see my girls soccer team play. Ed Dobson, pastor of Calvary Church in Grand Rapids and former college all-star soccer player at Liberty College, had volunteered to take the team in my absence. This was an amazing gesture since Calvary was a giant church, much bigger even than San Jacinto Baptist, and with a lot more going on. As the senior pastor of such a giant enterprise, Ed certainly had his hands full. Coaching a high school girls' soccer team could not have been convenient, but it speaks volumes about the man. People like Pastor Dobson began to appear in my path during this entire ordeal. I began to understand that I had no power over my predicament, that I was totally in the hands of other people. It was humbling and reassuring and a testament to the goodness of people to one another, especially in times of need. And greater than the people who came to my aid, I gained an immediate understanding of God's control over all things. One thing was for sure, He had my attention.

Ten days passed before I finally gained sufficient strength and permission from Dr. Zakem to go watch the soccer team play. It turned out to be a cold, misty day in Holland, and I was a pathetic sight on the sideline. Wrapped in a blanket sitting in a lawn chair thin and weak, I watched pre-game warm up. Rich May, a referee whom I had known several years, came over and brashly asked, "Geeze, what's the matter with you?"

Wielding the shock power of cancer, I said, "I'm dying from testicular cancer."

To my absolute astonishment, he said, "Oh, I've had that, you'll be alright," and held up his shirt. He had long scar down the middle of his chest and stomach, verifying the truth of his flippant revelation. Rich just grinned and jogged off. I sat stunned but filled with an entirely new outlook thanks to this unexpected messenger of hope. We lost the game, I got extremely sick and was hospitalized early, but that day changed everything for me. There was a chance after all; there was hope.

In reality, what was happening was that my cancer was being purged, and the rest of my body was along for the scary ride. After my first horrible treatment, when I thought "gradually get worse" meant a death sentence, my treatments actually got easier! After the first therapy withered me away, Dr. Zakem changed the procedure for the second. I was continuously fed intravenously throughout the course of the treatment. This kept both my weight and my strength up. By the time the second session was over, I actually left the hospital heavier than when I entered. This had a positive influence on my frame of mind since I was expecting each treatment to affect me more than the previous one, and if that were the case, my chances of survival looked slim.

I still had my hair after the initial treatment, but after the second, it began to fall out in chunks. One afternoon, with Sue sitting in the room, I was washing my face in the bathroom when I noticed a bunch of short whiskers in the washcloth. At first I was puzzled, but then it dawned on me that I was literally washing my beard off! I had sported a beard ever since my days in Dakota, and Sue had never known me without one.

"My beard is coming off!" I exclaimed.

"What?" Sue asked from the other room.

"My beard is coming off right in the washcloth." There were a few moments of silence as I tried to decide what to do. "Well, no sense in putting off the inevitable," I said and began to vigorously go about washing my beard off. As I did this, I could see a very curious Sue trying to get a look in the mirror at something she had never seen before . . . the bottom half of my face! When I finally emerged from the bathroom, Sue put her hands over her mouth, trying to suppress her laughter.

"You look good," she said between giggles, but you could tell seeing my chin struck her as a funny sight.

"Whatever," I replied laughing myself. "I feel naked! If this is gonna happen, it's gonna happen on mah terms," I declared with a hint of Panhandle creeping into my voice.

Finding humor in his situation, Scotty posed as Ghandi. It was the only time during their marriage that Sue saw him clean shaven.

I called Darcy, who had been the family barber for years, and asked her to bring her clippers when she came to visit. When she came, I had her shave all the remaining hair off my head; I was completely bald, face and all. What I discovered later about losing your hair to chemo was that it doesn't stop with your head or your beard. I lost the hair on my chest, in my armpits, my crotch, and my eyebrows. For a while, I constantly had annoying hairs fall into my eyes. They were my eye lashes falling out. Except for the hair on the lower part of my legs, I was as smooth as an eggshell. A weird aspect of this was realizing how pasty my complexion was without any "peach-fuzz" on my face, and without any eyebrows I looked like some sort of alien. As humorous as it was, the entire process scared me; I knew what was happening: my body was quickly deteriorating in front of my eyes.

Another strange side effect from the chemotherapy that I hated even more than losing all my hair was the loss of taste. Soon after the needle went into my arm, my sense of taste always disappeared. I had a fickle appetite because the chemo turned my stomach into knots, but what I did try to eat all tasted the same—like cardboard. The only satisfaction I got from eating was the texture of the different foods; for the course of the treatment and for several days afterwards, taste simply did not exist. My favorite day during recovery time was the day, maybe four or five after being released from the hospital, when suddenly I could taste again. I feared when it was all over that I would lose this forever. This made me gain a new appreciation for many simple things in life that we take for granted daily. "Taste," I thought one day, "who would have thought it was so important, such a gift?" There's no way to describe how suddenly being able to taste a cheeseburger or piece of supreme pizza or vanilla ice cream can almost feel erotic.

During one chemo session, I was pleasantly surprised when the door opened and some of my best friends from Dakota House filed in. Steve was accompanied by his wife, Jari, and with them were Art, and Stats. Their presence made it clear that everyone was expecting the worst and making sure they had a chance to say good-bye. It was great to see them, a comfort that I cannot express, but I hated the situation that brought them there. They brought me gifts including a Three Stooges video, a book filled with inspirational verses, and hamburgers from the outside world. The fact that they had made the trip from the Detroit area to Grand Rapids spoke volumes about our fondness for each other and the depth of our friendship. After they left I prayed that it was not the last time I would see them.

Sue was working during the day, and my friends and relatives came and went according to their schedules. It was not unusual for me to be alone as the five-day chemotherapy ran its course. One evening, as I lay alone in a fog with chemicals coursing through my veins, the phone rang. Clumsily, I grabbed it and put it to my ear. "Hello?"

A familiar voice on the other end replied like it was a question, "Scotty?" Immediately I recognized the soft drawl.: "Karen," I said, "yes, it's me."

"How are yew doin'?" she asked with a concerned tone. I could tell immediately that the news had reached her. I felt emotion rising within me as we spoke, but not like in the past. It was just good to hear from her. Karen and I had experienced some highs and lows, but overall we contributed an amazing flavor to each other's lives. Even though things fell apart between us, I had always felt she was an integral part of my life. I can't imagine the story of me not including her. And now, with my future uncertain, there was her small voice on the other end of the line.

"Oh, I'm hangin' in there," I answered. "I look kinda funny, without my hair and beard, but that's the least of my problems. How are things in Amarilla?"

"Yew don't have yer beard?" she asked in disbelief. "That must be a saht."

"Things are fahn here," she continued.

The conversation had started out fine, but then there was an awkward silence. I instantly reverted back to my Texas dialect. "Boy howdy, Ah haven't heard yer voice since . . ." I had to stop short and actually think about when she and I had last talked.

Then Karen finished it for me, ". . . since yew bought drinks at Graham Central Station for me and Ross."

I couldn't help but chuckle, "Oh yea, I was pretty brave back then."

"Yeah, that was an interestin' naht," Karen added.

"It's been about eight years, right?" I asked.

"Yes, sir," she answered.

"It doesn't seem that long ago."

"No, it doesn't," she agreed.

I was tired from the chemo, but the conversation continued, and I filled her in on all the sorted details of my situation. It was nice to hear from her, and I didn't want to say goodbye, but after awhile, we reached that point where silence took over. We both felt like something more should be said, and for all we knew, this could be our only opportunity to speak before I died. Finally, I broke the tension: "Karen, Ah'm, sorry about . . ." There was a slight pause before I finished the sentence. There were many things I could have concluded the thought with, but in the end I simply said, "us."

"No, no, no!" she quickly responded. "It was *mah* fault, Scotty."

"Naw, Ah took yew for granted . . . Ah took *us* for granted," I corrected.

"Scotty," she said in determined tone, "Ah cheated on yew . . . remember?"

"Karen," I countered, "if we're gonna give out awards for who cheated on whom, Ah'll get the winner's trophy." I continued quickly so she could not edge in a word. "Ah was jerk to yew, and it wrecked us . . . yew gave me what Ah deserved."

"Well," she said, "let's not dwell on the past. There's plenty of blame to spread around, but fer now yew just need to worry about gettin' better."

After a couple of seconds, I said, "Ah've learned a few things over these past few years, and one thing Ah've come to embrace, is that everything happens for a reason. Mah life would be pretty boring had I never met yew."

"Scotty, did yew ferget who ye're talkin' to?" Karen said. "Ah *know* yew, and yer lahf would NOT have been boring if yew hadn't met me."

"Well," I began after some thought, "yew certainly have played a special role in it, and Ah wanna say thank yew for that." I continued in a sincere voice, "There was a lot more good than bad, that's for sure."

"Yes there was," she agreed in her soft drawl.

We took turns trying to tie up the loose ends we left dangling eight years earlier. I was really feeling the effects from the chemo kicking in and knew I had better say good-bye.

"Ah'm afraid Ah have to go," I said. "Ah'm getting' real tarred."

"Alraht," she answered, "yew get yerself well, Okay?"

There was an awkward silence; saying goodbye was still hard. Finally in full Texas dialect, I said, "Yew tell Ross he's a lucky man."

"Yew tell Sue she's a lucky woman," she replied.

Then we both said goodbye and hung up.

The whole thing was surreal, and part of me wondered if the chemo made me dream it. But the next day I realized she did call, we had talked, and I smiled at the thought of it all. She was now an old friend from the past.

I lost all my hair and still needed recovery time, but by the time I received my final therapy in July, I left the hospital and went straight to the golf course with my sister Darcy and my mother! Things were looking better; I had regained a sense of hope.

My chemotherapy treatments came and went with the summer of 1991, and still being alive and actually feeling quite normal, I returned to coaching in August . . . this time it was the boys' team. My hair had grown back, and I was sporting my usual stubble-face whiskers. The only place that my hair did not return as before was in my armpits. For reasons unknown, it just didn't quite come back. I'm just glad it happened there and not my eyebrows or my face. I think Sue more than anyone was overjoyed when I grew my beard back. She liked that I sported a beard and the thought of having to look at me clean-shaven was something she would have to learn to love. To my relief, my sense of taste returned totally, and I have taken full advantage of tasting good food ever since.

Everything had taken on the air of normalcy when the "other shoe dropped." The chemo had gone as well as could be hoped for, but the usual routine at this point was a follow-up surgery called a "nodal-dissection." In this operation, surgeons remove any cancerous lymph nodes from your body. Since they act as a highway for cancer to travel throughout your body and may contribute to more cancer, oncologists like to eliminate the potential threat they pose by removing them. This is the surgery that left Rich May with his lengthy scar. I was in remission, and the doctors wanted to keep it that way. You see, the reason my chances were so slim at the onset of my diagnosis were because the testicular cancer had traveled throughout my body. This was the reason Dr. Kitts originally took that chest x-ray back in March. I had seen that x-ray, and both lungs were filled with white spots about the size of quarters. The view of a healthy lung would be dark and clear. He knew then what he wanted verified that following day at the office with all the pregnant women—that I had cancer that had gone undetected and unchecked for several months. It had spread throughout my body and needed to be addressed with all possible haste . . . a day or two here or there might cost me my life. Now that they had gotten me this far, they wanted to leave nothing to chance.

There was also a suspicious dark spot remaining on my liver that they wanted to remove at the same time as the nodal dissection. It had been my cancer-riddled, swollen liver that pressed on nerves in my lower back that kept me from sleeping months earlier.

It was this chronic pain that finally made me see Dr. Kitts, and now this infected liver would have to be dealt with. The same surgeon who relieved me of my cancerous testicle was scheduled to perform this surgery. It was an invasive, risky procedure with a SIX-MONTH recovery time! Once again, I had to prepare a team for bad news, and once again, an unexpected source would intervene on my behalf. I couldn't help but feel like God was pulling the strings.

On August 6th, Sue gave birth to our first child, Rebekah. In the middle of the excitement of becoming parents, there loomed anxiety as I prepared for the major follow-up surgery. I had a meeting with my soccer team explaining the situation and turning over the coaching reigns to a guy named John Anderson, a talented and responsible young man I had coached the previous four years. Little did I know that explaining the details of my upcoming surgery to the team was the first step in a minor miracle.

Later that same day, I received a phone call from Clif Ferguson, the father of a player named Mark. He informed me that he did not normally stick his nose into other people's business but that he had some concerns about my surgery. As it turned out, Cliff Ferguson was an anesthesiologist at Butterworth, the largest hospital in Grand

Rapids. I had no previous knowledge of this. He proceeded to inform me that after Mark explained to him what I had told the team, he felt he should call and talk to me. He said that whenever they encounter a patient like me at Butterworth, they always referred him or her to Indiana University, Purdue University Indianapolis (IUPUI). Apparently IUPUI was the cutting edge of research and treatment of testicular cancer in the United States. According to Cliff, no one in Grand Rapids typically performed this surgery, especially with the added complication of simultaneously removing a "wedge" of liver! Yet, I was already scheduled for these very things in Grand Rapids. At IUPUI, they perform these operations nearly on a daily basis. This information got my attention. When I shared with my mother what Mr. Ferguson had told me, she took less than three seconds to declare, "That's it then; we're going to Indianapolis." Dr. Zakem made it easy by helping me cancel the scheduled operation and releasing my records to Indianapolis. I sensed a little bewilderment that I exercised my own will here, but Dr. Zakem ultimately said, "It's your body and your life, so you do what you think is right." I felt totally at peace with my decision, and so a trip to Indiana and this risky surgery were scheduled. Not that I didn't trust the doctors in Grand Rapids, but it was a comfort knowing that the best doctors in the nation would be behind the scalpel at IUPUI.

The day we went to Indianapolis started before dawn. My parents, Sue, and our two-week-old daughter Rebekah piled into a van and made the five-hour drive south. My brother and sisters had all made plans to arrive later and spend the night at a nearby hotel in order to be around before and after the surgery. After an entire day of starving myself and drinking the prescribed pre-operation "shakes," I finally saw not one, but two doctors. With my parents and wife listening, Dr. Nichols began with, "Well, there's been a little miscommunication between here and Grand Rapids. After studying your charts and x-rays, we have determined that you are not quite the patient we expected to see." I remember thinking, "Yea, so where are you going with this?" He continued to explain, "For this surgery to be of any use, your chemotherapy needed to be less than 90% effective." My mind was racing as his tone was very matter-of-fact. "This can't be good news," I thought. As Dr. Nichols continued to talk, there was a silent tension in the room. Everyone knew he was building up to the point when he was going to drop the big bomb. "There's nothing we can do for you." As he spoke, I was mentally preparing to field those words and it was obvious that was the direction his statistics were leading to. Somewhere in my numbed mind I heard two percentages: ". . . chemotherapy must be less than 90% effective," and ". . . your treatment has been 96% successful . . . ." I was trying to make the math make sense; less than 90% to be of any use . . . mine was 96% effective. Suddenly at the same time it hit me, he spoke the words, "This surgery is probably unnecessary, and we'll most likely be sending you home." He actually said it calmly, like he was asking if I wanted a refill on my coffee. Everything I had prepared for turned on a dime at these words, and I was ready to explode with joy! Dr. Nichols continued to explain how there were still a few things to do to be sure, but I knew he would not have let that cat out of the bag unless he was reasonably sure that he was not performing the operation, that he would be sending me home. He also made it clear that even though the surgery was not immediately necessary, it might need to be done in the future if my cancer returned. I would have to come to Indianapolis for regular check-ups.

"Can I eat something?" I asked.

"Oh, certainly," he replied, realizing I had basically fasted all day in preparation. "I'll send a nurse right in, and she can order something for you."

As the hospital staff prepared to release me, I shoveled down three cheeseburgers, compliments of the hospital cafeteria. Since everyone had already reserved hotel rooms for the night, we all gathered there and had a celebration, then awoke and drove north the following day. On the drive toward Michigan, Sue was napping, and Rebekah was quietly fidgeting in her car seat. I looked out the window and realized summer was almost gone. Some farmers were harvesting the last of their corn, and there was anticipation in the air for the approaching autumn. I tried to digest all that had happened since the previous March. It had been a whirlwind of activity and emotion, so fast that I barely remember making decisions; things just happened, and I seemed to be along for the ride that I had no control over. Like a rollercoaster, it had been a ride of unexpected turns and dips, and now I was approaching the terminal at the end, checking to see if I still had everything and feeling exhilarated. "Had God shaken me to attention?" I wondered. I was fortunate. Had this happened a few years earlier, I may not have survived. I wondered why my brother Randy had not been saved. The cancer that killed him was now one of the most common and one of the most curable. "We have no control," I thought. One thing was for sure: if I managed to stay alive, my life would have a new sense of purpose. I felt the need to make a difference, and this experience might be a tool that could be of use.

"Still alive and kicking," I murmured as I looked at Rebekah in the rearview mirror. "You'll get to know me after all."

That afternoon, I strutted into practice, unannounced, like a man who had won the lottery. They were running some sort of drill and one by one, they began to stop and stare, not believing that it was me approaching. When it became obvious, they broke ranks and came running my way. I can never express how it felt to walk those steps and see the joy of those boys. Jon looked especially relieved that he didn't have to coach the team alone. He stayed on as an assistant for that year, and together we coached the team to a record with more wins than losses, a successful feat for our young squad.

Although I continued to visit IUPUI every month for the next year, eventually they said I did not need to return. The surgery I was scheduled to undergo in Grand Rapids turned out to be unnecessary after all. The spot on my liver disappeared over time, and it was determined to be scar tissue left from the immediate reaction of my body to the heavy dose of Sisplatinum I had received in August. Interestingly enough, there were several large and troublesome moles on my body that disappeared as well. They were present my entire life, and one in particular on my chest had periodically caught the attention of doctors. One day, standing in front of a mirror drying off after a shower, I suddenly realized it was gone. I don't remember any gradual process; it was suddenly, just gone. I searched through my chest hair looking for some sort of scar or faded sign, but I found virtually no trace of it. I can only assume that it, too, was cancerous and fell victim to my chemotherapy as well . . . a bonus side effect, I guess. Sue and I made a special visit to the Fergusons to personally thank Clif for interceding on my behalf. He certainly saved me from a risky, unneeded surgery and months of agonizing recovery.

The drama and the scare were over, at least for now. But hanging over my head was the fear that the cancer would return. I had cheated the reaper this time, but it was a close call, a very close call. I couldn't help but feel this was not over. In the meantime, life had to go forward. I set my sights on a vague date five years ahead. I had heard somewhere in the process of my cancer that after remission, being cancer-free for five years was an important milestone. As life rolled on for Sue, Rebekah, and me, every check-up was an exercise in anxiety, but I was alive, and not from anything *I* had done, but by sheer providence.

REBOOTING

CHAPTER 49

After the chaos and fear of 1991, I had to back up and try to restart my life. When my cancer was detected and the urgency of my condition was made clear, I quickly had curtailed everything I was involved with to undergo surgery and treatments. Now that I had survived, I needed to essentially hit the "reboot" button and get back to the business of living. First and foremost, I registered for classes at Grand Valley State University and resumed my quest to become a teacher. Grand Valley had been very accommodating when I suddenly had to drop out of my classes the previous March. Under special circumstances, I was reimbursed the cost of tuition after the deadline had passed, and no grades were posted for that semester. I have nothing but praise for how Grand Valley handled my situation. The university made it nearly effortless for me when I had to curtail my studies, and now when it was time to re-enter my program, it was done without any complications. I continued to coach for Rockford High School, and I was working part-time for Olson's American Marine and Rockford Hardware. Sue continued to work as a law clerk for Wheeler, Upham, and Uhl, and together we resumed planning outdoor trips for churches. Although I was still being monitored on a monthly basis, life moved ahead, and the next two years passed without incident.

In the springtime of 1994, two milestone events were in progress; I was completing my final two courses at G.V.S.U., and Sue was pregnant with our second child.

When I returned from Texas ten years before, my plan was to finish the schooling I had begun at Northern Michigan. The circumstances that unfolded in Rockford never let me return to Marquette. I had accumulated 117 credits at N.M.U., all of which transferred to G.V.S.U., but absolutely none of them had anything to do with education. I entered Grand Valley with a very high status, but changing my focus to education was nothing short of starting over. I had lost a semester dealing with cancer, but in the grand scheme of things, that was a minor setback. My new education program had taken me three-and-a-half years to complete, but now the end was in sight; I only had to finish my student teaching, a Spanish class, and a college algebra class I had taken as an independent study—that is, just me and the professor. Student teaching was the most time-consuming but easiest of the three; the Spanish and math classes were both like giant albatrosses hanging around my neck.

I had observed classes at Rockford and been a Teaching Assistant at Creston, an inner-city high school in Grand Rapids. Because my degree was in two areas—history and art—I had to assist in both types of classes. So halfway into a semester at Creston, working with a marvelous history teacher named Chris Avery, I was plucked out to go work in an art class in the suburbs of Jenison. Both were exceptional experiences.

I tried hard to get placed into Rockford High School for my student teaching because my plan was to teach there. It only made sense since I lived in Rockford, had coached there for several years, and the art teacher there was due to retire at any moment. In fact, I was always afraid he would retire before I finished my degree, especially when I had lost time due to my cancer. But happily for me, he was still teaching when I started my last semester at G.V.S.U. Student teaching there would definitely get my foot in the door when it came time to hire a new art teacher. I wanted to be that guy and was posturing myself to be on the short-list. But much to my dismay, I was told by the university that they did not have a willing teacher. This surprised me since I knew Mr. Stamp, the art teacher there, and he had indicated to me that he would be glad to have me on board. Instead, I was placed in the tiny farm community of Ravenna, thirty-five minutes away from Rockford. This made my daily routine extremely difficult to manage. I was driving from Rockford to Ravenna and then back to Rockford to coach. Periodically, I had to make additional trips to G.V.S.U. for my Spanish class and to meet with my math professor. It was a circus.

In the end, I was able to finally pass the algebra exam, but the Spanish class that I had so badly neglected unexpectedly posed a barrier to my graduation. It all came down to how I performed on the final exam. The day of the exam, I sat down at my desk and began to answer the questions. It became painfully obvious at the start that I was lost. As I picked my way through the test, I realized that if I failed, I would be faced with summer school just to graduate and enter the working world. It was an unsettling feeling for sure. When it was over, I knew it would take a miracle for me to pull a passing grade out of this mess. I decided to visit my professor to find out my fate.

I knocked on professor Hoeksema's office door. "Hey, Scott, come on in," he said in friendly recognition. He was not someone you would picture as a college Spanish professor. He simply did not look the part, not to mention his obvious Dutch name.

"What can I do for you?" he asked.

"Well, I need to know if I've passed your class," I started. I continued, "I don't think I've done very well and if I have to take it over, I need to know now, so I can get it done this summer."

As he turned toward his computer, he spoke, but it was not necessarily to me. "Well, let's see what we've got here." He tapped on the keys until he arrived at the grades for my class and then zeroed specifically in on my name. "Hmmm," he murmured as he scrolled and highlighted certain assignments and grades. "Hmmm," he moaned again. By the sound of his reactions to my scores, I was beginning to feel like my summer was going to be filled with Spanish.

"Let's see how you did on this final," he said as he switched from the computer to the stack of stapled papers he had just placed on the edge of an adjacent desk. He fumbled through the pile until he came to my name and pulled my exam from the middle. Without saying anything, he flipped through the pages. I could tell he was searching for any reason to give me the benefit of the doubt. A couple times he said enthusiastically, "Oh, that's good." Then he began to ask me some interesting questions.

"Why did you take this class?"

"It is required for my degree," I answered.

"How much more do you have to complete before you graduate?"

"This is it," I said. "I only need this class, and I'll be done." It was almost spoken as a plea.

"Are you doing anything else with Spanish after this?" he persisted.

"Not a thing. I only need it to graduate," I repeated. Then I continued, "That's why I need to know if I passed; if I didn't, then I need to take it this summer, so I can get a job next autumn."

"But nothing more to do with Spanish?" he asked again.

"Nothing," I said emphatically this time.

Professor Hoeksema leaned back in his chair and stroked the sides of his chin with his thumb and forefinger. My future depended on what he was about to say. After a few anxious moments, he slowly spun his chair around and with a rye smile, simply said, "You passed."

Every indication between the lines was that I, in fact, did not pass or at least was dangerously close to failing. The non-verbal communication was as clear as an August sky. What I interpreted in our exchange that day was, "Well, you failed my class, but you are so close to passing I am going to throw you a bone; plus, it is not in an area that has anything to do with your pursuits, so I am not going to let this class set you back . . . I'm going to fudge this a little in your favor."

"Thank you professor," was all I said. I never saw my test score nor did I want to. I just knew that he was not going to be an obstacle to me moving on. This was quite contrary to the attitude of my education professor, whose obstinance would almost cost me a golden opportunity. I shook Professor Hoeksema's hand and one last time, gratefully said, "Thank you very much." I turned and walked away, feeling a giant sense of relief. A few weeks later when my grades arrived in the mail, I was expecting to see a "D-" for my Spanish class, barely squeaking by. I was surprised to see that Professor Hoeksema had given me a "C."

When it got near the end, my student teaching class had set up mock interviews with local principals. The assignments for this exercise were random, and I was set to interview with the principal from East Kentwood. This was a large school on the south side of Grand Rapids and a rival of Rockford's. I noticed on the list was a principal from Rockford Middle School named Jamie Hosford, whom I knew. I pulled a switch-a-roo with another student who wanted to teach in East Kentwood but was scheduled to interview with Jamie, the Rockford principal. It wasn't until months later that I realized how important this little maneuver would be in the course of my life. It was the first step in a series of events that would once again make me ponder about God's plan for my life.

The night of the interviews went smoothly, and I felt confident that I had done a solid interview with Mr. Hosford. I was walking through the parking lot at the university, feeling rather proud that I had manipulated the system to get noticed. Suddenly, a nice SUV pulled up next to me, stopped, and the electric window whined down.

"Hey, Scott!" someone yelled from inside. I looked in to see Jamie Hosford leaning across the center console in order to speak to me. Jamie Hosford was an outstanding athlete in high school and earned All-American status at Grand Valley in football and wrestling. I had been around Rockford enough to be on a first-name basis with him.

"Hey, Jamie, how'd I do?" I answered quickly.

"You did fine," he said, "a really nice job." This was great to hear but not the reason he stopped to chat. In many ways, this spontaneous meeting in the parking lot was as providential as my chance meeting with Karen on the bluff at Castaway. A door was about to be opened, but at the time I was totally in the dark.

"Can you call me tomorrow? There's something I want to talk to you about."

"Sure, I'll call you," I answered a little perplexed.

"Call me at school in the morning, okay?"

"Okay," was all I answered, and he drove away.

From then until the next morning, my mind did summersaults trying to figure out what could be on Jamie's mind. I really didn't have a clue. "It has to be a good thing, right?" I kept asking myself.

I called Jamie the following morning, and he asked,

"How close are you to graduating from Grand Valley?"

"I have two weeks left," I answered.

"Well, here's my situation," he started. "I have an art teacher who is going into the hospital for some surgery. I need someone to sub for at least two weeks. I liked your interview; I'd like to give you first crack at this opportunity."

"I'd have to get out of my last little bit of classes in Ravenna and my last seminar class. If I can finagle that, then what else do I need to do?"

"You'll have to get your name on the official substitute list," he answered.

"How do I do that?"

"You'll have to call them and see what their requirements are. If you can get your name on that list by Thursday, call me. The job will be yours."

"Okay, I'll give you a call one way or the other by Thursday."

"Okay," he acknowledged, "I won't do anything until I hear from you."

I was excited beyond imagination and realized all I had to do was get my name on that Kent Intermediate School District (KISD) substitute list, and I could begin to draw a paycheck. After all the work, money, and drama I had been through, to finally get to a point where I could make money was a great feeling. But I couldn't get too fired up over it; there was still the matter of jumping through the hoops to get my name on that coveted list. The first order of business was to get Ravenna to sign off on my last week of student teaching and my student teaching seminar professor to waive the last week of class. The staff at Ravenna were excited that I had a sure-fire opportunity to get my foot in the educational door and hurriedly compiled the necessary papers to set me free. With their endorsement in hand, I didn't think the professor would be any kind of obstacle . . . I was wrong.

When I told my professor what was in the works and all I needed was his permission to go ahead, he acted a little incensed that something was happening beyond the realm of his authority.

"No, you can't do that. You have to finish the class," was his dogmatic answer.

"But there is only one class period left . . . ONE!" I replied in disbelief.

"You have to finish the requirements," was his cold reply.

"But isn't this what we're after, a teaching job?" I reasoned.

But no matter how much logic and pleading I threw in his direction, he was unyielding in his stance. I was incredulous! I could not believe that this professor was going to block an opportunity, not just to teach and make money, but to teach in the district where I lived, coached, and wanted to teach . . . for a single class period! I was determined not to let this chance slip away. I had an ace in my hand that I decided to play.

A few years earlier, when I first began to pursue my teaching degree, I developed a rapport with my Introduction to Education professor, Al TenEyk. He was a professor with whom I spoke with frequently and even sat down and ate lunch with a time or two. Having a personal connection with Al TenEyk became even more beneficial when he became the Head of the Education Department at G.V.S.U. When I needed to quickly drop my courses after my cancer diagnosis, it was Professor TenEyk I called. He simply said, "You do what you need to do; I'll take care of everything on this end." He not only dropped me from the rosters of my classes, but he helped me get my tuition reimbursed, citing my extenuating circumstances. I was in his debt for this, but I also knew he was in my corner and would surely go to bat for me in this current dilemma.

I called Professor TenEyk and explained my predicament. He, too, was miffed that a professor would purposely block an opportunity to work within my field. Knowing the time constraints of the situation, Professor TenEyk once again made things easy. "You come to my office by 3:00 this afternoon. I'll have what you need."

What happened next was a whirlwind of signatures, references, and paperwork; the absence of any of them would have stopped the entire effort. When I arrived at Professor TenEyk's office at 3:00, I had in my hands all the documents required from Ravenna High School completed and signed. Professor Ten Eyk said, "You're all set," and handed me the required documents from the university. Now all of these had to be submitted to the K.I.S.D. just to get me eligible to be tested, fingerprinted, and added to the official substitute list. This basically would allow me to call Jamie Hosford and inform him that I was officially certified to teach. This process usually was planned far in advance and took an entire day, but K.I.S.D. went out of its way to make it happen in a few hours, and that Thursday afternoon

I was officially a certified teacher. I called Jamie that evening and said, "Jamie, I'm on the list." He replied, "That's great. I'll see you bright and early Monday morning." The following week I began to teach art at Rockford Middle School.

The teacher I was subbing for was scheduled to be gone for two weeks. But her recovery from surgery had complications and delayed her return. Two weeks came and went, and I was still teaching her class. Ultimately, I finished the year for her, which had two very beneficial results for me. The first was that it gave me practical experience in the field in which I wanted to teach. Secondly, it allowed me to add Jamie Hosford as a reference on my resume, a very impressive addition that would pay off in the long run.

SOMETIMES, IT'S WHO YOU KNOW

CHAPTER 50

Somewhere in the middle of that time in May when I was teaching there was a Saturday graduation ceremony at G.V.S.U. My mom and dad, in-laws, and Sue came to watch me walk across the stage and receive my diploma . . . it had been a long difficult journey, but I had finally done it. I was now ready for the real world; it was time to find a teaching job.

I had sprinkled my resume to several schools in the Grand Rapids vicinity in hopes of landing some interviews. It was not a widespread shotgun delivery; however, they were sent to schools where I actually felt I would like to teach. Of course, my hope was that Rockford would call me and offer me a job. I felt since I lived there and had coached there for five years that my chances were good. The only glitch with this plan was that Mr. Stamp had not retired like I thought he would. He was still hanging in there teaching. Still, I was certain there were other jobs to be filled in the Rockford district. I went about my normal summer without worry, expecting that sooner or later, the calls would start rolling in.

After my experience teaching at Rockford Middle School, it all began to sink in. That last hectic week of class, student teaching, and finishing the school year for the ailing art teacher had left me little time to digest what was happening. I had finally jumped through all the hoops, I had my diploma, I possessed a certification, and I had some practical experience under my belt. I was feeling pretty good about where I was in life.

It so happened that summer, for the first time ever, the World Cup soccer tournament was being held in the United States. One of the field locations was the Pontiac Silverdome near Detroit. This would also be the first time ever that the World Cup would play games indoors; that is, in the domed Pontiac venue. This was a once-in-a-life-time-opportunity that I did not want to let get away, so I had purchased tickets for Sue and me to attend four games in Pontiac.

What helped tremendously was that my parents' cabin at Leisure Lake was not far from Pontiac. We decided to stay there and use it as the staging location for daily trips to the Silverdome. In doing this, we basically put ourselves out of touch with anything happening back on the west side of the state.

Returning late one evening from a day of watching the spectacle that is the World Cup, my mother said, "Darcy called you; she said it is urgent that you call her." My sister Darcy, who also lived in Rockford and was a photographer, was well-known around the high school. She was the sister whose basement became my sanctuary while struggling to get back on my feet years before. When I returned her call, she said, "Hey bro, Tom Popiel has been trying to get a hold of you."

"Who is he?" I asked.

"The principal of Cedar Springs High School. He knows you coach at Rockford, so he called them trying to track you down."

"So how'd you get involved in this?" I wondered to her.

"They know I'm your sister, so they contacted me to try and find you. I knew you and Sue were at the Lake, so that's why I'm calling. You better call him," she insisted.

She gave me the number of Tom Popiel, and I wasted no time in contacting him. When he answered the phone and I told him who I was, he said, "Man, you're a hard guy to get a hold of."

"Sorry, I'm on the other side of the state watching World Cup games," I replied.

"Well, we'd like to interview you for a teaching position," he announced.

"Thank you," I said. "When would you like me to come in?"

"Well," he began, "I know it's short notice, but I'd like you to come in tomorrow. Since it has taken so long to contact you, we've actually been interviewing candidates for a couple days now."

At hearing this, I knew I could not decline. I needed to make this happen.

"Sure," I answered enthusiastically, "I can come back to interview."

"Great," said Mr. Popiel. "I'll schedule you last in the morning so you have a chance to get here. Is ten o'clock good for you?"

"Yes, that'll work just right. I have tickets to the evening soccer match, so ten o'clock will work perfectly."

"Okay then, I'll look for you at ten."

"Thanks! I'll see you then," I replied. When I got off the phone, I looked at Sue with a wide grin and said, "I have an interview."

The next day, I drove across the state to Cedar Springs, sat on the hot seat in front of several faculty members as they grilled me with the typical questions, and then turned around and drove back to the lake and on to Pontiac and watched another World Cup soccer match. By the time Sue and I returned to the cabin, it had been a very long day for me.

I had given Tom the phone number at the cabin, so he could reach me without having to act like a detective. I knew he must have been highly interested in me to go through such pains to find me for an interview. As it turned out, twenty-five years earlier, Tom Popiel was a coach at Creston High School for a young man named Jamie Hosford. The same Creston where I assisted Chris Avery in her history class and the same Jamie Hosford whom I finagled a mock interview with and then subbed long-term for at Rockford Middle School. Jamie's name on my resume caught his eye, and he called him to ask about me.

While I was rubbing the sleep from my eyes and having a cup of coffee with my mother and Sue, the phone rang. My mother answered and unexpectedly handed it to me. "It's for you," she said.

"Hello?"

"Hi Scott, this is Tom Popiel from Cedar Springs High School," he said in a very formal fashion.

"Good morning, Tom."

"Listen," he began, "I would like to offer you a job here at Cedar Springs."

Cedar Springs was not my top choice, and I wanted to know if any other schools, especially Rockford, were looking my way. So in the middle of a tough job market, I had the gall to ask, "Can I think about it?"

"Yes, you can think about it, but don't think too long," he added. "You're not the only candidate we are considering."

Having a job in hand did not go without having impact on me; this is what all the work was for. But I wanted to see if Rockford was interested before I said yes.

"I'll let you know by this afternoon."

"That will be fine," said Tom.

I immediately proceeded to contact the principal at Rockford High School and boldly asked if they were considering hiring me in any capacity. What I found was there were no openings in Rockford for either history or art, the two areas in which I was certified to teach. They were not hiring.

It didn't take long for me to realize I had a job waiting for me; all I had to do was accept it. I let about an hour pass, and I called Tom Popiel. "Mr. Popiel," I started, "I would like to accept your offer to teach at Cedar Springs High School."

"Fantastic," he responded. "I am glad to hear you are joining our staff." It was only after I accepted the offer that he confided in me that he had called and talked directly to Jamie Hosford. When he asked Jamie about me, Jamie simply said, "Hire him; he's a keeper."

After one last World Cup game and a couple days of relaxing at the lake, Sue and I drove back toward a new life in Rockford. As the familiar countryside rolled past, I looked out the window and wondered about my future. I was excited knowing that I was beginning a new phase in my life. I couldn't help but contemplate how all the little things worked together to get me this job.

It all began by switching my interview from an East Kentwood principal to Jamie Hosford; his connection with Tom Popiel launched me to the top of the candidate list. Had Jamie's name not been on that resume, Tom might have simply passed it by. As solid as my resume was, in reality, it was only one in dozens of highly qualified, and in most cases, much younger candidates. I had plenty of experience and an attractive diverse list of achievements, but I was a little long in the tooth for a first-year teacher. It was a perfect example of "it's not always what you know, but who you know." And beyond that, what if Rockford had not made the connection between me and my sister Darcy when Tom called them looking for me? I realized that had any of these small things not happened exactly how they did, I might have continued to drive trucks for Olson's American Marine for who knows how long! I wondered about God's role in all this. "Coincidence?" I wondered silently. "I don't know about that," I silently answered myself. Looking out the window, I said to Sue, "Sometimes I guess it's just who you know." I wasn't necessarily referring to Jamie Hosford, but certainly he was an integral part of the whole thing.

Two months later, I began my orientation as a new teacher for Cedar Springs.

AMBUSHED

CHAPTER 51

It was the autumn of 1994, and I had begun my career as a high school teacher at Cedar Springs High School. My principal, Tom Popiel, had pulled my name out of dozens of applicants, mainly because he noticed a familiar name listed as a reference on my resume. I was still coaching both boys and girls soccer at Rockford, and Sue was pregnant with our second child. After living in my second-floor apartment for seven years, Sue and I had saved enough money, purchased our first house, and moved in on Halloween. It was only a few blocks away from the apartment, but another milestone in what was turning out to be a banner year for us. I was really enjoying my new profession, and teaching at Cedar Springs was a good decision. But in the back of my mind, I considered this as a temporary placement. I kept a constant eye on the opportunities in Rockford, and most specifically was waiting for the expected retirement of John Stamp, the Rockford High School art teacher. That was the job I coveted; it was only a matter of time. While I was still working on my degree, I had feared that he would pack it in before I was graduated, but now years later, he was still teaching. I patiently bided my time. Living in Rockford and already drawing a paycheck from the athletic department would certainly place me on the short-list whenever that position was vacated.

Sue was expecting to give birth sometime in mid-December. I had everything prepared and was anticipating a call during class some day. I was looking forward to the time when I got to say, "See ya!" and dash out of my classroom. But Christmas Break came around, and still no baby. I was working feverishly on finishing a portion of our basement and was nearly finished. One day, while completing the finishing touches on the new electrical system, Sue sat quietly reading in the recliner as I got down to the absolute final wire to be tightened into the electrical panel. Suddenly, from the other room, I heard her say, "Oh, oh, my water just broke!" I knew what that meant; the baby was on its way. Yet, I stood there with a screwdriver poised in mid air, only one set screw away from completing days of work. I stared at the screw while Sue was moving about in the other room saying, "Let's go, Scott, it's time."

"One stinkin' screw," I said out loud.

"What?" Sue said, hearing that I had spoken.

"Nothin', Ah'm coming," I said with the Panhandle dialect as I placed the screwdriver down on top of the panel, so I would remember where I had left off.

I was dirty from working all day and knowing how calm everything had gone for Rebekah's birth, I jumped into the shower for a quick clean-up. I had done the same thing when Sue's water broke for Rebekah, so I didn't think anything was out of order to do it now. When I got out of the shower, Sue was leaning with both hands against the wall in the hallway gritting her teeth, saying, "You better get a move on, this thing is happening!" At that moment, I realized that this birth was not going to be the same as Rebekah's.

We got into the car, and just like in the movies, I was speeding down the highway with my flashers on while Sue braced herself with one hand on the dashboard and the other on the door. Unbelievably, we had just finished our birth class the very night before. It concluded with a tour of where to drop off the expecting mother and where to park. I literally had been at our destination the previous night. I dropped Sue at the hospital entrance, and an orderly helped her into a wheelchair and said, "I have her; go ahead and park your car." After I had done this, I entered the lobby of the hospital, only to find Sue sitting alone in her wheelchair in front of an unmanned reception desk. Sue was trying to reposition herself, all the while saying, "They better get me into a room fast—this baby is coming!" I ran around like a lunatic until I got a nurse to finally admit Sue and get her into a room.

They did the usual check and said, "Oh, you're not ready yet, just relax," and left us alone in the room. Not long after they departed,

Sue began to writhe around in the bed. "I'm telling you, I am having this baby!" Immediately, I rang the panic button for the nurse. Once again after a quick check, the nurse assured us that the baby was not coming. Again after she left, Sue insisted the baby was, in fact, on the way. This went on several times until during one visit, the nurse suddenly said, "Oh my, you're right, this baby is coming right now!" She called for assistance, and the two nurses became a flurry of action, quickly changing the comfortable accommodations into a delivery room. I stood stroking Sue's forehead while the dominant nurse pulled on a pair of rubber gloves and positioned herself at the foot of the bed between Sue's elevated ankles while stating, "The doctor is on his way, but we better get ready to deliver this baby. Everything's okay," she assured us as she prepared to deliver the baby herself. Sue was gritting her teeth, trying her best to obey the instructions from the nurse when at the moment of truth, Doctor Ligon stepped into the room. He snapped on a pair of gloves while asking the nurse a couple of questions. He pulled up a stool at the foot of the bed and said, "Okay, push." Within five minutes of him stepping into the room, I was cutting the umbilical cord of our second daughter, Kaitlin. From the time I had parked the car until the delivery was a mere forty-five minutes. Dr. Ligon, after his brief appearance, simply looked at Sue and me and said, "Now *that's* the way to have a baby." The actual duration of time we had seen him that day was less than ten minutes. "A thousand dollars a minute," I thought. "I'm in the wrong profession."

A couple years passed without change. I was still waiting for an opportunity to switch from Cedar Springs to Rockford, we settled into our new home, and our family had grown to four with the addition of Kaitlin. It was April of 1997, and I was gearing up for the girls' spring soccer season. One day, quite unexpectedly at Cedar Springs, I received a call from the athletic director from Rockford.

"Hey Scott, Dave here," he began.

"What's up?" I asked.

"Can you come for a meeting after school today?"

It was a request with no previous mention. I had no idea what it could be about and answered a little perplexed, "Sure, I guess . . . what about?"

"Oh, something to do with the boys' season," was his vague reply.

"The *boys'* season?" I asked, totally mystified why something that happened in the autumn would be brought up in April. And as I hit the rewind button to the boys' season, nothing unusual registered; I was totally baffled as to what this meeting could be about. The tone he used made me nervous, but maybe it was something positive; after all, the year before I had led the boys to Rockford's first district championship in soccer. As I daydreamed, I had a fleeting vision of that hysterical evening when we won the championship, and my boys shaved my head in front of all our fans. But quickly, I returned to the reality that I was totally in the dark, and in the end I answered, "Sure, I can come in." So after school that day, I drove to Rockford High School and into Dave Price's athletic director's office.

Dave Price was a really nice guy who had helped me through the early years of the Rockford soccer program. He was not the director who had originally hired me twelve years earlier, but he had been very supportive of my efforts to create tradition and a solid foundation in a tough league.

"Come on," he said. "I'll take you down to the conference room," and he walked me through the clean halls of a school that had only been built four years earlier.

"What's this about?" I asked, getting the feeling that something was in the air.

"Well, you'll find out soon enough," was all he said. I began to get nervous at his reluctance to give any sort of details as to what was going on. When we entered the conference room, I was surprised to see the superintendent, the principal, my junior varsity coach, several school board members, and Jamie Hosford, who was now the director of personnel in the district, all seated at a large conference table. With only a couple of exceptions, these were all friendly faces whom I knew from previous encounters and being part of the athletic community in Rockford. I still had no clue as to what the meeting was about, but with all these big-wigs present, it must be serious.

Jamie began by asking me questions about a team-building weekend the boys' team attended at Spring Hill Camp back in August. I had to search my brain to recollect why they would be concerned over anything that happened during the two days I took my team to Spring Hill. To the best of my recollection, nothing unusual happened during the duration of our camp. We had trained, we had scrimmaged a local team, and we had bonded around campfires . . . all the usual stuff. "Why are they asking me about team camp?" I wondered to myself. Eventually, the questions zeroed in on an event that took place the last morning of camp while I was packing luggage into the back of my pick-up. It was so insignificant that I had forgotten that it even happened and had to really think hard to recall the details. It certainly wasn't anything that I felt was of any consequence.

On that morning back in August, the team was packing up to leave. We had been at Spring Hill Camp for the previous two days, and our time there was over. As I was throwing luggage into my truck, I heard a commotion coming from the middle of the compound thirty of forty yards away. When I looked, I saw the team gathered in a large group, laughing and generally just standing there. I didn't know what the attraction was, and I had no fore-knowledge about what was going on. I went to investigate and as I passed through the crowd of young men, I saw what was getting all the attention. One of our younger players, a nice kid named Brian Eckert, had been duct taped to a tree. He was facing the tree with his arms wrapped around the trunk and was wearing his soccer shorts, but he was definitely taped to the tree. As I passed through the mob, everyone was waiting to see what I would do, if I would put a stop to it or not. Brian did not seem to be in any stress and was simply taped like he was hugging the tree; he was just calmly standing there. When I got next to Brian, I stopped and surveyed the situation.

Very quietly I asked, "Are you okay, Brian?"

"Yeah, I'm fine, coach," he answered.

"Alright," I said. Since he said he was fine, I hammed it up a little and looked up and down, scratching my beard as if I was pondering the sight. Then calmly, without saying a word, strolled on my way. The crowd cheered at my silent approval. Then one player stepped from the mob and tried to pull Brian's shorts down, but the tape around his butt would not let it happen. Almost simultaneously, another kid grabbed a twig lying on the ground, scurried forward, and stuck it downward into the waistband of Brian's shorts. Once again because of the tape, the stick was barely able to stay in place, and in fact, looked as if it were going to fall right out. There was raucous laughter and at this point, I decided it was time to put an end to it before they went any further.

The previous year, the team grabbed a couple freshmen and shaving-creamed them while sitting around the fire one evening. Both of these were rather tame initiations in comparison to what many teams do, but I had made it clear to my upper classman that I would not allow anything malicious or degrading to be done to any of our players. Still, I saw no harm in some minor mischief. I felt they had picked Brian to try and bring him more into the fraternity of the team; he was, after all, a very quiet young man; selecting him for this made sense. What I learned later from the ring-leaders was that the target was originally a different kid who was loud and obnoxious . . . but he became suspicious and hid that morning. Brian simply walked by at the wrong time.

At the point when the stick was crammed into Brian's waistband, I came forward and said, "Alright boys, that's enough, let him loose from there." The boys quickly obeyed and slapping Brian on the back, the event was over. I remember my part in the entire thing was less than five minutes. Also present was my assistant coach, Dave, and a parent who had been video-taping the entire weekend, including Brian being taped to a tree.

When the soccer banquet at the end of the season rolled around, I happened to remember the incident and mentioned it as a gag award to Brian. I even presented him with a roll of duct tape and a stick. I never thought about it again until I sat before this panel of people asking me to recount the event for them. What really bothered me was that they kept referring to it as a hazing. This was as far from a hazing incident as anything I can imagine. I couldn't believe that this little blip of mischief was creating so much attention.

At one point, there was a break, and I walked with the athletic director to the drinking fountain. As we walked I asked, "Is this serious; I mean, can I lose my job over this?"

"I don't know," he said. Then he continued, "All I know is that this has been the worst day of my career."

Suddenly it hit me: that's exactly what they were building up to do—fire me! I couldn't believe it. What I discovered was that ever since the banquet, when I gave Brian his gag gift, his parents, especially his mother, began building a hazing case against me for allowing their son to be treated so poorly. It was such a non-issue to Brian that he had never even mentioned it to his parents. The irony, in fact, was that they didn't know it happened until *I* brought it up. They, on the other hand, were making it into something it wasn't and threatening the school with a lawsuit if it did not act against me. I was stunned.

Jamie Hosford, for all practical purposes, was facilitating this meeting. It was a surreal setting. After all, he was the guy who gave me my first teaching experience and could possibly be responsible for me getting hired at Cedar Springs. Now his position as a Rockford administrator dictated that he be the agent carrying out the ire of the Eckerts. As I surveyed those at the table, I remembered how many of them had come to my aid only a few years earlier when my young family was struggling through my cancer. Now once again they were helping decide my fate, only this time like puppets being blackmailed by an angry mom. I was definitely feeling betrayed. But I understood their dilemma because nothing puts a school district more on the defensive than parents with lawyers. With the possibility of bad press for one of the state's darling school districts, damage control takes precedent; everyone is expendable.

Once during the winter, Brian's father even arrived at our house to ask for our copy of the video of the team weekend. I was not home at the time, but Sue gladly obliged since he said it was for something they were putting together for Brian's birthday. That was simply a lie to get the tape. Evidently, they had systematically gone around and obtained all the copies of the weekend they could. I had never even watched it.

After my walk to the drinking fountain, Dave and I returned to the conference room, and the interrogation continued. Interestingly enough, Brian's parents were not present. I had been relatively close to them during the soccer season and had even sat and comforted Brian's mother when her father had died. I think they did not want to face the absurdity of what they were accusing me of. On my part, it was really frustrating to not face my accusers; I had no opportunity to ask a single question. At the end of the meeting, the superintendent simply said, "We would like you to resign, and we would like you to do it quietly." This request was not only asked of me, but also of my assistant coach who said, "Fine, give me a piece of paper, and I will resign right now." I could tell he was incensed. He continued, "This is easy for me. I'm a minor part of all this, but what about *him*? He's devoted his life to building this program." As he said this, he was pointing at me. He only received blank stares. Then he coarsely ripped a piece of scrap paper from a notebook close by and scribbled out his resignation, signed it, slammed the pen down on it and said, "There! You should all be ashamed of yourselves!" and left the room.

I was in shock and to be frank, wasn't sure what to do. I said, "I would like to think about this, if you don't mind."

"Okay, but we would like this to happen soon," replied the superintendent.

Mr. Price and I then rose and left the room together. As we walked down the hallway, he repeated what he had said earlier. "This is the worst day of my career."

That evening, I told Sue how everything had come crashing down. I explained the details to her, and together we tried to reason what was best to do. The next day at school, I had even more surprises.

While in class, I received a call from the Cedar Springs superintendent, Nyla Rypma, who had obviously had a conversation with administrators from Rockford. Rockford had contacted her to put pressure on me to resign without a fight. She was concerned about what this might mean for my teaching career if I fought it and it spilled out beyond athletics. The pickle that I was in was the fact that I had only been teaching for a couple of years and had not yet received tenure status. This left me vulnerable and not assured of protection by the legal power of the education union. Nyla was genuinely concerned that she could lose her new art teacher if this thing spun into a giant news story.

During my lunch, I went and sought counsel from the one guy whom I felt knew his way around this type of situation: my principal, Tom Popiel.

Tom was definitely "old school" and had risen through the ranks of education the old-fashioned way. He began as a classroom teacher and coach and then became an athletic director, and finally a principal. He was a large man with a full head of blonde hair who was an automatic presence when he entered a room. He reminded me a little of Rodney Dangerfield, but I had learned to respect his straight-forwardness in the short time I had known him. He was definitely a little crude and sometimes profane but had years of experience and always "called a spade a spade." I would put a lot of stock in whatever his perspective in my matter would be. I sat across the desk from Tom and asked, "I'm sure you have heard what is happening to me at Rockford."

"Yes," he said, "it really stinks." Then he continued, "I've seen this type of thing before; nobody comes away a winner."

"What do you think I should do . . . I mean, what would *you* do?"

"Well," he started, "like you, I'm sure, I would want to fight this thing . . . I mean it is so trivial in nature yet so devastating in its result."

"Yeah," I agreed, "didn't see it coming at all."

"It sounds like they have been preparing this for months and then ambushed you."

"That's exactly what happened," I agreed.

"I haven't even had a chance to have a conversation with these people. They were not even present at the meeting . . . very frustrating."

"As much as I know you feel the injustice of this, and as much as I know you want to fight it, I think you need to step back and consider the big picture," Tom began.

"If you fight this and lose . . . which you could because you're not tenured . . . your teaching career could be over." As he spoke, the gravity of the situation began to sink in; it wasn't merely about retaining my coaching position, but it was about my future and the future of my family. The more Tom counseled, the more I realized I had to do what they asked; I had to resign. It was not going to be easy; I loved coaching at Rockford. Trying to explain this to my girls' team was going to be emotional.

The last thing Tom told me was, "I know this is hard to understand right now, but in time, this will all fade, and you will be involved in other things. Time," he added, "is the only thing that is gonna make this tolerable. In the meantime, you're just gonna have to bend over and let 'em screw you."

His counsel was difficult to hear, but I knew he was right. That day on the way home from school, I dropped in unexpectedly to the Rockford superintendent's office. When his secretary told him who was waiting in the lobby, he made time to meet with me. After some uncomfortable pleasantries, I asked him straight out, "Is there any way to keep my coaching position?"

"Under the circumstances, I would have to say no," he replied.

"So even if I don't resign, your plan is to fire me?"

"It will be a lot messier, but yes, you are not going to keep your job . . . one way or the other."

"Do you really think this thing that happened to Brian is a hazing and that I am responsible for it?" I asked sincerely, wanting to know.

"Yes," he answered matter-of-factly. "We consider this a hazing, and our hands are tied. You were the head coach; therefore, you were responsible."

I looked down at the floor and tried hard to keep my emotions in check. It was difficult to hear that I would always be tagged with this on my record. What he told me really sounded like a party line that had been rehearsed to justify the action. To this day, I don't believe what happened at team camp was malicious or that it had any negative effect on Brian. I have always felt that if it had been at all traumatic, he would have told his parents, said something to me, or quit the team . . . he did not. I also don't believe that Rockford's superintendent *really* felt it was a hazing. Like any large school district, many things happened in Rockford, things monumentally worse than my little incident, yet Rockford's administration was masterful at managing bad press. That's precisely what I think was happening in my case. It was a no-brainer for them, knowing that without tenure, I was a man without any legal leverage. I knew at that point I would have to give up my program; I would have to go quietly like they asked.

"All right then," I began, as I reached into my satchel and produced a letter of resignation I had prepared earlier. "Here's my resignation."

As he accepted my letter, he said, "I will be glad to recommend you for any position you seek elsewhere." I couldn't help but think if I had *really* done something wrong, he would never have offered his reference. I knew then this was all politics, not justice.

I had a graduate class that evening, but my mind was elsewhere. On the way home, I stopped at Joy Alexander's house and gave her the bad news. She was a leader on the team and a player whom I loved dearly, and together we burst into tears at the whole thing, and she hugged me. That evening, at home, it all finally came crashing down, and I sat slumped against the wall in our dining room, trying to get my head wrapped around all that happened. The most heart-wrenching part of the whole deal was when Rebekah, four at the time, walked up and knelt before me and said, "I'm sorry they're taking away your team, daddy."

The next week, there was a board meeting. Accepting my resignation was on the agenda. In the days between me tendering it and the board meeting, the news had gotten out. The newspaper called me relentlessly, trying to pry out the details for the scoop. Perhaps the most difficult part of the resignation was the stipulation that it was done "quietly." This gave me no possibility to tell my side . . . and believe me, I wanted to tell my side.

The soccer parents were outraged when they got wind of what was happening and how it was being handled. The night of the board meeting, perhaps one hundred parents had gathered ready to block any decision pertaining to my resignation. Much to the disdain of the parents who had assembled to speak on my behalf, the board declared a "closed session" and retired to a private room. In the time they were left to stew among themselves, Jamie Hosford herded them into a large room and counseled them to be careful of what they planned to do; it might actually hurt me more than help me. At this, they sent a representative to my house; a trusted parent named Tony knocked on my door and asked me point blank, "Coach, you have a ton of support. What do you want us to do?"

"Awe, Tony," I began, "you don't know how much this means to me, but I think you had better tell them all not to do anything."

He looked a little shocked at this, but when I explained the rock and the hard place in which I was situated, he understood.

They quickly hired another coach, and the soccer season played itself out in mediocrity, with drama hanging over it from the start. I felt sorry for my girls, but there was nothing I could do. When they had their first game, I simply could not stay away. I actually went to the sideline and asked the new coach, "Hey, do you mind if I just sit here? I won't interfere or try to coach or anything."

Santos, the new coach, was a nice Mexican guy who got thrust into this awkward situation. Out of a sense of compassion, he agreed to let me hang around the sideline. As the game was being played, Dave Price walked by and was surprised to see me sitting on the team bench. Very quietly he came over and said, "Scott, you can't be over here."

"C'mon Dave, I'm not doing anything. I'm just sittin' here."

"I'm sorry, but you just can't be here. I know it's hard, but you've got to let it go."

It was a humiliating walk, but I made the long trip out of the stadium and out of the Rockford soccer program. It hurt deeply and in the end, was so unfair. The other result of all this was the giant wrecking ball it sent smashing through the plans I had made to teach at Rockford. I couldn't imagine with this on my record that they would consider hiring me on staff. It took some time, but slowly, as the Rockford administration surely hoped for, the entire thing faded away, and life went on.

It seemed like all the things that were going so well were imploding. I wondered to God, "What's the big picture, here, Lord? How can everything be going so well and suddenly be going so bad?" I couldn't believe with all I had experienced in life that I had the forgetfulness to ask that question. The next year, John Stamp finally retired from Rockford, and I watched my dream job pass me by. I didn't even try to apply for it. I knew with all the same administrators in place that it would be a waste of time, and once again, I recall thinking how unfair it all was.

After school one day, when all my students had left, I sat daydreaming out the window, contemplating what was next for me. It was time to set a new direction and get on with life.

20/20 HINDSIGHT

CHAPTER 52

For the next year, I did not coach soccer. It was impossible not to feel like I had been unceremoniously kicked aside without recognition for what I had achieved with Rockford's soccer program. It didn't help that the house Sue and I had purchased was literally in front of the soccer stadium. As much as I wanted to watch both the boys' and girls' teams, I stayed away from the activity basically going on in my back yard. It was during this time that I began to embrace hunting. It kept me away from any temptation to stay apprised of the soccer games behind the house . . . especially in the autumn. Goose and deer hunting became my new obsession and in the spring, I sought sanctuary in the woods bagging turkeys.

The year after my demise at Rockford, the athletic director at Cedar Springs paid me a visit.

"Hey Scott, I wanted to let you know that we are starting a soccer program here next fall, and I thought you might be interested."

Cedar Springs was a small district and was only arriving at a point where they had enough players and support to add soccer to their athletics. Dan Zang, the athletic director, knew all about the Rockford ordeal, and he also knew that I had gotten the shaft. He wanted my experience and was encouraging me to apply for the coaching position soon to be posted. He also had seen me work with the students at Cedar Springs, and he understood that whether or not a hazing had really taken place at Rockford, one thing was for certain: I loved kids. He really soothed my ego when he told me with a wide grin, "Rockford's loss is our gain." I never considered this as something coming my way—starting yet another program. It was intriguing since they had no where to go but up. I interviewed for the job, but it was just a formality. In short time, I was hired as Cedar Springs' first boys' soccer coach. It seemed that everyone was in the know as to my past but recognized it for what it was, and they were excited that I was available to take the helm at Cedar Springs. I was given an unexpected second chance at a school that I originally planned to only stay at temporarily. Funny how things work out.

For several years, I coached the boys' soccer team and added the girls' junior varsity job when that program began. It was a great new direction, one that I had not even considered, and I began to realize that Cedar Springs would be where I spent my career as a teacher and a coach. At least that was what I thought, but as the years went by, I once again found that my plan was not always God's plan. There were yet more unforeseen twists and turns coming my way.

It was 1998, and Sue and I had added our son, Cameron, to the family. Once again, I was cheated out of the opportunity to get a call at school and race out of the room in a frenzy. Cameron was born at the end of January, on Superbowl weekend! Like the previous couple of years had been for me, Cameron's delivery was a difficult one. Unlike the girls, Sue's water did not break, but she began experiencing contractions, and we made the trip to the hospital. It was, in fact, time to deliver, but he was positioned wrong, and there was some work to be done beforehand. Throughout an entire night, I had to wake up Sue and walk her around the hospital floor. Hopefully, the movement would reposition the baby. By the time morning had come, we knew every painting on every wall on the fourth floor of Butterworth Hospital.

I awoke on the narrow sofa in Sue's room with a flurry of activity happening all around me. I was exhausted from a night with little sleep and sat on the edge of the cot with my head in my hands. For everything that was happening, I couldn't for the life of me shake the cobwebs out of my head. Finally, I rose and stumbled into the bathroom to splash water on my face. While in there, the head nurse hollered at me, "You better pick up the pace, dad, or you're going to miss the big event." At this, I snapped into reality like a drunk finding an instant sense of soberness. After a half an hour or so of contractions and systematic pushing, I was cutting my third umbilical cord, but this time of my first and only son.

My dad's health had been deteriorating for years and in August, at the beginning of the boys' soccer season with my Cedar Springs team, he died. I had been through a lot of difficult times, but losing my father was something like I had never known before. We had many rough moments, but I loved him beyond words. Even though I had basically been on my own since I graduated from high school, I had counted on him, especially during rough days. Now that he was gone, I felt an unusual sense of loneliness. There was an emptiness that weighed on me for years and at times, even to this day. Someone would say, "You look just like your old man," or someone would say one of my father's famous sayings, and he would appear in my mind. I could see his infectious grin or hear his voice; I could see him tinkering with a project in his shed or just sitting on the porch drinking a Black Label with Ernie Harwell calling the play-by-play of the ballgame from the window. Those were days I wish I had back.

For the next several years, things did not change. Our family was growing, and the kids were all taking on their different personalities. Both Rebekah and Katie followed in my footsteps and became soccer nuts. Cameron, on the other hand, wanted nothing to do with soccer or anything for that matter. It took a long time for a diagnosis to happen, but we soon discovered that Cameron had several behavioral issues that needed to be dealt with. He had a combination of Asperger's Syndrome, Oppositional Defiance Disorder (ODD), Obsessive Compulsive Disorder (OCD), and Attention Deficit Hyperactivity Disorder (ADHD). His behavior was like a Venn diagram; on any particular day, he could be within any of the three different areas, or in any combination. On really special days, he could have a little of everything going on all at once . . . really fun to be around. Our job as parents was trying to figure out what he was dealing with the most each day and then push or not push the buttons that would either make him tolerable, or explosive. With me working, most of this daily nightmare fell to Sue. As he got older, it slowly improved, but it was a long, difficult process.

The Hazel Family at Mackinaw City 2009. (left to right) Rebekah, Cameron, Sue, Kaitlin. Scotty, standing in back.

When Rebekah entered high school, she made the junior varsity soccer team her freshman year. In order not to miss her games, I resigned not only the girls' coaching position at Cedar Springs, but also the boys' job in the fall. I had begun coaching travel teams in the autumn and decided to lighten my load by giving up the boys' team. In truth, I actually was opening up more hunting time in the autumn. I still could have coached the boys but decided I wanted to hunt more. I had also discovered over the years that I enjoyed coaching the girls better anyhow. Don't get me wrong, I loved the boys' teams, and we had a blast, but there is something extremely satisfying about helping girls reach an athletic potential that most of them don't even realize they possess.

The news that I was no longer coaching got around and one day, Rebekah came home from practice and said her coach wanted to talk to me. The junior varsity coach for Rockford, Amira Ponne, was a short athletic woman who had played collegiate soccer at a high level. When I went to talk with her the following day, she said, "I hear you're not coaching high school ball at Cedar any more."

"That's right," I answered, "I would miss all of Rebekah's games if I did."

"Well, if you're not doing anything, I could use your help here."

"Hmmm, that's an interesting idea," I pondered aloud.

"What would you want me to do?" I asked, contemplating exactly what my role would be.

"Do you know anything about goalkeeping . . . I could sure use someone to train my goalkeepers while I work with the rest of the team?"

Now I had not ever done much with goalkeepers, but I knew all the rules pertaining to them. I knew I could at least teach them the tactics of the position. When I was the head coach at both Rockford and Cedar Springs, I never had someone specifically designated to train the keepers; I did it myself. I knew it was a very specialized position, and I could easily find drills to help train their fundamentals. In addition, only having to concentrate on the goalkeepers would streamline my responsibilities. In an instant, the whole idea was very intriguing.

"Well, I'll be honest, Amira, I have worked with keepers when I coached teams before, but I would never consider myself a goalkeeper's coach . . . but I can give it the ol' college try."

"I would love that," she replied enthusiastically.

Knowing what had happened to me in 1996, I realized I probably better make sure it was okay with the school. It had been ten years, but many people were still around from the time when I was asked to resign.

"Let me think about it," I said, "I'll let you know tomorrow." I really didn't need to think about it; I just wanted to make sure I didn't resurrect old demons . . . it had been a long recovery for me, and if I thought about it at any length, I became depressed over the entire thing all over again.

First, I went and talked to Heidi Greenland, the varsity coach and head of the program. Heidi was actually a player for me when the program was young, so she was well aware of what happened to me in Rockford.

"Heidi," I began, "Ponne has asked me to help her with the junior varsity."

"That's a great idea. I think you'd enjoy that," she responded.

"But what about the hazing deal?" I asked right out.

"Oh, I don't care about that. I'd love to see you back here at Rockford," she said without any hesitation.

"Well, I thought I had better ask before I just started showing up on the sideline."

"I appreciate that, Scotty, but I don't have a problem with it . . . welcome aboard."

"Yeah, well, I better go talk to Erickson, but I thought I better ask you first."

Tim Erickson was the old defensive coach for the football team and the latest athletic director at Rockford. Like Heidi, he was around when the hazing accusation came out, and I knew I would have to get his approval before I accepted Ponne's offer to help coach the J.V.

I knocked on Tim's office door. "Hey, Scott, come on in," he greeted me enthusiastically. "Haven't seen you in awhile! What's up?"

"Well, Ponne wants me to help her coach the J.V. girls and before I say yes, I need to know if my past is gonna be a problem."

"Your past?" he asked with a sense of confusion.

"You know," I said, "my *past* . . . the hazing thing with the Eckerts?"

"Oh, that . . . totally forgot about that," he said. Then he added, "That's a black mark on this district . . . that was a shame."

"I already asked Heidi, and she doesn't care if I help," I noted.

"Well?" I asked again.

Without answering me, he asked, "I thought you were coaching up in Cedar?"

"I was," I replied, "but my daughter plays here, and I didn't want to miss her games, so I resigned . . . that's why I am available at all."

"So basically you're a volunteer parent, right?"

"I guess so."

"Then you have every right to be part of the program; you're a parent of a player, of a student." Then after thinking a little more, he added, "I don't see any problem with you helping Ponne with the J.V. squad."

"Alright, then," I said, "that's all I needed to hear."

The next day, I showed up at the J.V. practice with my cleats on and a pair of goalkeeper gloves and began to train Amira Ponne's goalkeepers. For the next three years, I slowly became a fixture in Rockford soccer once again. Part of me felt like I was pulling a fast one; I mean, being an assistant coach for the J.V. girls squad was pretty low-profile. In some ways, I felt like I was sneaking in the back door. It was odd being back in the black and orange colors of Rockford High, but it felt satisfying. I found I enjoyed having a small, specific role rather than being the head honcho calling the shots. Plus, it saved me from the mandatory barrage of meetings required of a head coach. I could simply do my thing and go home, even forget about it if I chose to. I discovered that being in the shadows, I could analyze the game a lot better. I was enjoying myself.

Three years later, the year that Rebekah was to be a senior, Heidi resigned as Rockford's head soccer coach. Ponne applied and was hired as the new varsity coach and had no hesitation in stating, "If I get this job, you're coming with me." Before I knew what was happening, there I was back on the sidelines of the varsity girls' soccer team for Rockford. This is a place I never thought I would be again. It was special because my daughter was playing right in front of me. She may not have enjoyed it so much—I am rather a loud mouth from the bench—but I loved being that close to her and the action.

After two years of this, Ponne, expecting her second child, decided to give up coaching to spend more time with her family. The J.V. coach, Steve Thomas, applied and got the vacant varsity job. He knew me mainly because by this time, my daughter, Kaitlin, was playing on his J.V. team. Steve and I had not talked all that much, and he seemed to have his own favorite personnel. After Heidi had resigned, Steve had also applied for the varsity job but settled for the J.V. position when Ponne was hired. I wasn't sure if he had a grudge over that or not, and I wasn't sure how he felt about me, as Ponne's assistant. When the time came for the parent meeting and I had not received a call from him, I pretty much knew my coaching days at Rockford were over for a second time. Then, after I had resigned myself to the belief that I was through, Steve called late the night before the meeting and asked if I would like to stay on as the goalkeeper's coach. Once again, I was going to have the chance to be close to the action with a kid playing on the team. Once again I would remain part of the program that I had started years earlier. I gladly accepted the invitation.

Even though I felt a giant injustice had been perpetrated against me in 1996, the new life given to me by Amira, Heidi, Steve, and Tim gave me a certain amount of vindication. It was exactly how Tom Popiel had predicted; time would pass, and new things would happen; I would get over it. I had no clue that getting over it meant I would be part of it again . . . that was a bonus. An interesting twist in this second chance was that Dan Zang, the former Athletic Director, had been passed over as a principal candidate in Cedar Springs and was instantly scooped up by Rockford. Dan Zang, the A.D. who also counseled me during my rough times, was now my children's principal and in some ways, my new boss as an assistant coach for Rockford High School. In retrospect, I couldn't help but once again realize that my plan and God's plan were so different.

Driving home from a game one night after a tough victory away from home, I bobbed and weaved through the traffic on U.S. 131. As I exited at the Rockford exit, I caught myself looking out the passenger side window at the old Olson's American Marine building. This was where I had worked when I crawled back to Michigan with my tale between my legs in the mid-1980s. I began to ponder all that had happened since I graduated from G.V.S.U. It had been sixteen years, but it all seemed a blur. Every so often, I had the opportunity to sit back and try to let my mind catch up with reality . . . this was one of those times. Driving alone without any music blaring, I forced myself down memory lane. This sense of melancholy had been a trademark of mine for years . . . all the way back to drinking alone at home with fading embers in the fireplace or in college with the dim lights of my "thoughtful environment." It took nearly thirty-five years of 20/20 hindsight, but I realized that all the bad stuff combined to get me to this point of satisfaction. At this point, it was a happy stroll and as I closed in on Rockford, I quoted the words of my father whenever he felt content: "I wonder what the poor people are doin'?"

THE CIRCLE IS COMPLETE

CHAPTER 53

Once I set my sights on becoming a teacher, I felt I had a lot to offer and that I would be good at it. Things didn't work out like I had planned or even imagined, but that was nothing new. I had gotten used to thinking something would happen a particular way, only to have a giant curve ball pitched my way. I had settled in at Cedar Springs High School and was becoming more and more involved with the things that fulfilled me: building relationships with students and programming activities. I loved teaching my classes, but I really enjoyed developing rapport and planning the school's events. My very first year teaching, 1994, I also got suckered into coaching the freshman volleyball team. Like many young teachers who yearn to find a way to get involved, saying no to anything is difficult. It was very fun but from a competitive perspective it was, as they say, "like trying to make chicken salad out of chicken shit." Because of a Saturday tournament, it was the only time in over twenty years that I missed going to the Spring Hill winter retreat. In my list of priorities, this was unacceptable, so after a single year coaching volleyball, I resigned.

I also was advising the freshmen class for student government. It was loads of extra time, but I enjoyed it and actually got paid extra to do it. Eventually, I would inherit the overall job of student activities advisor.

When my father died, it was August of 1998, just a couple weeks before school began and the boys soccer team was already training.

Trying to get my head wrapped around teaching and coaching was difficult; it seemed insignificant in relation to the grief I was dealing with. Cedar Springs had built a brand new high school, and I was in a room that smelled like fresh linoleum. Two weeks after my dad's funeral, when I entered that room to prepare for the coming year, there was a computer sitting on my desk. I sat down and just stared at it. "What the heck am I going to do with this?" I said out loud.

I was a dinosaur when it came to technology. I had finished my degree typing papers on a typewriter; I wanted nothing to do with all the new gadgets coming out. I felt the more people got connected through cyber space, the further they removed themselves from reality, from society. It was almost ironic; the more people got connected the more disconnected they became. I was informed that all our record keeping, communication, and data collection would be done on our new computers. I held out as long as I could until they mandated I switch from my hand-written records to the new technology. I was a reluctant participant. Over time, I got used to it and began to see the benefits and appreciated the speed of it all.

It was students who tutored me the most. They showed me the applications in a useful, practical manner. They had grown up in this new culture; it was being forced on me in my middle age. It was not uncommon for me to become exasperated while unsuccessfully attempting to do something on the computer. Many times when this happened, I would grab the closest kid to my desk and demand, "C'mere and show me how to do this!" I was amazed at the capabilities and shocked at how far behind the times I had let myself fall. One day a student asked me if I had an e-mail account. I had a vague idea what it was but must admit I didn't really have a clue as to its potential.

"No, I don't have e-mail," I said somewhat embarrassed. "What would *I* do with that?"

"Here, let me help you set one up; you'll love it," said my student as he got up from his desk and came up to guide me through the motions of establishing e-mail right there in my art room. In time, I was using e-mail to communicate with people like everyone else in the world . . . it was handy.

Years later in 2004, I sat down one morning and logged into my e-mail account. On the top line of my inbox I saw a message was waiting for me with a return address that stopped me in my tracks. I don't recall it exactly, but it included the name Karen. I just stared at it.

"No way, it couldn't be," I thought. I tapped my middle finger on the desk, trying to decide first of all, if it was really the Karen from my past, and secondly, if I should open it or not. I mean, "What could she possibly want?" I wondered. Listed in the subject category it simply read, "Hey." After a few anxious moments, I grabbed the computer mouse, placed the indicator on the e-mail with the familiar name, and clicked it.

I could tell by the first couple of tentative sentences that it was, in fact, Karen.

"*Dear Scotty,*" it began.

"*I looked you up on 'People Search' and I hope I have found the correct address for the correct person.*" She continued with a couple of pleasantries but got directly to the reason she had taken the time and effort to find me. *"I don't know if you have heard this or not, but I wanted to make sure you knew . . . Kevin Gambrel died suddenly the other day."* This news stunned me, and I sat back in my chair and stared out the window. I thought of all the times I had laughed with Kevin and all the conversations we had about God. I thought of the interesting twist Kevin had in the relationship between me, Karen, and Ross. I couldn't help but think of how Kevin had given up his cozy American life to go to China. "This does not make sense," I thought. "This was a Godly man." As I reminisced on my memories of Kevin, I fought to hold back the tears. I couldn't reason why I was alive, and he was not. I was the one who struggled so much with my Christian walk and survived my cancer, yet Kevin, so much a beacon of goodness, was taken in a flash.

Karen and I caught up on the years gone by, but mainly this reconnection was all about Kevin's sudden death. She told me that he had suffered a heart attack in the bathroom at school during the school day. It was devastating for his family, of course, but as expected, his death was tragic for his school, Tascosa High, where he had himself attended. With amazing potential ahead, Kevin had only taught at Tascosa for two months. Weird to think of how many times as a student he might have been in the very bathroom where he would die years later. As strange as it was to have a conversation with Karen, the reason for her to look me up impacted me even more. It seemed impossible, but my friend, Kevin, was dead.

Kevin's death was only one of several unexpected deaths that really grabbed my attention. A few years earlier, in 2001, another friend of mine named Mark died after fighting cancer for several years. This death really had an impact on me. Mark Olson was the owner of Spring Hill Camp. In the twenty-plus years that I had attended Spring Hill, he and I got to know each other. His was an amazing vision that started out small with his father and then exploded under his direction. Under his guidance, Spring Hill had become one of the best camps in the country, one that could even rival the capabilities of Young Life camps like Castaway Club.

He was truly a Godly man whose heart was focused on reaching kids for Christ. Nothing was impossible for Mark, and he always thought big. He had a young, large family, a wife and four or five kids, I think. They were all part of his vision for Spring Hill. When he finally died, I took a day off work to drive to the camp and attend his funeral; that's how much his life meant to me . . . it was the least I could do for a man who had made such a giant impact on literally thousands of kids and on me. Once again, it was a young death that made no sense to me. "Why him and not me," became a question I would ponder after several deaths of men and women I knew who were toeing the Christian line better than I.

There were a couple other deaths of students and parents that slapped me into thought. One of these deaths was Mrs. Eckert, Brian's mother. I was saddened by this because I knew Brian as a player, but also because I never got a chance to find out why she had ambushed me with all her legal guns blazing. Never in the twelve years that passed since the incident was I ever afforded an opportunity to ask that question, to face my accusers. Was it really a hazing? Did I really damage her son? I hoped that a day would come when we could talk, and now that was impossible.

Just as easily as these people died, whether tragically or by disease, *I* could have died. My family could be the one without a husband and a father. Trying to find any rhyme or reason for it will drive anyone nuts. As difficult as it is to wrestle with middle-aged parents and friends dying, it is the student deaths that are the most difficult to come to terms with. They are all tragic and nearly all the result of poor decisions. With that in mind, I have tried to make my life meaningful. In spite of my shortcomings, and there are a bunch, I try to make a difference.

Admittedly, I am still a little rough around the edges, and I'd be a liar if I said I didn't enjoy the occasional beer or rated "R" movie. At wedding receptions, I enjoy dragging Sue out onto the dance floor. My children hide their faces most of time, but at age fifty-three, I am that guy with the moves from 1975. Occasionally when we find ourselves in a Catholic church for a wedding or an Easter mass, I have no problem taking communion like I did when I was a kid at St. Pius X. This makes my Baptist relatives cringe, but my Catholic kin love it. Me, I don't think it is any big deal one way or the other . . . it's communion and no matter where I am, I understand what it means.

Overall, I continue to strive to be a positive influence on teenagers. This has become my calling. As much as I can in a public school, I am not afraid to talk about my Christianity. There are limits, of course, but if students open the door to a conversation about religion, I gladly walk through it without any reservations. Many times I simply "public school-ize" my advice and try to help them make wise choices; it doesn't take a Bible to be smart. I make my room available for a weekly Bible study and for over ten years, I have facilitated a winter weekend at Spring Hill for an average of 100 kids; 100 public school kids! It has become one of the favorite events of the school year and if I was ever forced to pull the plug on it, there would probably be a mutiny! It is rewarding beyond description when they come to me afterwards and tell me how the weekend has changed their lives. What I have realized is that all my crazy experiences, good and bad, help me to better understand young people and counsel them on decisions. It is easy for me to say, "I have been where you are." Perhaps God's plan for me was to shovel a ton of craziness my way over a forty-year timeframe just so I could speak with authority on many issues. No matter how you look at it, the circle is complete; now *I'm* the guy in front of kids trying to point the way. In many ways like when I attended Young Life, I am Dale Moore to many of my students.

It was during my time as a teacher that I found I had a gift for telling stories. It's not that I didn't tell stories before; admittedly, I can drone on about anything, but now I have a captive audience who genuinely seems to enjoy what I am peddling. Much of what I have shared in this book I have shared with students first. Usually, we will be discussing some topic that will send me back to something that happened in my life, and I will be candid in trying to provide a life-lesson. In the education world, they refer to these impromptu situations as "teachable moments." These are the things I remembered about the teachers I loved and tried to emulate, the trait that I wanted to possess myself.

When I spoke, I always focused on the hard roads that I had taken as a young man and the pitfalls in which I fell. I also hold nothing back when referring to my failures and the unforeseen events of life, like cancer and basically being fired at Rockford. Some obvious morals to the stories are that there are consequences of making unwise decisions and to be prepared for the unexpected, two things which I am highly qualified to address with authority. I usually incorporate tons of humor, and I always speak about my personal experiences. Whenever possible, I also make it clear that in spite of my sporty personality, I was sold out to God, that I was a born-again Christian, and I always try to do what is right. I also make it clear that I still find myself doing many things wrong, making mistakes, but that I never stop trying.

I knew I was making a difference with students, or at least giving them a setting that they enjoyed, when younger siblings would attend my classes and ask to hear a story that they vaguely heard over a dinner conversation. They knew the gist of many of the tales I had told their older brothers or sisters and would refer to them by title, but they wanted to hear all the details from the man who lived them; they wanted the experience for themselves. It became a trademark of taking any class taught by Mr. Hazel; "He tells great stories!" kids would tell each other. In fact, it is because of my students that this book was written at all. After a class one day during which I told a personal anecdote, one of my brightest pupils, a young lady named Mallory Sattler, casually passed by my desk and still smiling about my story, said, "Mr. Hazel, you need to write these stories down; you should write a book."

"Yeah," I answered sarcastically, "who would read it?"

"*I* would," she said earnestly, "You have lived a crazy life . . . you have done some interesting things."

"Really?" I asked. "You honesty think people would want to read about this stuff?"

"Absolutely!" she replied. "I know I would, and if I would, I think at least other teenagers would, too."

"Yeah, maybe," I replied, internally rolling the idea around.

Her suggestion stuck in my head, and I began to dabble around with the concept of putting my stories, my life, down in writing. I wasn't sure if it was interesting enough or not and if I did write, what would I do with it when I finished? When I finally decided to take Mallory's suggestion to put my stories down in writing, the initial question was, "Where do I start?"

Another result stemming directly from recounting tales in my classroom was encouragement from staff and students to do some public-speaking engagements, to seek a larger audience. To my surprise, people began to recommend my name whenever they were asked about having a keynote speaker for an event. In February of 2001, I booked the nationally renowned speaker Laurie Stewart to give a presentation at Cedar Springs High School. What unexpectedly happened was the beginning of a friendship between Laurie and me. As we got to know each other and I explained how it was that I came to be a teacher at Cedar Springs, Laurie came right out and said, "You should be speaking yourself; you have a lot to tell."

"Really?" I asked, trying to act modest.

"You have a way with words," she continued, "these kids hang on everything you say . . . I think you have a lot to offer; you would be a great speaker."

Perhaps the first glimpse of this potential happened when I spoke to several hundred people at an event during our "Pride Week" in the spring of 2003. As the activity advisor at Cedar Springs, I contracted a popular band out of Chicago to play at the Pride Week grand finale assembly. Because I spent most of our budget on the band, I couldn't afford to bring in a speaker to complete the event, so I just decided to do it myself. I felt confident that I could pull this off, and the accolades I received afterwards only encouraged me to pursue speaking more seriously. I was just trying to fill the gap and found that not only kids, but adults really enjoyed what I had to say.

This was the beginning of many speaking engagements that would follow.

Over the course of the next few years, and in part to the encouragement I received from Laurie Stewart, I was asked to speak at three graduation commencements, a handful of baccalaureates, a high school in LaGrange, Indiana, and at Saginaw Valley State University; all of which I felt honored to do. There were many other lesser engagements, but these were larger events that made me wonder if I had something to offer as a speaker. But perhaps the presentation I was most excited about was when a former player of mine asked if I would speak at a team-building weekend for girls' soccer at Spring Hill.

After all those times that I had taken kids to hear great speakers at Spring Hill, I was going to be that guy on the stage. I only hoped that I could deliver like all those guys I had seen before when I served as a chaperone. The interesting twist was that the guy who hired me was the same guy who put the stick in Brian Eckert's waistband that ultimately cost me my coaching position at Rockford. I had never held any of those boys responsible for what happened to me; they were merely young men enjoying the fraternity that is high school sports. He and I were close as player and coach and remained close as he got older, and he coached his own high school teams at Rockford, Cedar Springs, and then Forest Hills Northern High School. I was his mentor. It was ironic that he and I were back at the scene of the crime, so to speak, working together to influence the lives of young athletes. "God has a funny sense of humor," I thought.

When I first accepted the invitation to speak, I realized I really had to put something special together. I found myself sitting in my den, staring out the window and rummaging my mind for grand ideas. I suddenly had an epiphany: "I have spent a lot of time looking out windows." It occurred to me that in many of the milestone moments of my life, I have contemplated the situation while taking in the view out whatever window was closest. And now as I tried to put together a dynamic presentation for my protégée, I was once again looking out windows. It was spring, and I was anticipating another enjoyable season coaching the Rockford girls with Steve Thomas. It was unseasonably warm for March in Michigan, and I could already see tulips reaching for the sunlight. I knew that whatever presentation I put together, I would be revealing intimate aspects of my past not only to my team, but to my daughter who was part of the squad. This was not going to be like talking to strangers. This would peel back layers of things that most people would keep hidden about themselves . . . scary, but necessary if I was going to be real to these young athletes.

I decided to tell my story . . . the whole crazy thing. But as I scratched my head and looked out the window in deep thought, I realized the starting point would have to be something they could relate to; it would have to be when I was their age.

I had survived failed romances, failed business ventures, tornados, poverty, job loss, personal tragedy, and the scare of cancer. I also had seen the difference that people can make in a person's life and how God is necessary for peace and fulfillment in life. As with the beginning of this book, my presentation at Spring Hill ultimately zeroed in on a fact that I had come to realize late in my life: that in the chaos of life, a single person can indeed make an impact. The answer to the often asked question, "Can I make a difference?" is "yes." When I trace back the trail of all I have been through since high school—Young Life, Castaway Club, Indiana Deb, Karen, Amarillo, Dakota House, Becky, Lloyd, Kevin, LaVisa, the Prodigal Son, Rockford, Susan, coaching, cancer, Cedar Springs, and Spring Hill—it all begins with the persistence of one caring friend: Joey.

Thirty-five years after it had happened, I understood that the sequence of events that define my life, starting with Joey's invitations to attend Young Life. As I sat and thoughtfully connected the dots, it became obvious that a single person with a seemingly insignificant act of kindness can have monumental results. As a history teacher, I know how the course of events can twist on any small action. What I suddenly grasped was that without Joey's invitation, there would have been no Young Life. Without Young Life, there would have been no Castaway. Without Castaway there would have been no Karen and possibly no salvation decision. Had there been no Karen, there would have been no Texas. Had there been no Texas, there would be no Lloyd, no Kevin Gambrel, no skill as a carpenter, and no training up in the Christian walk. Had there been no Christian walk, there may not have been a Becky. Had there been no Becky, there would have been no compassion, no example, no temptation.

Had there been no temptation, there would have been no break-up, no flight to Texas. Had there been no return to Texas, there would be no failed business, no final farewell, and no lessons for the prodigal son. Had there been no impoverished return to Michigan, there would be no refuge in Rockford. Had there been no Rockford, there would have been no Rockford Baptist Church, no coaching, and no forging my faith by trials. No Rockford Baptist would mean no Sue, no children, no Grand Valley, no teaching degree. Without a teaching degree, there would be no Cedar Springs, no students, no stories, no Spring Hill. It goes on and on. Take out any link in this chain of events, and everything that happened afterwards would not even be in my vocabulary . . . awesome and frightening. It helps me understand that when life deals what seem to be traumatic blows, time might reveal their part in something much bigger, much more perfect. It helps strengthen my faith in Him who really understands how things fit into the big picture.

Now that I conclude my book, the stories defining my life, the circle is complete. I started with my awakening in high school, to the excitement that life can bring with all the traps, triumphs, and tribulations and with the kid who started the ball rolling with a simple invitation.

It is now 2012 and almost summer, and as I tap out the last few lines of my memories, I find myself one last time looking out the window in deep thought. I don't have much, if any, of the Panhandle dialect left in my speech, but occasionally a "howdy" or "y'all" pops out of nowhere. When it happens, like in the past, people might stop and ask, "Where are you from?" and I smile and think of thunder-boomers marching across the high plains of Texas. Just as easily as some drawl might slip out, an "eh" or "yah" from my days as a Yooper might make an unexpected appearance. When this happens, I reminisce on the power of Lake Superior and the brotherhood of fraternity. As I envision scenes from my past, outside the window there is a light breeze blowing the new leaves back and forth, and one more time I catch myself day dreaming as the trees sway. I smile as I think of Sue and my family, my job, and of the things I love to do in life; it has all finally come together with purpose. I remember the bible verse which states, ". . . that all things work together for good to those that love God . . ." (Romans

8:28) and I realize that even though it took forty years and countless setbacks and pitfalls, this certainly is true for me.

"How different would my life be had Joey not cared?" I wondered. Just the thought makes the hair on the back of my neck stand up. So much that defines who I am would never have happened had if not been for her. I put my chin in my hand and my elbow on my knee and daydreamed out the window, "God is good," I say in a whisper. "Thank you, Joey."

Joey, 1977

ACKNOWLEDGEMENTS

I would like to extend my thanks to all those who encouraged me to write, mostly students who convinced me that my story was worth telling. A special thanks to Mallory Sattler and Mackenzie Frederick who first got a glimpse of what I was putting down and gave me the initial 'thumbs up.' My utmost gratitude to Brooke Johnston who became my guinea pig, student editor, and critic. Thanks to Clifton Young, Professor of English, Muskegon Community College and friend whose expertise and opinion was of great help.

Also, thanks to Maddy Crandall for transferring Professor Young's editing to the manuscript. Special thanks to Pastor Larry Rowland, Rockford Baptist Church, for his council on content and input as an author himself. Far and above all appreciation and gratitude I can give, thanks and love to my wife, Sue, for putting up with me and allowing me to tell my story. Thank you, my dear, for loving me in spite of myself.

Scott Hazel

CPSIA information can be obtained at www.ICGtesting.com
Printed in the USA
BVOW031450281112

306686BV00006B/1390/P

9 781477 252550